Publications of the

CENTRE FOR REFORMATION AND RENAISSANCE
STUDIES

Essays and Studies, 5

SERIES EDITOR   Konrad Eisenbichler

Victoria University

in the

Fantasies of Troy

Classical Tales and the Social Imaginary in Medieval and Early Modern Europe

Edited by

ALAN SHEPARD *and* STEPHEN D. POWELL

Toronto
Centre for Reformation and Renaissance Studies
2004

CRRS Publications
Centre for Reformation and Renaissance Studies
Victoria University in the University of Toronto
Toronto, Ontario M5S 1K7
Canada

Tel: 416/585-4465
Fax: 416/585-4430
Email: crrs.publications@utoronto.ca
<www.crrs.ca>

Library and Archives Canada Cataloguing in Publication

    Fantasies of Troy : classical tales and the social imaginary in medieval and early modern Europe / edited by Alan Shepard and Stephen D. Powell.

(Essays and studies ; 5)
Includes bibliographical references and index.
ISBN 0-7727-2025-8

    1. Troy (Extinct city)—In literature. 2. Troy (Extinct city)—In art. 3. Trojan War—Literature and the war. 4. Trojan War—Art and the war. 5. Arts, European. I. Powell, Stephen David, 1966– II. Shepard, Alan, 1961– III. Victoria University (Toronto, Ont.). Centre for Reformation and Renaissance Studies. IV. Series: Essays and Studies (Victoria University (Toronto, Ont.). Centre for Reformation and Renaissance Studies) ; 5.

PN56.T76F35 2004   809'.93358   C2004-905672-7

Cover illustration: Dish with scenes from the story of Aeneas and the Trojan Wars. Tin-glazed earthenware. Italian, Urbino, from the workshop of Guido Durantino; dated 1535. From the collection of the George R. Gardiner Museum of Ceramic Art (Toronto). By permission.

Cover design: Ian MacKenzie, Paragraphics

Typesetting and production: Becker Associates

Contents

Acknowledgments   vii

Contributors   ix

1   Introduction   1
Alan Shepard and *Stephen D. Powell*

AFFILIATION AND APPROPRIATION

2   How Troy Came to Spenser   15
James Carscallen

3   "Fairer than the evening air": Marlowe's Gnostic
Helen of Troy and the Tropes of Belatedness and
Historical Mediation   39
Michael Keefer

4   In Search of the Trojan Origins of French:
The Uses of History in the Elevation of the
Vernacular in Early Modern France   63
Paul Cohen

5   *Togail Troí*: The Irish *Destruction of Troy* on the
Cusp of the Renaissance   81
Brent Miles

6   The Disappearance of the Trojan Legend
in the Historiography of Venice   97
Sheila Das

RHETORIC, TRANSLATIO IMPERII, AND TROJAN LEGACY

7   Smiting High Culture in the "Fondement":
The Seege of Troye as Medieval Burlesque   117
Pamela Luff Troyer

8   Imagining the Masculine: Christine de Pizan's Hector,
Prince of Troy   133
Lorna Jane Abray

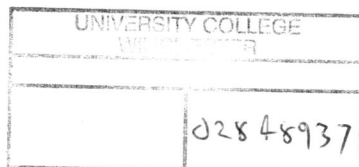

9   *La Troade* de Garnier: destins malheureux
    et exemples héroïques   149
    Stéphanie Bélanger

10 "What's Hecuba to him . . .": Trojan Heroes and
    Rhetorical Selves in Shakespeare's *Hamlet*   161
    Andrew Hiscock

11 Embracing Troy: Surrey's *Aeneid*   177
    Stephen Guy-Bray

12 Appropriating Troy: Ekphrasis in Shakespeare's
    The Rape of Lucrece   193
    Christopher Johnson

EXEMPLARITY IN TROYNOVANT

13 Slanderous Troys: Between Fame and Rumor   215
    Elizabeth Jane Bellamy

14 Falling into History: Trials of Empire in Spenser's
    Faerie Queene   237
    Rebeca Helfer

15 According to "the common received opinion": Munday's
    Brute in *The Triumphes of Re-United Britannia* (1605) 253
    Scott Schofield

16 The Fall of Troynovant: Exemplarity after the
    Death of Henry, Prince of Wales   269
    Michael Ullyot

Index   291

Acknowledgments

We would like to thank our contributors for giving us the opportunity to publish their work and the series editor, Konrad Eisenbichler, for his interest in the volume; the Centre for Reformation and Renaissance Studies at the University of Toronto for sponsoring a 2002 conference, "Troy in the Renaissance," from which most but not all of these papers emerged; the Social Sciences and Humanities Research Council of Canada for a grant to aid the publication of the volume; and two graduate students at the University of Guelph who provided expert research assistance, Debra Henderson and Robyn Read.

Contributors

Lorna Jane Abray is Associate Professor and Chair of History at the University of Toronto. She is the author of *The People's Reformation: Magistrates, Clergy and Commons in Strasbourg 1500-1598* (1985) and of articles on reformation and gender history in the early modern period.

Stéphanie Bélanger est professeur contractuel au Collège militaire royal du Canada. Elle a obtenu son doctorat à l'Université de Toronto, et elle a publié quatre articles dans son champ d'études, les figures de l'héroïsme dans les dramaturgies françaises du XVIIe siècle.

Elizabeth Jane Bellamy is Professor of English at the University of New Hampshire. She is the author of *Translations of Power: Narcissism and the Unconscious in Epic History* (1992) and many articles on early modern poetry.

James Carscallen is Professor Emeritus of English Literature at the University of Toronto and author of *The Other Country: Patterns in the Writing of Alice Munro* and of articles, mainly on English literature of the Renaissance.

Paul Cohen is *Maître de conférences* at the University of Paris-8 (Vincennes-Saint Denis), where he teaches early modern European history. He is working on a book on the emergence of French as a national language in the sixteenth and seventeenth centuries, and has published several articles on early modern French cultural history.

Sheila Das is Assistant Professor of Italian in the Department of Classics, Modern Languages and Linguistics at Concordia University (Montreal). She has published articles on Paolo Sarpi's major historical narrative, *Istoria del concilio tridentino*, and is currently writing on Renaissance political prose.

Stephen Guy-Bray is Assistant Professor of English at the University of British Columbia. He is the author of *Homoerotic Space: The Poetics of Loss in Renaissance Literature* (2002), and of articles, mainly on sixteenth and seventeenth-century poetry.

Rebeca Helfer is Assistant Professor of English at the University of California, Irvine. She is completing a manuscript with the working title *The Art of Recollection: Ruin and Cultural Memory in Spenser's Poetry*.

Andrew Hiscock is Lecturer in English at the University of Wales, Bangor. He has published *Authority and Desire: Crises of Interpretation in Shakespeare and Racine* (1996) and *The Uses of this World: Thinking Space in Shakespeare, Marlowe, Cary and Jonson* (2004) and co-edited *Dangerous Diversity: the Changing Faces of Wales from the Renaissance to the Present Day* (1998). Hiscock is at work on *Shakespeare and Early Modern Dramatists*, a forthcoming collection, and on a new study of discourses of memory in early modern literature.

Christopher Johnson is Assistant Professor of Comparative Literature and the Program in Literature at Harvard University. He has published articles on early modern lyric, translation, and the rhetoric of science. He is working on a book manuscript, *Hyperboles: The Rhetoric of Excess in Early Modern Literature and Thought*.

Michael Keefer, an Associate Professor of English at the University of Guelph, is the author of *Lunar Perspectives: Field Notes from the Culture Wars* (1996) and of articles on Renaissance literature and philosophy and on contemporary literary theory and cultural politics. He has edited Marlowe's *Doctor Faustus* (1991); his new critical edition of the 1604 and 1616 versions of *Doctor Faustus* is forthcoming.

Brent Miles is finishing his doctorate at the Centre for Medieval Studies, University of Toronto, and teaches in the Celtic Studies Program at St. Michael's College, University of Toronto. He writes on medieval Irish and Welsh literature and Insular medieval Latin.

Stephen Powell is Associate Professor of English at the University of Guelph. Among his publications are articles about medieval romance and the editing of Chaucer.

Scott Schofield is a Ph.D. Candidate in English at the University of Toronto and a Graduate Fellow at the Centre for Reformation and Renaissance Studies. His thesis examines the representations of Tudor-Stuart monarchy in London drama and pageantry (1603–1613).

Alan Shepard is Professor in the School of English and Theatre Studies at the University of Guelph. *Marlowe's Soldiers: Rhetorics of Masculinity in the Age of the Armada*, his study of late sixteenth-century London theatre, the rhetoric of national security, and the narratives of empire, appeared in 2002.

Pamela Luff Troyer is writing a doctoral dissertation at the University of Denver on Ælfric's mediation of sedition in his *Lives of the Saints*. Her work focuses on the political uses of hagiography and the transmission of classical stories in medieval England.

Michael Ullyot is a Graduate Fellow at the Centre for Reformation and Renaissance Studies, University of Toronto. He has recently completed a Ph.D. thesis on exemplarity, humanist pedagogy, and the life and death of Henry, Prince of Wales.

Introduction

ALAN SHEPARD AND STEPHEN D. POWELL

For modern audiences, the story of the Trojan War and the Fall of Troy almost always belongs to Homer, or perhaps Virgil. The story seems important to us, moreover, precisely because it is Homer's or Virgil's, because of its literary merits, not because we recognize it to be about our own genealogy or identity or the future. So influential is our investment in Homer and Virgil that we overlook how often their poems' master narratives are bent to serve modern cultural needs. As the thinking goes, if Homer and Virgil are great poets, then they must believe the things we believe.[1] What Sylvia Federico aptly calls the "cultural ownership of Troy"[2] is today related to a putative symbiosis between the poems and modern values; we seldom think of Troy as a physical place—Heinrich Schliemann's 1870 discovery of the ruins of Troy notwithstanding; and we think even less often about the extended literary tradition of competing Troy stories that once performed massive cultural work.

In medieval and early modern Europe, when dozens of versions of the Troy legend were in circulation and readers and auditors sometimes understood the legend's actors to be their own ancestors, the legend was made to perform weighty tasks—commenting on imperial prerogative, dynastic succession, even destiny. Indeed, in those times the legend's durability was tied far less to literary value than to its usefulness. It is well known that the myths of Trojan origin were commonplace in many parts of Europe, that Brutus (great-grandson of Aeneas) was said to be the founder of Britain and Francion (son of Hector) the founder of France. Such myths served to legitimate the identities, distinctiveness, and gloriousness of various individuals and groups. But the myths also brought with them their own warnings. By linking their pasts to Troy, medieval and early modern Europeans were surely also questioning their own futures. Bluntly, if Troy

---

[1]For a recent discussion of the ways the Trojan legend is read and adapted today, see "A Little Iliad," Mendelsohn's review of the 2004 Hollywood movie *Troy*, directed by Wolfgang Petersen.

[2]Federico, *New Troy*, p. xii.

could fall, so too could they. In composing, transmitting, and reading what we are calling their "fantasies of Troy," then, medieval and early modern Europeans were engaged in both the hyperveneration of Trojan valour and the dark imaginings of the certainty of Trojan disaster, often at the same time.[3]

The fifteen essays collected here all treat now-evaporated fantasies of Troy, analyzing their competing narrative variations from the late Middle Ages through the early modern period. One way or another, the fantasies are all about empire in its various guises. Yet in their expression they occupy a wide generic range—from learned poetry written for court, like Spenser's *Faerie Queene*, to the burlesque of the medieval *Seege or Batayle of Troye*, from treatises written on linguistic history to philosophical explorations of representation. The reason for the intense interest across this generic range, we believe, is the centrality of the Trojan legend within the medieval and early modern European social imaginary or, more precisely, imaginaries.

To borrow Charles Taylor's recent definition, the "social imaginary" characterizes how people "imagine their social existence, how they fit together with others, how things go on between them and their fellows, the expectations that are normally met, and the deeper normative notions and images that underlie these expectations."[4] Expressions of the social imaginary in a given time and place are inextricably linked to literacy practices as well as the oral transmission of stories. As Taylor explains,

> I adopt the term "imaginary" (i) because my focus is on the way ordinary people "imagine" their social surroundings, and this is often not expressed in theoretical terms, but is carried in images, stories, and legends. It is also the case that (ii) theory is often the possession of a small minority, whereas what is interesting in the social imaginary is that it is shared by large groups of people, if not the whole society. Which leads to a third difference: (iii) the social imaginary is that common understanding that makes possible common practices and a widely shared sense of legitimacy.[5]

Taylor means to describe the modern gulf between intellectualized social theory and popular culture as it is now "shared by large groups of people," a distinction that is less valuable in characterizing the medieval and early modern periods, where theorists of the day (poets, for example) were visibly in charge of the "complex systems of presumption"[6] that found expression

---

[3] Whereas Federico, in *New Troy*, frames her discussion of fantasies of the Trojan legacy with Freud and Lacan, our use of "fantasies" is not meant to invoke psychoanalytic theory.

[4] Taylor, *Modern Social Imaginaries*, p. 23.

[5] Taylor, *Modern Social Imaginaries*, p. 23.

[6] Vogler, "Social Imaginary," p. 625: "Crudely put, *imaginaries* are complex systems of presumption—patterns of forgetfulness and attentiveness—that enter subjective expe-

in central legends such as the Fall of Troy. We need look no further than the rood screen and the Latin mass of pre-reformation Europe or the early modern anatomy theatre to see how the invisible and the incomprehensible were integral to medieval and early modern communal formations. A belief in the inscrutability of certain myths was also a part of the medieval and early modern social imaginary.

Some but not all of the texts discussed in these essays—poems, rhetorics, linguistic treatises, and historiographies, among others—were composed by elites to substantiate their own interests, to be sure. Yet their fantasies of Troy often had as target audiences ordinary people and the collective frameworks and foundational myths of their societies. The stories, rehearsing familiar tales and making them locally relevant, were aimed at capturing and furthering the "complex systems of presumption" that undergird a society's "widely shared sense of legitimacy," as Taylor says. Just as the Christian narrative was tended by priests but lived out in ordinary people's lives in front of the rood screen, so too were the stories about Troy transmitted by writers but also lived out in the ways people embraced the normative presumptions about love, for example, or war.

As the English writer and soldier Barnabe Rich expressed it in 1609, however, crying out in vain against his society's infatuation with the Troy material, "what shall I say of our great Grandsire *Aeneas* . . . . I wonder that our English Nation, for the glory of antiquity shoulde bee so fond to recount their Genealogy from such a desteyned progeny."[7] More than almost any other set of stories, aside from those in the Bible, the legends of Troy provided medieval and early modern people with structures and vocabularies for exploring principal matters and for establishing parameters for social interaction. That such a dominant narrative component of the social imaginary, entertained right across Europe, could be based upon an ancient and (for most) foreign myth of failure and loss complicated but did not slow either its adaptation or its use in justifying medieval and early modern aspirations—toward empire, or at least toward cohesive notions of national identity.

The essays in this collection have been chosen to illustrate the sometimes surprising ways in which such adaptations have been made to the Troy legend, hitherto little explored by scholars beyond the hyper-canonical texts that may come instantly to mind. This last fact explains the absence from this collection of the extended treatment of two such texts—Chaucer's *Troilus and Criseyde* and Shakespeare's *Troilus and Cressida*. These two have

---

rience as the expectation that things will make sense generally."
    [7]Rich, *A Roome for a Gentleman*, D3r, D2r.

been extensively studied elsewhere.[8] The literary texts under consideration here, with only a few exceptions, have been much less frequently discussed by scholars.[9]

This collection, then, is bound together by a curiosity about a story told and retold dozens of times by medieval and early modern writers, about how that story contributed for centuries to the constitution of the social imaginaries of several different nations, each one understanding itself to be destined for greatness without end, each one relying on the cultural practices of storytelling to help make it so, and each one—as several essays make clear—gradually leaving the Trojan myths behind.

AFFILIATION AND APPROPRIATION

In this first section we present five essays devoted to questions of writers' efforts to affiliate their own work and their various national literatures with Trojan legends. The first two essays, by James Carscallen and Michael Keefer, synthesize the manifold versions and purposes of the Troy material across Europe and the vast expanse of time, from antiquity to romantic medievalism in late early modern Germany, while focusing on Spenser and Marlowe in late sixteenth-century England. Essays by Paul Cohen, Brent Miles, and Sheila Das concentrate on the use and status of the Troy material in France, Ireland, and the city-state of Venice. Taken as a group, the essays chart the waxing and waning of the Troy legend as a preferred source of nationalist myth-making in the service of empire and as a ready-made framework for articulating the origins of people destined for greatness. The emphasis in this grouping is less on questions of empire *per se* than on the historiographical and literary practices of the writers who affiliate with and appropriate the Troy material into the social imaginaries of their particular cultures' aspirations.

Carscallen's piece poses a philosophical question about the power of the imagination to create wholeness from a story which, though told and retold, is itself shot through with contradictions, a story that could go in many different directions. The essay offers a tour of several earlier treatments of the "discursive hybridity" (as Keefer reminds us) of the Troy story by Heliodorus, Chrétien de Troyes, Robert de Boron, Chaucer, Lydgate,

---

[8]Recent scholarship on the Troilus texts in Chaucer and Shakespeare includes Federico's chapter on *Troilus and Criseyde* in *New Troy;* Benson's "Troy" in his *Chaucer's* Troilus and Criseyde; James' chapter on *Troilus and Cressida* in *Shakespeare's Troy;* and Wilson and Milowicki's "*Troilus and Cressida*: Voices in the Darkness of Troy."

[9]*The Faerie Queene* is certainly much discussed, but its "Trojan" content is less often at the centre of discussion.

Malory, Caxton, and others. Dismissing the notion that *The Faerie Queene* is exclusively a British poem, Carscallen takes it to be an exemplar of the impetus to affiliate with Homer and the legion of adapters in order to produce stories that unite opposites such as love and chivalry, that create a world of peace and love, however temporal. Carscallen ends with Spenser's treatment of the relationship of destiny and love (love in the public, national sense) in Artegall's romance of Britomart in *The Faerie Queene*.

While Carscallen's essay surveys the historical memory of a host of medieval writers who borrow the Troy story for various ends, Keefer's primarily looks forward from the sixteenth century to discuss some of the processes by which later poets affiliate their stories with Troy. Keefer's concern is with the "hermeneutics of recovery," the "sedimented textual history" of a story such as Troy, and specifically with the ways the playwright Christopher Marlowe is actively engaged with other, sometimes ancient discourses that take up questions of the transference of cultural legitimacy and the translation of empire. Keefer argues that Marlowe's rendition of Helen of Troy substantially departs from what scholars often assume is a brittle demonology in *The Tragedy of Doctor Faustus*. Engaged in his own act of recovery, Keefer locates Marlowe's spectral Helen in three particular contexts to show that as a trope, the silent Helen of *Faustus* becomes a vehicle for thinking about divine justice and divine wisdom. To make his argument, Keefer reaches back to Euripides' two Helens, to Gorgias' reading of Helen's dilemma as an instance that proves the healing power of poetry, to Jean Calvin's warnings about "spiritual fornication"; and forward to Goethe's and Hölderlin's treatments of Helen and Faust in the context of romantic medievalism—all to bring into relief some of the literary practices of fantasizing about Trojan personae as place-holders in questions of earthly mores and divine justice.

Paul Cohen demonstrates that the Troy materials played a significant role in the linguistic history of early modern France, where affiliation was a strategy of nationalist individuation. Cohen studies the ways the Trojan legend was deployed in two related controversies about the origin of the French language and the origin of French culture. For many early modern French writers the putative origin of both language and culture was the same: Greece, not Rome. French was not a debased form of Latin, in this view, and thus evidence of Gaul's subservience to Rome, but rather a descendant of Greek, gloriously brought to Gaul by the survivors of Troy, notably Hector's son Francion. Variations of this melding of philological untruth and historical myth were common in sixteenth-century writings, even among many who might well have known better. Some, like Peter Ramus, went so far as to suggest that Gaul was the ultimate origin of Greek culture. These arguments prompt Cohen to speculate on the cultural significance of language and linguistic history in the period, the desire to liberate French "from its historical dependence on classical Rome," and the probability that many understood such claims of Gallic pre-eminence to be untrue. Cohen's argument points to some of the ways in which early modern writers understood the myth of Trojan origin to be culturally essential, yet also utterly fictional.

While the majority of essays in this collection are devoted to examining the increasing uses to which the Troy legends were being put by medieval and early modern writers, the final two essays in this group, by Brent Miles and Sheila Das, explore evidence from Ireland and Venice of the limits of affiliating with Troy, signs of the material's being exhausted. Miles considers the reception of the Trojan legend in late fifteenth-century Ireland, arguing that a model of Irish literary history that ignores medieval and early modern engagement with classical texts is misleading. Such a model fails to recognize the stylistic, thematic, and narrative influences of such texts on the more often studied native Irish texts. *Togail Troí*, a tenth-century text derived in part from Dares Phrygius, was undoubtedly popular, as it survives in three separate editions that testify to expansions and revisions; Miles finds evidence that this work helped to shape the native Irish tradition. Yet by 1500 the *Togail Troí* had ceased to have a direct influence on Irish literature, and Miles seeks an explanation of that in fifteenth-century manuscript copies of classical texts. These manuscripts mark off such texts as the *Togail Troí* as non-Irish, "as something apart, ultimately belonging to the antiquity of continental Europe."

Sheila Das takes us from the periphery of Europe to its centre to discuss the historiography of Venice, an empire whose need for affiliation with Troy materials also waned. Distinguishing Venice from other jurisdictions, Das explains the gradual diminishment of the myths of Troy from the historiography of Venice. She argues that the Troy material proved more useful to Venice in the medieval period as a myth of liberty and stability; the material proved less useful as a warrant for authorizing or justifying imperialist expansion in the wake of certain crises of Italian independence by city-states and in the light of fifteenth-century humanism. Two humanist treatises on the foundation of Venice—Bernardo Giustiniani's *De origine urbis Venetiarum* (1493) and Gasparo Contarini's *De magistratibus et republica Venetorum* (1531)—prove that the Troy material was gradually fading from view in Venetian historiography. Das challenges certain widely agreed-upon notions held by contemporary scholars that the Myth of Venice was instrumental in the city's efforts to expand its empire. Suggesting that a widely published historiography is as much an "international language" as the visual images of empire that have formed the core of evidence to which modern scholars have pointed, Das shows both how and why major figures such as Contarini came to consider the Trojan legend largely irrelevant to contemporary efforts to bolster the foundational myths of Venice.

RHETORIC, TRANSLATIO IMPERII, AND TROJAN LEGACY

The second group of essays is devoted to focused analyses of medieval and early modern literary texts that perform normatizing functions for their readers, that aid readers in imagining and then surrendering to collective agreements about matters of local identity and national destiny. Fundamentally these agreements rely on literary practices that express praise or blame, and they often draw exemplars from the Troy material. The readings here, of French and English works, open up some of the ways the Trojan legend is recast—through rhetorical means—to meet specific concerns.

Mostly, such concerns are serious, in keeping with a general sense that the fall of Troy was a weighty and tragic subject and that the origins of French and English national identities lay in the descendants of Troy. In the first of these essays, however, Pamela Luff Troyer argues that the late medieval English *Seege or Batayle of Troye* should be read as a comic if still pointed exploration of the impact of the Trojan legend on cultural formation. Troyer examines the way three of the four surviving manuscript copies of the poem deviate radically and humorously from the traditional tale. Recognizing that such variations are less likely to be the result of authorial incompetence or scribal meddling than scholars once imagined, Troyer reads these deviations from tradition as evidence of the poem's attempt to burlesque the weighty subject it was treating. Hector's death, for example, is a matter of comic scorn: he is stabbed in the posterior by a less than chivalrous Achilles as he covetously and foolishly bends over to examine a shiny helmet. Indeed, throughout the poem, Troyer claims, the Greeks, and even more the Trojans, are made to seem comically ridiculous, "their own worst enemies." The result is to turn upside down the notion of Trojan ancestry for the earliest Britons, but, Troyer argues, that result is less important than the text's larger goal of carnivalesque entertainment, a low-grade satire on the foolishness of grandiose aspiration.

As Lorna Jane Abray argues, however, the legend of Troy has more dangerous implications for the social imaginary of gendered discipline in late medieval France in the far more serious treatment it is given in various texts by Christine de Pizan. Reading Christine's portrayals of Hector, Abray argues that these depictions move quickly and decisively from the formulaic praise accorded to Hector as one of the Nine Worthies to views of an immature and reckless hero who brings disaster rather than triumph. For Christine, Hector represents the "failure to discipline boys into men" and the dangers of equating physical strength with masculinity and thus martial worth. Writing in a historical moment in which France was threatened by such undisciplined leaders—the dukes of Orléans and Burgundy clamouring to wrest control from the mad King Charles VI—Christine shapes her presentation of Hector accordingly. Rather than the ancestor of Francion, Hector thus becomes a rhetorical marker of the contemporary dangers confronting France.

In Robert Garnier's *Troade*, a play published in 1579, the Trojan legend is again brought to bear on contemporary French troubles, this time the sixteenth-century wars of religion, though with almost precisely the opposite effect. In her essay, Stéphanie Bélanger reads the way the myth of the Trojan foundation of France is connected to notions of divine justice and retribution and thus to a belief that bloodshed in a noble cause will eventually lead to historical justification. In Garnier's play, as in other French plays of the period, such as Antoine de Montchrestien's *Hector*, the Trojan defeat is shaped as a noble last stand against Greek perfidy, which manifests itself in unfair warfare and violence against women and children. For Garnier, Bélanger argues, the glorious destiny of the defeated Trojans is evidence of divine retribution. Thus, just as the Trojans were riven by war and yet live in glorious history, Garnier proposes, so too will France come through its bloody present to a divinely ordained glorious future.

Andrew Hiscock is likewise concerned with how the Trojan legend is recast, not by contemporary political events but rather by ongoing cultural debates in sixteenth- and early seventeenth-century England about the nature of memory, the function of education, and the shaping of subjectivity, about "translating learned knowledge into significant human action." While Abray and Bélanger map the legend's appropriations onto contemporary events, then, Hiscock shows that *Hamlet* actually joins with treatises on education to theorize such appropriation. Through his various references to the Trojan legend, Hamlet attempts to form a stable frame of reference for his present actions, even though his use of the past is at odds with the positions of others, including Gertrude and Claudius. Such recollections of the past, however, are inherently translations, which Hiscock urges us to understand within an early modern understanding of translation: "not as examples of slavish replication, but as creative acts of self-definition."

Stephen Guy-Bray's essay considers the Earl of Surrey's translation of books two and four of the *Aeneid* (published 1554–1557), comparing it both to the original and to Gavin Douglas' translation into Scots from a few decades earlier. Guy-Bray seeks to rethink Surrey's work as deliberately original, and not as an instance of near-plagiarism on Douglas' part, and he works to understand the philosophical motivations for Surrey's choices—his choice to translate books two and four, for one thing, but also his rendering of key parts of the poem into tightly compressed, unrhymed English verse that is a faithful replication in English terms of the Latin original (as opposed to Douglas' bloated rhyming couplets). Surrey's early use of what would come to be called blank verse seems to point forward to later English writers, but Guy-Bray argues that it is actually Douglas' translation that is more "modern," translating both the content and the form. Instead, Surrey used blank verse to approximate Latin prosody in English words. When Surrey does deviate from the original, moreover, it is for the same reason that he has chosen to translate books two and four, which describe the destruction of Troy and the ill-fated love of Dido and Aeneas—because he wishes to emphasize that memory of the past is painful. Remembering Troy's fall, then, is painful, as Surrey's contemporaries would have agreed, but not necessarily a sign of future English glory.

Christopher Johnson also comments on the painfulness of the contemplation of Troy's fall, this time in the visual depiction in the second half of Shakespeare's 1594 poem *The Rape of Lucrece*. Johnson argues that this famous section of the poem is notable both for its self-conscious concern with the nature of mimesis and for its commentary on the nature of identity. By looking at the picture of Troy's fall, Johnson claims, Lucrece "learns that identity is more performative than rhetorical." At the same time, the ekphrasis "suggests that the 'lacrimae rerum,' with which Virgilian ekphrasis memorably epitomizes the fall of Troy, no longer could be assuaged in the waning years of Elizabeth's *Troynovant*." Indeed, for Johnson, the ekphrasis works in the poem to bring the Trojan story to life for a suffering Lucrece, while for the reader it brings Troy's fall into the world of Shakespeare's contemporaries. In both cases, however, such re-presentation of Troy is not only temporary (as all ekphrasis is) but also problematic, as Lucrece commits suicide and as the reader, too, is forced to "reenter the stream of time and action."

Exemplarity in Troynovant

In the final section, four essays are devoted to the consequences of widely entertained fantasies of London–as–Troynovant as the Tudor dynasty gave way to the Stuart regime. The affiliation of the two great cities, linked by Brutus, had taken on real urgency in the latter years of Elizabeth's reign.[10] By the 1590s, both myths had come to seem a bit tired—not yet obsolete, but wearied, and with diminishing impact on the social imaginary that constituted Londoners' sense of destiny in the wake of the Spanish Armada

---

[10]For a discussion of the differences in function and status of the Troy legend in the reigns of Elizabeth and James, see James, *Shakespeare's Troy*, especially ch. 1.

and other threats, martial and civilian, associated with the transition from Elizabeth to James.[11] Two of the essays, by Elizabeth Jane Bellamy and Rebeca Helfer, offer readings of Spenser's *Faerie Queene* devoted to the poet's engagement with questions about the role of poetry in the affairs of state. So while Bellamy and Helfer return us full circle to Spenser, theirs is a more political poet than Carscallen's syncretizing one. The final two essays, by Scott Schofield and Michael Ullyot, present arguments about the role and status of the Troy material in two London Lord Mayors' Shows, in 1605 and 1612, pageants designed as with *The Faerie Queene* to glorify England's (and London's) past and future. These essays show that the Troy legend was nearly exhausted as a fund of stories to be borrowed, burnished, and heeded, even though in retrospect we can see that Troynovant itself had several decades to go before its own Fall would literally come to pass in the Great Fire in 1666.

Writing of the imperial agenda of late sixteenth-century England, Bellamy concentrates on the Britomart-Paridell episode in *The Faerie Queene*, reading it as a way for Spenser to suggest the obsoleteness of the Trojan mythology for contemporary England. Bellamy's essay anticipates Ullyot's on the 1612 Lord Mayor's Show in that both take up questions of the instability of the exemplary figure drawn from ancient history and the ideological burden of "propping up" various Renaissance genealogies. Bellamy argues that we may read a figure such as the faerie-knight Paridell as a demonstration of an alternative script for refugees from Troy, much as Prince Henry has been recast as a contemporary Hector whose own contingency is on display. In the end, Bellamy takes us beyond Spenser's treatment to Chaucer's in *The House of Fame* to suggest that no genealogy can be divorced from its own literary history and that any poet's use of an exemplar—whether it be Hector, Paris, or Paridell—is at some level suspect and vulnerable to questions about the truth content of poetry as an ideological force to be grappled with.

Spenser's ambiguous stance toward Elizabethan imperialism is also the subject of Helfer's study, which focuses on the trial of Jove in Nature's Court in *The Faerie Queene* along with the poet's narration of English history in books II and III. Arguing that that forensic setting is itself one sign of Spenser's ambivalence toward Jove's claims that empire can be without end, Helfer develops a set of arguments regarding the poet's inheritance of Virgil's poetic legacy. So while humanists and others in the sixteenth century were pressing the Troy material more vigorously than before, Helfer argues, Spenser was

---

[11] On the dissolution of the Troy myth, national security, and the London theatres in the 1580s and 1590s, see Shepard, *Marlowe's Soldiers*, especially ch. 2.

crafting a poetic meditation along similar lines, asking slyly whether the *translatio imperii* was not just another trope for disguising ruthless imperial ambitions. Spenser is seen here as being almost skeptical toward Queen Elizabeth's aims of empire-building. In Helfer's view, then, *The Faerie Queene* may be a poem celebrating Elizabeth's links to both Jove and Troy, but it is also a poem that leaves open Spenser's view of the contingencies of history and the instrumental uses of fictions of empire.

Schofield considers the paradox that while historiographers and anti-quaries were moving away from the legend of England's ancestral relation-ship to Brutus, certain playwrights and pageant makers were continuing to exploit well-established myths in order to score political points with the crown. Schofield takes as his case study Anthony Munday's 1605 London Lord Mayor's show, a civic pageant ostensibly designed to celebrate the entry of a knight and Merchant Taylor, the city's Lord Mayor, as Brute. As Schofield explains, however, Munday makes an extravaganza that virtually ignores the new mayor, while celebrating King James' insistence that his accession has resurrected an ancient Great Britain rooted in the myth of Brutus. Schofield marshals several competing versions of foundation myths for England by the likes of William Camden, Sir Robert Cotton, Samuel Daniel, Michael Drayton, Polydore Vergil and others, to show us the extent to which the notion of England's claims to be linked to Brutus were being treated skeptically by Munday's contemporaries.

The spectacle of another Lord Mayor's Show is a jumping off point for Ullyot's study of the effects of the sudden death of James' son Henry, Prince of Wales in 1612 on the contemporary uses of the Troy material and on the category of *exemplarity* more broadly. Henry's death coincided with Thomas Dekker's civic pageant for Sir John Swinnerton's entry into London, *Troia-Noua Triumphans*. Instead, as the pageant proceeded, Prince Henry lay dying at court, and his death a few days later unleashed a torrent of elegies that reignited London's previous relationship to the Troy material. Where the city's link to Brutus had previously been a metaphor of great joy in the accession of King James, after the death of Prince Henry all had changed: as Ullyot demonstrates, poets especially appropriated bits of the Trojan legend indiscriminately in their efforts to elegize the prince, whose death was instantly and regularly compared to Hector's. Ullyot's essay recovers a number of the elegies produced on the occasion in order to make a larger argument about the impact of a sudden, singular event on the uses of the Troy material by contemporary writers. Their poems remind readers that the category of "exemplar" is itself a fiction, that exemplary figures from the past—legendary figures and historical ones alike—are mortally vulnerable to the contingency of time.

WORKS CITED

Benson, C. David. *Chaucer's* Troilus and Criseyde. London: Unwin Hyman, 1990.

Federico, Sylvia. *New Troy: Fantasies of Empire in the Late Middle Ages*. Medieval Cultures 36. Minneapolis: University of Minnesota Press, 2003.

James, Heather. *Shakespeare's Troy: Drama, Politics, and the Translation of Empire*. Cambridge Studies in Renaissance Literature and Culture 22. Cambridge: Cambridge University Press, 1997.

Mendelsohn, Daniel. "A Little Iliad." *New York Review of Books* 24 June 2004: 46–49.

Rich, Barnabe. *A Roome for a Gentleman*. London, 1609. STC 20985.

Shepard, Alan. *Marlowe's Soldiers: Rhetorics of Masculinity in the Age of the Armada*. Aldershot: Ashgate, 2002.

Taylor, Charles. *Modern Social Imaginaries*. Durham: Duke University Press, 2004.

Vogler, Candace. "Social Imaginary, Ethics, and Methodological Individualism." *Public Culture* 14 (2002): 625–627.

Wilson, Robert Rawdon and Edward Milowicki. "*Troilus and Cressida*: Voices in the Darkness of Troy." *Reading the Renaissance: Culture, Poetics, and Drama*. Ed. Jonathan Hart. New York: Garland, 1996. 129–144.

Affiliation

and

Appropriation

How Troy Came to Spenser

JAMES CARSCALLEN

I: HISTORY

This paper will come as a kind of broad-jump hopscotch through the vast
literature of Troy. I would like to show if I can how the city's story attained the
full meaning for which it had the potential. This is not to say that later writers
are necessarily better than earlier ones—Homer at the beginning is as great as
any. But they had different aims, and if I dwell on Spenser at the end it will be
because of his talent, and inclination for, gathering varied materials into a
structure at once comprehensive and coherent—and by the same token mean-
ingful.[1] His story of Troy becoming his own England is thus a kind of scripture:
a play scripture or "para-scripture," if we like, but a scripture all the same, by
which I mean an account of a culture's experience, taken as a whole, that gives
this experience a satisfying shape and sense. I am going to treat the Matter of
Troy first as history, or pseudo-history, with justice as its end; later I will turn
to the love that caused the Trojan War, and try to show how love can both
disrupt and, in a higher form, transform the simpler story of justice.

Whether believing in it or not, Spenser used the so-called "Tudor myth":
the notion, that is, that England's present rulers were descended, through
those of ancient Britain, from an eponymous Trojan settler named Brutus.
But England belonged to a western Europe in which almost everybody was
claiming Trojan ancestry;[2] for what everybody knew or knew about was of
course the Trojan scripture that Virgil had produced for Rome. Christian
Europe also knew—as it seems Virgil did, through some channel[3]—of another

---

[1]To have an extreme contrast, we can think of the Trojan epistles in Ovid's
Heroides. Ovid cares about what his writers are feeling and seeking in a particular
situation: the larger story, while assumed to be familiar, counts only as it makes this
situation possible.

[2]To refer to only one author, Guido delle Colonne in his Trojan history (see the
discussion below) knows that Rome, England, and France were founded by Aeneas,
Brutus, and Francus respectively; he has also read of other Trojan foundings—of Venice
by Antenor and Sicily by Sicanus.

[3]Hadas, *Hellenistic Culture*, pp. 238–241, 253–256.

scripture, the Jewish: and in this last it possessed the highly developed history of a people first chosen, next drawn down into what proved a land of bondage, and finally, after wandering and struggle, reaching a Promised Land where they could establish their city. That city had itself been brought low, to be sure, but for believers in a Messiah it had at least been provisional, pointing through further ordeals to a great restoration. Since, moreover, the new Jerusalem would be of a higher order—an abiding city, a light to lighten the nations—the relation between earlier and later became typological: the story was now not just longer but more significantly structured.

But there was an important scripture that western Christendom did not know: the Homeric poems venerated by the Greeks, which were pretty well lost in the Latin world by the end of Antiquity, and recovered and re-absorbed only slowly at the end of the Middle Ages. In a large measure our knowledge of the Trojan story comes from other sources, generally much later than the Homeric poems though often representing traditions at least as old. As is well known, our two *general* accounts of the war, long accepted as eye-witness reports and debunked only in the early eighteenth century,[4] were those of Dares the Phrygian and Dictys of Crete. These were probably written in the first century CE, though Dares' sixth-century Latin translator added new information about events before the war; Dictys had already dealt with events immediately following it.

The prelude and postlude are actually of more importance to us here than the main accounts themselves: for they put the war as a whole into a larger context, with all the possibilities that that opens. When an earlier Trojan king, Laomedon, nervously refuses hospitality to Jason and his Argonauts, Greeks return to plunder his city and carry off the princess Hesione. Laomedon's son Priam does the necessary refortifying—it was from this detail that later tradition developed its notion of Troy as the greatest of all cities. In the same addition to Dares the sending of Paris to Greece has revenge for its motive, and with such a motive there can go a strong sense of injustice, becoming all the stronger if Priam's city in turn is plundered and laid waste. In other words, the Trojan War had causes and results as well as events; these could be matter for praise and blame; and in particular it was possible to see the fall as that of a noble city wantonly destroyed. This is not the view of Dictys, for whom the war is primarily one of Greek reason and justice against Asiatic barbarism. It is not clearly the view of Dares either, though he has often been thought more of a Trojan advocate than he really is. Nor does Dictys suggest any real recovery for the

---

[4]See Frazer's ed. of Dictys and Dares, *The Trojan War*, p. 7.

city: Troy is as finished as Carthage. This is why Virgil's recasting of the story was so important for its future career. Like Euripides before him he shows us nothing of Trojan crimes; he describes all the horrors of the Greek victory; and in place of a minor figure in Homer and a downright unsavoury one in Dares and Dictys he gives us the *pius Aeneas*. Embellishing an existing Latin tradition,[5] Virgil has Aeneas called out by Venus, his mother, to bring the surviving Trojans to Italy and unite them there with indigenous Latins. A new race now exists, a chosen people destined to build a new city and, on its own terms, give a biblical kind of blessing to the world.[6]

Of the various national and civic legends following the lead of the *Aeneid*, by far the best known throughout western Europe was Geoffrey of Monmouth's *Historia Regum Britanniae*, written under Henry I of England and almost—though not quite—uncontested during the Middle Ages. In principle Geoffrey has almost the whole history that we are going to need (and quite as much as the Tudors felt themselves to need). Starting where Virgil starts, with the fall of the city, he brings Brutus with his people to a far western island empty of human inhabitants; there, as Diana has revealed to him, his descendents are to found "a second Troy" to which "the round circle of the whole earth"[7] will be subject. And when the British, having indeed done well on the island, are mostly driven from it by the Saxons, an angel prophesies that in time they will "reoccupy their lost kingdom" (xii.17). Yet taken in isolation these announcements give a false impression of Geoffrey's work. Primarily it is a simple chronicle, with a strong sense that one thing follows another but a weak sense of events working out a destiny (what Geoffrey really enjoys is then-and-there battles and strategy). And at the end he is less a seer inspired by a vision of restoration—which in any case would just be a return to where things were—than a condemning medieval preacher who, like Gildas before him, sees British sin leading to British downfall.

Geoffrey's *imaginative* contribution to the fully formed history we are assembling is his strong sense, equally medieval, of what I have called the provisional. As I have noted, it is possible to see cities like David's Jerusalem or Priam's Troy as neither original nor ultimate but as temporary greatness flanked by periods of failure and exile. Geoffrey gives us such a city,

---

[5]Brill's *New Pauly*, s.v. *Aeneas*. According to a decree of Julius Caesar the *gens Iulia* was descended from a son of Aeneas called "Iulus" as well as the traditional Ascanius.

[6]The two crucial passages in the *Aeneid* are I.278ff. and VI.851–853; and the *Aeneid*, as a whole, makes its terms those of firm government.

[7]Geoffrey of Monmouth, *History of the Kings of Britain*, i.11. Subsequent citations are noted parenthetically.

temporary as a British capital, in his Troia Nova or Trinovantum, later to be called London (iii.20). More important, he has the mighty and tragic Arthur—Arthur in context, that is, bringing the line of British kings to its climax, defying Roman demands, and confounding the Emperor himself before succumbing to treachery at home. And it is Geoffrey who first puts Arthur in a still larger context, the Matter of Troy that we have seen in his work. Once again, he may not have cared much: he clearly cared little about a "once and future" Arthur, for while we hear of the wounded king being taken to Avalon, we hear nothing about any return. Still, given the prophecies Geoffrey mentions, a great opportunity was now there for tellers of the story to take.

For some centuries they failed to do so. On the Continent the Arthurian legend, while absorbed into that of the Holy Grail by Chrétien de Troyes and Robert de Boron and developed in the great romance cycles that followed Robert, sees consummation outside history. Malory, who would like to see it in his own England, is good at finding parallels (if not typological prefigurings) between Arthur's Britain and the proud England of Henry V, itself now vanished; he even mentions the "Breton hope" of Arthur's return. But he mentions this last briefly and wistfully; there is nothing of conviction here. What happened next was simply a dynastic accident: it so happened that Henry V's widow married, or at least cohabited with, her Welsh clerk of the wardrobe, and that their grandson won the Battle of Bosworth. As a result England had a reigning house that could claim British ancestry, making it royal for good measure; the same house could claim, or have it claimed for them, that the Troy once fallen and provisionally revived under Arthur had finally realized its destiny in themselves. And Spenser could write *The Faerie Queene*, of which at this stage I will say only one thing. Virgil never quite asserts that Rome is another Troy—he is more concerned with a renewed Golden Age; Spenser, with Geoffrey behind him (not to say various Tudor antiquaries whom I have left unmentioned) does speak of "Troynovaunt."[8] He also has a ringing claim that this new Troy (the third, actually, after Troy and Rome) will

---

[8]The Sibyl tells Aeneas that he will have to endure another war like the original one (I.88ff.). More important here, Jupiter reassures Venus that in time descendents of Troy will conquer Mycenae and Argos: the Greek cities, in other words, that conquered Troy. Indeed Julius, the "Troianus . . . Caesar," will extend his rule to Ocean itself (by conquering Gaul and invading Britain) (I.281–288). But Troy precisely did *not* do these latter things, and Virgil is more aware of Rome as vindicating Troy than as recreating it.

For the whole matter of Tudor descent from the British royalty of Geoffrey's history, see Millican, *Spenser and the Table Round*.

equal its great predecessors, even bring an eternal and loving peace.[9] The typology that appears only casually and fitfully in Geoffrey is fully alive for Spenser.

There are further steps that Spenser makes less plain, though I will later try to show how he suggests them. To see them indicated elsewhere, we can move from England to the Burgundy of the great dukes—or at any rate to the successor world where, in the year 1500, Jean Lemaire de Belges set about his *Illustrations de Gaule et Singularitez de Troye*.[10] A weird and sometimes wonderful work related to the age's universal histories,[11] the *Illustrations* both takes the Trojan genealogy back to the Flood and brings it down through the Trojans Francus and Bavo to the French and Imperial families of Lemaire's own day. The moral of his story is quite clear. Not only must these kinsmen be reconciled with each other, but in a great "croisée"[12] they must reconquer the lands of another kinsman, King Priam, lands now held by the Turkish invader. It is not enough to found a new and greater city: greatness must include that of saving the old and reuniting with it.

Such an idea goes much farther back than Lemaire: in founding his new capital, for instance, the Emperor Constantine had wanted to use the site of Troy, even if his staff talked him down to a more practical location nearby. In Lemaire's mind, moreover, the European powers should undertake their *croisée* not just as Trojans but as Christians: for the descendents of Francus and Bavo whom he is trying to connect were connected earlier under the Emperor Charlemagne, and Charlemagne's family, Lemaire assures us, bestowed its lands on the Church.[13] The theocratic Franks later recovered a city both honoured even above Troy and, for Lemaire, closely associated with it, the city of Tasso's *Gerusalemme Liberata*, Jerusalem set free. And the *Liberata* can show us something more again: not just a successful reunion of Christianity with its original home but, by the same act, the releasing of a sacred power—a greater thing than Virgil's just rule—that, filling the world, will also transform it. On the one hand, what Godfrey of

---

[9]See Spenser, *The Faerie Queene* (subsequently cited as *FQ*), III.ix.44–45 and III.iii.49.

[10]Lemaire's dates are 1473–?1515. See *Oeuvres de Jean Lemaire de Belges*, ed. Stecher. Vol. I contains the first book of the *Illustrations*, Vol. II the second and third books. In my references I give Lemaire's book numbers, which are important, along with Stecher's page numbers.

[11]Apart from Boccaccio's *De genealogia deorum* (1373), Lemaire's main source is Annius of Viterbo's *Antiquitates* of 1498, which for the first time enabled writers to take the French line back, not just to Francus as in Fredegar, but to the first age of the world.

[12]Lemaire, *Oeuvres*, vol. I, p. 350; vol. III, p. 473.

[13]Lemaire, *Oeuvres*, vol. III, p. 259.

Bouloigne liberates is very particular, the Holy Sepulchre before which we see him standing at the end of the poem; on the other, we hear of Christianity not only regaining the lands Islam has usurped but taking salvation—what Christ's burial and resurrection brought about—to the source of the Nile and the endless realms beyond the ocean.[14]

With his quest for a transforming relic Tasso has been seen as echoing the story of the Grail; even more suggestive here, I feel, is another tradition with which he will have been familiar. The matter of Jason had been attached to Troy ever since the Latin translator of Dares, and in 1430, to mention one well publicized event, Philippe le Bon had founded the Order of the Golden Fleece. Whatever Philippe may have had in mind, we know that he was attached to Jason[15] just as he was attached to Trojan ancestry[16] and the idea of a Crusade. In Burgundian authors close to him, as also in the earlier *Ovide moralisé*, Jason's *croisée* was made into that of a Christ-like deliverer;[17] in orders imitating Philippe's, the Fleece appears as the fire of the Holy Spirit, while in alchemy it becomes the regenerating *mysterium*. Jason may take his prize back home; the Crusaders may stay to rule in Jerusalem (or Constantinople); later Roman Catholic expansion may achieve crossings previously unimaginable: but the real goal reached by the crossing and recrossing here is a placeless holiness that redeems all places.

I will be coming back to the significance of this claim; to return briefly to Lemaire, though, I would like to point out one way in which his powerful structure is rather less than powerful. It does, to be sure, give the Trojan War a cause both definite and morally significant: abandoning their spouses, the infatuated Paris and Helen flee to Troy and a delighted Priam. The result is disaster, and the reason, clearly, has been evil love and its approval. It also happens that in Lemaire's account restoration involves a good counterpart: for the genealogy by which he connects the rulers of Europe with Troy and

---

[14]See in particular Tasso, *Gerusalemme Liberata*, XIV.8ff., XV.27ff., XVII.93ff. There had been a prophecy in Ariosto (*Orlando Furioso* XV.18ff.) of the triumph of Cross and Empire in all the newly discovered East; but the Biserta from which the Saracen assault originates in Boiardo and on which Ariosto's Franks focus their ultimate counter-assault points back historically to Carthage and mythologically to the underworld source of uprisings in late classical tradition. Tasso's counterpart of Biserta is Egypt (XVIII); his sacred city and tomb, able to emanate sacred power if liberated, are something quite different.

[15]Lefèvre, *L'Histoire de Jason*, p. 97.

[16]Bayot, *La légende*; Doutrepont, *Littérature française*, pp. 171–176.

[17]Lefèvre, *L'Histoire de Jason*, pp. 102ff. For Lefèvre the Fleece is what Jason overcomes to redeem mankind. For Filastre in *Le Thoison d'or* (1468–1473) the Fleece is itself sacred: "une âme pure et sainte" presented to God in the Temple of Jupiter, i.e. in the Church (see Doutrepont, *Littérature française*, p. 164).

each other is full of dynastic marriages.[18] Significantly, though, that is all these are: love need have nothing to do with them. And this brings me to the complicating of our subject that I warned about earlier. The story of Troy is a love-story, the war itself, as in many another legend, is over a woman. And to see what that entails we must now ask what happens to history when love comes into it.

II: LOVE

To approach this question, I first need to indicate a framework for it—and make some generalizations without having space to discuss them fully. I have already claimed that when history, like any story, takes on greater structure, it takes on greater meaning—what structure expresses. It thus becomes more fully what it is, and by this criterion we can say that Homer has no real history at all: for since the sequence of events in his world depends on the gods, and the gods are capricious and unpredictable, the overall result can have no real shape.[19] In the Stoic ambiance of the *Aeneid* the sequence of things does have shape and meaning, since it has become the process by which reason moves to its practical realization as justice; and men, who in Homer are much like the Homeric gods,[20] have become good or bad as they obstruct or further this process. Now for a further assertion: when we sense meaning we are also sensing integration—not surprisingly if structure, being a matter of order, is also a matter of unity. When we say, for instance, that the *Aeneid* "means something," an important reason is our feeling that the new city will somehow be one with the old. To take a further step, the steadfast *pietas* underlying this oneness enables us to identify it with love: here the love that T.S. Eliot calls "in itself unmoving, only the cause and end of movement."[21]

At the same time, love in the complementary sense of desire or attraction is the principle of movement itself: the dynamic of a story rather than the *stasis*

---

[18]The most important attempt in the later Middle Ages to organize mythology and history by genealogy was Boccaccio's *De Genealogia*, one of Lefèvre's and Lemaire's leading sources.

[19]Both the *Iliad* and the *Odyssey* have powerful structures as individual stories, and we could speak of Providence ordaining these structures. But this intention is *ad hoc*, even if the poems we have originally belonged to larger cycles. Because of the Homeric conception of divine (as of human) nature, there can be no *general* design here, and in that sense no history.

[20]That is, they do the kind of thing they do as casually and unreflectingly as Odysseus destroying Ismaros on his way home to Ithaca (*Odyssey* IX.47ff.).

[21]Eliot, *Burnt Norton*, V, p. 175.

that it moves towards. In both this second way and the first we can say that all stories, including all histories, are love-stories, whether or not love appears in them as content. And to account more fully for the shape of the Trojan history, we will have to conceive love in still a third way, as neither *stasis* nor the seeking of it but as an irrational force that disrupts such a movement and has to be cast out for an orderly settling of affairs. Passionate love can, of course, be something more acceptable; we will even be seeing it as an ally of reason and of the destiny through which reason triumphs. Yet here too something has to be cast out: something that, however unruly, contains what our story needs if it is to reach true wholeness. To complete this paper's own story we will need finally to ask what this something is;[22] in the meantime we can go back to our thoughts on Homer.

If there is a sense in which Homer has no history, in the same sense he has no love. He has sex, of course, and domestic affection, but the Briseis who causes the quarrel between Agamemnon and Achilles is primarily booty, something of which Achilles demands his proper share. So is Helen, what Paris brought home from a raid. Nor, we can add, is either Helen or Paris blamed for what happened;[23] love, the doing of Aphrodite, is just one of those things. But as we approach the hellenistic world we can sense the ground shifting. In Euripides, again a crucial figure, we find on the one hand that Helen has become monstrous, responsible for the war, and on the other that the war's most notable victims are the women who, outrageously, are taken off to be concubines. Sexual responsibility and sexual sensibility are now realities that matter. And if there is no accompanying sense of *history* in Euripides, there is certainly one when the same judgments are made in Virgil. Virgil, moreover, shows something else I have mentioned: the disruption that passionate love can cause. Dido, whom I feel to be pointedly contrasted with Helen in the Underworld episode, is no monster, and in offering the bounteous refuge of her realm and person to a storm-driven exile she is quite sincere. But the *pietas* governing Aeneas' historical mission, like all proper dedication in classical thought, demands the subduing of

---

[22]By "this paper's own story" I do not mean the historical evolution of the Trojan matter. It is true that an *account* of this history, such as the present paper, naturally tends towards the literary form that all discourse takes, but my own "story" corresponds only in part to actual chronological development.

[23]In Books III and VI Paris is blamed for failing to fight, not for loving except as it impedes fighting; certainly he is not blamed for raiding. In the same books Helen blames herself (though no-one else blames her) for foolishness—again not love; and even Helen makes no distinction between personal responsibility and the compulsion brought by Aphrodite.

instinct and any attachment resulting from it. Aeneas' marriage with Lavinia is something quite different. Its function is to bring the fusion of newcomers with Latins that makes possible the *pax romana*, and it has nothing to do with "being in love"—something that has to be sacrificed before the hero can properly land in Italy at all.[24]

Love could get farther by other routes. We might have guessed that Ovid, mischief-maker that he was, would sing not of arms and the man but of the new empire of Cupid, and imagine himself as marching bound and bleeding in Cupid's triumph[25]—something we will meet again. What nobody has ever quite explained is the development, from Ovid's spoofing submission among other things, not only of a medieval fealty to love but of one that could enter into the serious business of war itself. We see this happening in the *romans anciens* of the mid-twelfth century when the *Roman d'Énéas* works love into the relation between Aeneas and Lavinia. This takes some doing, since the two are on opposite sides in a siege: if Lavinia wants to write an Ovidian epistle to her love, she accordingly has to wrap it around a carefully aimed arrow.[26] And significantly, the playing up of love here goes with a playing down of what for Virgil is the relation's main point: the union of peoples and a historical succession of leaders. But at any rate Aeneas is now a lover who need not put love behind him; and when Benoît de Ste. Maure writes a slightly later romance on the Trojan War itself, he takes for granted that a proper knight will also be a lover, indeed that love will inspire his prowess in fighting. In the story of Troilus and Briseida (which Benoît works up from mere names in Dares and interweaves among his battles) what is wrong is not love but infidelity to it.

So the story of Troy now glorifies both chivalry and love, governed by similar and connected codes. And this was to remain the case for centuries: it must have been second nature for Caxton, bringing out his *Eneydos* in 1590, to intend it for the gentleman apt "in faytes of armes, in love, and in noble chyvalrye."[27] I have quoted Caxton, though, because of

---

[24]Structurally the Dido story is a prologue to the main one, that beginning with Aeneas' arrival in Italy. Within the Italian story the glowing prospect of alliance with Latinus and marriage with Lavinia is suddenly blocked by forces of passion, whether strictly erotic or not: the respective furors of Juno, Allecto, and Turnus complete with Bacchic dances and, of course, war.

[25]More precisely arms and war: "arma gravi numero violentaque bella" (Ovid, *Amores* I.i.1). Ovid does of course sing of arms and the man when he includes a résumé of Virgil's Roman history in the final book of the *Metamorphoses*. On Cupid's empire see *Amores* I.i.12–13; on Cupid's triumph, *Amores* I.ii.

[26]See *Enéas, Roman du XIIe Siècle*, ll. 8795ff.

[27]*Caxton's* Eneydos, *1490*, p. 3. Lefèvre's work was done about 1464; Caxton's came

a remarkable inconsistency. By also translating Jean Lefèvre's *Recoeil des Histoires de Troyes*, itself a translation, he takes us back to Guido delle Colonne and his *Historia Destructionis Troiae* of 1287, in which both love and chivalry come under strong attack. Guido does not have Virgil's sense of historical destiny, but he does have a keen sense of propriety and even more of prudence. Any indulging of impulse, such as the mutual attraction between Paris and Helen when they meet at a festival, is a co-operating with the Fates who, being bent on destruction, will bring immense harm at the slightest opportunity.[28] And this was the view taken over by Lydgate in his own version of Guido, the *Troy Book*. Indeed Lydgate turns Guido's single-minded Fates into someone more mysterious as well as more fully medieval, the fickle lady Fortune, who at the same time is more than just fickle, since she is as determined on our ruin as the Fates themselves. What makes her changeable is mainly that, in order to ensure a proper downfall, she first raises us up. And what makes this tactic even more bewildering is that the prosperity she brings us to is not simply high estate: as Lydgate's master Chaucer had shown in *Troylus and Criseyde*, a man in Fortune's grace may become a model of valour, comradeship, generosity, and indeed all the virtues. These hardly seem the trap of a witch—and Lydgate himself, for all his disdain of fortune and vanity, is writing to supply models of "verray knythod"[29] to his master the young Prince Hal.

If we turn to a somewhat later work, based mainly if freely on Caxton and taking the Guido tradition to its full implication, we will be able to see medieval love and chivalry at their worst—as well as the way this worst can seem best. Shakespeare's *Troilus and Cressida* paints a very unflattering picture of its heroine, to say nothing of Helen; and even Troilus, while the wronged party and faithful for the short time of the action, is by no means the nice guy he is in Chaucer. Hector *is* a nice guy, a true gentleman; and quite as important as the love-story is one in which he challenges to single combat any Greek knight who values his honour and his lady. In the event an unarmed Hector is ambushed and killed by Achilles and his Myrmidons: there could hardly be a more terrible offence against honour. What, though, are we to make of honour itself here, and of the love that it fights for?

In effect Hector himself raises this question. When Priam's sons are considering a Greek demand that Helen be returned, Hector takes a stand at least generically like Guido's, since it is one of prudence if not avoidance

---

out about 1474.

[28]See Guido delle Colonne, *Historia Destructionis Troiae*, p. 42.

[29]*Lydgate's Troy Book*, Prologue, l. 76.

of risks. Helen, he says, has cost us tens of thousands of men, yet she is of no value to us: the sensible thing would be to give her back. And when Troilus retorts that Helen is valuable if valued, Hector appeals to justice itself, the "law of nature" requiring "that all dues be rendered to their owners."[30] Then, quite suddenly, he goes over to his brothers' side, agreeing that "our joint and several dignities" (2.2.193) are at stake. "Dignity" here means honour; and the honour in question requires, not justice—returning Helen, that is—but fighting to keep her in the interest of prestige.

It is as if Hector were rejoining a club. Within a club we do find justice, not to say loyalty and generosity. We also, to be sure, find aggression, since the members are sure to be competing at billiards or whatever. Still, these are just games, as is the club itself: within the enclosure of its agreed-on rules members can pretend to fight while keeping away from the real fighting outside. What is remarkable about the Middle Ages, though found to some degree far more widely, is the effort made in the period to turn the whole world into a club, with real life becoming play and play real life. Chivalry was the pretence that even knights at war were engaged in a game; and as the violence of tournaments shows, the game had to be nothing less than war. But of course war is *not* a game: whatever its open or tacit conventions of fair play,[31] neither side keeps them unless they serve its interest. And even the game that, superficially at least, war can really become is an unfair one in a way that games in this world always are. Acceptance to a club or team, after all, means that somebody else is turned down and inevitably treated with superiority or callousness, as we can see from Pandarus' contempt for the common soldiers or the use of Helen as a football. It is Hector's tragedy that, whatever his reason may know, his delight in the chivalric kind of honour makes him believe in the game, while his humanity is seduced into thinking this honour the same thing as itself. And with Hector's tragedy goes that of the more commonplace Troilus: for love was a game like chivalry in the Middle Ages, and never more so than when most serious. Like Hector Troilus is shockingly betrayed, and like Hector he more deeply betrays himself. Remembering how Virgil's justice excluded love, we can now see the even greater human crisis when love is itself what excludes. And to bring such love to justice, one discrimination to another, is no solution: we will somehow have to bring both the love and the justice to something beyond either.

To see what this might be, I am first going to turn back to another classical tradition, sharing a great deal with Virgil but, in the form that

---

[30]Shakespeare, *Troilus and Cressida*, II.ii.176–177, 174.
[31]Hector uses this phrase at V.iii.43 in Shakespeare's *Troilus and Cressida*.

concerns me, differing in a respect important here. And while this tradition will also take us away from Troy for a bit, I hope the reader will find the point of arrival worth the detour. Love for one alone (preferably at first sight), with unassailable virginity before marriage and unwavering constancy after it, and the same love sustaining the lovers as, guided by Heaven, they surmount all obstacles to reach wedded bliss: this may sound Victorian, like the love that Tennyson's Arthur considers the best inspiration for virtuous knighthood.[32] Yet I am actually thinking of Heliodorus' *Aethiopica*, written around 230 CE, much the best of the Greek romances but typical enough of the genre and very typical in its high conception of love.[33] Like the *Aeneid* it has the complex structure that became explicit in the hellenistic period: as Heliodorus says, "extreme contraries [are] . . . composed into a harmony,"[34] while at the same time a false counterpart is cast out. But in the *Aeneid* love itself is the false harmony: the destined true one is the union of the Trojan and Latin peoples. In the *Aethiopica*, on the other hand, not only is the truest harmony that of love, but the fulfilment of this love is the will of destiny. And destiny, helping the two lovers through their sensational adventures while helping the fair Chariclea to sensational ingenuity, both unites her with her long-lost parents, the rulers of Ethiopia, and unites their dark southern race with that of her noble Greek lover Theagenes.

Only rarely has a case been made for the influence of the Greek romances on the *chansons de geste*. These arose much later, of course—our textual evidence begins only with the late eleventh century, but that brings us up to the age of the Crusades, or in other words of soldiers and pilgrims

---

[32]See Tennyson, *Idylls of the King*, *Guinevere*, ll. 472–480.

[33]The tradition I am sketching here is important since it can digest history and specifically the Matter of Troy. Equally important is the tradition of Nature and natural love, coming through Alan of Lille's *Planctus Naturae*, Jean de Meun's conclusion of the *Roman de la Rose* and, to mention one significant later poem, the fourteenth-century *Échecs amoureux*, which was partly translated, perhaps by Lydgate and perhaps before 1412, as *Reson and Sensuallyte* (see Sieper's edition). Both Jean and the *Échecs*, if in opposite ways, fail to reconcile the instinctive and normative conceptions of Nature. But at a crucial point—Diana's picture of the Arthurian age (ll. 3140ff.)—the latter work reaches an ideal of virtue in love that is neither abstinence nor the opposite but heroic constancy to a single beloved. And the author can both imagine a Golden Age of constant love, physical or not, and a fall from it associated with the Judgment of Paris. The repair of the fall, though, has no association with history.

[34]Heliodorus, *Aethiopian Story*, p. 276. Complex *recognition* is fully present in the fifth-century tragedians and Aristotle's *Poetics*. But a tragedy as Aristotle knows it consists entirely of recognition, and the complete story with recognition as resolution first appears overtly in New Comedy and romance.

coming back from a partly Greek world where romances remained popular. And influence or none, we can almost see Chariclea in the plucky and resourceful heroine from the perilous south who so often gets her trapped beloved out of assorted scrapes and on to matrimony and his proper rank at home. The romance cast of barbarous enemies, again, ranging from pirates to tyrants, is interestingly like that of the *chansons*; yet we should also notice a couple of the differences here. In the *Aethiopica* the destiny of the lovers, for all its beneficial side-effects, is really a private one: they in particular are the gods' favourites, and once they reach happiness the gods are satisfied. The historical circumstances, moreover, while definite enough, are of only accidental concern to the lovers. But the *chansons de geste* breathe real concern for the fiendish Saracens threatening the citadel of Charlemagne; the success or failure of the Christian heroes is that of Christendom itself. And while this does not make the *chansons* Trojan, it helps explain both something Trojan that came out of them and the particular form it took.

The *chansons*, with their central interest in Charlemagne and the Saracens, proved extraordinarily resilient in northern Italy. They also became suffused there with Arthurian courtesy and fantastic adventure, so that serious love and patriotism now wore chivalric dress. And near the end of the fifteenth century the Count Matteo Boiardo, turning back from his early humanist efforts, added something else again: like the Burgundian-minded Jean Lemaire across the mountains, he saw fit to provide a Trojan lineage for his patrons, the Dukes of Ferrara. In the *Orlando Innamorato*,[35] well on its way to completion when Boiardo died in 1494, these varied elements combine effortlessly. Roland fights for Christendom; he also falls in love, getting into exotic adventures as a result; and Ruggiero, the hero who upstages him as the work proceeds, is pure boyish enthusiasm for chivalry and its "allegrezza e cortesia" (II.i.2). At the same time Ruggiero is one of our heroic lovers; and his heroic lady Bradamante, if not as brainy as Chariclea, is a strength in another way, being a *virago*—a knight herself. The love of the two, furthermore, is guided by destiny: here, however, and very significantly, there is nothing private about this destiny.

Ruggiero's blood runs back to Hector, and it is God's will that, helped by Bradamante, he pass it on well Christianized to the Este family of Ferrara. In a world where succession now ran strictly by blood-line and primogeniture, this should not be surprising; of course destiny would get help from marital alliances, as we have found in Lemaire. But there is something more here: Ruggiero and Bradamante would never have married if they had not happened to meet and fall in love—to which we can add that they are drawn

---

[35]The first "complete" edition was 1495; I have cited Bruscagli's ed. in my text.

together by each other's courtesy even before Ruggiero knows Bradamante's sex. Historical destiny, specifically Trojan destiny, has come together both with heroic love and with courtesy and chivalry; and this unprecedented combination (which may not have seemed remarkable at all to Boiardo) displays its full significance in his successors. In Ariosto's *Orlando Furioso*, a half-continuation of the *Innamorato*, not only is there a much greater sense of a crucial time and a crucial threat to the Christian empire, but the union of the lovers is equally crucial. For the finest Trojan blood flows here in both, and when its two streams become one in the womb of Bradamante (who assumes new importance as a result), an enhanced blood flows on through the Estensi to make possible their own version of the Augustan Golden Age.

Here, though, we will need to make more reservations. What Ariosto passed on to Spenser (of this kind, I mean—he passed on much else) was largely matter without form. He has no real story to tell about the lovers: they are already betrothed at the beginning, their marriage comes at the end, and in the middle we find mainly contrived delays and misunderstandings. What makes the pair even more marginal is the fact that, far more than Boiardo, Ariosto separates the serious destiny of love from its silliness. The latter, while still delightful, becomes in Orlando a madness that has to be cast out along with the love causing it. It is the release from love in the Christian champion and the resulting surge against the Saracens that constitutes Ariosto's chief subject: the matter of Ruggiero and Bradamante, while formally primary and much inflated at the end, is in reality fairly incidental. And even if, as is likely enough, Ariosto would have preferred to draw his Trojan matter more tightly into his scheme, luck was against him. The Estensi could be made bringers of world peace only by enormous sleight of hand; in any case they had no connection by blood or their political past with the Carolingian world. And once more, the traditional Matter of France does not connect Charlemagne's empire with Troy as we have seen Lemaire doing: it seems too concerned with immediate Saracen threats and Christian responses.[36]

III: SPENSER

But if Ariosto had bad luck, Spenser had singularly good: there lay ready to hand, if he wanted it, a well-structured and basically complete Trojan-

---

[36]A court poet of Charlemagne's named Dungal did trace his master's descent to the Trojans. See Barraclough, *The Crucible of Europe*, p. 42. But the *chansons de geste* are something else.

British history. Also available, if he wanted it, was Ariosto's vesting of the Trojan destiny in a pair of lovers. And for reasons I will partly deal with, he did want both things. But this meant a formidable task of integrating—something for which, as I have suggested, he had a special knack. To clear our ground, we can note to begin with that Spenser lived to finish only six of the twelve books that he planned for *The Faerie Queene*, though I agree with those who say that the six form a coherent unit of their own. In any case they make quite clear that the poem is not primarily about Troy or its British descendents at all. Basically it is a set of missions against vice—one vice and mission per book; the missions are sent out by Gloriana the Faery Queen, and the protagonist of each book is a specialist in the relevant virtue. It seems that during the poem's evolution (something at which we can only guess, though guesses can be educated) first Arthur came into it and then, as something distinct, a more elaborate British element—Trojan like Arthur, since Spenser is following the tradition of Geoffrey of Monmouth.

While we have seen in part what the British matter consists of in the resulting poem, a rather fuller account is in order here. A line of British rulers comes down from the Trojan Brutus, and at the time when Spenser's action is set these have founded a noble if provisional Troynovaunt. Arthur is very much present, waiting to become a king at the end of the twelve-book poem; but more to the foreground in what we have is a British prince called "Artegal," loosely associated with Arthur in name as in family.[37] Of even greater importance, greater than in Ariosto, is the princess Britomart, not only a doughty warrior in her own right—since she is yet another virago—but with Artegal as her consort the destined mother of the British line to come. The present Britain, in spite of Troynovaunt, is struggling for

---

[37]Efforts to establish a precise family connection between Arthur and Artegal are somewhat misplaced, as always when Spenser avoids an issue: the relation between the two figures is of a different kind. By the same token Artegal and Britomart are different in *function* from Arthur. It is true that the British chronicles shown to the latter (and leading up to his father) are called those of Elizabeth's "auncestries" (II.x.1), but in fact neither the "linage" (2) stretching from the past in the chronicles nor that stretching onward from Britomart in Merlin's prophecy (III.iii.21ff.) is a strict blood-line. Spenser like Geoffrey is keeping to an older idea of succession. It is significant, then, that the succession from Britomart is *imagined* as a blood-line ("from thy wombe a famous Progenie / Shall spring" [III.iii.22]), whereas the (unmentioned) idea of a blood-line coming to Elizabeth from the Faery Queen Gloriana, Arthur's future bride, would be highly awkward both in itself and in its doubling of the line coming from Britomart and Artegal. For Spenser Gloriana is Elizabeth's analogue or mirror-image, and even the "auncestry" that he associates with her in the same context shares this mirror quality (see II, Proem, especially 4).

its life against pagan (here Saxon) invaders; but after its defeat and enslave-
ment to a series of conquerors, the British succession will burst forth to rule
again and bring an eternal peace. At the same time it will flatten "the great
Castle" (III.iii.49)—for which read "Castille," since that is Spenser's version
of the threat from the dire south that in the *chansons de geste* had already used
Spain as a base.

At this point we need to see how the lovers' story achieves coherence
simply in itself, the coherence that had been impossible for Ariosto. In the
material inherited by the *Furioso* from the *Innamorato* Bradamante, already
a virago because she wants to be, meets and becomes betrothed to Ruggiero.
Later and independently (as Ariosto takes up the tale) she comes to know
of the great lineage to descend from her, but there is nothing about this
knowledge to alter her subsequent behaviour. In *The Faerie Queene*, on the
other hand, it is *because* she has learned of her destiny that Britomart—be-
wildered at first by love—sets out to find the consort-to-be whom she has
seen in a magic mirror. Because the world is dangerous she disguises herself
as a male knight, and because searching in such a world will mean real
fighting (Britomart is not Tasso's Erminia) she gets fully into her role of
virago. It is accordingly as knights in armour that she and Artegal first
encounter one another and, naturally, do battle. Then, when he manages
to shear away her "ventayle" (IV.vi.19) or face-piece, the situation changes
completely. He submits in adoration of her beauty, she sees her knight of
the mirror in his own revealed face—and recognition brings betrothal to
make a perfectly coherent story.

So far so good: but now let us ask how and why Spenser makes such
a story cohere as well with the very different ones into which he has
introduced it. Both questions lead beyond the subject of story by itself, what
this paper is about, but we should note one fact concerning the extant poem
that is significant here: Spenser concentrates the Matter of Britain around
the middle two of its six books. To which I will add another fact not
obviously related to the first one, and hence needing to be squared with it:
in a poem consisting of stories about virtues, Books Three and Four are
concerned with the virtues relating to love. Since these books are also the
ones in which Britomart falls in love with Artegal and the two reach
betrothal, that may seem all the squaring we need. Yet by itself the presence
of British love in books that are about love in a different way gives us only
coincidence; the defending of the relevant virtues as the matter of the books,
moreover, may seem to have no connection with Britain or its destiny.

What do these virtues amount to—the virtues Spenser calls chastity
and friendship? Chastity may but normally does not remain virginity: its
essence is the mental firmness needed in love, positively the faithfulness of
lover to beloved, negatively the ability to say no to anyone who would

come between them. It is thus the appropriate form in the present context of the steadfastness that we have also seen in, say, Aeneas, and that for Spenser is one characteristic of the world itself as a good thing. Friendship is the complementary ability to say yes, the virtue that brings concord. Concord itself, like love, is primarily sexual in the poem; but, like love again, it is something more general as well, something applicable to the entire world, here as functioning harmoniously. The flanking virtues in this perspective, those of Books II and V, have to do, not with the kinetic force that love is in the poem, but with the static order whose virtues are respectively temperance—the order of a world as duly constituted—and justice, the order of a world put right again when it has gone wrong.

Now let us try to integrate, and first to see how the Matter of Britain, especially that of Britomart and Artegal, is organically bound to the virtues of chastity and friendship. Britain also occurs, to be sure, in the books of temperance and justice, but only in the middle books do we have specifically British missions along with those of the books themselves. And the virtues required for these extra missions are, in the first place, British in the most intrinsic way. At one point in Book III Britomart stops for a night's lodging; over supper she hears another British guest recount the destruction of Troy—a story of the past and its tragedy that leaves her shaken with grief. She pulls herself together by affirming something present, the Troynovaunt that is already a city to be proud of; and most important, her very reason for travelling is that she knows the course and, beyond more tribulation, the glorious outcome of the Trojan story. All of which means that, to be who she properly is and do what she accordingly must, Britomart needs to understand and accept her part in a *process*, a fully historical one in its complexity of structure and amplitude of context. To have this need is to be British, since Britain in the poem, unlike Fairyland, has an identity that can only realize itself through the vicissitudes of time. And it is because of her understanding and acceptance of this fact that Britomart can remain constant in vicissitude, or in other words have the British virtue of steadfastness.

But we have been seeing how steadfastness, in the form of chastity, is equally a virtue of love; as we saw earlier, it is through love that history fulfils itself like any story, if in a pre-eminent way since history is the story of a world as a whole. And so two things work together: Britomart's historical destiny requires her chaste love, while chaste love enables her to play her part in destiny. The same thing is true with the virtue of friendship, but less plainly because of friendship's special character: of all the virtues in *The Faerie Queene* it comes closest to healthy natural inclination, and so may hardly seem a virtue at all. We should think again, though, of the episode in Book IV where Britomart and Artegal abandon their enmity. For several reasons the two have been fighting with immense acrimony: when he sees her beauty and she his identity, their concord thus comes as an act of virtue, however effortless. It had to come, moreover, by means of previous discord,[38] for as in Book III, we are dealing with something that can be what it is only through time and vicissitude. And lastly we again have two things working together: Artegal's love and Britomart's obedience to her calling (helped, of course, by her own love). Destiny, in other words, has again required one of love's virtues, while the virtue is such as to serve destiny.

If the foregoing explanation has needed to be somewhat tortuous, we can see a clear epitome of the issue here by going back to Britomart at the supper-table. The guest who recalls history is a roving and roving-eyed knight called Paridell—with a family-line going back, needless to say, to Paris. And even in telling his affecting tale Paridell is covertly flirting with someone else at the table: a roving-eyed wife called Hellenore who is if anything worse than Helen in Shakespeare. Presently Hellenore has burned her husband's house down "for sport, or for despight," says Spenser (III.x.12), comparing her to the Helen who delights to see Troy in flames. She then runs off with the dashing Paridell for an affair that lasts as long as such things usually do. It is against shenanigans like these that Spenser sets Britomart mourning the loss of the first Troy, praising Troynovaunt, and declaring her faith in the Trojan glory to come. In the supper scene there is no way for Britomart to declare *how* it is to come, since she must not reveal her sex or her destined marriage with Artegal; but both the shape of Spenser's Trojan story—the shape as no-one else had quite shown it—and the means by which this shape fulfils itself stand out here with great simplicity and cogency. What false love brought low true love will raise up again, aided by destiny to be an aid to destiny.

It remains for us to ask how destiny aids what is *not* destiny, the non-historical missions of chastity and friendship that define the poem's books as entities of their own. What may clarify things here is a circumstance somewhat odd in itself. Britomart is not only the woman meant for Artegal and bearing the British future in her person: she doubles as the "patron" or champion of chastity, standing in for a non-British knight called Scudamore who, to judge from fairly clear evidence,[39] was the patron Spenser originally

---

[38]The *Liberata* contains a similar story, of Clorinda and Tancredi, complete with the shearing away of Clorinda's helmet (III.xxi); but it is a tale of tragic accident (with transcendence, to be sure), not of concord possible only through discord.

[39]See Spenser's problematic letter to Raleigh (ed. Hamilton, p. 738). At the time of writing it Spenser intended Scudamore to undertake the adventure and Britomart to finish it "by reason of the hard Enchauntments." But Scudamore here starts from Gloriana's court, and since—as I have surmised—Britomart is a relative latecomer to the

intended. The significant thing here is that Scudamore by himself is unable to do his job; and the reason will not only help us with our present question but lead us to the heart of this paper's subject.

Scudamore's lady, a chaste maiden named Amoret, has been imprisoned by the very unchaste magician Busyrane. Like other villains at the end of Spenser's books, Busyrane represents vice at so high a level of organization as to parody the order of virtue itself: unchastity here is strangely like chastity, and most obviously in its constancy. This constancy, however, is anything but a seeking of concord: the power over another that it craves is precisely the opposite. Amoret has enough strength to resist Busyrane, but cannot get free from him or out of his castle; nor can Scudamore get in, since the castle is surrounded by fire. Britomart, on the other hand, having a magic of her own emblematized by her enchanted lance,[40] *can* pass through fire; and so, in the first place, she can discover the strange ritual enacted in the castle every night.[41] A trumpet sounds in the dark; a great storm arises with earthquake, fire, and wind;[42] and then, to music of utmost *allegrezza*, a "jolly company" (xii.5) enters to perform a "maske," or pageant, of love. At its climax the pageant, like some other play we have seen, proves the opposite of jolly: for in the Ovidian triumph it turns out to be, a ruthless young Cupid, "victor of the gods" (xi.49), rides as triumphator, while Amoret as captive must march before him carrying her heart in a basin.[43] Pursuing the triumph backstage, Britomart learns what is behind all this: in a bare, empty room the "vile enchanter" (xii.31) himself is trying to compel

---

poem, I will suggest that Spenser originally intended Scudamore himself to finish the task, as would be normal in the poem.

[40]See *FQ* III.iii.60.

[41]See *FQ* III.xii.1ff.

[42]See I Kgs 19:11–12 (wind, earthquake, and fire) and Ex. 19:16–18 (thunder, lightning, thick cloud, "the voice of the trumpet exceeding loud," and smoke "as the smoke of a furnace").

[43]There is not only Ovid here but, partly derived from him, a more general medieval conception. Guido's Fates differ from their originals, the impassive dealers of individual lots, by their malice, its general application, and the reason for it, which is resentment, since they target those highest as being happiest. The Fortune by whom Lydgate replaces the Fates, while again personally malevolent, is less simple in her psychology as well as her tactics. When Jason's expedition arrives at Troy she actually implants suspicion in Laomedon: by great punishment of such a minimal offence she wants to "Schewen her myght and her cruelte" (Lydgate, *Troy Book*, Part I, ll. 723ff.). In the latter part of *Troilus and Criseyde* we find the same tyrannical, sadistic Fortune closely associated with a similar Cupid (Chaucer, *Troilus and Criseyde*, IV.1ff., 288ff., V.582ff., etc.). Neither these figures themselves nor their assocation were by any means confined to Chaucer and Lydgate: it is the tradition in which Venus and Cupid are virtually identical that lies behind Spenser's Busyrane episode, with its parody of both truer destiny and truer love.

Amoret's love, using of course the same magic that compelled her captivity. But Britomart is too much for him, and with the undoing of Busyrane's spells Amoret is healed and set free.

Why, though, could she not have freed herself—or have been freed by Scudamore? To do some summing up here, the total vice that parodies virtue comes as not just badness but illusion, and temporally as not just change but fickleness. In both ways, that is, it comes as falsehood, and in itself it has the falsehood of paradox—or more precisely it has the false paradox that, in Busyrane's world, binds pleasure to pain and play to grim earnest in an un-uniting union, a mockery of true integration. We will see the same falsehood on other terms, with the betrayal that it brings, if we think again of the Fortune of Chaucer and Lydgate, the "honour" of *Troilus and Cressida*, or the love in all these that leaves an anguished Troilus crying "O beauty, where is thy faith?"[44] And what is being falsified is nature itself, as is most plain, perhaps, in the sado-masochism of Busyrane and his castle. Amoret, who possesses only natural virtue, cannot overcome unnatural vice: she needs help from a greater strength, that given to Britomart by her supernatural destiny. To sense the full presence of this latter, we can note an important parallel here: the fire-storm recalls those accompanying theophanies in the Bible; the trumpet in darkness recalls that of Sinai in particular; and Busyrane takes his name from "Busiris," supposedly the Pharaoh of the Exodus. Sinai, of course, is not Egypt, and Cupid's law is that of love—as in Jesus' new commandment, we may want to say. But once again we are dealing with evil parody: this is not the law that is love, but the love that is law, the commandment that is bondage. Unless upheld by a power that can pass through fire or sea, nothing will escape it.

IV: THE FULFILMENT OF THE STORY

We have been seeing how destiny—the shaper of history—not only achieves its purpose through virtuous love, but enables virtuous love to fulfil its own purpose. And yet the very act of putting the matter thus simply can make us see what a precarious arrangement we have been dealing with in the last pages. It is not just that we cannot count on lovers loving for the sake of destiny while destiny looks down benignly on love or even justice. Even when working together, these principles remain separate in themselves and hence, inevitably, foes as much as friends. There is only one way of resolving our difficulty: a new way of understanding, even if a way contrary

---

[44]Shakespeare, *Troilus and Cressida*, V.ii.66.

to all natural possibility—or that of a "supernatural" possibility on what are really the same terms.[45] We need an *identification* here that, by the most intense of paradoxes, would also be the greatest affirmation of distinctness. Without such an identification separate principles, whether singly or in league, can only resist and if possible exclude what they cannot assimilate, as we first found when we saw Virgilian justice repressing love. No doubt the excluded is also the unaccommodating; it may even have become a perverse league of its own like Busyrane's pleasure and pain. But the cause lies on both sides, or rather on exclusion as such and a world that necessitates it; and as I have already suggested, it is always in the vanquished and excluded that the key to a saving integration must be sought. When we reject Falstaff—or Dido or Turnus or even Busyrane as a human being with human needs—it is the wholeness of humanity that we are rejecting. The resulting establishment, however grand its façade, must ultimately collapse; but with what it has put in its dungeon we could make something more sound.

Looking into the future, Spenser's Merlin sees a Troynovaunt of "eternall union" where "sacred Peace shall lovingly perswade / The warlike minds, to learne her goodly lore" (III.iii.49). In other words, he sees a Virgilian conjunction of peoples bringing a just peace—even a loving peace, willingly accepted. What we have to ask now is both whether such a resolution of history could really be stable and whether it could really be acceptable. The para-scripture of Troy—to take Troy as the good city in this world[46]—says yes to both questions. The canonical scripture of the Bible

---

[45]In Alan of Lille's classic presentation Nature seeks to preserve the "lawful marriage" (*The Plaint of Nature*, Pr. 4) of opposites by which God constituted the universe. Man has brought a fall through the coupling of similars—specifically homosexuality, but Alan's real concern is unnatural coupling as such. Yet distinctness and common ground are both essential to relation; whichever of these we make primary, the "vice" here is as natural as the "virtue." As for the latter, Alan's Nature and her "lawful marriage" rely on the Desire that not only is "sweet shipwreck, light burden" (Met. 5), and so on, but has Byblis and Myrrha for examples.

[46]See Barney, s.v. "Troy." According to Barney the Middle Ages "typically" associated Troy with worldly pride, and the Judgment of Paris (involving an apple, of course) with the sin of Adam. While overly sweeping, Barney's generalization enables us to make important distinctions. The Fall of Troy might (as here) be simply assimilated to that of man, in which case the restored Jerusalem of the Book of Revelation would logically be the New Troy as well. Virgil, having no notion of a heavenly city, sees Troy as a pre-eminently good earthly one, and its Roman counterpart as divinely intended not only to triumph but to endure. Augustine, in deliberate rebuttal, sees both Troy (*City of God*, III.ii) and *Roma aeterna* as worldly cities, evil as such and doomed to permanent failure. Spenser's British version of Virgil's Rome is something else again: the good city made possible in this world through grace, but distinct from the New Jerusalem seen in the distance by his patron of holiness (*FQ* I.x.55ff.).

says no to the first: it tells us we have no abiding city here.[47] Yet if only in making the New Jerusalem the outcome of a historical process it compromises itself: for it binds its city to time and space, the dimensions of separation—or exclusion. It seems, then, that the consummation we are looking for cannot be found in either of our kinds of scripture, at least as taken on their own terms. I tried earlier to show something of it in the fullest implication of historical crossing; and for a view more relevant at present we can turn briefly to the end of the entire *Faerie Queene*, or to what little we can discern of an end never written. One thing we know is that a "paynim" king harassing Queen Gloriana would have been defeated, almost certainly by Arthur, and presumably as in the military victories of the traditional Arthur or Charlemagne. But then, and quite certainly, Arthur would have married Gloriana—though a match between the hero of Britain and the Faery Queen is something else that had never occurred before Spenser. What can it suggest for us?[48]

Arthur in this ending would be not just British but Trojan in the fullest sense I have given the word. He would be Trojan through the historical character of his victory even apart from his ancestry; he would be equally Trojan in my larger sense through being a lover, one who has been ardently seeking Gloriana from the beginning of the poem. But there is a further way again of being Trojan, one we have not yet properly considered: a way in which we could apply the term to Gloriana herself. If Troy is the city of things inescapably *there*—the compulsions of justice and desire—it is also the city that is past and to come, departed from and journeyed to, a place that has haunted the European mind because it is *not* there. Gloriana is the lady of imagination: and imagination or fancy, which can be the most mischievous of impositions, is in a truer function the key that we forfeited in imposing the rational and objectively real. Imagination does not conjure the world of these things away, but it enables us both to see a different world and, seeing the real one in a different light, to live in it without being its prisoners. Imagination, moreover, can bring these two worlds into a wholeness greater than either. Fairyland, as Spenser suggests, mirrors the real Britain of Elizabeth Tudor as if from beyond an ocean; yet it is right here, as he also suggests.[49] It could not be here as a given dynastic

---

[47]Heb. 13:14.

[48]I say "suggest" since the marriage as something in space and time would only give us a city like the others we have just considered.

[49]See *FQ* II, Proem. Defending the reality of Faeryland by noting that real places may be unknown ones (but may also get discovered), Spenser appeals to the New World as his prime example. But even in so doing he makes this world sound fabulous: it lies

establishment, even one deriving from a true succession assured by a true-love romance. But it could belong to a presence greater than things that are only here or there, only real or fanciful in ways that exclude each other. This presence would be the genuine union of two cities or peoples as well as the end of the one genuine scripture. And liberated from inner and outer compulsion, its transforming power would be that of genuine love.

WORKS CITED

Alan of Lille. *The Plaint of Nature*. Trans. J.J. Sheridan. Toronto: Pontifical Institute of Mediaeval Studies, 1980.

Ariosto, Lodovico. *Orlando furioso*. Ed. Marcello Turchi. 2 vols. [N.p.]: Garzanti, 1974.

Barney, Stephen A. "Troy." *The Spenser Encyclopedia*. Ed. A.C. Hamilton et al. Toronto: University of Toronto Press, 1990. 701–702.

Barraclough, Geoffrey. *The Crucible of Europe*. Berkeley and Los Angeles: University of California Press, 1976.

Bayot, Alphonse. *La légende de Troie à la cour de Bourgogne*. Bruges, 1908.

Boiardo, Matteo. *Orlando Innamorato*. Ed. Riccardo Bruscagli. 2 vols. Turin: Einaudi, 1995.

Brill's New Pauly. Leiden: Brill, 2002.

Caxton, William. *Caxton's Eneydos*. Ed. W.T. Culley and F.J. Furnivall. EETS ES 57. London: Oxford University Press, 1890.

Dares: see Dictys.

Dictys of Crete and Dares the Phrygian. *Trojan War: the Chronicles of Dictys of Crete and Dares the Phrygian*. Trans. R.M. Frazer, Jr. Bloomington: Indiana University Press, 1966.

Doutrepont, Georges. *La Littérature française à la cour des ducs de Bourgogne*. Paris, 1909. Rpt. Geneva: Slatkine, 1970.

Eliot, T.S. *Burnt Norton. The Complete Poems and Plays*. 1969. Rpt. London: Faber, 1978.

Enéas: Roman du XIIe siècle. Ed. J.-J. Salverda de Grave. Les classiques français du Moyen Age 44, 62. 2 vols. Paris: Champion, 1925–1929.

Geoffrey of Monmouth. *The History of the Kings of Britain*. Trans. Lewis Thorpe. Harmondsworth: Penguin, 1966.

Guido delle Colonne. *Historia Destructionis Troiae*. Trans. Mary Elizabeth Meek. Bloomington: Indiana University Press, 1974.

Hadas, Moses. *Hellenistic Culture*. New York: Norton, 1959.

Heliodorus. *Aethiopian Story*. Trans. Sir Walter Lamb. London: Everyman, 1961.

Lefèvre, Raoul. *L'Histoire de Jason: ein Roman aus dem 15. Jahrhundert*. Ed. Gert Pinkernell. Frankfurt: Athenäum, 1971.

---

across a western ocean like Celtic otherworlds. At the same time, one of its regions is "fruitfullest Virginia" (*FQ* Proem.2), ruled by and named after Elizabeth; and presently Spenser is saying that his queen may see "thine owne realmes in lond of Faery." In the same proem, that is, he virtually makes Faeryland congruent with Elizabeth's dominions, including Britain itself.

Lefèvre, Raoul. *The Recuyell of the Historyes of Troye.* Trans. William Caxton. 2 vols. London: David Nutt, 1894.

Lemaire de Belges, Jean. *Oeuvres.* Ed. J. Stecher. 3 vols. Louvain, 1882–1885.

Lydgate, John. *Reson and Sensuallyte.* [Translation of Les échecs amoureux.] Ed. Ernst Sieper. EETS ES 84, 89. London: Oxford University Press, 1901.

Lydgate, John. *Troy Book.* Ed. Henry Bergen. Part I, EETS ES 97. London: Oxford University Press, 1906.

Millican, Charles B. *Spenser and the Table Round.* Cambridge: Harvard University Press, 1932.

Shakespeare, William. *The History of Troilus and Cressida.* Ed. Virgil Whitaker. Harmondsworth: Penguin, 1958.

Spenser, Edmund. *The Faerie Queene.* Ed. A.C. Hamilton. 2nd ed. Ludlow: Longman, 2001.

Tasso, Torquato. *Gerusalemme Liberata.* Ed. Bruno Maier. 2 vols. Milan: Rizzoli, 1982.

Tennyson, Alfred. *Poems.* Ed. Christopher Ricks. 2nd ed. Ludlow: Longman, 1987.

"Fairer than the evening air":
Marlowe's Gnostic Helen of Troy and the Tropes of Belatedness and Historical Mediation

MICHAEL KEEFER

War ich das alles? bin ichs? werd ichs künftig sein,
Das Traum- und Schreckbild jener Städteverwüstenden?
[Was I all that? Am I that now? Shall I be that in future,
The dream image and the dread image of those destroyers of cities.][1]

GOETHE'S BELATED HELEN

Helen of Troy, whom the chorus of Aeschylus' tragedy *Agamemnon* pun-ningly names "*helenas, helandros, heleptolis*" ["the ruin of ships, men, and the city"],[2] is a figure at once of desolation and desire; and the city to whose name hers is forever attached, and for the destruction of which this choral speech blames her, is an emblem of historical memory, of unassuageable loss, and in successive embeddings of the matter of Troy from Virgil to the vernacular poets of Western Europe, an emblem also of a translation of empire and a concomitant transference of cultural legitimacy.

In Goethe's *Faust*, these motifs are commingled in those scenes where Faust chivalrously rescues Helen from the anger of Menelaus and teaches her to speak in rhyming couplets,[3] thereby giving dramatic expression to a belief in intimate correspondence between classical Greece and Germany that remained a prominent element in German culture from Winckelmann's celebrated *Geschichte der Kunst des Altertums* (1764) and Hölderlin's odes and hymns to the writings of Martin Heidegger. There is a delicate magic to Helen's acquisition of the trick of rhyming—though what might seem the more difficult feat of speaking in German she has already accomplished

---

[1]Goethe, *Faust, Der Tragödie zweiter Teil,* III, ll. 8839–8840, p. 256. The translation is Fairley's, from *Goethe's Faust*, p. 151.

[2]Aeschylus, *Agamemnon*, ll. 689–690, in *Eschyle*, vol. 2, p. 34.

[3]Goethe, *Faust*, Part II, Act III.

without noticing it. That must be the point: Heidegger, a century after Goethe, insisted that the classical Greek and German languages share a deep, and elsewhere unparalleled, ontological adequacy,[4] and he found Hölderlin's expression of a classicizing spirituality convincing to the extent that he saw no incongruity in citing the third stanza of the hymn "Wie wenn am Feiertage" (understood as a poetic exposition of the concept *die Natur*) as an authoritative guide to the meaning of Aristotle's term *physis*.[5]

Although my principal concern in this essay is with the earlier *raptus Helenae* performed by Marlowe's Doctor Faustus, I would like briefly to pause, for purposes of comparison, over Goethe's and Hölderlin's acts of affiliation to and appropriation of classical Greece. What one might think of as the characteristic mood of Hölderlin's poetic incantations, a passionate Hellenism in which divine presences summoned up by an uncanny apostrophic magic brighten the spring air and the orchards of his native Swabia,[6] was also accompanied by a powerful intuition of belatedness:

> Aber Freund! wir kommen zu spät. Zwar leben die Götter,
>   Aber über dem Haupt droben in anderer Welt.
> [But, my friend, we have come too late. The gods do live,
>   But on high, over our heads, in another world.]

The urgency of Hölderlin's invocations of immanent divinities is arguably motivated by this sense of ontological separation and historical distance, and a corresponding feeling of vastation and abandonment:

> Nemlich, als vor einiger Zeit, uns dünket sie lange,
>   Aufwärts stiegen sie all, welche das Leben beglükt,
> Als der Vater gewandt sein Angesicht von den Menschen,
>   Und das Trauern mit Recht über der Erde begann . . . .
> [For, when some time ago now—to us it seems ages—

4See Heidegger, *An Introduction to Metaphysics*, p. 57: "For along with German the Greek language is (in regard to its possibilities for thought) at once the most powerful and most spiritual of all languages."

5See Heidegger, "On the Essence and Concept of φυσισ" in *Pathmarks*, p. 184; for the full text of Hölderlin's "Wie wenn am Feiertage," see *Selected Poems and Fragments*, pp. 172–176. Elsewhere Heidegger writes that Nietzsche "understood the great age of Greek beginnings with a depth that was surpassed only by Hölderlin" (*An Introduction to Metaphysics*, p. 126).

6See, for one of many possible examples, Hölderlin's ode "Der Zeitgeist," ll. 13–16: "Wohl keimt aus jungen Reben uns heil'ge Kraft; / In milder Luft begegnet den Sterblichen, / Und wenn sie still im Haine wandeln, / Heiternd ein Gott . . ." ("True, from young vines we gather a holy strength; / In mild spring air, or when they are wandering / In orchards calmly, men will meet a / Brightening god" [*Selected Poems and Fragments*, pp. 30–31]).

> All those gladdened by life mounted up from this world,
> When the Father turned his countenance away from men,
> . . . mourning rightly broke out over the earth . . . .][7]

In his hymn "Die Wanderung," Hölderlin opens up the question of historical difference by inquiring how it is that the Graces, the daughters of heaven, have come to "barbarians": "wie kommt / Ihr, Charitinnen, zu Wilden?" His suitably paradoxical response is to say that all that is divinely born ["alles Göttlichgeborne"] becomes "a mere dream for anyone who would make it his by stealth, and punishes the one who would liken himself to it by force—while often taking by surprise him who had it least in mind":

> Zum Traume wirds ihm, will es Einer
> Beschleichen und straft den, der
> Ihm gleichen will mit Gewalt;
> Oft überraschet es einen,
> Der eben kaum es gedacht hat.[8]

In the lines preceding these, the spiritual forces that Hölderlin evokes in this poem are very clearly gendered, as "Gratien Griechenlands," "Himmelstöchter," "Dienerinnen des Himmels" [the Graces of Hellas, heaven's daughters, the servant girls of heaven][9]: these are the powers who resist the stealthy appropriations of latecomers by fading into the insubstantiality of dreams. There are overtones of serpentine as well as human cunning in the verb *beschleichen* ("to steal up upon," "to surprise," "to cheat"); and this verb, while rhyming with the forceful declaration of likeness or equality [*gleichen . . . mit Gewalt*] which these same heavenly powers punish, is also contrasted in these lines with another form of surprise: an unasked gift of the divine, which manifests itself in lively impetuosity (*überraschen*, "to take unawares," has these connotations, and is cognate with the English "rashness"). Those of the implicitly masculine *Wilden* who retain what one might take to be a barbarian propensity for stealth and force receive only a dream or simulacrum; the feminized divine bestows itself in a manner that anticipates desire.

This poem participates in a hermeneutical discourse that is more fully unfolded and explicated in Goethe's *Faust*. In that play's first scene, Faust proclaims equality with the Earth Spirit he has so vehemently invoked ["Ich bins, bin Faust, bin deinesgleichen"], and is devastatingly rebuked for his

---

[7]Hölderlin, "Brot und Wein," stanzas 7.1–2, 8.1–4; *Selected Poems and Fragments*, pp. 156–157. I have modified Hamburger's translation of these lines.

[8]"Die Wanderung," stanzas 9.6–7, 11–15; *Selected Poems and Fragments*, p. 188.

[9]"Die Wanderung," stanzas 8.9–10, 9.8; *Selected Poems and Fragments*, p. 188.

presumption: "Du gleichst dem Geist, den du begreifst, / Nicht mir!" ["You are equal to that spirit you can grasp—not me!"].[10] Faust will shortly discover that another less tremendous spirit—one that has attempted to take him by surprise, and that is determined to cheat him—can also evade his control. Mephistopheles, who contemptuously remarks, "Du bist noch nichts der Mann, den Teufel festzuhalten!" ["You're not the man to hold the devil in your grasp!"], instructs the subordinate spirits who have sung Faust asleep to "Play on him with sweet dreams, plunge him into a sea of delusions!" ["Umgaukelt ihn mit süßen Traumgestalten, / Versenkt ihn in ein Meer des Wahns!"].[11]

Goethe's Prologue in Heaven evokes in its opening lines an abyssal sublimity of space and time ("Die Sonne tönt nach alter Weise / In Brudersphären Wettgesang . . . " ["The sun resounds among the singing spheres with its ancient music . . . "])—which Mephistopheles, though himself a primordial being, undercuts with cynical colloquialisms: "I like to see the old man from time to time," he says ["Von Zeit zu Zeit seh ich den Alten gern . . . "]. He possesses a synoptic awareness of human history from its beginnings, but only as an endless repetition of the same: "Der kleine Gott der Welt bleibt stets von gleichen Schlag / Und ist so wunderlich als wie am ersten Tag" ["These little lords of creation haven't changed in the least. They're just as queer as they were on the first day"].[12]

Faust's encounter with the Earth Spirit, who is likewise a quasi-originary being, puts him up against a force that looks rather like temporality itself: "Geburt und Grab, / Ein ewiges Meer, / Ein wechselnd Weben, / Ein glühend Leben: / So schaff ich am sausenden Webstuhl der Zeit / Und wirke der Gottheit lebendiges Kleid" ["I am birth and the grave, an eternal ocean, a changeful weaving, a glowing life. And thus I work at the humming loom of time, and fashion divinity's living garment"].[13] Following his rejection by this spirit (but prior to his meeting with the demonic power of negation), Faust declares to his famulus Wagner the impossibility of recapturing the past: "Past ages, my friend, are a book with seven seals. What you all call the spirit of the times is just your own spirit with the times reflected in it":

---

[10]Goethe, *Faust, Der Tragödie erster Teil*, ll. 500, 512–513, p. 21.

[11]Goethe, *Faust, Der Tragödie erster Teil*, ll. 1509, 1510–1511, p. 47.

[12]Goethe, *Faust, Der Tragödie erster Teil*, ll. 243–244, 350, 281–282, pp. 13–15. The translation of these lines is Barker Fairley's, from *Goethe's Faust*, pp. 6–7 (with a small alteration to the translation of line 350).

[13]Goethe, *Faust, Der Tragödie erster Teil*, ll. 504–509, p. 21. The translation is Fairley's, from *Goethe's Faust*, p. 10 (with an alteration to the last line—as before, in the direction of literalism).

Mein Freund, die Zeiten der Vergangenheit
Sind uns ein Buch mit sieben Siegeln.
Was ihr den Geist der Zeiten heißt,
Das ist im Grund der Herren eigner Geist,
In dem die Zeiten sich bespiegeln.[14]

The Helen sequence in Part Two of *Faust* returns to this hermeneutical thematic, adding to it the question of gender. Even before their magical translation from the palace of Menelaus to Faust's castle, Helen and her attendants are, as Mephistopheles says, no more than ghosts, ironically fearful of leaving a daylight that is no longer theirs.[15] As Faust himself had been, they are to be played upon by sweet dreams and delusions—though once Helen has consented to a translation to Faust's castle, a neverland construct of Romantic medievalism that with deliberate naiveté conflates the period of barbarian invasions with the high-medieval Frankish conquest of the Pelopponese seven centuries later,[16] she is pointedly aware of her multiplication in the mirroring minds of her abductors and appropriators:

Einfach die Welt verwirrt ich, doppelt mehr;
Nun dreifach, vierfach bring ich Not auf Not.
[When there was only one of me, I caused trouble in the world. More trouble when there were two. Now that I am threefold, fourfold, it's one calamity after another.][17]

But what exactly are the consequences of this Faust's cohabitation with Helen? He repeats with her the legend of Helen's afterlife cohabitation with Achilles on the white island of Leuke, down to the detail of their son Euphorion[18]—who in Goethe's dramatic allegory becomes, at the moment

---

[14]Goethe, *Faust, Der Tragödie erster Teil*, ll. 575–579, p. 23; *Goethe's Faust*, trans. Fairley, p. 11.

[15]"Gespenster!—Gleich erstarrten Bildern steht ihr da, / Geschreckt, vom Tag zu scheiden, der euch nicht gehört." *Faust, Der Tragödie zweiter Teil*, III, ll. 8930–8931, p. 259. ("You ghosts. There you stand like dummies, dreading to leave the daylight that isn't yours" [*Goethe's Faust*, trans. Fairley, p. 153].)

[16]The castle courtyard is specified by the stage direction as *"umgeben von reichen, phantaschichen Gebäuden des Mittelalters"* ("surrounded by rich and fantastic medieval buildings"), Faust, p. 265. Such a building might be taken to evoke the castles built by Villehardouin and other great nobles during the Frankish occupation of the Pelopponese (a period that seems to be remembered in distorted fashion in Faust's speech in ll. 9443–9481, pp. 273–275 [Fairley, p. 161]). Lynkeus' speech to Helen at ll. 9273–9332 (Fairley, p. 159) explicitly evokes the period of barbarian invasions and the fall of the western Roman empire.

[17]*Faust, Der Tragödie zweiter Teil*, III, ll. 9254–9255, p. 268; *Goethe's Faust*, trans. Fairley, p. 159.

[18]For a summary account of the legend, see Calasso, *The Marriage of Cadmus and Harmony*, pp. 121–122, 124.

of his death and disappearance, Lord Byron: an image at once of aspirations for the restoration of freedom to modern Hellenes and of the poetic, erotic, and ethical power to be gained from an affiliation to Greek culture. After a last embrace, Helen is also de-corporealized, leaving in Faust's arms her garment and her veil, which Mephistopheles predicts will "sweep [Faust] through the ether, above all that is commonplace" ["Es trägt dich über alles Gemeine rasch / Am Äther hin . . . "].[19]

The verb which for Hölderlin signified the surprising and unantici-pated nature of the feminized divine's gift of itself (*überraschen*) recurs here, though in disseminated form (*über . . . rasch*). And like the gods whose presence is invoked and intuited in Hölderlin's odes, Helen's choral atten-dants disperse themselves as blessings of fertility, divine presence and Bacchic potential into a landscape that is finally as much German as it is Arcadian.[20]

MARLOWE'S HELEN AND THE 'SIN OF DEMONIALITY'

Two centuries earlier, Marlowe's Doctor Faustus also made Helen of Troy his paramour—but with less happy consequences, for the male protagonist at least. In this play, if we can trust a preponderance of its critics, the motifs from the matter of Troy that Goethe makes explicit in his re-working of the legend of Faustus, in particular the sense of historical depth and the play with questions of historical difference and belatedness, seem to be largely absent. I want to propose that this view arises from a reductive and narrowly demonological contextualizing of Marlowe's Helen within what was until recently a dominant tendency in Marlowe scholarship, and to outline other more rewarding contexts (still largely neglected by most critics of the play)—in the writings of Jean Calvin; in the intriguingly problematic representations of Helen by Herodotus, Euripides, and other classical writers; and finally, in the use made of Helen by Gnostic sectarians whom Marlowe appears to have read about during his years of theological study at Cambridge.[21]

However we contextualize the Helen sequence in Marlowe's play, one of our focal points must be Faustus' enraptured apostrophe, which contains a great deal more than the cloying eroticism of the best-known filmed

---

[19]Goethe, *Faust, Der Tragödie zweiter Teil*, ll. 9952–9953, p. 288; Fairley, p. 168.

[20]Goethe, *Faust, Der Tragödie erster Teil*, ll. 9985–10038; Fairley, pp. 169–170.

[21]This latter part of my analysis is in some respects anticipated by Forsyth's essay "Heavenly Helen"; by my own remarks in "Right Eye and Left Heel," pp. 88–89, and in the introduction to my edition of *Doctor Faustus* (1991), pp. xxxviii–xlvii; by Moore in "Aspiring Minds and Lumps of Clay," ch. 7; and by Nuttall in *The Alternative Trinity*.

version of the play, in which Richard Burton aims the lines, through much flapping about of veils and streamers, in the direction of a smug Elizabeth Taylor:

> Was this the face that launch'd a thousand ships
> And burnt the topless towers of Ilium?
> Sweet Helen, make me immortal with a kiss;[22]
> Her lips suck forth my soul, see where it flies!
> Come Helen, come, give me my soul again;
> Here will I dwell, for heaven be in these lips,
> And all is dross that is not Helena.
> I will be Paris, and for love of thee
> Instead of Troy shall Wittenberg be sack'd . . . .

Forgive the interruption, but is there a scholar anywhere who does not respond to this Wittenberg man's notion of his *alma mater* in flames, or cannot take pleasure in imagining one or two close colleagues at the heart of a similar conflagration? Yet the thought of long-haired Achaeans running bronze-clad through Wittenberg, spearing astonished academics in the streets of their plundered and burning city, is perhaps not uppermost in Faustus' mind. He seems rather to be supplying his erotic raptures with a medievalized chivalric frame:

> Instead of Troy shall Wittenberg be sack'd,
> And I will combat with weak Menelaus
> And wear thy colours on my plumed crest;
> Yea, I will wound Achilles in the heel
> And then return to Helen for a kiss.[23]

One may be tempted to remember that "weak Menelaus" was strong enough, in Book Three of Homer's *Iliad*, to disgrace the "godlike" Paris, or Alexandros, as Homer prefers to call him, in single combat. Yet that episode also ends with a kiss: Aphrodite, goddess of love, wraps her favourite rapist in a cloud, carries Paris back within the walls of Troy, and delivers him to Helen's boudoir.

But who or what is Marlowe's Helen? What is the meaning of her appearance in this play? To these questions Marlowe scholars have had a

---

[22]Compare *Dido Queen of Carthage*, IV. iv. 121–123: "If he forsake me not, I never die, / For in his looks I see eternity, / And he'll make me immortal with a kiss." The feminizing of Faustus that this echoing of Dido's words might suggest becomes explicit later in the speech when he identifies Helen with Jupiter, and himself with "hapless Selene."

[23]Marlowe, *Doctor Faustus*, ed. Keefer, V. i. 91–103, pp. 82–83.

very direct and simple answer ever since the publication in 1946 of Sir Walter Greg's frequently reprinted and much-cited essay on "The Damnation of Faustus." In Greg's belief, "'Helen' . . . is a 'spirit,' and in this play a spirit means a devil. In making her his paramour Faustus commits the sin of demoniality, that is, bodily intercourse with demons"—and "the nice balance between possible salvation and imminent damnation is upset" once he has fallen into "the direst sin of which human flesh is capable."[24] In other words, the appearance of Helen in this play marks the decisive point at which Faustus becomes unredeemable. As Roma Gill put it, more melodramatically, "Helen's lips 'suck forth' [Faustus'] soul in more than metaphor. The kiss signals the ultimate sin, demoniality, the bodily intercourse with spirits. Now the Old Man gives up hope of saving Faustus; the Good Angel leaves him. After such knowledge there is no forgiveness."[25]

This view of the matter has not gone unopposed. T. W. Craik objected in 1969 that "The case, reduced to this summary form, is ludicrous"; in his view, "the literal-mindedness with which it has been invented and applied, and the materialistic view of sin which it implies . . . make the theory of Faustus' damning demoniality . . . repugnant to the whole nature of Marlowe's play."[26] But despite objections to the interpretive or theological reductiveness of Greg's essay, his invocation of "demoniality" seemed to many mid- and late-twentieth century critics to provide the obviously appropriate context to the appearance of Helen in the play.[27] A cursory reading of the seventeenth-century theologian and demonologist Ludovico Maria Sinistrari, from whose work *De daemonialitate et incubis et succubis* Greg derived the term *daemonialitas*, might have inclined them to think otherwise.

If Sinistrari's dates (1622–1701) were only slightly later, and his other writings less well substantiated, one might suspect this learned casuist to be an invention of Jonathan Swift. By paragraph 49 of *De daemonialitate* he is earnestly debating the question of whether incubi and succubi cultivate the

---

[24]Greg, "The Damnation of Faustus," in Leech, *Marlowe*, pp. 105–107.

[25]Marlowe, *Doctor Faustus*, ed. Gill, p. xxvi.

[26]Craik, "Faustus' Damnation Reconsidered," pp. 194, 196.

[27]Critics who have accepted Greg's "demoniality" thesis include, in addition to Gill, Gardner, "The Tragedy of Damnation," pp. 339–340 n. 13; and Szönyi, "Traditions of Magic," p. 7 n. 14. For other responses ranging from a qualified and revisionary acceptance to outright skepticism, see Sachs, "The Religious Despair of Doctor Faustus," pp. 642–643; Ornstein, "Marlowe and God," p. 1383; Manley, "The Nature of Faustus," p. 228; French, "The Philosophy of Dr. Faustus," p. 140; Kiessling, "Doctor Faustus and the Sin of Demoniality," pp. 205–211; Brandt, "Marlowe's Helen," p. 120 n. 3; and Honigmann, "Ten Problems in *Dr Faustus*," pp. 174–175. Bevington offers a survey of responses to Greg's thesis in "Marlowe and God," pp. 8–9.

arts and letters, have possessions, and make war among themselves (he decides, in each case, that they do).[28] Although he is unsure whether they are subject to Original Sin, Sinistrari concludes that since they are rational beings, Jesus Christ came to save them also; they must therefore have sacraments like those of the human church (paras. 61–62).[29] By paragraph 114 he seems almost to be an advocate of demoniality, finding little if any crime against religion in the act, and professing himself unable to understand why it should be understood as more wicked than bestiality and sod-omy—the former being definitely worse than the latter, since it involves conjunction with a lower species, and hence a debasing of human dignity. Coitus with an incubus, on the other hand, joins us with an entity who is, like us, rational and immortal—but who, "being nobler in body, and certainly more subtle, is more perfect and more worthy than man; and thus a man who joins himself with an incubus does not degrade, but rather dignifies his nature . . . ."[30]

If Sinistrari is to be our guide in matters demonological, Faustus' union with Helen looks more like an act of spiritual self-improvement than clear evidence that he is, in Hart Crane's wonderful phrase, a "bent axle of devotion."[31] We might of course seek out a less visibly unbalanced guide to such matters than Sinistrari. And yet the discursive contexts inscribed within this play are not merely demonological: they involve an actively revisionary engagement with other more ancient discourses—as is emble-matically made evident when Faustus tells how with "sweet pleasure" he has "conquer'd deep despair": "Have I not made blind Homer sing to me / Of

---

[28]Sinistrari, *De daemonialitate*, pp. 82–83.

[29]Sinistrari, *De daemonialitate,* pp. 106–111.

[30]Sinistrari, *De daemonialitate,* pp. 200–202: "In coitu autem cum Incubo, in quo nulla habetur qualitas, vel minima, criminis contra Religionem, difficile est rationem invenire, per quam tale delictum Bestialitate et Sodomia gravior esset. Siquidem gravitas Bestiali-tatis prae Sodomia, prout supra diximus, consistit in hoc, quod homo vilificat dignitatem suae speciei jungendose cum bruto, quod est speciei longe inferioris sua. In coitu autem cum Incubo diversa est ratio: nam Incubus ratione spiritus rationalis, ac immortalis, aequalis est homini; ratione vero corporis nobilioris, nempe subtilioris, est perfectior, et dignior homine; et hoc modo homo jungens se Incubo non vilificat, immo dignificat suam naturam . . . ."

[31]Crane, "For the Marriage of Faustus and Helen," I, l. 52, *Complete Poems*, p. 29. To be fair, it should be added that Sinistrari does allow for another kind of coitus, which is demoniality with demons rather than with incubi and succubi—though in this work he is very little interested in it. He thinks even coitus with incubi or succubi to be damnable if the person involved believes his partner to be a devil. Greg's identification of Marlowe's Helen as a demonic spirit may be correct; his belief that Sinistrari provides the most hopeful context within which to interpret her is, I think, unhelpful.

Alexander's love and Oenon's death?" (This is an element of the tale of Troy that was narrated in the post-Homeric *Kypria*, but passed over in silence by Homer himself: Faustus would have been the first to hear it from his lips.) "And hath not he that built the walls of Thebes / With ravishing sound of his melodious harp / Made music with my Mephastophilis?"[32]

Given this evidence of discursive hybridity, shall we then seek out wider contexts, keeping in mind that there remains something ineradicably uncanny about the notion of sexual commerce between corporeal and disembodied beings?

SPIRITUAL FORNICATION

What Sir Walter Greg was—forgive the term—groping towards in his reflections on "the direst sin of which human flesh is capable" is a category explicitly linked to Helen of Troy by that magisterial reformer and Elizabethan best-seller Jean Calvin, whose spirited account of what he called "spiritual fornication" occurs in a passage of his *Institutes of the Christian Religion* devoted to "the abomination of the Mass":

> Offered in a golden cup, it has so inebriated all kings and peoples of the earth, from highest to lowest, and has so stricken them with drowsiness and dizziness, that, more stupid than brute beasts, they have steered the whole vessel of their salvation into this one deadly whirlpool. Surely, Satan never prepared a stronger engine to besiege and capture Christ's kingdom. This is the Helen for whom the enemies of truth today do battle with so much rage, fury, and cruelty—a Helen indeed, with whom they so defile themselves in spiritual fornication, the most abominable of all.[33]

The stupefying contents of a golden cup, a deadly whirlpool which engulfs the victims of that poisonous *pharmakon*, a siege engine, a temptation to defilement and spiritual fornication: as the frenzy of shifting metaphors may suggest, the danger of this Mass, this Helen, is a function of its uncontrollable instability and supplementarity. Through their very promiscuity, Calvin's metaphors might be said to enter into a metonymic relationship with the central shift or slippage that makes the Mass an "abomination": that transgression of ontological categories and of differences in material substance which occurs when the wine in the elevated cup undergoes a purported transubstantiation into the blood of Christ.

There is of course a Homeric intertext to Calvin's words: he is remembering those lines in Book IV of the *Odyssey* in which Helen removes

---

[32]Marlowe, *Doctor Faustus*, ed. Keefer, II. iii. 25–30, p. 41.
[33]Calvin, *Institutes of the Christian Religion*, IV.xviii.18, vol. 2, p. 1445.

the grief of Menelaus, Telemachus and Peisistratus by casting into their wine a medicine she obtained in Egypt,

> . . . free of gall, to make one forget all sorrows,
> and whoever had drunk it down once it had been mixed in the wine bowl,
> for the day that he drank it would have no tear roll down his face,
> not if his mother died and his father died, not if men
> murdered a brother or a beloved son in his presence . . . .[34]

But Calvin's conflated allusion to this passage and to the siege of Troy produces undeniable confusions. The drugged potion of forgetfulness with which Helen obliterates sorrow is the offering of the Mass; these liquids are also "a Helen" (with the suggestion of a potential plurality of Helens). The "enemies of truth," the Roman Catholics who do battle for this Helen and defile themselves with her, are implicitly equated with the defenders of Troy, thus aligning the Reformers with the Achaean or Greek be-siegers—whose primary aim was to recover possession of Helen. But if Helen is also a siege engine being used against Christ's kingdom, are the Reformers now the defending Trojans and the Roman Catholics the besieging Greeks? Helen is bewilderingly both inside and outside the walls, the object of siege warfare and its primary instrument.

Calvin's initial focus is upon the soporific and stupefying power of the abomination that he equates with Helen; "spiritual fornication," whatever precisely that may involve, appears to follow as the defiling consequence of a drugged or inebriated condition. In an analogous manner, Marlowe's Faustus, having given his fellow scholars a glimpse of "Helen of Greece," only comes to desire her as his paramour after the Old Man's denunciation of his "most vile and loathsome filthiness" has brought him to a more powerful than ever sense of his desperate spiritual condition—an awareness which he tells a menacing Mephastophilis he wishes to "extinguish":

> One thing, good servant, let me crave of thee
> To glut the longing of my heart's desire:
> That I might have unto my paramour
> That heavenly Helen which I saw of late,
> Whose sweet embracings may extinguish clean
> These thoughts that do dissuade me from my vow
> [. . .] to Lucifer.[35]

---

[34] *The Odyssey of Homer*, trans. Lattimore, IV.221–225, p. 71.
[35] Marlowe, *Doctor Faustus*, ed. Keefer, V. i. 11, 41, 82–88, pp. 78, 79, 81–82.

If Marlowe's Helen is a figure not just of desire but also of a willed forgetfulness of grief, this may reflect the poet's awareness both of Homer and of more contemporary texts by which Homer's had been mediated. But his relationship to such mediations is unlikely to have been one of mere acquiescence. There is evidence in *Doctor Faustus* that Marlowe's six years of theological study at Cambridge had given him a thorough understanding of Calvin's doctrines[36]—and evidence both there and elsewhere that he detested them. On the issue of the sacrament that so agitated Calvin, Marlowe is reported by the spy Richard Baines to have held scandalously unorthodox opinions:

> That if there be any god or any good Religion, then it is in the papistes because the service of god is performed with more Cerimonies, as Elevation of the mass, organs, singing men, Shaven Crownes & cta. That all protestantes are Hypocriticall asses . . . . That if Christ would have instituted the sacrament with more Ceremoniall Reverence it would have bin had in more admiration, that it would have bin much better being administred in a Tobacco pipe.[37]

HELEN'S SPECTRALITY

An unstable and uncanny figure in Calvin's muddled allegory, Helen is only marginally less so in classical texts. As the daughter of Zeus, she is consistently represented in classical Greek writings as a numinous figure, whose beauty and (in many versions) ethical irresponsibility are alike quasi-divine attributes. "[T]he only woman in Homer who clearly has distinctive epithets of her own,"[38] her close linkage to the powers of Olympus is made evident in a variety of ways—in the favoured afterlife as an inhabitant of the Isles of the Blest that Homer confers upon Menelaus for the sole virtue of being her consort,[39] or in the story that Stesichorus was blinded as a punishment for abusing Helen in one of his poems, and only recovered his sight after publishing a palinode in which he declared that she was never at Troy, but only a phantom image of her.[40]

Two rather obvious things need to be said about the classical Helen. The first is that this most hauntingly desirable of all women undergoes a repeated

---

[36]See Stachniewski, *The Persecutory Imagination*, pp. 17–84, 292–331; my introduction to *Doctor Faustus*, pp. xlvii–lv; and Nuttall, *The Alternative Trinity*, pp. 22–41.

[37]MacLure, *Marlowe: The Critical Heritage*, p. 37 (with u/v silently modernized).

[38]Parry, *The Making of Homeric Verse*, p. 97; cited by Calasso, *The Marriage of Cadmus and Harmony*, p. 91.

[39]Homer, *The Odyssey*, IV. 561–570, pp. 79–80.

[40]See Plato, *Phaedrus* 243a–b, in *The Collected Dialogues of Plato*, ed. Hamilton and Cairns, p. 490.

dematerialization, not just in Stesichorus, or in the *Helen* of Euripides, in which the trope of Stesichorus' palinode becomes the subject of an entire play, but in other sources as well—among them Herodotus, in whose *Histories* the story that Helen spent the years of the Trojan War in Egypt is narrated in circumstantial detail, backed with the authority of the temple priests of Memphis, and supported by the claim that although Homer rejected this true story "as less suitable for epic poetry than the one he actually used, he left indications that it was not unknown to him."[41] Roberto Calasso can thus claim that "Helen is the power of the phantom, the simulacrum—and the simulacrum is that place where absence is sovereign."[42]

Secondly, Helen very clearly becomes, in post-Homeric Greece, a vehicle for thinking about divine justice, another kind of sovereign absence. Euripides, reflecting on the catastrophe of Troy in the wake of Stesichorus and Herodotus (and in the midst of the unfolding catastrophe of the Peloponnesian War), seems to have recognized the strategic power of Helen-as-simulacrum in the sustaining of any poetic legitimation of the justice of divine power. Such a theodicy would seem to require one of two diametrically opposed moves: either that Helen be separated from affiliation to Olympian Zeus and reattached to her human paternity in Sparta, or else that she be altogether disconnected, except as bodiless image or *eidolon*, from the siege of Troy.[43] Euripides proceeds to demonstrate the futility of both moves.

In *The Trojan Women*, Andromache, crying out against the Hellenes who are about to murder her son Astyanax, also denounces the *casus belli*: "Helen, Tyndareos' daughter! You were never daughter of Zeus!" But detaching Helen from her divine father and making her the daughter, rather, of Tyndareos of Sparta, results in an immediate proliferation of phantom paternal agencies of devastation:

> You had many fathers; the Avenging Curse was one,
> Hate was the next, then Murder, Death, and every plague
> That this earth breeds. I'll swear Zeus never fathered you
> To fasten death on tens of thousands east and west![44]

---

[41]Herodotus, *The Histories*, II. 116, p. 126. The Helen-in-Egypt story occupies all of II. 112–120 (pp. 124–128).

[42]Calasso, *Marriage of Cadmus*, p. 123.

[43]There is a clear parallel between this move and the docetic Christology of some early Christians, usually Gnostics, who claimed that Christ himself did not suffer upon the cross, but only a phantom image of him. See Filoramo, *A History of Gnosticism*, pp. 124–126, 149, 160–161.

[44]Euripides, *The Women of Troy*, in *The Bacchae and Other Plays*, p. 115.

The repeated denial of any link between Helen and Zeus does not absolve that god of responsibility: when Hecabe calls out to Zeus, with a counter-claim to affiliation and to justice—

> Zeus, our maker, begetter, Lord of our land!
> We are Dardanus' children! See: is our torment just?

—the chorus answers: "He sees, and the flames burn on."[45]

In his *Helen*, Euripides dramatizes a version of what Herodotus and the penitent Stesichorus had represented as the "true" story: in the protagonist's own words,

> The Helen who went to Phrygia as a prize for Troy to defend and the Greeks to fight for—that Helen was not I, only my name. Zeus did not forget me: I was taken by Hermes, wrapped in a cloud, borne through the secret places of the upper air, and set down here in the palace of Proteus, whom Zeus picked out as the most honourable of all men, so that I might preserve my chastity inviolate for Menelaus.[46]

But the problem of theodicy re-emerges in the words of the Messenger when, only a few lines after declaring that "The ways of the gods are involved and mysterious . . . and all is for the best," he appears to contradict himself by remarking on the ways in which their priests and prophets withheld what would seem to be vital information:

> Calchas saw his friends dying in battle for the sake of a phantom, yet he gave them neither word nor sign; no more did the Trojan Helenus—his city was sacked for nothing. You may say it was because the god did not wish them to speak.[47]

The sophist Gorgias, Euripides' contemporary, adds another dimension to the ethical-theological discourses surrounding this phantasmatic Helen when in his *Encomium of Helen* he argues that—even assuming she did indeed abandon her husband and accompany Alexandros to Troy—she can in no way be blamed. For if Helen acted by the will of fate and of the gods, they are at fault; and if she was carried off by violence she is to be pitied rather than condemned.

> But if it was *logos* which persuaded her and deceived her heart, not even to this is it difficult to make an answer and to banish blame as follows. *Logos* is a powerful lord, which by means of the finest and most invisible body effects

---

[45]Euripides, *The Women of Troy,* in *The Bacchae and Other Plays*, p. 132.
[46]Euripides, *Helen*, in *The Bacchae and Other Plays*, p. 136.
[47]Euripides, *Helen*, in *The Bacchae and Other Plays*, pp. 158–159.

the divinest works: it can stop fear and banish grief and create joy and nurture pity.[48]

Poetry provides a proof of this: "Fearful shuddering and tearful pity and grievous longing come upon its hearers . . . ." And other kinds of ordered speech reinforce the argument:

> Sacred incantations sung with words are bearers of pleasure and banishers of pain, for, merging with opinion in the soul, the power of the incantation is wont to beguile it and persuade it and alter it by sorcery. There have been discovered two arts of sorcery and magic: one consists of errors of soul and the other of deceptions [apatemata] of opinion. All who have and do persuade people of things do so by molding a false argument . . . . What cause then prevents the conclusion that Helen similarly, against her will, might have come under the influence of logos, just as if ravished by the force of the mighty?[49]

Helen is here the victim of *logos*—but she might also be said to merge with it, as another body, in some accounts almost invisible, in others an insubstantial shining-forth, but always "effect[ing] the divinest works." In writing this *Encomium*, Gorgias was without doubt remembering that same passage of Book IV of the *Odyssey* which Herodotus cited as evidence that Homer knew of Helen's Egyptian sojourn, and which Calvin would allude to in his rant against "spiritual fornication"—for Gorgias also notes that "The effect of speech upon the condition of the soul is comparable to the power of drugs over the nature of bodies."[50] Like the incantations of which the old sophist speaks, Helen in Book IV of the *Odyssey* brings pleasure and banishes pain, beguiling her auditors with drugs—and also with the stories she proceeds to tell them: "Sit here now in the palace," she says, "and take your dinner and listen / to me and be entertained."[51]

The Helen who was actually in Troy is thus intimately connected with what Gorgias says of "the magic violence of speech"[52] and the therapeutic sorcery of poetic incantations. But as Calasso insists, the Helen who was *not* in Troy is still more scandalously connected to the deceits of poetry. According to the version of events given by Herodotus,

---

48Sprague, *The Older Sophists*, p. 52. In this and the following quotation I have made minor emendations, preserving "logos" where the translator gives "speech," and substituting the gender-neutral "sorcery" for "witchcraft" as a translation of *goeteia*.

49Sprague, *Older Sophists*, p. 52.

50Sprague, *Older Sophists*, p. 53.

51Homer, *The Odyssey*, IV. 238–239, p. 71.

52This phrase is not Gorgias' own, but comes from one of his most profound interpreters—Untersteiner, *The Sophists*, p. 106.

For ten years the war had raged around an absent woman, whom the Trojans would have been more than happy to hand over to the Achaeans, if only they had actually had her. Why on earth did Homer keep quiet about that extraordinary fact in the events leading up to the war? Herodotus answers: "because this story was not suitable for epic composition." It is an explanation that leaves us dumbfounded. So the centuries-old accusation against Homer, that he was a craftsman of deceit, turns out to be true, does it? For overridingly literary motives, Homer kept quiet about the supreme scandal of the Trojan War: that blood had been spilled for a woman who was not actually there, for an impalpable ghost.[53]

★   ★   ★

Does it seem extravagant to suggest an association between Marlowe's Helen, the Helens of Euripides, who are bound up with an interrogation of divine justice, and the Helen of Gorgias—who, through a slippage of signifiers that seems to be the mark of her uncanny power, is also to be identified with the deceptive ability of *logos* and of poetry to "stop fear and banish grief"? Let us remember again that Marlowe's Faustus does not ask to have Helen for his paramour solely in order "[t]o glut the longing of [his] heart's desire," but also because he anticipates that her "sweet embracings may extinguish clean / These thoughts that do dissuade me from my vow / . . . to Lucifer."[54] Like the medicinal drug which Helen stirred into the wine in the palace of Menelaus, sexual congress with Helen is to make Faustus temporarily oblivious to his anguish and despair. (It is not clear that Faustus wholly believes the trick will work, for an accurate awareness of the reality of his situation burns up through the glamour of his words: "Brighter art thou than flaming Jupiter / When he appear'd to hapless Semele . . . ."[55] But didn't Gorgias warn us that the domain of *logos*, of drug-like incantations, was also one of *apatemata*, or deceptions?)

It is worth reflecting, in this light, on the poetic and deceptive power that enters Faustus' speech when he addresses Helen. Only fifteen lines previously he has abjectly renewed his blood-pact with Lucifer and betrayed to demonic assault the Old Man who attempted to correct him. How many critics of the play, after subjecting themselves to the rhetorical splendours of this speech, have been able to notice that Faustus must be supposed to speak these lines with his own blood, the visible sign of his cowardice and shame, still dripping from his arm?

But what did Marlowe know of an ancient writer as obscure as Gorgias? We cannot be sure that he had read the *Encomium of Helen*—but if he knew the text *On Nature or that which is not [Peri tou me ontos]*, in which Gorgias

[53]Calasso, *Marriage of Cadmus*, p. 129.

[54]Marlowe, *Doctor Faustus*, ed. Keefer, V. i. 83, 86–88, pp. 81–82.

[55]Marlowe, *Doctor Faustus*, ed. Keefer, V. i. 106–107, p. 83.

enunciates a philosophy of paradoxical skepticism, it is possible that he would have sought out Gorgias' closely related pronouncements on rhetoric and poetry in the *Encomium*. Stephen Greenblatt has described as thoroughly Gorgian both Marlowe's fascination with "the magic violence of speech"[56] and also the recurrent predicament of his protagonists, who are "forever cut off from the knowledge of being, forever locked in the partial, the contradictory, and the irrational," and hence obliged "through the power of language [to] construct deceptions in which and for which they live."[57] Greenblatt is alluding here to *Peri tou me ontos*, in which Gorgias supplements his rhetoric of deceptions with what amounts to a skeptical "empty ontology": in summary form, his argument is "first and foremost, that nothing exists; second, that even if it exists it is inapprehensible to man; third, that even if it is apprehensible, still it is without doubt incapable of being expressed or explained to the next man."[58] Although Greenblatt does not remark on the fact, there is no doubt either that Marlowe was familiar with this formulation of an implicitly tragic epistemological gap between human discourse and its referents: when, in his opening speech, Faustus advises himself to "Bid *on kai me on* farewell," he is unmistakably quoting from Gorgias' *Peri tou me ontos*.[59]

THE GNOSTIC HELEN

These contexts may take us some distance towards answering—or at least complicating—the question of who or what Marlowe's wordless Helen may be, as well as the further question of the extent to which her appearance in the final act of *Doctor Faustus* evokes textual mediations and historical depths that may be comparable in significance to those which are much more explicitly in play in Goethe's *Faust*. The question of *why* she appears in this play can, on a preliminary level, be more easily explored. As I have argued elsewhere, Helen was drawn into the legend of Faustus as a direct consequence of a logic of

---

[56]Greenblatt, *Renaissance Self-Fashioning*, p. 215 (quoting Untersteiner, *The Sophists*, p. 106).

[57] Greenblatt, *Renaissance Self-Fashioning*, p. 215.

[58]Sprague, *The Older Sophists*, p. 42. The term "empty ontology" is borrowed from Poster, "Persuasion in an Empty Ontology." I have surveyed the evidence for knowledge of Gorgias in a forthcoming essay, "Ben Jonson's Skeptical Friend: Gorgias in the English Renaissance."

[59]Marlowe, *Doctor Faustus*, ed. Keefer, I. i. 12, p. 6. The quotation is from one of the first sentences of Gorgias' text: *"oute de to on estin . . . oute to me on . . . oute to on kai me on . . ."* ([N]either does the existent exist nor the nonexistent . . . nor the existent and nonexistent . . ."). See Diels, *Die Fragmente der Vorsokratiker*, vol. 2, p. 243; and Sprague, *The Older Sophists*, p. 43.

legitimation which motivated the Lutheran theologians—Luther himself, his colleague Philip Melanchthon, and Melanchthon's student Augustin Lercheimer—who were primarily responsible for the elaboration of demonologically inflected narratives about this magician.[60] According to patristic writings which Luther and Melanchthon read and cited (among them the apocryphal *Acts of Peter* and *Acts of the Holy Apostles Peter and Paul* and the pseudo-Clementine *Recognitions*), the apostle Peter engaged in a series of rhetorical and magical contests with the Samaritan magician and antichrist Simon Magus. But Simon's existence is also attested to by the canonical *Acts of the Apostles* and by refutations of his teachings by patristic apologists and heresiologists including Justin Martyr, Irenaeus of Lyon, and Hippolytus of Rome.[61]

According to the view of sacred history expounded in the pseudo-Clementine *Recognitions* (which Luther adopted in his major work of scriptural exegesis, the *Commentary on Galatians*),[62] the prior appearance of an exponent of the demonically inspired False Prophecy amounts to a certification of the authenticity of the exponent of True Prophecy whom God then inspires to dissipate falsehood and disseminate his sacred truth. Simon fits this pattern: he preceded St. Peter and was refuted by him. Luther's and Melanchthon's immediate predecessors included a magician and astrologer whose titles and claims of expertise suggest affiliations to a number of ancient magicians and prophets—among them Simon Magus. On his earliest recorded appearances in 1506, this "Georgius Sabellicus, Faustus junior, magus secundus" is said to have boasted "that the miracles of Christ the Saviour were not so wonderful, that he could do all the things that Christ had done, as often and whenever he wished."[63] By the time of his death in the late 1530s, Doctor Georgius Faustus, as he came to call himself, had become famous throughout Germany as (in the words of the town council of Nuremberg) a "great sodomite and necromancer."[64]

---

[60]See Marlowe, *Doctor Faustus*, ed. Keefer, pp. xxxvii–xlii.

[61]In the *Acts of Peter* the contests between the apostle and Simon Magus are wholly magical in nature (see Hennecke, *New Testament Apocrypha*, vol. 2, pp. 282–316).

[62]See Clement, *Recognitions* III. 59, 61. Compare the accounts of the historical master-narrative of Luther's *Commentary on Galatians* provided by Edwards, *Luther and the False Brethren*, pp. 112–115 and by Headley, *Luther's View of Church History*, pp. 64–66, 233.

[63]This blasphemous boast appears in the earliest surviving account of the historical Dr. Faustus, a letter written by the Benedictine abbot and humanist Johannes Trithemius to Johannes Virdung von Hassfurt in August, 1507. See Palmer and More, *The Sources of the Faust Tradition*, p. 85. For analysis of the letter, see Harmening, "Faust und die Renaissance-Magie," and Baron, *Doctor Faustus from History to Legend*, pp. 23–39.

[64]Palmer and More, *Sources of the Faust Tradition*, p. 90. This characterization of Dr. Faustus, which appeared in the records of the City Council of Nuremberg in May, 1532, echoes the claim of Trithemius that when in the spring of 1507 Faustus was appointed

Late in his own life, Philip Melanchthon seized upon the opportunity of authenticating his and Luther's quasi-apostolic role as Reformers by pointing to the parallel: just as St. Peter had been preceded and opposed by the antichrist Simon Magus, so also he and Luther were preceded and (so he suggested) opposed by Faustus, whom Melanchthon went out of his way to mis-identify as having been born in a village only steps away from his own home-town of Bretten.[65] Simon Magus was associated, in the stories told about him by his Christian enemies, in his own theological pronouncements, and apparently also in the flesh, by a woman whom he claimed was Helen of Troy;[66] the presence of Helen in the Lutheran legend of Faustus is one sign of its functional derivation from the patristic legend of Simon Magus. This heresiarch claimed to be the originary and supreme divine power; the woman whom he called Helen, and whom he said he had redeemed from prostitution in a brothel in Tyre, was his *ennoia* or First Thought. Though divine in nature, she was made captive by subordinate powers whom she had engendered, and imprisoned by them in a succession of female forms, including that of Helen of Troy, within the world they made:

> Now this Simon of Samaria, from whom all sorts of heresies derive their origin,
> formed his sect out of the following materials:—Having redeemed from slavery

---

schoolmaster in the town of Kreuznach, "he began to indulge in the most dastardly kind of lewdness with the boys" ("mox nefandissimo fornicationis genere cum pueris uidelicet uoluptari coepit"), and when this was discovered, had to flee (Palmer and More, p. 86).

[65]In two posthumously published texts, Melanchthon claims that "Ioannes" Faustus was born near his own birthplace, and that Faustus repeated Simon Magus' attempt in the apocryphal *Acts of Peter* (and many derivative texts) to fly up into heaven (see Palmer and More, *Sources of the Faust Tradition*, pp. 99, 101). Melanchthon's student Augustin Lercheimer recounted in 1597 an odd little kitchen debate that supposedly took place between Faustus and Melanchthon in the latter's house in Wittenberg (Palmer and More, pp. 121–122). As I remarked in "Right Eye and Left Heel," these texts construct a ratio in which Melanchthon's relationship with a magician who repeated the acts of St. Peter's antagonist Simon Magus confers an implicitly apostolic status on the Reformer. Earlier sources identify Faustus' Christian name as Georgius; the name Ioannes and the claim that he studied magic in Cracow suggest that Melanchthon conflated Faustus with Trithemius' correspondent, the Heidelberg astronomer and magician Johannes Virdung von Hassfurt, who had indeed studied in Crakow, and whom Melanchthon had known in his youth (Virdung cast his horoscope).

[66]The full accounts of Simon's Helen theology provided by Irenaeus and Hippolytus are evidently based upon Simonian materials (see Irenaeus, *Against Heresies*, I. xxiii, pp. 87–88; Hippolytus, *Refutation of All Heresies*, VI.ii–xv, pp. 196–214, especially VI.xiv, pp. 210–212). A much abbreviated version appears in *The Clementine Homilies* (II.xxii–xxv, pp. 232–233); in the generally parallel *Recognitions of Clement*, Helen is renamed Luna, though there remains a reference to the Trojan War (II.vi–ix, xi–xii, pp. 98–100). In the apocryphal *Acts of Peter*, and the much later *Acts of the Holy Apostles Peter and Paul,* there are no references to Helen, and only residual traces of Simon's doctrines.

at Tyre, a city of Phoenicia, a certain woman named Helena, he was in the habit of carrying her about with him, declaring that this woman was the first conception of his mind, the mother of all, by whom, in the beginning, he conceived in his mind [the thought] of forming angels and archangels. For this Ennoea leaping forth from him, and comprehending the will of her father, descended to the lower regions [of space], and generated angels and powers, by whom also he declared this world was formed. But after she had produced them, she was detained by them through motives of jealousy, because they were unwilling to be looked upon as the progeny of any other being. As to himself, they had no knowledge of him whatever [. . .]. She suffered all kinds of contumely from them, so that she could not return upwards to her father, but was even shut up in a human body, and for ages passed in succession from one female body to another, as from vessel to vessel. She was, for example, in that Helen on whose account the Trojan war was undertaken; for whose sake also Stesichorus was struck blind, because he had cursed her in his verses, but afterwards, repenting and writing what are called *palinodes*, in which he sang her praise, he was restored to sight. Thus she, passing from body to body, and suffering insults in every one of them, at last became a common prostitute; and she it was that was meant by the lost sheep [Matt. xviii.12].

For this purpose, then, he had come that he might win her first, and free her from slavery, while he conferred salvation upon men, by making himself known to them.[67]

This theology conflates the Greek myth of the birth of Athena, central motifs of Jewish Wisdom literature, and a proleptic allegorizing displacement of Paris' rape of Helen; the Trojan War thereby becomes a metaleptic repetition of the true cosmogonic narrative. Like the Helen of some of the classical texts to which I have referred, this Simonian Helen is a shimmeringly ambiguous figure—physically present, but paradoxically so as a mere *eidolon* of the divine reality which may be intuited as underlying her appearance at the siege of Troy. According to the fourth-century C.E. pseudo-Clementine *Recognitions*, Simon claimed his consort to be "Wisdom, the mother of all things, for whom, says he, the Greeks and barbarians contending, were able in some measure to see an image of her; but of herself, as she is, as the dweller with the first and only God, they were wholly ignorant."[68]

Marlowe activates this Simonian context when (in direct contrast to the treatment of Helen in the prose Faustbook which was his primary

---

[67]Irenaeus, *Against Heresies*, I. xxiii, pp. 87–88. In this narrative the notion, made explicit in the second century by Valentinus and his followers, that this Ennoia or divine Wisdom engendered the cosmos either as a kind of abortion or else as the result of rape by the lower powers, is already clearly implicit. For a brief account of the Valentinian cosmogony, see Filoramo, *A History of Gnosticism*, pp. 67–77.

[68]Clement, *Recognitions,* II. xii, p. 100.

source) he integrates elements from Wisdom literature into Faustus' speech to Helen:

> O, thou art fairer than the evening air
> Clad in the beauty of a thousand stars;
> Brighter art thou than flaming Jupiter
> When he appear'd to hapless Semele,
> More lovely than the monarch of the sky
> In wanton Arethusa's azur'd arms,
> And none but thou shalt be my paramour.[69]

Minus the mythographic allusions, this is a selectively cut synopsis of Solomon's paean to Wisdom in the apocryphal Wisdom of Solomon. According to Solomon, Wisdom

> is the breath of the power of God, and a pure influence that floweth from the glory of the Almighty: therefore can no defiled thing come unto her. For she is the brightness of the everlasting light, the undefiled mirror of the Majesty of God, and the image of his goodness. [. . .] For she is more beautiful than the Sun, and is above all the order of stars, and the light is not to be compared unto her. [. . .] I have loved her, and sought her from my youth: I desired to marry her, such love had I unto her beauty.
>
> Wisdom of Solomon 7: 25–26, 29, 8: 2; spelling modernized

What Faustus has deleted is, very significantly, the language that links this celestial beauty to the majesty and power of the Judaeo-Christian God, and that insists on its immunity from defilement. (But the deleted or repressed returns at once in the gender inversions of his allusions to Semela and Arethusa.)

Marlowe, in short, is aware that Helen, before reaching his Faustus, has passed through the embraces, not just of Menelaus, Trojan Paris, and the sophist Gorgias, but of the heretic and antichrist Simon Magus as well. Jean Calvin, whose inheritance Marlowe despised, fought with all his strength against the enticing magic of what he denounced as spiritual fornication. Marlowe, in contrast, seems to insist on the mental (and possibly corporeal) pleasures of this "spiritual fornication." But he also, more importantly, opens the way to a recovery of history through a hermeneutics of eroticism that anticipates what we have seen in the writings of Goethe and Hölderlin—and that is certainly no less complex than their evocations of "Gratien Griechenlands," "Dienerinnen des Himmels," or of Helen herself, in its recognition of the mediations constituted by prior appropriations of the desired classical form. The further question of whether Mar–

---

[69]Marlowe, *Doctor Faustus*, ed. Keefer, V. i. 104–110, p. 83.

lowe's Helen is, like the Helens of Euripides, part of a dramatic interrogation of divine justice is not one to engage with here. Let it suffice to say that through this evanescent image of Helen, which is also a fleeting simulacrum of her textually sedimented history, Marlowe has offered us a dangerous taste of eroticized wisdom—perhaps even of the Wisdom of perversity.

⋆   ⋆   ⋆

A three-sentence postlude. Thomas Greene, in his classic *The Light in Troy*, found "at the heart of the humanist enlightenment" something that he called "necromantic superstition."[70] I would prefer to say that the Homeric *nekuia* of Book XI of the *Odyssey* provides us with a necromantic hermeneutics of recovery, of engagement with the past through a gift to the dead of blood—or possibly, to think again of Faustus and Helen, of other bodily fluids as well. Greene eloquently describes the haunting consequences of this hermeneutic of necromancy, or necromantic superstition: "It produced buildings and statues and poems that have to be scrutinized for subterranean outlines or emergent presences or"—he says at last—"ghostly reverberations."[71]

WORKS CITED

Aeschylus. *Eschyle*. Ed. and trans. Paul Mazon. 2 vols. Paris: Les Belles Lettres, 1920–1925.

Baron, Frank. *Doctor Faustus from History to Legend*. Munich: Wilhelm Fink, 1978.

Bevington, David. "Marlowe and God." *Explorations in Renaissance Culture* 17 (1991): 1–38.

Calasso, Roberto. *The Marriage of Cadmus and Harmony*. Trans. Tim Parks. Toronto: Knopf, 1993.

Calvin, Jean. *Institutes of the Christian Religion*. Ed. John T. McNeill. Trans. Ford Lewis Battles. 2 vols. 1960. Rpt. Philadelphia: Westminster, 1973.

Clement I (Bishop of Rome, pseud.). *Recognitions of Clement*, and *The Clementine Homilies*. *The Ante-Nicene Fathers*, vol. 8. Ed. Alexander Roberts, James Donaldson, and A. Cleveland Coxe. Buffalo: The Christian Literature Co., 1886.

Craik, T. W. "Faustus' Damnation Reconsidered." *Renaissance Drama* n.s. 2 (1969): 189–196.

Crane, Hart. *The Complete Poems and Selected Letters and Prose of Hart Crane*. Ed. Brom Weber. Garden City, NY: Anchor, 1966.

Diels, Hermann, ed. *Die Fragmente der Vorsokratiker*. 4th ed. 3 vols. Berlin: Weidmann, 1922.

Edwards, Mark U., Jr. *Luther and the False Brethren*. Stanford: Stanford University Press, 1975.

---

[70]Greene, *The Light in Troy*, p. 93.

[71]Greene, *The Light in Troy*, p. 93.

Euripides. *The Bacchae and Other Plays*. Trans. Philip Vellacott. 1973. Rpt. Harmondsworth: Penguin, 1976.

Filoramo, Giovanni. *A History of Gnosticism*. Trans. Anthony Alcock. Oxford: Blackwell, 1990.

French, A. L. "The Philosophy of *Dr. Faustus*." *Essays in Criticism* 20 (1970): 123–142.

Forsyth, Neil. "Heavenly Helen." *Études de lettres* 4 (1987): 11–21.

Gardner, Helen. "The Tragedy of Damnation." *Elizabethan Drama: Modern Essays in Criticism*. Ed. R. J. Kaufman. New York: Oxford University Press, 1961. 320–341.

The Geneva Bible: A Facsimile of the 1560 Edition. Ed. Lloyd Eason Berry and William D. Whittingham. Madison: University of Wisconsin Press, 1969.

Goethe, Johann Wolfgang. *Faust*. Ed. Hanns W. Eppelsheimer. Munich: Deutscher Taschenbuch, 1962.

Goethe, Johann Wolfgang. *Goethe's Faust*. Trans. Barker Fairley. Toronto: University of Toronto Press, 1970.

Greenblatt, Stephen. *Renaissance Self-Fashioning: From More to Shakespeare*. Chicago: University of Chicago Press, 1980.

Greene, Thomas M. *The Light in Troy: Imitation and Discovery in Renaissance Poetry*. New Haven: Yale University Press, 1982.

Greg, W. W. "The Damnation of Faustus." *Modern Language Review* 41 (1946): 97–107. Rpt. Leech, *Marlowe: A Collection of Critical Essays*. 92–107.

Harmening, Dieter. "Faust und die Renaissance-Magie: zum ältesten Faustzeugnis (Johannes Trithemius an Johannes Virdung, 1507)." *Archiv für Kulturgeschichte* 55 (1973): 56–79.

Hattaway, Michael. "The Theology of Marlowe's *Doctor Faustus*." *Renaissance Drama* n.s. 3 (1970): 51–78.

Headley, John M. *Luther's View of Church History*. New Haven: Yale University Press, 1963.

Heidegger, Martin. *An Introduction to Metaphysics*. Trans. Ralph Mannheim. 1959. Rpt. New Haven: Yale University Press, 1975.

Heidegger, Martin. *Pathmarks*. Ed. William McNeill. Cambridge: Cambridge University Press, 1998.

Hennecke, E., ed. *New Testament Apocrypha*. Ed. W. Schneemelcher. Trans. R. McL. Wilson et al. 2 vols. 1963–1965. Rpt. London: SCM, 1973–1974.

Herodotus. *The Histories*. Trans. Aubrey de Sélincourt. Rev. John Marincola. London: Penguin, 1972.

Hippolytus, Bishop of Rome. *The Refutation of All Heresies. Hippolytus, Bishop of Rome*, vol. 1. Trans. J. H. MacMahon and S. D. F. Salmond. Ante-Nicene Christian Library 6. Edinbugh: T. and T. Clark, 1868.

Hölderlin, Friedrich. *Selected Poems and Fragments*. Ed. Jeremy Adler. Trans. Michael Hamburger. London: Penguin, 1998.

Homer. *The Odyssey of Homer*. Trans. Richmond Lattimore. New York: Harper & Row, 1967.

Honigmann, Ernst. "Ten Problems in *Dr Faustus*." *The Arts of Performance in Elizabethan and Early Stuart Drama: Essays for G.K. Hunter*. Ed. Murray Biggs, Philip Edwards, Inga-Stina Ewbank, and Eugene M. Waith. Edinburgh: Edinburgh University Press, 1991. 173–191.

Irenaeus, Bishop of Lyons. *Against Heresies. The Writings of Irenaeus*, vol. 1. Trans. Alexander Roberts and W.H. Rambaut. Ante-Nicene Christian Library 5. Edinburgh: T. and T. Clark, 1868.

Keefer, Michael. "Right Eye and Left Heel: Ideological Origins of the Legend of Faustus." *Mosaic* 22 (1989): 79–94.

Kiessling, Nicolas. "Doctor Faustus and the Sin of Demoniality." *Studies in English Literature* 15 (1975): 205–211.

Leech, Clifford, ed. *Marlowe: A Collection of Critical Essays*. Englewood Cliffs, N.J.: Prentice-Hall, 1964.

Ligota, C.R. "'This Story is Not True': Fact and Fiction in Antiquity." *Journal of the Warburg and Courtauld Institutes* 45 (1982): 1–13.

MacLure, Millar, ed. *Marlowe: The Critical Heritage 1588–1896*. London: Routledge & Kegan Paul, 1979.

Marlowe, Christopher. *Doctor Faustus*. Ed. Roma Gill. The New Mermaids. 1965. Rpt. London: Benn, 1973.

Marlowe, Christopher. *Dido Queen of Carthage* and *The Massacre at Paris*. Ed. H.J. Oliver. The Revels Plays. London: Methuen, 1968.

Marlowe, Christopher. *Christopher Marlowe's 'Doctor Faustus': a 1604-version edition*. Ed. Michael Keefer. Peterborough: Broadview, 1991.

Moore, Roger Emerson. "Aspiring Minds and Lumps of Clay: Christopher Marlowe and the Gnostic Body." Ph.D. diss. Vanderbilt University, 1995.

Nuttall, A.D. *The Alternative Trinity: Gnostic Heresy in Marlowe, Milton, and Blake*. Oxford: Clarendon, 1998.

Ornstein, Robert. "Marlowe and God: The Tragic Theology of *Dr. Faustus*." *PMLA* 83 (1968): 1378–1385.

Palmer, Philip Mason and Robert Pattison More, ed. *The Sources of the Faust Tradition: from Simon Magus to Lessing*. 1936. Rpt. New York: Haskell, 1965.

Parry, Milman. *The Making of Homeric Verse*. Oxford: Clarendon, 1971.

Plato. *The Collected Dialogues of Plato*. Ed. Edith Hamilton and Huntington Cairns. 1963. Rpt. Princeton: Princeton University Press, 1980.

Poster, Carol. "Persuasion in an Empty Ontology: The Eleatic Synthesis of Philosophy, Poetry, and Rhetoric." *Philosophy and Rhetoric* 27 (1994): 277–299.

Sachs, Arieh. "The Religious Despair of Doctor Faustus." *Journal of English and Germanic Philology* 63 (1964): 625–647.

Sinistrari, Ludovico Maria. *De daemonialitate et incubis et succubis*. Ed. Isidore Liseux. Paris, 1875.

Sprague, Rosamond Kent, ed. *The Older Sophists*. Columbia: University of South Carolina Press, 1972.

Stachniewski, John. *The Persecutory Imagination: English Puritanism and the Literature of Religious Despair*. Oxford: Clarendon, 1991.

Szönyi, György E. "Traditions of Magic: From Faustus to Dee at European Universities and Courts." *Cauda Pavonis: Studies in Hermeticism* 10 (1991): 1–8.

Untersteiner, Mario. *The Sophists*. Trans. Kathleen Freeman. Oxford: Blackwell, 1954.

Walker, A., trans. *Apocryphal Gospels, Acts, and Revelations*. Ante-Nicene Christian Library 16. Edinburgh: T. and T. Clark, 1870.

In Search of the Trojan Origins of French: The Uses of History in the Elevation of the Vernacular in Early Modern France

PAUL COHEN

In 1565 Henri Estienne, the renowned humanist, committed Protestant, accomplished Parisian printer, son of the great Latinist and royal printer Robert Estienne, and one of the foremost Hellenists of his day, published a learned tome entitled *Treatise on the Conformity of the French Language with the Greek*.[1] Within these two hundred some pages, Estienne mobilized his deep familiarity with Greek along with his considerable erudition to construct elaborate linguistic arguments towards what might seem a curious end: to demonstrate that the ancient language that most closely resembled French was not Latin, but rather Greek.

In this work and in others, Estienne presented a wide range of evidence to demonstrate the French tongue's linguistic filiation with Greek. He highlighted general similarities, like the fact that both tongues possessed copious lexicons, that both favoured brevity, and that speakers of both spoke a host of local dialects. He identified grammatical resemblances, like the fact that in both languages, articles (a part of speech, Estienne remarked, absent from Latin) are systematically employed before nouns, the present tense can be used to refer to the future, and the infinitive of a verb can be used as a noun. Estienne also constructed dozens of etymologies pairing French words to their allegedly Greek counterparts. If certain of his associations were plausible albeit historically incorrect—tracing the French *chef* ("head" or "leader") to the Greek χεφαλή (kephalê, meaning "head") rather than the Latin "caput"—others were considerably more unexpected—deriving the French *bailler* (whose medieval meaning was "to carry") from the Greek βάλλειν ("to throw" or "to hit") rather than the Latin *bajulare* ("to carry").[2]

---

[1]Estienne, *Traicte De La Conformité du language François avec le Grec*. Unless otherwise indicated, all translations are my own.

[2]Comparing the characteristics and qualities of French and Greek generally, Estienne declared: "the perfection of a language . . . consists in the fact that it is easy to pronounce,

Modern histories of language, of course, recount a very different narrative of the origins of French, and to us its Latin origins seem virtually self-evident.[3] Curious as Estienne's philological hypothesis might seem, however, we certainly cannot dismiss it as the product of linguistic ignorance: not only was Latin widely spoken in his father's household and among the cosmopolitan workers who staffed Robert Estienne's workshop during Henri's childhood, but Robert taught his young son Greek before Latin.[4] Nor can we dismiss Estienne as an isolated eccentric. Indeed, a flood of sixteenth-century publications put forth similar claims. The jurist Léon Trippault studied the etymology of French words, first in his *Celtic-*

---

pleases the ear, is copious and abundant in words of all kinds" [la perfection d'un language . . . gist en ce qu'il soit aisé à prononcer, contentant bien l'oreille, copieux & abondant en mots de toutes sortes] in *Traicte de la Conformité*, Preface, sigs. [¶iiii] r – [¶v] r. Concerning dialects, Estienne observed that French encompassed a variety of regional forms "which we might call its dialects. And just as it shares this in common with the Greek language, it likewise receives similar benefits from it. Just as the Greek poets took advantage according to their needs of particular words from certain regions of Greece, so could our French poets profitably do with several words which are nonetheless only in use in certain places in France" [qu'on peut appeler ses dialectes. Et comme ceci luy est commun avec la langue Greque, aussi en reçoit-il une mesme commodité. Car ainsi que les poetes Grecs s'aidoyent au besoin de mots peculiers à certains pays de la Grece, ainsi nos poetes François peuvent faire leur proufit de plusieurs vocables qui toutesfois ne sont en usage qu'en certains endroits de la France] (Estienne, *Project*, p. 133). On the use of articles in French and Greek, see *Traicte de la Conformité*, book 1, ch. 1, pp. 3–4; on the use of the present tense to indicate the future, book 1, ch. 3, pp. 51–53; on the use of the infinitive of a verb as a noun, book 1, ch. 3, pp. 63–66. On Estienne's etymologies of "chef" and "bailler," see *Traicte de la Conformité*, book 3, pp. 142, 144. See also the brief analysis of Estienne's reasoning in Clément, *Henri Estienne*, p. 281, and the standard etymologies tracing "bailler" and "chef" to Latin, in *Dictionnaire historique*, pp. 164–165 and 399–404.

[3]For a recent overview of the history of French that presents the standard account of the French language's Latin origins, see Chaurand, ed., *Nouvelle histoire*, chs. 1–3. For a step-by-step rebuttal of Estienne's linguistic arguments laid out in the *Traicte de la Conformité* from a late-nineteenth century positivist perspective, see Clément, *Henri Estienne*, esp. part 2, ch. 1, pp. 205–212 and part 3, ch. 3.

[4]On Robert Estienne's workshop, see Armstrong, *Robert Estienne*, pp. 15–16. Henri Estienne has this to say concerning his childhood education: "as for Greek, my late father Robert Estienne educated me in this language virtually from my childhood, and even before I began learning anything about Latin: (I advise all my friends to educate their children in this way, for several good and important reasons: even if the custom today is otherwise)" [quant au Grec, feu mon pere Robert Estiene m'y feit instituer quasi des mon enfance, & mesmes avant que d'apprendre rien de Latin: (comme je conseilleray tousjours à mes amis de faire instituer leurs enfans, pour plusieurs bonnes & importantes raisons: combien que la coustume soit aujourdhuy autrement)]. *Traicte De La Conformité*, Preface, sig. [¶¶viii] r.

Hellenism, Or, Etymology of French Words Taken From Greek With General Proofs of the descent of our language (1580), and then in a French-Greek dictionary published five years later, in order to demonstrate that "we pulled a part of our language from that of the Greeks [.]"[5] A French Hellenist named Blasset composed a short Greek-Latin-French dictionary in mid-century for the very same reasons.[6]

But when did Greek have occasion to influence French? It was one thing to weave elaborate etymological explanations demonstrating the lexical ties between French and Greek. It was quite another to explain how Greek had made its way from the Attic peninsula to France. While Estienne himself maintained a respectful silence on this question, many of his Hellenist colleagues turned to medieval historical writings for explanations. Like many of their counterparts across Europe, seventh-century scholars in France had invented a myth of the Trojan origins of the Gauls. At the end of the Trojan war, one of Hector's sons, Francion, fled Troy and set sail to found Gaul. For language-obsessed sixteenth-century humanists, it was an easy step to fold language into this heady historical mix. In his *Dialogue on the origins of the French language, and of its kinship with Greek* (1554), Jacques Périon argued that Gaul's first kings had come from Greece and had brought Greek with them.[7]

I propose in this paper to think about the cultural meanings embedded within what seems to be a sixteenth-century error of linguistic judgement. What are we to make of the demonstrations of Franco-Greek linguistic affinity and the Trojan claims of Henri Estienne and like-minded humanist Hellenophiles? Why did men of letters so deeply immersed in languages in general, and so well-versed in Greek and Latin in particular,[8] spill so much

---

[5]Trippault, *Celt-Hellenisme*; and *Dictionnaire François-Grec*, sig. aiii v: "nous avons tiré partie de nostre langage, de celuy des Grecs [.]"

[6]Blasset, "Excellence de l'affinité de la langue grecque avec la francaise," Bibliotheque Nationale Manuscrits Francais 1309, cited here from "Un Helléniste du XVIe siècle," ed. Henri Omont.

[7]Périon, *Joachimi Perionii . . . Dialogorum de linguae Gallicae origine, eiusque cum Graeca cognatione,* book 1 and book 2, fols. 32r–41r.

[8]If mastery of Latin was clearly widespread in learned circles during the Renaissance, the extent to which humanists were familiar with Greek at this time remains an open question. While a small number of French men of letters acquired a very real mastery of Greek—including Henri Estienne, his father Robert Estienne, the royal adviser Guillaume Budé, and Guillaume Postel—most humanist-trained elites probably attained only a minimal knowledge of Greek. On the prevalence of Latin in the early modern period, see Waquet, *Le Latin ou l'empire d'un signe* or the shorter overview in Burke, "'Heu Domine, Adsunt Turcae.'" On the state of the study of Greek in the fifteenth and sixteenth centuries, see Huit, "Notes sur l'état des études grecs," Delaruelle, "L'Étude

ink to argue claims that seem to fly in the face of grammatical fact? I suggest
that the answers to these questions have much to tell us about the cultural
and political importance of language and history in early modern France.

Henri Estienne's own text offers a number of clues to help orient our
reading of these arguments. Estienne formulated the following justification
to explain his reasons for compiling the *Treatise on the Conformity of the French
Language with the Greek*:

> how closely the French language resembles Greek, not only in the great
> number of words . . . but also in the many beautiful ways of speaking: so that
> through this comparison everyone might see to what extent Latin, Italian,
> Spanish are distant from Greek, with which our own is a close neighbor: . . .
> the Greek language is the queen of languages, and if perfection is to be found
> in any language, it is in this one that it can be found . . . . [I]n the same way
> the French language, because it is so close to that language which attained
> perfection, must be esteemed excellent above the others.[9]

In this passage, Estienne mixes philological analysis, a historical understanding of linguistic change, and the use of dynastic metaphors to assign
French all the qualities of linguistic royalty. If Greek is the queen of
languages, then French is its uncontested heir. Estienne works to distance
French from the Latin tradition—and hence from the influence of France's
sixteenth-century Romance-language rivals—and to tie French instead to
the glory of ancient Greece. I will argue that these words embody the central
features which characterize the ensemble of the "Trojan origins of French"
myths mobilized by early-modern French men of letters. Fashioning myths
of linguistic origins was a central component of the humanist campaigns to
elevate national vernaculars. Poets, philologists, and humanists strove to
invest their vernacular idioms not only with well-regulated grammars and
rich lexicons, but also with glorious historical pasts. Furthermore, the men
of letters who set out to elevate their vernaculars saw their idioms locked

---

du grec à Paris," Stevens, "How the French Humanists of the Renaissance Learned
Greek" and "The Motivation for Hellenic Studies in Renaissance France," and Weiss,
"Greek in Western Europe at the End of the Middle Ages."

[9]Estienne, *Traicte De La Conformité*, Preface, sig. [¶iiii] r–v: "combien le language
François est voisin du Grec, non seulement en un grand nombre de mots . . . mais aussi
en plusieurs belles manieres de parler: afin-que par ceste comparaison chascun voye
combien le Latin, l'Italien, l'Espagnol, sont esloignez du Grec, duquel le nostre est
prochain voisin: . . . la langue Grecque est la roine des langues, & que si la perfection se
doibt cercher [sic] en aucune, c'est en ceste-la qu'elle se trouvera. . . . pareillement la
langue Françoise, pour approcher plus pres de celle qui a acquis la perfection, doibt estre
estimee excellente pardessus les autres." For a discussion of Estienne's historical approach
to ranking languages, see Cattelaens, "Henri Estienne: historien de la langue français."

in a European-wide competition for linguistic and literary prestige. The historical excavation of a particular language's origins represented one of many learned battlefields in this linguistic war. In history and philology alike, then, novel scholarly practices, standards of proof and rules of evidence were mobilized to construct new myths in the service of specific political and cultural projects.

RECONSTRUCTING THE ORIGINS OF FRENCH

Central to the humanist project was the restoration of classical Greek and Latin in all their Platonic and Ciceronian glory. Scholars under Antiquity's spell argued that the dissemination of Greek and Latin was a crucial means of transforming their contemporaries into truly virtuous men and women. To restore the classical tongues would unlock the wisdom of Antiquity and revive the true eloquence of Athenian democracy and the Roman Senate. Those working on language, then, cast themselves as privileged participants in an intellectual revolution, authors of a break with the medieval past, heralds of a golden age of learning and letters.[10]

If the Renaissance revival of classical languages was an essential component of the humanist project, it was by no means the only goal of linguistic reformers. While Ciceronians mastered the twists and turns of Latin rhetoric and antiquarians proclaimed the virtues of Greek, others set out to reform vernaculars. Because of their lack of a fixed grammar, vernacular idioms lacked the complexity and stability that contemporaries believed were necessary attributes of a learned tongue. If French was to be saved from the quicksands of time and reborn as an idiom of learning and literary creation, it needed to be remade in Latin's image. This objective demanded a wholesale transformation of the internal workings of the French language, and to this end scholars turned out dozens of treatises codifying French poetics, vocabulary, spelling, and grammar.[11]

Whereas some struggled to define French linguistically, others sought to trace where French had come from. The search for the origins of French

---

[10]For useful starting-points on the humanist revival of Antique languages, see Waquet, *Le Latin ou l'empire d'un signe* and Grafton and Jardine, *From Humanism to the Humanities.*

[11]For discussions of the influence of humanism in France and the campaign to elevate French, see Atkinson, "Naïveté and Modernity," Cohen, "Courtly French, Learned Latin, and Peasant Patois," esp. ch. 6, Demaizière, "L'Expansion du français en France," Fumaroli, "Le Génie de la langue française," Gadoffre, *La Révolution culturelle,* Kibbee, "Language Variation and Linguistic Description in 16th-Century France," and Trudeau, *Les Inventeurs du bon usage.*

was of genuine philological concern, since it provided a means to reconstruct the etymology of words and to better understand grammatical structures. But it was also an essential effort to legitimate French as a language of literature and learning. Historians untangling the Celtic heritage of the Gauls, the influx of Greek through the Phocean colony in Marseille, the impact of Latin after the Roman conquest, and the Germanic influence of the Franks all searched for signs of the French language's future greatness in its past.[12] A noble language necessarily had a noble lineage, and historians sought to tease out this filiation. Scholars applied the notions of *translatio imperii* and *translatio studii* to the French case to demonstrate that the learning of classical civilizations had passed into France long ago. How and when this transfer of empire and learning had taken place was an open question to which they devised numerous competing hypotheses. The reconstruction of the history of French, then, was as much a part of the project to elevate French as was the constitution of a well-regulated grammar or a copious lexicon.

Where did French come from? For some, the answer was simple: French had evolved from the Latin left by the Romans after the conquest of Gaul. Consider the view of one sixteenth-century historian of French literature:

> As for language, that which our predecessors used after the Romans were chased from Gaul up until King Hugue Capet and his children, I believe that we should call it Romance rather than French: since most of its words are taken from Latin. The long period of mastery which the Romans enjoyed in this country implanted their language [.][13]

While such explanations for the history of French both fit the known historical record and accounted for many of the French language's linguistic characteristics, some contemporaries nonetheless found them problematic. If these accounts were true, it became possible to argue that French was no

---

[12]For discussions of linguistic history in early modern France, see Kibbee, "Renaissance Notions of Medieval Language" and Clerico, "Le Français du XVIᵉ siècle," esp. pp. 149–159. On early modern historical methods, see Desan, *Penser l'histoire à la Renaissance*, Franklin, *Jean Bodin and the Sixteenth-Century Revolution in the Methodology of Law and History*, and Kelley, *Foundations of Modern Historical Scholarship* and *Faces of History*. On the importance of classical and Celtic myths of national origins in sixteenth-century France, see Dubois, *Celtes et Gaulois*.

[13]Fauchet, *Recueil*, book 1, ch. 3, p. 13: "Quant au langage, duquel nos predecesseurs ont usé depuis que les Romains furent chassez de la Gaule, jusques au Roy Hue Capet & ses enfans, je croy qu'on le doit appeller Romand plustost que François: puis que la plus part des parolles sont tirees du Latin. La longue seigneurie que les Romains eurent en ce pais, y planta leur langue [.]"

more than a corrupt derivation of the Latin left by the Romans after their triumph over the Gauls. France's vernacular, then, might be viewed as the legacy of their ancestors' defeat and the cultural superiority of a foreign power. Worse, the cultural supremacy of Ancient Rome might even imply France's subsequent inferiority to Italy in the early modern period.

Many scholars therefore believed that for French to come into its own, it was necessary to free it from its historical dependence on classical Rome. In their efforts to liberate themselves from the Roman yoke, historians searched for alternate historical sources of French. The Greek hypothesis seduced many. Scholars convinced that Greek preceded Latin not only chronologically but in the linguistic hierarchy also sought to demonstrate that French derived principally from Greek rather than Latin. The Hellenist Blasset explained in a poem his reasons for composing a short Greek-Latin-French dictionary:

> Considering that the French language
> Gains favor with every day,
> ....
> And that everywhere our language is illustrated
> By great minds, who give it such luster,
> I wanted to compile this little work,
> Which reveals the French language's affinity
> With Greek, demonstrating the dignity
> That our language had even in Antiquity,
> ....
> In order to demonstrate that from ancient Greek
> The illustrious French Language is descended [.][14]

The Trojan version of the origins of the French kingdom and the tale of Francion's voyage from Troy to Gaul provided the historical evidence to tie the French language to Greek. Like Rome with Aeneas, France now had a foundation-myth "legitimated" by the classical tradition. Medieval scholars were long accustomed to incorporating such stories into historical narratives for justificatory purposes. Breton monks, for example, rewrote

---

[14]Blasset, "Excellence de l'affinité de la langue grecque avec la francaise," dedicatory poem addressed to two Greeks, Diassorinus Chius and Constantinus Cydonius, who worked in the royal library in Fontainebleau cataloguing the Greek manuscripts assembled by François I, pp. 161–162: "Considerant que le françois language / De jour en jour prent un grand avantage, / . . . / Et que par tout nostre langue est illustre / Par bons esprits, qui luy donnent tel lustre, / J'ay bien voulu faire ce petit oeuvre, / Qui du françois l'affinité descueuvre / Avec le grec, monstrant la dignité / Que nostre langue ha dès l'antiquité, / . . . / Pour demonstrer que du grec ancian / Langue françoise illustre est descendue [.]"

this tale to trace their province's origins to Troy, and thereby to argue that Brittany was the new beneficiary of *translatio imperii*.[15] Historian Jean Lemaire de Belges, who composed his voluminous *Illustrations of Gaul and Singularities of Troy* (1511–1512) to demonstrate Troy's origins among the Gauls, made it quite clear that this creative historical genealogy was aimed at refuting Italian claims to cultural and historical preeminence:

> to demonstrate in this French language, which the Italians with their habitual contempt call Barbarous (but which is not), the very venerable antiquity of the blood of our Princes of Gaul as much Belgian as Celtic: . . . to satisfy those who wish to know, that not only by popular opinion and common reputation, but also based on good reasons and true authorities, the Gallican and French nation, both Eastern and Western, is of entirely pure Herculean and Trojan extraction and that the virtues and feats of the great Hercules of Libya and of the most valiant Hector were manifested in the person of the emperor Charlemagne.[16]

Historical narratives like these allowed France and its monarchs not only to reflect proudly upon their Celtic-Trojan past, but also to look forward to a reconstitution of this fanciful pan-Occidental-Oriental Gallican-French nation. Lemaire de Belges promises Louis XII's wife Anne de Bretagne, to whom this work is dedicated, that France's kings will one day reunite its Trojan and French dynastic domains and refound the city of Troy.[17]

15For a discussion of Breton myths of Trojan origins, see Mathey-Maille, "Mythe troyen et histoire romaine"; for a discussion of how medieval writers historicized classical myths like the Troy story in romance literature, see Blumenfeld-Kosinski, *Reading Myth*.

16In *Les Illustrations de Gaule et Singularitez de Troye*, book 1, ch. 1, and book 3, "Peroration De Lacteur Aux Nobles Lecteurs Et Auditeurs De Ce Livre", quoted here from Lemaire de Belges, *Oeuvres*, vol. 1, pp. 11–12 and vol. 2, pp. 468–469: "esclarcir en ce langage François, que les Italiens par leur mesprisance acoustumee appellent Barbare (mais non est) la tresvenerable antiquité du sang de nosdits Princes de Gaule tant Belgique, comme Celtique: . . . satisfaire à ceux qui desirent congnoitre, que non seulement par opinion vulgaire et commune renommee, mais par vives raisons et vrayes autoritez, la nation Gallicane et Françoise, tant Orientale comme Occidentale, est de extraction toute pure Herculienne et Troyenne et que les vertuz et prouesses du grand Hercules de Libye et du trespreux Hector furent representees en la personne de lempereur Charles le grand." For a study of the composition of this work, see Abelard, *Les Illustrations de Gaule et singularitez de Troye*.

17Prologue dedicated to Anne de Bretagne of *Illustrations*, book 3, quoted here from Lemaire de Belges, *Oeuvres*, vol. 2, p. 251: "jespere encores voir que ces deux maisons et nations de France Orientale et Occidentale, lesquelles vous nommez aujourd'huy Hongres, Allemans, Lansquenets, dune part François et Bretons de lautre part, seront si unies ensemble par bonne et prospere alliance, quelles iront par communs accords et voeuz refonder en Asie, cestadire Turquie, la grand cité de Troye" [I still hope to see that the two houses and nations of Eastern and Western France, which one calls today

Such ideas formed the basis of Pierre de Ronsard's ambitious epic poem, the *Franciade* (1572).[18] His poem recounted the story of Francion (also called Francus), son of Hector, who escaped the sack of Troy to found the city of Paris in Gaul. Ronsard intended his poem to be France's *Aeneid*, to constitute a literary and historical foundation for a new era of cultural and political might. Indeed, Ronsard composed his work as an answer to a call for an epic poem in French that Du Bellay had issued over two decades before in his *Defence and Illustration of the French Language*.[19] Ronsard hoped that his *Franciade* would demonstrate resoundingly that France's vernacular was now capable of carrying the most prestigious of literary genres—the epic poem—as well as of providing a myth of national foundations tying France to a glorious Hellenic past.

Where some sought the origins of French in Greece, others looked further east. Guillaume Postel, for example, argued that Hebrew stood at the origin of French. Just as Estienne had chosen to link French to the idiom he considered greatest, Greek, Postel asserted his vernacular's filiation with Hebrew, to him the greatest of the three idioms of Antiquity. For Postel, such origins demonstrated the superiority of French over other vernaculars.[20]

Creative rewritings of the past were by no means a specialty of French historians. Italian scholars had put their pens to the glorification of Italian culture—and to specific Italian dynasties or city-states—in similar ways. In

---

Hungarian, German, *Lansquenet* (French term for German mercenaries) on the one hand, French and Breton on the other hand, will be united together in a good and prosperous alliance, and will by a common accord and wish refound in Asia, that is to say Turkey, the great city of Troy].

[18]Ronsard never completed his epic poem, first published as *Les Quatre Premiers Livre De La Franciade*, consulted here in Ronsard, *Oeuvres complètes*, vol. 16.

[19]Du Bellay, *Deffence*, book 2, ch. 5, entitled "Du long poëme Francoys," in which Du Bellay exhorts France's poets to imitate the Italian writer Ludovico Ariosto (1474–1533), author of *Orlando furioso*: "si tu as quelquefois pitié de ton pauvre Langaige, si tu daignes l'enrichir de tes thesors, ce sera toy veritablement qui luy feras hausser la teste, . . . s'egaler aux superbes Langues Greque & Latine, comme a faict de nostre tens en son vulgaire un Arioste Italien, que j'oseroy . . . comparer à un Homere & Virgile. Comme luy donq', . . . choysi moy quelque un de ces beaux vieulx romans Francoys, comme un *Lancelot*, un *Tristan*, ou autres: & en fay renaitre au monde un admirable *Iliade* & laborieuse *Eneïde*" [if you sometimes have pity on your poor Language, if you deign to enrich it with your treasures, truly it will be you who will help it raise its head . . . to equal the superb Greek and Latin languages, as did an Italian Ariosto in his vernacular in our time, who I would dare compare to a Homer and a Virgil. Like him then . . . pick for me one of those beautiful old French romances, like a *Lancelot*, a *Tristan*, or another, and revive for the world an admirable *Iliad*, a well-crafted *Aeneid*], pp. 128–129.

[20]See Launay, "Le *De originibus* de 1538." For an overview of Postel's thought, see Bouwsma, *Concordia Mundi*.

the 1540s Florentine academicians for example dedicated verse and histories to the Grand Duke Cosimo I de Medici which argued that Tuscany had been founded first by Noah and then by Hercules—and that Florence had founded Rome.[21] Ariosto used his *Orlando furioso* (1516) to show that his patrons the Este, the ruling house of Ferrara, were descended from one of Roland's companions in arms during the medieval wars against the Moors. And certain Italian Hellenists had set to work to demonstrate that Latin was merely a derivation of Greek—thereby discrediting the alleged greatness of the Roman tongue. Such work provoked angry rebuttals from Latinists.[22]

Tracing French back to Greek or Hebrew may have freed the French from Roman ancestry, but it still kept them in the shadow of one or the other of the great civilizations of Antiquity. Some historians therefore rewrote the myth of Trojan origins in order to make more radical claims. Gallic culture did not originate in Greece, they argued; Greek civilization originated in Gaul. André Favyn, historian and lawyer in the Parlement of Paris, explained that

> the Gallic language (that is to say, the Greek language) brought to Greece by the Gauls, who numbered 600 thousand, with their women and children, traveled through Germany, Italy, and Asia, where they lived . . . . They established in Asia their language government and Religion, notably in Thrace, Macedonia and the adjacent islands and neighboring provinces . . . Lucian demonstrates very clearly, that the Greek language was the ancestor of the Gallic [language].[23]

As far as these scholars were concerned, the problem of the origins of the French language was now resolved. France did not descend from any of the great classical empires, since France itself was the first great civilization of Antiquity, the progenitor of Greek—and by filiation Roman—culture. Peter Ramus argued just this in his grammar:

---

[21]After Pier Francesco Giambullari published his work of poetry *Il Gello* (composed in 1545) on this theme, Giovanni Battista Gelli pursued this theme in his "Dell'Origine di Firenze" (c. 1544), in which he demonstrated that Tuscany was "la prima provincia che fusse dopo il diluvio habitata" [the first province to be inhabited after the Flood]. Discussion and quotation from Plaisance, "Culture et politique à Florence," pp. 177–182.

[22]Tavoni, "On the Renaisance Idea that Latin Derives from Greek."

[23]Favyn, *Histoire de Navarre*, p. 28: "la langue Gauloise (c'est à dire la Grecque) portee en Grece par les Gaulois, lesquels au nombre de 600 mille, avec leurs femmes & enfans passerent en Alemagne, Italie, & Asie, lesquelles ils habiterent, . . . Ils planterent en l'Asie leur langage Police, & Religion, & nommement en la Thrace, la Macedoine, & isles adiacentes avec les provinces voysines . . . Lucian . . . monstre fort clairement, que la langue Grecque estoit l'originaire Gauloise."

But what need is there to invoke those Romans? Do we not have the Gauls, do we not have the French, who were the Varros, the Caesars, the Corvinuses, the Augustuses, and the Claudiuses of the Gallic or French language? Certainly Grammar and all the other liberal disciplines were long ago in the Gallic language in the schools of our Druids owing nothing at all either to the Greeks or to the Latins: and this learning afterwards having left Gaul with the Gauls went to Greece, where it was greatly cherished and honored, and from there it was invited to Italy, and in every part of the world [.][24]

In this vision of human history, the Gauls were the inventors of knowledge and the source of all learning. To Ramus and Favyn, the *translatio studii* had followed a circular route: learning was born in France, had passed into Greece, then Rome, and was now returning to its home in France.

While Ramus' grand assertions of Gaul's Antique glory had obvious appeal, other historians interested in demonstrating the existence of a flourishing French culture in the past settled for more modest claims. Claude Fauchet, president of the *Cour des Monnaies*, published a history of the French language and French poetry in 1581 in which he argued that the Middle Ages had constituted a golden age for French letters:

This language which I call French, was once more esteemed than it is today, because of the victories of our Kings, . . . languages grow stronger as the princes who use them expand [their realms]. And because our Kings were once very feared, I believe that their language was learned by more people. As in the time of Saint Louis . . . it was very esteemed: because the nobles and men of Justice in England spoke French . . . . Because the French language had been carried to England by William the Bastard Duke of Normandy, . . . The French language was no less prized in Sicily, Jerusalem, Cyprus and Antioch, because of the conquests of Robert Guichard and the Pilgrims who traveled to the Holy Land [.][25]

---

[24]Dedication "A La Royne, Mere Du Roy" in Ramus, *Grammaire*, sig. ✷iii v: "Mais quest il besoing de vous alleguer ces Romains? Navons nous point de Gaullois, navons nous point de Francoys, qui ayent este les Varrons, les Caesars, les Corvinus, les Augustes & Claudius de la langue Gaulloyse ou Francoyse? Certes la Grammaire & toutes aultres disciplines liberalles estoyent anciennement en langaige Gaulloys es escolles de nos Druides sans en rien tenir ny des Grecs, ny des Latins: & depuis estants sorties de la Gaulle avec leurs Gaulloys sont passees en la Grece, ou elles ont este fort cheries & honnorees, & de la ont este invitees en Italie, & en toutes les parties du monde [.]"

[25]Fauchet, *Recueil*, book 1, ch. 5, pp. 39, 43–44, 46–47: "Ceste langue que j'appelle Françoise, fut jadis plus prisee qu'elle n'est, à cause des victoires de nos Rois, . . . les langues se renforcent, à mesure que les princes qui en usent s'agrandissent. Et pour autant que nos Roys ont jadis esté fort redoutez, j'estime que leur langue estoit apprise de plus de gens. Comme du temps de saint Louis . . . elle estoit fort prisee: car les nobles d'Angleterre, & les gens de Justice parloyent François . . . . Or la langue Françoise avoit

One no longer needed to travel back to Antiquity to find evidence of French greatness. Medieval history, after all, taught that France had once possessed a linguistic empire virtually as grand as Ancient Rome. Fauchet criticized those who reified classical civilization. To Fauchet, those who truly loved France should seek edification not from Greece or Rome, but from "the wonderful studies and pleasant distractions, which while resting from war so many illustrious Kings, Dukes, Counts, Barons and Knights once dedicated themselves [.]"[26]

Not only was French more widely spoken in the Middle Ages, Fauchet and others argued, its literary achievements were held in great esteem all across Europe. Indeed, it became something of a trope in French literary histories during the sixteenth century to declare that the French had invented vernacular poetry.[27] Such interpretations made it possible to demonstrate the precedence of French over other vernaculars as a literary idiom. Indeed, many sought to prove that other vernaculars, particularly Italian, had derived in some way or another from French. Henri Estienne devoted dozens of pages of his *Project of a Book entitled On the preeminence of the French language* (1579) to cataloguing the French words and expressions which had been incorporated into Italian.[28] The Italian printer Jacques Corbinelli, who published Dante's *De Vulgari Eloquentia* in Paris in an edition dedicated to the French king Henri III, declared that French was "il primo volgare" [the first vernacular]—of which Italian was a mere derivation—and that Dante had in fact composed his text in Paris.[29]

---

esté portee en Angleterre, par Guillaume le Bastard duc de Normandie, . . . La langue Françoise n'estoit pas moins prisee en Sicile, Jerusalem, Chipre & Antioche: à cause des conquestes de Robert Guischard, & des Pelerins qui passerent en la terre sainte, . . . Elle fut encore plus estimee à Naples, à cause de Charles Comte d'Anjou, frere du Roy S. Louis: lequel conquist ce Royaume, & prenoit grand plaisir en la poesie Françoise, . . . Ainsi donc y ayant en ce temps la plusieurs Cours en Europe, qui avoyent des seigneurs nourris de laict François, d'avantage de gens le parloyent. Et qui plus est, les façons de faire, mots de guerre & de paix, se prenoyent en la Cour de France, . . . à cause des richesses de nos Rois, qui reluisoyent plus que leurs voisins [.]"

[26]Dedication "Au Roy De France Et De Polongne" of Fauchet, *Recueil*, sig. aii r–v: "les belles estudes & gentilles occupations, où durant le repos de la guerre se sont autrefois employez tant d'illustres Rois, Ducs, Comtes, Barons & Chevaliers [.]"

[27]Fauchet, for example, declared that "nos François ont monstré aux autres nations d'Europe l'usage de la ryme consonante ou omioteleute [*sic*]" [our French (poets) showed the other nations of Europe the practice of consonant or *omioteleute* rhyme], *Recueil*, book 1, ch. 7, p. 67.

[28]For Estienne's catalogue, see *Project*, pp. 208–280.

[29]Quoted in Fumaroli, "*Aulae Arcana*. Rhétorique et politique à la cour de France sous Henri III et Henri IV," p. 144.

MYTH AND HISTORY

The historical origins of French became a malleable substance in the hands of France's humanist-trained poets and historians. Did contemporaries take claims of Hebrew or Trojan descent for French and France seriously? Many scholars after all dismissed such myths of linguistic and national origins as ridiculous fictions. One contemporary wrote that the Trojan hypothesis was nothing more than a set of "fabulous Inventions,"[30] and Ramus refuted certain claims in his treatise on the Gauls.[31] Indeed, the formation of new historical hypotheses and rebuttals was a central feature of humanist polemic.

Furthermore, the fact that the "origins of languages" *topos* was the object of satire suggests that contemporaries could adopt a position of critical distance with respect to such accounts when they so chose. Consider Toulouse, a city in the non-French-speaking south, where the distinct Romance language Occitan was still in wide use in the early modern period. In the preface to a volume of Occitan verse, Toulouse's best-loved Occitan poet Pierre Goudelin (Goudouli in Occitan) traced the origins of both Toulouse and its language back to one of Noah's nephews, Tolus:

> At the moment when by the will of God languages were created . . . at the sepulcher of the Giant Nimrod's temerity [the Tower of Babel], who will say that ours [Occitan] was not among them? According to the common opinion, Noah's little nephew Tolus founded Toulouse, it appears thus to us that he carried a certain specific language from among those which had contributed to the confusion of the building with which the giants were supposed to reach Heaven, and in order to thwart the threat of another Flood. I say these things in order to fight against lies, in favor of the Moundino, Toulousain, Toulousenco language [.][32]

Early modern readers weaned on Ronsard's *Franciade*, Lemaire de Belges' histories of Gaul, and Henri Estienne's linguistic genealogies would have found such arguments familiar. Goudelin in fact chose the most forceful

---

[30]Matthieu, *Devis*, fol. 19r: "fabuleuses Inventions."

[31]Ramus, *Traicté Des Façons & Coustumes Des Anciens Gaulloys*, the French translation of *Liber de moribus veterum Gallorum* (1559) by Michel de Castelneau.

[32]Goudelin's preface, "A Touts D'amb'un trinfle d'abertissomen," *Ramelet Moundi*, pp. [15–16]: "Quand del mandomen de Diu las lengos se troubéguen à la sepultuo de la temeritat del Gigan Nenbrot, qui dira que la nostro nou fouresso pas de l'azempre? Segoun l'oupiniu comuno, Tolus petit nebout de Noë foundéc Toulouso, l'aparenço dits douncos per nous que be pourtao qualque lengatge particulié, d'aquelis qu'abiôn serbit à la counfusiu del bastimen doun las girouëtos dibiôn frega le Cél, & despita le majenc de tout autre Delutge. Assò siô dit de fregado countro les trufandiés, en fabou de la lengo Moundino, Toulousano, Toulousenco [.]"

such argument possible: rather than link Occitan to one of the three languages of Antiquity, he traced it straight to the linguistic source, the idioms spawned at the Biblical confusion of languages at Babel. Goudelin, of course, did not expect his readers to believe that Occitan was in fact the first and greatest of humanity's tongues. Rather, his linguistic history is a learned philological joke, a pastiche of Estienne-like myths of linguistic origins, entirely consistent with the carnivalesque use of Occitan in Toulouse's festival life.

While it may well be impossible to ascertain whether a deeply learned scholar like Henri Estienne, armed with an impressive mastery of classical Greek and Latin, really "believed" his hypotheses, what is certain is that some contemporaries committed to such arguments also declared themselves to be unconcerned with the historical accuracy of their claims. Ronsard addressed this question directly in the preface to his *Franciade*:

> History only recounts things the way they are, or were, without disguise or ornament, and the Poet contents himself with the plausible, to that which could be, and that which is already received by common opinion . . . . I say this because the majority of us think that the Franciade is a history of the Kings of France, as if I had undertaken to be a Historiographer and not a Poet. In short this book is a Romance like the Iliad and the Aeneid [.]

Ronsard then proceeds to demolish the historical veracity of Homer's *Iliad* by arguing that it would have been impossible for the Greek army to spend ten years away from home. Just as Homer and Virgil spun fantastic fables for the noble cause of glorifying their respective peoples, so Ronsard claims the right to erect his own French myths:

> Imitating those two great figures, I have done the same thing: . . . it is possible that Francion undertook such a voyage, all the more so because he could have done so, and on this foundation of possibility I have built my Franciade upon his name . . . . Having thus a great desire to honor the house of France, and above all King Charles IX, my Prince . . . just as women who are ready to give birth choose good air, a healthy house, a rich godfather to protect their child, in the same way I have chosen the richest argument, the most beautiful verses and the most distinguished godfather of Europe to honor my book and support my work [.][33]

---

[33]"Au Lecteur" in Ronsard, *Oeuvres complètes*, vol. 16, pp. 4–5, 7–9: "L'Histoire reçoit seulement la chose comme elle est, ou fut, sans desguisure ny fard, & le Poëte s'arreste au vraysemblable, à ce qui peut estre, & à ce qui est desja receu en la commune opinion . . . . Je dy cecy pource que la meilleur partie des nostres pense que la Franciade soit une histoire des Rois de France, comme si j'avois entrepris d'estre Historiographe & non Poëte. Bref ce livre est un Roman comme l'Iliade et l'Aeneide . . . Suivant ces

The historical tradition one mobilized to praise the king did not have to be true—it simply had to be glorious.

⋆   ⋆   ⋆

History as well as philology, then, offered scholars a rich pallet of possible narratives with which to declaim the greatness of French and even, when opportune, France's regional idioms. Sixteenth-century French writers proposed a range of accounts which still astonish for their diversity and creativity. Estienne Pasquier, one might say, played it safe by incorporating them all into his account of the origins of French: French was in his view a mixture of the Gauls' Celtic idiom, the Greek spoken by Hellenic colonists in Marseille, the Roman legions' Latin, and the Franks' Germanic tongue.[34] Whether one searched back to the Middle Ages or Antiquity, to Gaul, Rome, or Greece, among the Hebrews or the Occitan-speaking troubadours, the object of their search was the same: to find or forge for French a noble pedigree.

WORKS CITED

Abelard, Jacques. *Les Illustrations de Gaule et Singularitez de Troye de Jean Lemaire de Belges*. Geneva: Droz, 1976.

Armstrong, Elizabeth. *Robert Estienne, Royal Printer: An Historical Study of the Elder Stephanus*. Cambridge: Cambridge University Press, 1954.

Atkinson, James B. "Naïveté and Modernity: The French Renaissance Battle for a Literary Vernacular." *Journal of the History of Ideas* 35 (1974): 179–196.

---

deux grands personnages, j'ay fait le semblable: . . . il est vraysemblable que Francion a fait tel voyage, d'autant qu'il le pouvoit faire, & sur ce fondement de vraysemblance j'ay basti ma Franciade de son nom . . . . Ayant donc une extreme envie d'honorer la maison de France, & par sur tout le Roy Charles neufiesme, mon Prince, . . . comme les femmes qui sont prestes d'enfanter choisissent un bon air, une saine maison, un riche parrain pour tenir leur enfant, ainsi j'ay choisi le plus riche argument, les plus beaux vers & le plus insigne parrain de l'Europe pour honorer mon livre, & soutenir mon labeur [.]"

[34]Pasquier, *Recherches*, book 8, ch. 1, p. 673: "la langue dont nous usons aujourd'huy selon mon jugement est composée, part de l'ancienne Gauloise, part de la Latine, part de la Françoise" [according to my judgement the language which we use today is composed in part by the ancient Gallic language, in part by Latin, in part by Frankish]. On the contribution of Greek, Pasquier noted that "c'ait esté depuis que les Gaulois furent reducts sous la servitude de Rome, qu'ils frequenterent l'Université de Marseille, & que par cette mutuelle frequentation, ils emprunterent plusieurs mots Grecs, & dont ils embellirent leur langue" [it was after the Gauls fell into servitude under Rome that they began to frequent the University of Marseille, and by this mutual frequentation, they borrowed several Greek words, with which they embellished their language], ch. 2, p. 677.

Blasset. "Un Helléniste du XVIe siècle. Excellence de l'affinité de la langue grecque avec la française." Ed. Henri Omont. *Revue des études grecques* 30 (1917): 158–166.

Blumenfeld-Kosinski, Renate. *Reading Myth: Classical Mythology and Its Interpretations in Medieval French Literature*. Stanford: Stanford University Press, 1997.

Bouwsma, William J. *Concordia Mundi: The Career and Thought of Guillaume Postel (1510–1581)*. Cambridge, MA: Harvard University Press, 1957.

Burke, Peter. "'Heu Domine, Adsunt Turcae': A Sketch for a Social History of Post-Medieval Latin." *The Art of Conversation*. Ithaca: Cornell University Press, 1993. 34–65.

Cattelaens, Monika. "Henri Estienne: historien de la langue française." *Henri Estienne. Actes du colloque organisé à l'Université de Paris-Sorbonne*. Cahiers V. L. Saulnier, no. 5. Paris: École Normale Supérieure de Jeunes Filles, 1988. 77–84.

Chaurand, Jacques, ed. *Nouvelle histoire de la langue française*. Paris: Seuil, 1999.

Clément, Louis. *Henri Estienne et son oeuvre française (étude d'histoire littéraire et de philologie)*. Paris: A. Picard et Fils, 1898. Rpt. Geneva: Slatkine, 1967.

Clerico, Geneviève. "Le Français du XVIe siècle." *Nouvelle histoire de la langue française*. Ed. Jacques Chauraud. Paris: Seuil, 1999. 147–224.

Cohen, Paul. "Courtly French, Learned Latin, and Peasant Patois: The Making of a National Language in Early Modern France." Ph.D. diss. Princeton University, 2001.

Delaruelle, Louis. "L'Étude du grec à Paris de 1514 à 1530." *Revue du seizième siècle* 9 (1922): 51–62, 133–149.

Demaizière, Colette. "L'Expansion du français en France et l'émergence d'une grammaire française au XVIe siècle." *La Langue française au XVIe siècle: Usage, enseignement et approches descriptives*. Ed. Pierre Swiggers and Willy Van Hoecke. Louvain: Leuven University Press, 1989. 32–53.

Desan, Philippe. *Penser l'histoire à la Renaissance*. Caen: Paradigme, 1993.

Dictionnaire historique de la langue française, 2 vols. Ed. Alain Rey. Paris: Dictionnaires Le Robert, 1992.

Du Bellay, Joachim. *La Deffence et illustration de la langue francoyse*. Ed. Henri Chamard. Paris: Marcel Didier, 1970.

Dubois, Claude-Gilbert. *Celtes et Gaulois au XVIe siècle: Le développement littéraire d'un mythe nationaliste*. Paris: Librairie Philosophique J. Vrin, 1972.

Estienne, Henri. *Project Du Livre intitulé De la précellence du langage François*. Paris: Mamert Patisson, 1579. Rpt. Geneva: Slatkine, 1972.

Estienne, Henri. *Traicte De La Conformité du language François avec le Grec*. Geneva: Henri Estienne, [1565]. Rpt. Geneva: Slatkine, 1972.

Fauchet, Claude. *Recueil De L'Origine De La Langue Et Poesie Françoise, Ryme et Romans*. Paris: Mamert Patisson, 1581. Rpt. Geneva: Slatkine, 1972.

Favyn, André. *Histoire de Navarre, Contenant l'Origine, les Vies & conquestes de ses Roys*. Paris: Laurent Sonnius, 1612.

Franklin, Julian H. *Jean Bodin and the Sixteenth-Century Revolution in the Methodology of Law and History*. New York: Columbia University Press, 1963.

Fumaroli, Marc. "*Aulae arcana*. Rhétorique et politique à la cour de France sous Henri III et Henri IV." *Journal des savants* (1981): 137–189.

Fumaroli, Marc. "Le Génie de la langue française." *Les Lieux de mémoire* III. *Les France 3. De l'archive à l'emblème.* Ed. Pierre Nora. Paris: Gallimard, 1992. 911–973.

Gadoffre, Gilbert. *La Révolution culturelle dans la France des humanistes: Guillaume Budé et François Ier.* Geneva: Droz, 1997.

Goudelin, Pierre. *Le Ramelet Moundi.* Toulouse: R. Colomiez, 1617.

Grafton, Anthony and Lisa Jardine. *From Humanism to the Humanities: Education and the Liberal Arts in 15th and 16th Century Europe.* London: Duckworth, 1986.

Huit, C. "Notes sur l'état des études grecs au XIVe–XVIe." *Revue des études grecques* 14 (1901): 140–162.

Kelley, Donald R. *Faces of History: Historical Inquiry From Herodotus to Herder.* New Haven: Yale University Press, 1998.

Kelley, Donald R. *Foundations of Modern Historical Scholarship: Language, Law, and History in the French Renaissance.* New York: Columbia University Press, 1970.

Kibbee, Douglas A. "Language Variation and Linguistic Description in 16th-Century France." *Historiographia Linguistica* 17 (1990): 49–65.

Kibbee, Douglas A. "Renaissance Notions of Medieval Language and the Development of Historical Linguistics." *Journal of Medieval and Renaissance Studies* 22 (1992): 41–54.

Launay, Marie-Luce. "Le *De originibus* de 1538: une rhétorique des origines." *Guillaume Postel 1581–1981.* Paris: Editions de la Maisnie, 1985. 305–316.

Lemaire de Belges, Jean. *Oeuvres.* Ed. J. Stecher. 4 vols. Louvain: J. Lefever, 1882–1885. Rpt. Geneva: Slatkine, 1969.

Mathey-Maille, Laurence. "Mythe troyen et histoire romaine: de Geoffroy de Monmouth au *Brut* de Wace." *Entre fiction et histoire. Troie et Rome au Moyen Age.* Ed. Emmanuèle Baumgartner and Laurence Harf-Lancner. Paris: Presses de la Sorbonne Nouvelle, 1997. 113–125.

Matthieu, Abel. *Devis De la langue francoyse, à Jehanne d'Albret, Royne de Navarre, Duchesse de Vandosme, etc. Par Abel Matthieu natif de Chartres.* Paris: Richard Breton, 1559. Rpt. Geneva: Slatkine, 1972.

Pasquier, Estienne. *Les Recherches De La France D'Estienne Pasquier, Conseiller Et Advocat general du Roy en la Chambre des Comptes de Paris.* Paris: Laurens Sonnius, 1621.

Périon, Joachim. *Joachimi Perionii Benedictini Cormoeriaceni Dialogorum de linguae Gallicae origine, eiusque cum Graeca cognatione, libri quatuor.* Paris: Sebastien Nivellium, 1555. Rpt. Geneva: Slatkine, 1972.

Plaisance, Michel. "Culture et politique à Florence de 1542 à 1551: Lasca et les *Humidi* aux prises avec l'Académie Florentine." *Les Écrivains et le pouvoir en Italie à l'époque de la Renaissance (deuxième série).* Ed. André Rochon. Centre de recherche sur la Renaissance Italienne, 3. Paris: Université de la Sorbonne Nouvelle, 1974. 149–242.

Ramus, Peter (Pierre de La Ramée). *Grammaire De P. De La Ramee, Lecteur du Roy en lUniversite de Paris, A La Royne, Mere Du Roy.* Paris: André Wechel, 1572. Rpt. Geneva: Slatkine, 1972.

Ramus, Peter (Pierre de La Ramée). *Traicté Des Façons & Coustumes Des Anciens Gaulloys, Traduit du Latin de P. de la Ramée, par Michel de Castelnau.* Trans. Michel de Castelnau. Paris: André Wechel, 1559.

Ronsard, Pierre de. *La Franciade*. 1572. 2 vols. *Oeuvres complètes*. Ed. Paul Laumonier. Vol. 16. Paris: Société des Textes Français Modernes, 1950–1952. Rpt. in one volume. Paris: Nizet, 1983.

Stevens, Linton C. "How the French Humanists of the Renaissance Learned Greek." *Publications of the Modern Language Association* 65 (1950): 240–248.

Stevens, Linton C. "The Motivation for Hellenic Studies in Renaissance France." *Studies in Philology* 47 (1950): 113–125.

Tavoni, Mirko. "On the Renaissance Idea That Latin Derives From Greek." *Annali della Scuola Normale Superiore di Pisa* 3rd Series, 16 (1986): 205–235.

Trippault, Léon. *Celt-Hellenisme, Ou, Etymologic Des Mots Francois Tirez Du Graec. Plus. Preuves en general de la descente de nostre langue*. Orléans: Eloy Gibier, 1580. Rpt. Geneva: Slatkine, 1973.

Trippault, Léon. *Dictionnaire François-Grec, De M. Leon Trippault, Conseiller du Roy, au siege Presidial d'Orleans*. Orléans: Eloy Gibier, 1577.

Trudeau, Danielle. *Les Inventeurs du bon usage (1529–1647)*. Paris: Éditions de Minuit, 1992.

Waquet, Françoise. *Le Latin ou l'empire d'un signe XVIᵉ–XXᵉ siècle*. Paris: Albin Michel, 1998.

Weiss, Roberto. "Greek in Western Europe at the End of the Middle Ages." *Medieval and Humanist Greek*. Ed. Carlo Dionisotti, Conor Fahy, and John D. Moores. Medioevo e Umanesimo, 8. Padua: Antenore, 1977. 3–12.

Togail Troí:
The Irish Destruction of Troy
on the Cusp of the Renaissance

BRENT MILES

By any measure Ireland, plagued with colonial wars and religious conflict throughout the sixteenth and seventeenth centuries, made a modest contribution to the phenomenon of the European Renaissance. This observation ought to imply no necessary judgement on Irish culture. Because it had never been conquered by Rome, Ireland knew no erosion of civilization like that which Renaissance thinkers believed to have happened in their own lands in the Middle Ages. However, the realities of trade and pilgrimage, among other things, had left Ireland with its own contacts with Europe, and the mounting success of the Tudor English colony in Ireland throughout the sixteenth century ensured that a Renaissance culture of some sort would have a life on Irish soil. Indeed, the brutal implementation of Tudor policy to extirpate the native culture of the "wylde Irishe," and moreover to replace it with the "civilized" culture of England in its flush of Renaissance pride, has coloured subsequent critical discussions of Renaissance Ireland. The immensely influential Irish literary critic Daniel Corkery argued that "whatever of the Renaissance came to Ireland met a culture so ancient, widely based and well-articulated, that it was received only on sufferance: it had to vail its crest and conform to a new order; it did not become acclimatised, as had happened elsewhere; it was rather assimilated, assimilated so thoroughly that its features can no longer be discerned."[1] This strong native culture, we presume, may be contrasted with that of less hardy nations such as England, France or Germany, which fell victim to Renaissance effeminacy.

While more recent work has tended to shy away from Corkery's undisguised nationalist bias, his view remains fascinating for its modern reflection of a confident, pre-modern culture of learning in Ireland which

---

[1]Corkery, *Hidden Ireland*, p. 149; see also pp. 11–16.

subsequent political developments were not able wholly to efface. Several centuries saw the families of the original 1169 Anglo-Norman invasion of Ireland largely assimilate to Irish culture, leaving most of the island divided between, on the one hand, Anglo-Irish lords with only nominal allegiance to England, and, on the other, the native aristocracy of so-called "Gaelic Ireland." English control of its colony, the so-called "Pale," had seldom been weaker when, faced with rebellion among his own subjects in Dublin in 1534, Henry VIII articulated a new Tudor resolve to reduce the whole of the island to a colony of England. The Tudor campaign culminated in the Battle of Kinsale, 1602, where the English achieved an incontrovertible military victory over the Gaelic aristocracy. This cataclysm, and the self-imposed exile of the native aristocracy which soon followed in 1607, we now mark as the political defeat of Gaelic Ireland. It is clearly with this history in mind that Corkery's "Renaissance" is conceived as a hostile force coming to Ireland from outside, and presumably on the coat-tails of the English conquest. "Renaissance Ireland" remains an unusual collocation, critics mostly preferring "Gaelic" and "Tudor" Ireland to denote the period. However, there has been an emerging acceptance of the notion of a Renaissance culture in Gaelic Ireland, and the supposedly foreign nature of the political and cultural innovations evoked by the term today need be neither rejected on principle, nor accepted on faith.[2] My essay addresses the cusp of this Renaissance Ireland, namely the late fifteenth century, a period which anticipates the marked innovations of the sixteenth century. The discussion falls around a series of texts in Irish treating of the antique tale of the fall of Troy. Late medieval Irish engagement with the tale of Troy argues for a native Irish agency in the later reception of Renaissance ideals in Gaelic Ireland, and perhaps offers a parallel to scholarly interests on the Continent.

Not well-known outside Irish scholarly circles, *Togail Troí*, "The Destruction of Troy," was one of the central literary texts of medieval Ireland. The work is in part a translation of a text from antiquity, the *De excidio Troiae historia*, written in Latin in the sixth century, but purportedly the work of a Greek eyewitness to the war, Dares Phrygius.[3] Dares' plain narrative of the Trojan War came to be standard in the Middle Ages, while Homer's version was unknown. Benoît de Saint-Maure's *Roman de Troie*, written c. 1172 and based on Dares' text, though it is the immediate inspiration for the ensuing medieval tradition of Troy, does not represent

---

[2]Mac Craith's survey "Gaelic Ireland and the Renaissance" is the best introduction to the subject; see also Bradshaw, "Manus 'The Magnificent.'"

[3]The only edition remains Meister's *Daretis Phrygii de excidio Troiae historia* (1873); for origin and dating of Dares' text, see Frazer, *The Trojan War*, pp. 11–13.

the first medieval effort to bring the tale to life in a vernacular. *Togail Troí* is the work of an anonymous tenth-century monastic author in its earliest version, and predates the French work by roughly two hundred years. As with later continental works, *Togail Troí* is also based on Dares' *De excidio*. *Togail Troí* is in fact one of a series of vernacular Irish adaptations of classical texts, all of which suggest there was a "school" of scholars devoted to fostering the heritage of antique Greece and Rome in Ireland. Also sometime in the mid-tenth century an Irish scholar produced *Scéla Alaxandair*, a vernacular version of the principal classical accounts of the conquests of Alexander the Great. In the eleventh through the thirteenth centuries anonymous Irish authors also created, most importantly, versions of Lucan's *Pharsalia*, Vergil's *Aeneid*, Statius' *Thebaid*, the same author's unfinished epic *Achilleid*, and a short, folkloric transformation of Homer's *Odyssey*. It is striking how much the Irish anticipate continental Europe of the twelfth-century Renaissance, and especially the French, in this flurry of classical adaptations from Latin into the vernacular. In contrast to continental authors, the Irish wrote all of this in prose. All of the classical tales in Irish were copied several times, and *Togail Troí* received at least three separate editions, meaning that the tale was expanded and rewritten in the succeeding generations to give us three separate extant recensions, preserved in at least nine manuscripts. The earliest extant recension, incorporating text from the original tenth-century translation, is from the eleventh century. This copying and revision, comparable in extent to that lavished on the Irish heroic epic *Táin Bó Cúailnge*, mark *Togail Troí* as a popular text.[4]

Critics have long treated these adaptations of non-Irish narratives as if they were inherently less valuable than "native" tales of Irish heroes, with their preservation of Irish history. Yet the possible importance of the classical tales in the development of medieval Irish literature has recently been examined. Hildegard Tristram has persuasively argued that a spate of interest in classical tales in the tenth century gave a new direction to medieval Irish *literati*, in that the classical tales provided a new model for the writing of texts in an epic language on a grand scale. The adapting of Latin texts such as the *De excidio* into extended narratives in Irish may have given Irish authors the experience they needed to compose extended prose narratives from their own native lore, the culmination of this process being the transformation of oral tales into the written prose epic *Táin Bó Cúailnge*,

---

[4]For a discussion of the classical tales as well as a bibliography of editions, see Stanford, *Classical Tradition*, pp. 73–89. See Mac Eoin, "Verbalsystem," for an account of the history of *Togail Troí*, and pp. 193–202 especially for the dating of the texts; see also Myrick, *From the* De Excidio Troiae Historia *to the* Togail Troí, pp. 85–87.

"The Cattle Raid of Cooley." Descriptions of battle in *Togail Troí*, influenced ultimately by like descriptions in Vergil's *Aeneid*, may have had an influence on native, "saga" prose.[5] A striking Irish "heroic" style, which continued to influence Irish prose into the modern era, can be found in nascent form throughout the first recension of *Togail Troí*. Although scholars have mostly traced this prose style to an irrecoverable tradition of medieval storytelling, there is an emerging willingness to acknowledge a literate component to the style as well. The following description of the Trojan hero Hector shows many of the distinctive mannerisms of Irish heroic prose, including extensive employment of alliterating dyads and triads (in the prose passages below, alliteration in the original, which the translation attempts to reproduce, is underlined):

> *Roleth, tra, clu 7 erdercus Hectoir mic Priaim sechnón na huile Assia 7 na huile Éorpa. Ba cocur cecha deisse etir primcathracha in domain. Óenchathmílidh co n-úath, con-erud, co luinde leoman, co crúas choradh, co mbuille míled, co n-ainbthinche onchon, oc cathugud 7 oc comérge 7 oc comersclaigi, co n-uathiud a chathrach fri láechu athlama ána íarthair in betha.*[6]

> [And the fame of Hector son of Priam spread throughout all Asia and all Europe. He was the talk of every pair of persons in the principal cities of the world. Unique battle-soldier with fear and with fright, with lion's fierceness, with hero's hardness, with soldier's striking, with leopard's storminess, fighting and rising and defending with the few of his city against the swift, splendid heroes of the Western World.]

The influence of Vergilian heroic similes is observable in the following passage from the second recension of *Togail Troí*, a passage which, moreover, may be the source for imitations in Irish saga:

> *Ron gabsaide condalbdus risin n-imned ra immir Hectoir forsin sluag. Tanic co díumsach dásachtach amal tic banni dían dílend a hucht airslébi co trascrand feda 7 fidbada remi cona scailend i fánaib 7 i fánglentaib na ferund. Is amlaidsein ra essairg Achíl tromsluagu na Tróianna immi di cach aird.*[7]

> [He (Achilles) was seized with sympathy on account of the suffering Hector set upon the host. He came, vainglorious and violent, as comes the furious rush of the flood from the breast of the hill, leveling tree and treeslope before it until it sinks into the depressions and hollows of the earth. Thus did Achilles smite the hosts of the Trojans on all sides.]

---

[5]See Tristram, "Tradition," esp. pp. 22–24, for the genesis of written epic; for battle descriptions in *Togail Troí*, see Mac Gearailt, "Change and Innovation," pp. 486–488, 490–493.

[6]Stokes, "Destruction of Troy," ll. 1067–1073.

[7]Best and O'Brien, *Book of Leinster*, vol. 4, ll. 32775–32779; this passage is discussed by Mac Gearailt, pp. 487–488.

The number of separate rewritings of *Togail Troí* attests to the importance which Irish *literati* attached to the text. However, the heroes of the Trojan War were also assimilated, after a fashion, into native literary culture, just as they were later on the Continent. An excerpt from the twelfth-century anonymous bardic poem *Clann Ollaman Uaisle Emna* highlights one Irish bard's interest in the heroes of the Trojan War. This long poem recounts the genealogy of the rulers of the province of Ulster, a line whose founders not coincidentally are also the principal heroes of *Táin Bó Cúailnge*, "The Cattle Raid of Cooley." Stanzas 3–6 commence the praise of the Ulster royal line with an evocation of the heroes of Troy:

Comoirrdeirc Asia re hUlltaib	Asia is as famous as Ulster
im écht, im allaid, im uaill;	in deed, in fame and in pride;
Priaim ainm Conchobair Codail	Priam is the name of Conchobhar of Codal
borrfadaig im Thoraig thuaid.	who rages around northern Troy.
Coimfhedma Treóil is Cú Chulainn	Troilus and Cúchulainn are equal
im chomlonn, im ré is im rath;	in battle, in lifespan and in fortune;
Fergus Énias re luad loingse	Aeneas is Fergus in consideration of exile,
glé-dias buan nar choimse i cath.	a brilliant, constant pair, boundless in battle.
Alexandair Naíse nertmhar—	Powerful Naoise is Alexander—
rena néim Troí ocus Táin;	their beauty caused Troy and the *Táin*;
Echtair mar Chonall cert Cernach	Hector is like honest Conall Cearnach,
nert ro-garb re hernach n-áig.	a fierce strength against the iron of battle.
Cosmail gach áen-fher d'iath Emna	Each single man of Eamhain's land
d'fhir ar Tróe muirnig na máer;	has a counterpart in spirited, lordly Troy;
ropo data a n-áirem uile,	it would be pleasant to count them all,
gach sáir-fher don chuire cháem.[8]	every hero of the fair company.

What is perhaps most interesting about this section of the poem is the poet's obvious historical consciousness. The pagan heroes of the Heroic Age of Greece and Asia Minor are cogently put in to the company of the pagan heroes of Ireland's own "Heroic Age," the heroes of its own pre-medieval epic. The synchronizing of European and biblical history with the events of Ireland's own cherished past is in fact a passion of medieval Irish learning. The "use" of such borrowed learning is evident, for example, in these lines from a poem about world history by twelfth-century poet Gilla in Chomded Ua Cormaic:

Tarthatar aís Hercoil óig	In the time of young Hercules
tri meic aille Herimoin;	were the three splendid sons of Éireamhón;
tarraid in triar cétna cain	the same three fair ones
Greic ar Tróe ca trentogail.	lived in the time of Greece's destruction of Troy.

---

[8]Byrne, "Clann Ollaman," pp. 61–62.

Cethri bliadna iar Troí gním gaeth	Four years after Troy, that clever feat,
cu tomaidm Locha Da Chaech;	to the eruption of Loch Dá Chaoch;
Cermna Sobairche derb días	Cearmna and Sobhairce, steady pair,
i rre Samsoin is Aenias.[9]	lived in the age of Samson and Aeneas.

The classical tales in Irish, especially *Togail Troí*, continued to be copied in the fifteenth century. Yet this period also apparently saw the end of fresh adaptations. Moreover, by 1500, *Togail Troí* and references to its heroes virtually disappear from sight in Gaelic Ireland. This is a significant discontinuity given the importance of the classical corpus in the four centuries preceding, and given that the native literary culture by no means ends with the Tudor conquests of the sixteenth century. On the contrary, the sixteenth century is the period of our so-called Renaissance Ireland. The seventeenth century, distinguished by historians writing in Irish such as Geoffrey Keating, as well as by a large corpus of scholarly and devotional literature in print, has been called the "Golden Age of Irish Prose." Considering that these were times of such literary productivity, why did the Irish lose interest in their own rich imaginative investment in the "matter of Troy"? The late fifteenth century, the period of transition from medieval to Renaissance in Ireland, may provide some clues.

For the sake of convenience we can take the third, last recension of *Togail Troí* as an example of the late medieval engagement with the classical tales. This recension is preserved in two fifteenth-century manuscripts. The first, Royal Irish Academy MS D iv 2, is typical of the great books of the Irish Middle Ages, which is to say, it is encyclopedic in conception. The manuscript is a sprawling collection of native tales from Ireland's heroic pagan period, tales of its later Christian kings, and native *dinnsheanchas*, or Irish place-name lore. The manuscript also contains *Togail Troí*, the Irish *Odyssey*, the Irish *Pharsalia*, two additional tales from antiquity, "The Tale of the Minotaur" and "The Parricides of the Children of Tantalus," and, to leave nothing out, an Irish translation of the French "Legend of the Holy Grail." Irish manuscripts are difficult to date in the absence of a scribal colophon, as is the case here, but the dating of the manuscript to the middle of the fifteenth century is most likely accurate.[10]

The encyclopedic gathering of texts evident in RIA MS D iv 2 is typical of the manuscripts of medieval Ireland. Manuscripts were not seen by their makers as volumes in a library, but rather as libraries in themselves. This is

---

[9]"*A Rí ríchid réidig dam*," in Best and O'Brien, *Book of Leinster*, vol. 3, ll. 17855–17862; see also Myrick, *From the* De Excidio Troiae Historia, pp. 81–85, for similar mentions of the Trojan War in Irish annals and poetry.

[10]See Mulchrone, *Catalogue of Irish Manuscripts,* pp. 3297–3307.

especially true of the great patrons' books written for the Gaelic aristocracy, important manuscripts which generally had proper names of their own, and which, as one scholar has recently noted, would sit in a patron's collection much as a Rembrandt would be displayed in the homes of later collectors.[11] There are cases in which books were employed as a form of currency. For example, in 1462, *Leabhar an Rátha*, the "Book of Pottlerath," was used to ransom Edmund Butler, nephew of James, the fourth Earl of Ormond, after he had been taken captive by Thomas FitzGerald, the eighth Earl of Desmond. The O'Donnells, governing territory in Donegal where the production of patrons' books was rare, actively pursued the acquisition of books from other provinces. *Leabhar na hUidhre*, the "Book of the Dun Cow," was acquired from parties in Connaught in the mid-fourteenth century, relinquished to the O'Connors of Sligo as ransom for the son of the O'Donnells' chief historian sometime around 1340, and then carried back to Donegal in triumph by Aodh Ruadh Ó Domhnaill after the taking of Sligo Castle in 1470. The value of such books did not necessarily lie in the richness of their decoration, which, in comparison with patrons' books from workshops on the Continent, is extremely modest. It is just as reasonable to view these books as collections of prestigious texts above all else. These patrons' books in fact have much in common with "scholars' books," written by scholars for their own use, which were typically aggregative and encyclopedic in the fashion of the "great books." We can see this phenomenon in the "Ó Cianáin Miscellany" of c. 1345, a scholar's manuscript which is nonetheless the first significant gathering of important Irish texts from the later Middle Ages and a valued specimen of Irish decoration in its own right.[12]

The second manuscript of the third recension of *Togail Troí* is altogether different from the first. Kings' Inns Library MS 12–13 is a scholar's book, written by Maoílechlainn Ó Cianáin and finished in 1492. The manuscript is a collection of classical tales, and classical tales only. In addition to *Togail Troí*, Ó Cianáin has included the Irish *Odyssey*, "The Parricides of the Children of Tantalus," a text called "The Third Troy in the time of Astyanax," and the Irish *Aeneid*. Not encyclopedic in the usual manner, this manuscript represents a gathering of texts along one extraordinary theme, namely derivation from classical antiquity. We cannot pretend that no manuscript gathering of materials along thematic principles was ever made

---

[11]Carney, "Literature in Irish," p. 693.

[12]For an overview of Irish manuscript practice, see Henry and Marsh-Micheli, "Manuscripts and Illuminations," pp. 789–807; see also Carney, "Literature in Irish," pp. 690–694.

in earlier times in Ireland. However, a complete manuscript devoted to classical tales alone is unprecedented before 1492. Although some of these tales had been classics of Irish literature in their own right, the consciousness of these tales as something apart, ultimately belonging to the antiquity of continental Europe, is here uniquely suggested by manuscript context. A second fifteenth-century manuscript, Franciscan A 11, written by Daelgus Ó Duibhghennán, consists of the second recension of *Togail Troí* as well as the Irish *Aeneid*. However, its text breaks off abruptly in the *Aeneid* in mid-sentence, making it difficult to speculate whether Ó Duibhghennán's original work was meant to be comparable to Ó Cianáin's compilation. Copies of other recensions of *Togail Troí* are extant from the fifteenth century, but these have been rebound or altered, as with the Franciscan manuscript, or continue the normal encyclopedic principle of Irish medieval manuscripts. With due appreciation of the fragmentary evidence and the difficulty of dating Irish manuscripts, it is still possible to recognize in Ó Cianáin's late medieval "classical" manuscript a departure from earlier medieval practice.[13]

Manuscript production in Ireland was the prerogative of professional scholarly families. Maoílechlainn Ó Cianáin belonged to the illustrious Ulster learned family of the Ó Cianáins, a family responsible for some of the most important "great books" of medieval Ireland. These include the earliest extant patron's book, *Leabhar Meig Shamhradháin*, the "Book of Magauran," written for Tomás Mág Shamhradháin (d. 1343), and the "Ó Cianáin Miscellany" mentioned above. The historian Tadhg Ó Cianáin accompanied his aristo-cratic patrons to the Continent in 1607, where he composed his history of the aristocracy's flight, *Imthecht na nIarla*, "The Flight of the Earls." This manuscript of classical tales written by Maoílechlainn Ó Cianáin is, then, representative of a tenacious scholarly tradition much valued in Gaelic Ireland, and reflects professional practices in the book industry of the day.

Yet while Ó Cianáin worked within an inherited tradition, his remark-able choice of materials is evidence of innovation on his part. Put another way, such a manuscript was not conceived as a library in the earlier fashion of so many collections which went before it, but was perhaps conceived to sit in a library. This might be for example the library of a humanist scholar, or maybe the scholar's patron, a Renaissance prince. The innovation is subtle, but significant. Ó Cianáin's discreet selection of translations from Greek and

---

[13]For Ó Cianáin's manuscript, see de Brún, *King's Inns Library, Dublin*, pp. 30–33; for the Franciscan manuscript, see Dillon, *Franciscan Library, Killiney*, pp. 22–23. Poppe, "The Classical Epic from an Irish Perspective," is an important recent discussion of the manuscript context of the classical tales in the Book of Ballymote especially.

Roman antiquity may reflect the pretensions of the movement we will subsequently call humanism.

It follows that Ó Cianáin's manuscript reflects practices of manuscript collection as well as production in the late fifteenth century. Unfortunately, information on libraries in Ireland in the pre-modern period is meagre, in part because collections were broken up in the turmoil of the English conquest. However, it is clear that both Anglo-Irish and Gaelic Ireland once had thriving ecclesiastic and secular libraries. An extant booklist from the library of the Franciscan house in Youghal, originally written in 1491, shows a collection which is overwhelmingly religious in character and exclusively in Latin. The learned scribal families to whom we owe our books in Irish from the period were working independently from church patronage. Aside from the efforts of the O'Donnells to acquire noted patrons' books, however, our only other substantial record of collections in Ireland are two lists of library holdings from the "Rental" of the Earl of Kildare. The Rental was begun in 1518 in the time of the ninth earl, but the earlier of the two lists may have been made before 1505 in the time of the eighth, known as the "Great Earl." In either case, the earls of Kildare were foremost the local magnates of a strong Anglo-Irish family that had long accommodated itself to the culture of Gaelic Ireland, yet which had recently made astute concessions to the Tudors. The earlier booklist includes works in Latin, French, and English, as well as in Irish. Latin holdings include unspecified works of Vergil, Juvenal, and Terence, as well as literature of the church. Items in French include chronicles, Mandeville's *Travels*, and a "boke of Farsses"; English items include an Arthurian romance, Ralph Higden's *Polychronicon*, the *Siege of Thebes*, and translations of works by Christine de Pisan and Geraldus Cambrensis. Irish items represent a selection of saints' lives, chronicles and translated works, and native saga. The booklist is evidence that an Irish aristocrat at the turn of the sixteenth century could acquire a substantial library of materials both native and imported from abroad if so inclined, be it by dint of literary interest or as a show of urbanity and wealth.[14]

Most of the materials in the earlier booklist were likely to have been manuscripts. The Irish materials were without question in manuscripts, as printing in the Irish language did not begin until 1567. However, the new medium was known earlier through printed books imported from England.

---

[14]See Ó Clabaigh, *Franciscans in Ireland*, Appendix 1, pp. 158–180, for an edition of the Youghal booklist; for the Earl of Kildare's library, Mac Niocaill, *Crown surveys,* pp. 312–314, 355–356; for the date of the booklists, O'Grady, *Irish Manuscripts in the British Museum*, pp. 154–155.

We can assume that the first book printed in English, Caxton's *Recuyell of the Historyes of Troye*, printed in Bruges in 1474, reached the libraries of Ireland, as we have from the late fifteenth century an Irish translation of part of it, *Stair Ercuil ocus a Bás*, "The History of Hercules and his Death," done by Uilliam Mac an Lega. This Uilliam, incidentally, was one of the most productive scholar-scribes of the fifteenth century. Much of his work is extant, including *Leabhar na Carraigi*, the "Book of Carrick," which formed part of the book-ransom for Edmund Butler. There is confusion surrounding Uilliam Mac an Lega's exact identity, in that he may be identical with another scribe, Illann Mac an Lega Ruadh, the head of a learned medical family to whom we owe a large corpus of translations of continental medical texts.[15]

Where *Stair Ercuil ocus a Bás* is concerned, we would do better to call Mac an Lega's work an adaptation rather than a translation: he gives himself leave to conform the story to the style and archaic language of the earlier vernacular adaptations, and especially *Togail Troí* itself. This is typical of Irish literary translations of the period, which, stylistically, tend to give little evidence of their origin in a foreign literature. We clearly see Mac an Lega's fidelity to the medieval tradition in the following passage describing Hercules' slaughter of the people of Thebes following his killing of Lycus and Megara. The passage has no equivalent in Caxton, and typifies Mac an Lega's additions to his source:

> *Docuaidh immorro igha uathmar angidhi eoid a cenn Ercuil tre comradh Lingcuis, 7 do nocht a lann asa haithli 7 doróne da orduin cudruma comora do Lingcus. Ocus doróne in cetna do Megra . . . Ocus nir luaithi sruth sanntach síradhbul sleibhi ag dul re fantaibh naid srotha falcmara foirrderga fola in la sin isin cathraigh ac sileadh as meidibh míled 7 a slesaibh saerclann socineol iarna toitim la hErcuil a ndigail a clemna 7 a carat. Conidh amlaidh sin ro ghabh Ercuil in Teibh for Lingcus.*[16]
>
> [A terrible, cruel pang of jealousy went through Hercules because of what Lycus had said, and he bared his sword and made two even, equal pieces of Lycus, and did the same with Megara. . . . And a headlong, mighty mountain-stream flowing down the slopes would not be swifter than the copious, crimson streams of blood in the city that day, flowing from the necks of soldiers and from the sides of well-born nobles who had fallen before Hercules in vengeance for his father-in-law and his friends. So that it was thus that Hercules won Thebes from Lycus.]

This passage, recalling similar evocations of post-battle gore in the native sagas, can be compared with the epic simile of Achilles' rage from *Togail Troí* given above. Mac an Lega was an accomplished literary artist in his own right,

---

[15]See Henry and Marsh-Micheli, "Manuscripts and Illuminations," pp. 803–806; the fullest recent discussion of Mac an Lega is Ross' *Bildungsidol–Ritter–Held*, esp. pp. 30–49.

[16]Mac an Lega, *Stair Ercuil ocus a Bás*, ll. 884–895.

displaying a mastery of clear narrative prose, which is as rare in Irish writers of his generation as it is among writers of any time or place. He boldly improves on Caxton, expanding the odd scene, but mostly editing his source text to produce a tighter, less tedious narration. Archaic language is mostly restricted to a few passages of heightened artistry, the greater part of the narrative being composed in language that is reasonably close to the idiom of contemporary speakers. However, Mac an Lega's *Stair Ercuil* does not represent a new direction in Irish prose. Mac an Lega's text is quite the opposite, a virtual homage to the medieval tradition. Traces of mannerisms pioneered in tenth- and eleventh-century texts like *Togail Troí* and *Táin Bó Cúailnge* can be found throughout *Stair Ercuil*, a tribute to the serviceability and tenacity of the tradition.

    This homage to Irish tradition is more than just a stylistic matter. We can compare the context of Caxton's telling of Hercules' deeds to that of Mac an Lega's. As in the case of Ó Cianáin's manuscript of classical tales, Mac an Lega's selection of material represents a calculated choice. Mac an Lega has translated from only the first two books of the *Recuyell*, and specifically the deeds of Hercules, which occupy most of the narrative up to Book III and precede the war against Priam's Troy. Mac an Lega has removed the story of Hercules from its Trojan setting in Caxton, and has, in effect, placed it afresh within the context of the native Irish Troy. This resetting of the tale would have been perceived by those familiar with Ireland's own medieval literature, or with the varied riches and deficiencies of its libraries. As far back as the tenth century, *Togail Troí* actually did include a brief account of Hercules' feats. These represent an addition to Dares' text and presumably reflect the author's desire to dignify and as much as possible "complete" Dares' plain narrative with what could be gleaned from elsewhere about the Greek and Trojan heroes. Unfortunately, this account was desultory, so much so as to strike the reader as incongruous with the larger text. It is a noticeable aesthetic failing of *Togail Troí* that its version of the tale of Hercules fails to make of the adventures anything other than a bare narrative list. Mac an Lega perhaps wanted to mine Caxton's book to amend a deficiency in the native Irish corpus. Mac an Lega did not bother to translate Book III of Caxton, the account of the Trojan War proper, perhaps because this would only have duplicated the story already told in *Togail Troí*. *Stair Ercuil ocus a Bás*, as executed by Mac an Lega, amends the earlier native corpus by providing a full account of Hercules' career apart from his participation in Troy's destruction.

    These efforts by Mac an Lega are symptomatic of scribal efforts in general in fifteenth century Ireland. Literary creation had fallen into abatement, and was supplanted by the work of scribes and builders of libraries. These scholars were perhaps concerned to preserve the native literary corpus against the incursions of English culture. The story cannot be so simple, however, as Gaelic political power was on the ascent throughout this period. Irish, having long since overtaken French as the preferred language among Anglo-Norman lords in Ireland, seriously threatened to replace English as well. The period is also rich in translations into Irish, predominantly from Latin and English. Perhaps one aim of scribes and translators was to promote an Irish equivalent to burgeoning libraries of materials available from overseas, which may have been augmented with relatively inexpensive printed books from England especially. Foreign printed books would have been distinct for their non-encyclopedic format, among other things. I have argued that Maoílechlainn Ó Cianáin's volume of classical tales, as well as perhaps the similar incomplete collection of Daelgus Ó Duibhghennán, suggest such a bibliophilic trend in Gaelic Ireland.

It would be wrong to equate this activity to preserve the native corpus with Irish conservatism alone. Our relative lack of knowledge about the reality of intellectual life in Gaelic Ireland in this period encourages us to suspend judgement, just as it dissuades us from claiming to know more than we do. The ostensibly conservative activity of professional scholar-scribes actually anticipates the most innovative scholarly venture of the next century. This is the compilation of *Betha Colaim Chille*, "The Life of Columcille," by Manus Ó Domhnaill. Ó Domhnaill's activities are an indispensable index of where Irish culture was heading, and what it might have achieved, had it not been for the continued political defeats endured by Gaelic Ireland in the succeeding years. Ó Domhnaill was involved in the rule of his father's territories in Donegal from at least 1510, and was himself lord of Donegal between 1537 and 1563. In 1532, Ó Domhnaill assembled from old books all the materials he could find in Latin and Old Irish about the Irish saint Columcille. Ó Domhnaill then edited this material and translated it into the comprehensible idiom of the modern Irish of his day. Writing of his own efforts in his preface:

> *Bidh a fhis ag lucht legtha na bethad-sa gorab é Maghnas . . . [Ó] Domhnaill, do furail an cuid do bi a Laidin don bethaid-si do cur a n-Gaidhilc, 7 do furail an chuid do bi go cruaid a n-Gaidilc di do cor a m-buga, innus go m-beith si solus sothuicsena do cach uile.*[17]
>
> [Let it be known to readers of this *Life* that it was Manus Ó Domhnaill who ordered the Latin part of this *Life* to be translated into Irish, and who ordered the part of it that was in difficult Irish to be turned into easy Irish, so that it might be clear and easy to understand for all.]

---

[17] Ó Domhnaill, *Betha Colaim Chille*, p. 6.

This is the first time an Irish scholar articulates the need to translate important works from Old Irish, incomprehensible to all but scholars even in Ó Domhnaill's day, into the contemporary vernacular. This activity can be likened to the representation of the culture of classical Rome through the medium of Latin's descendants, for example, French or Italian. What is most interesting, however, is that Ó Domhnaill was neither a cleric nor a member of a professional learned family, but very much a layman, actively engaged in the government of a territory. He was also a noted author of love poetry, a gifted diplomat and, as Brendan Bradshaw has argued, a "prince-aesthete" after the inspiration of Castiglione's *Book of the Courtier*. Bradshaw has argued that we can see in Ó Domhnaill's career the unmistakable impress of Renaissance theory as well as practice, and that Ó Domhnaill merits the title "Renaissance Prince" for that reason. Mícheál Mac Craith has not hesitated to reiterate the claim that *Betha Colaim Chille* is a "distinctively Renaissance product," nor to deny the clear imprint of Christian humanism in Ó Domhnaill's scholarly ambition and pious intent.[18]

The work of earlier fifteenth-century scholars and bibliophiles such as Maoílechlainn Ó Cianáin and Uilliam Mac an Lega shows that later literary efforts which we are apt to label "Renaissance" in Ireland may represent an evolution of native medieval scholarship and all its concerns as well as an openness to trends from abroad, and inevitably those from Tudor England. But the confusion which can follow the application of the term *Renaissance* to Ireland, and especially to the culture of Gaelic Ireland, is nowhere clearer than in the infamous scholars' feud between Daniel Corkery and Pádraig de Brún. Writing in 1930 in the wake of Ireland's independence, de Brún mourned the failure of Irish writing to receive the imprint of the Renaissance, identifying this as a *bacaighe*, a "lameness" in the tradition persisting to the present day. Corkery, whose ideas I considered at the beginning of this essay, responded with a fierce defence of the native tradition:

> *Sé rud a deirim-se ná gurbé an buadh is mó atá againn féin ná dúthchas cruinn a bheith againn sa Ghaedhilg, go bhfuilimíd, toisg é sin a bheith amhlaidh chun tosaigh ar gach tír gur chuir cló an Renaissance, isteach uirthi; go bhfuilimíd, sa méid sin, níos comhgaraí ná iad don tSean-Ghréig.*[19]

---

[18]See Bradshaw, "Manus 'The Magnificent,'" p. 23; Mac Craith, "Ireland and the Renaissance," p. 59.

[19]Corkery, "Na hEorpaigh Seo Againne," p. 4, quoted from Mac Craith, "Gaelic Ireland," p. 58; de Brún, "Ars Scribendi," p. 4, quoted from Ó Buachalla, "Ó Corcora agus an Hidden Ireland," p. 121.

[I affirm that our greatest accomplishment is that we have a definite national culture in Irish, and that it is for that reason that we are superior to every country with which the Renaissance interfered, and that we are, in that respect, closer than they to ancient Greece.]

De Brún's remarks had in truth little aim other than to encourage the translation of the Greco-Roman classics into Irish, an activity de Brún himself pursued with much success for the remainder of his career. Corkery's response may be overstated, yet his views cannot fail to be influential even today. Breandán Ó Buachalla makes the sad observation that neither party in this contest seems to have given much thought to the fact that many of the classics had been translated into Irish, and that a substantial proportion of the corpus of medieval Irish, hence of Irish tradition, consisted of such works already.[20] A mistaken equation of "Renaissance" with that period's engagement with classical literature would be in itself rather too naive to characterize this dispute between two great *littérateurs* of modern Ireland. Yet something of that sort has contributed to produce this ultimately fruitless exchange. To be sure, antiquarian preoccupation with Ireland's own classics, its early medieval literature, is probably the most distinctive feature of Irish scholarship following the recovery of Irish culture after centuries of chaos brought by Viking raiders and Anglo-Norman adventurers. The fourteenth-century "literary revival" in Ireland is the period when the "great books" appear again, which is to say it is an antiquarian's revival as much as a poet's; the parallel to the revival of classical learning on the Continent is obvious. This revival continues uninterrupted into the period of so-called Renaissance Ireland. It is noteworthy that Manus Ó Domhnaill draws attention to the disasters of the Viking raids as the cause for the loss of the original *Life* of Columcille, and of the necessity of collecting and reediting to restore that ancient text for his own generation. Ó Domhnaill may or may not borrow from the European myth of the eclipse of classical civilization resulting from barbarian attacks against Rome and the recovery of that civilization by the Renaissance. The coalescence of revival and Renaissance is nowhere clearer than in *Betha Coluim Chille*. But ignoring the long Irish engagement with the classics of Greece and Rome, simply because the tradition was begun so spectacularly in the early medieval period, may introduce a distortion into our attempt to write a fair literary history of the later period.

---

[20]Ó Buachalla, "Ó Corcora," p. 122.

WORKS CITED

Best, R. I. and M. A. O'Brien, ed. *The Book of Leinster, formerly Lebar na Núachongbála*. Vols. 3–4. Dublin: Dublin Institute for Advanced Studies, 1957–1965.

Bradshaw, Brendan. "Manus 'The Magnificent': O'Donnell as Renaissance Prince." *Studies in Irish History presented to R. Dudley Edwards*. Ed. Art Cosgrove and Donal McCartney. Naas: University College Dublin, 1979. 15–36.

Byrne, Francis John. "Clann Ollaman Uaisle Emna." *Studia Hibernica* 4 (1964): 54–94.

Carney, James. "Literature in Irish, 1169–1534." *A New History of Ireland II*. Ed. Art Cosgrove. Oxford: Clarendon, 1993. 688–707.

Caxton, William. *The Recuyell of the Historyes of Troye*. Written in French by Raoul Lefevre. Trans. William Caxton. Ed. H. Oskar Sommer. 2 vols. London: David Nutt, 1894.

Corkery, Daniel (as Domhnall Ó Corcora). "Na hEorpaigh Seo Againne." *Humanitas* (1930): 2–6.

Corkery, Daniel. *The Hidden Ireland: A Study of Gaelic Munster in the Eighteenth Century*. 1924. Rpt. Dublin: M. H. Gill, 1979.

de Brún, Pádraig. "Ars Scribendi." *Humanitas* (1930): 2–5.

de Brún, Pádraig. *Catalogue of Irish Manuscripts in King's Inns Library, Dublin*. Dublin: Dublin Institute for Advanced Studies, 1972.

Dillon, Myles, Canice Mooney and Pádraig de Brún. *Catalogue of Irish Manuscripts in the Franciscan Library, Killiney*. Dublin: Dublin Institute for Advanced Studies, 1969.

Frazer, R. M., Jr., trans. *The Trojan War: The Chronicles of Dictys of Crete and Dares the Phrygian*. Bloomington: Indiana University Press, 1966.

Henry, Françoise and Geneviève Marsh-Micheli. "Manuscripts and Illuminations, 1169–1603." *A New History of Ireland II: Medieval Ireland 1169–1534*. Ed. Art Cosgrove. 2d ed. Oxford: Clarendon, 1993. 781–815.

Mac an Lega, Uilliam. *Stair Ercuil ocus a Bás. The Life and Death of Hercules*. Ed. and trans. Gordon Quin. Irish Texts Society 38. Dublin: Irish Texts Society, 1939.

Mac Craith, Mícheál. "Gaelic Ireland and the Renaissance." *The Celts and the Renaissance: Tradition and Innovation*. Proceedings of the Eighth International Congress of Celtic Studies. Ed. Glanmor Williams and Robert Owen Jones. Cardiff: University of Wales Press, 1990. 57–89.

Mac Eoin, Gearóid. "Das Verbalsystem von *Togail Troí* (H. 2. 17)." *Zeitschrift für Celtische Philologie* 28 (1960–1961): 73–136, 149–223.

Mac Gearailt, Uáitéar. "Change and Innovation in Eleventh-Century Prose Narrative in Irish." *(Re)Oralisierung*. Ed. H. L. C. Tristram. Tübingen: Günter Narr, 1996. 443–493.

Mac Niocaill, Gearóid. *Crown surveys of lands 1540–41: with the Kildare rental begun in 1518*. Dublin: Irish Manuscripts Commission, 1992.

Meister, Ferdinand. *Daretis Phrygii de excidio Troiae historia*. Leipzig: Teubner, 1873.

Mulchrone, Kathleen. *Catalogue of Irish Manuscripts in the Royal Irish Academy, Fasciculus 26*. Dublin: Royal Irish Academy, 1942.

Myrick, Leslie Diane. *From the De Excidio Troiae Historia to the Togail Troí: Literary-Cultural Synthesis in a Medieval Irish Adaptation of Dares' Troy Tale*. Heidelberg: Winter, 1993.

Ó Buachalla, Breandán. "Ó Corcora agus an Hidden Ireland." *Scríobh* 4 (1979): 109–137.

Ó Clabaigh, Colmán N. *The Franciscans in Ireland, 1400–1534: From Reform to Reformation.* Dublin: Four Courts, 2002.

Ó Cuív, Brian. "The Irish Language in the Early Modern Period." *A New History of Ireland III: Early Modern Ireland, 1534–1691.* Ed. T. W. Moody, F. X. Martin and F. J. Byrne. Oxford: Clarendon, 1976. 509–545.

Ó Domhnaill, Manus. *Betha Colaim Chille. Life of Columcille.* Ed. A. O'Kelleher and G. Schoepperle. Champaign-Urbana: Graduate School of the University of Illinois, 1918.

O'Grady, Standish Hayes. *Catalogue of Irish Manuscripts in the British Museum.* Vol. 1. London: British Museum, 1926.

Poppe, Erich. "The Classical Epic from an Irish Perspective." Introd. to *Imtheachta Aeniasa: The Irish Aeneid.* Ed. George Calder. Irish Texts Society 6. 2nd ed. London: Irish Texts Society, 1995.

Ross, Bianca. *Bildungsidol–Ritter–Held: Herkules bei William Caxton und Uilliam Mac an Lega.* Heidelberg: Winter, 1989.

Stanford, W. B. *Ireland and the Classical Tradition.* Dublin: Figgis, 1976.

Stokes, Whitley. "The Destruction of Troy, aus H.2.17, mit englischer Uebersetzung." *Irische Texte* 2, 1. Ed. Whitley Stokes and Ernst Windisch. Leipzig: S. Hirzel, 1884. 1–142.

Tristram, Hildegard L. C. "Aspects of Tradition and Innovation in the *Táin Bó Cúailnge.*" *Papers on Language and Medieval Studies Presented to Alfred Schopf.* Ed. Richard Matthews and Joachim Schmole-Rostosky. Frankfurt: Peter Lang, 1988. 19–38.

The Disappearance of the Trojan Legend in the Historiography of Venice

SHEILA DAS

As Venice emerged fully independent from Byzantine rule in the Middle Ages, the city set about the task of defining its own self-image. It was to do so in typical medieval style—by establishing ties to a classical past.[1] Venice, as with many other states, sought the associations of authority and continuity that could be suggested by fashioning its current existence as part of an inheritance of classical values and achievements. Among Italian cities, however, Venice was a rarity since it actually did not have an obvious Roman heritage—demonstrable, for instance, in archeological ruins—to lend credibility to claims of an ancient Roman foundation. Ancient provenance, therefore, had to be fabricated. In this endeavor, Venetian chroniclers increased the temporal distance and so loosened the historical bonds. They turned to literary sources and the pre-Roman era from which they were able to draw the material necessary to assert a noble Trojan lineage for the Republic.[2]

Comprehensive accounts of the Trojan foundation of Venice appear in the chronicles of Martin da Canal and Marco and indicate, therefore, that the myth was fully formulated by the thirteenth century.[3] The ensuing centuries, however, witness a shift from this medieval tradition, as Venice, unlike its counterparts in the rest of Europe, continually chose to minimize

---

[1]Venice became independent from Byzantine control in the eighth century when Byzantium recognized the rule of the locally elected doge.

[2]Hay, *Europe*, pp. 47–50. This was by no means an exception in medieval Europe. Even if accounts of Trojan origins did not "bulk large" in medieval chronicle, they were popular enough to overshadow previous claims to mythical origins.

[3]Carile, *Le origini di Venezia*, pp. 63–65. Carile has indicated that Martin da Canal and Marco centre their history of the origins on the Trojan settlement, and therefore consolidate the Trojan foundation in the originary myth, something that in the eleventh century was not yet stabilized, as bear witness the five versions of Giovanni Diacono's *Origo civitatum italie seu venetiarum*, the last of which offers the hypothesis of Trojan settlements in the terraferma—led by Antenor.

its claim to Trojan origins. Taking its place was another myth, and another eastern translation: the recovery of the relics of St. Mark the Evangelist. But by the fifteenth century even the Marcian theme was losing favour, at least in the historiographic tradition of the Republic, as Venice aimed to construct a more objective, or less fantastic, view of its own past.[4]

Within the narrow confines of its historiography, the Venetian abandonment of the Trojan myth during the Renaissance may not seem startling. But within the greater European context, which shows countries and cities throughout the continent beginning to devise legends that would link them to Trojan ancestry, the Venetian case strikes one as a rather peculiar cultural aberration. Humanist advances in historiographical method cannot account for it, since the Trojan foundational myth proliferated in other countries that were equally aware of and similarly subject to the same demands for verification and authenticity in their historical writing. Venice, then, at odds with what seemed to be the rage in the European mytho-historical scene, emerges as an anomaly. For just when other nations were desperately trying to create or elaborate upon a Trojan legend and so establish their unique claim to the Trojan, usually imperialist, destiny, Venice put its own Trojan tradition aside.[5]

The aim of this paper is to trace the lines of that tradition in order to recover clues as to the disappearance of the Trojan myth from Venetian historiography. A chronological approach affords the most obvious way to highlight the historical mutations of the myth, and so I shall begin with a sketch of the legend from its earliest and most fully formed composition, which is found in Venice's late medieval chronicles. Following from this, I shall examine other myths that became popular in the historiography of the *Serenissima* and that effectively supplanted the Trojan legend in the course of the Renaissance. Finally, I will compare these mythical transformations with Venice's historical realities to offer a hypothesis of the motivations behind the rise and fall of Troy in the historiography of Venice.

I

By the thirteenth century, the basic elements of the mythical Trojan foundation of Venice had been established. Two chroniclers can be credited

---

[4]This is not the case with art, as St. Mark or his winged lion figured in paintings and ornaments in the most prestigious works throughout the Renaissance: Battista d'Agnolo del Moro, *Saint Mark at the Recruiting Table*, Titian, *The Triumph of Faith*, Vittore Carpaccio, *The Lion of Saint Mark*, Palma Giovane, *Allegory of the League of Cambrai*, Giovanni Bellini, *Virgin Between the Saints Nicholas, Peter, Benedict and Mark*. See Wills, *Venice Lion City*, pp. 15, 35, 48, 66, 231.

[5]Yates, *Astrea,* pp. 50-51, 60-63, 130-133.

for this: Martin da Canal, who composed his *Les Estoires de Venise* in 1267, and Marco (known only by this one name), who wrote his chronicle in 1292.[6] Both recall the legendary Trojan settlement of Venice as the originary event of a three-fold myth informing Venice's foundation. In brief, the myth generally begins by professing the Trojan settlement of Venice.[7] It then proceeds with an explanation of the move onto the salt flats of the lagoons themselves, by citing either Attila's or the Lombards' invasions as prompting the *Veneti* to flee from the *Terraferma*. The final layer of the myth reports St. Mark's *praedestinatio* of Venice as his final resting place and the fulfillment of that in the later translation of his remains, which thereby yokes Mark as patron saint to the Republic.[8]

Keeping in mind the tripartite nature of the Venetian foundational legend, let us now turn to examine the Trojan component. I will begin here with Marco's chronicle (1292). Except in one particularity, it resembles da Canal's story quite closely. He begins:

> And so the Trojans . . . reached an unoccupied mound of earth where the city of Venetiae is now built, and deliberating among themselves about the place which was surrounded by water and free from all rule, they resolved to build dwellings by themselves there.[9]

Marco identifies the Trojans who arrived at the Venetian marshes as a group. Further, he identifies their decision to build their city on that site because of the freedom suggested by the location itself: not only protected by the water surrounding it but, in fact, neither conquered nor inhabited. This interpretation stems from the historical and literary sources of Virgil and Benoît de Saint-More (*Le Roman de Troie*),[10] which cite the departure of Antenor and other Trojans to northern shores. Common characteristics of

---

6Da Canal, *Archivio Storico Italiano*, p. 338. Marco, *Codex Marco*, rpt. in Carile, "Aspetti della cronachistica," pp. 121–126.

7Muir, *Civic Ritual*, p. 2. There is also a variant which credits Gallican emigrants as Venice's original settlers, but its fortune falls entirely outside the purview of the task at hand. For our purposes, it is enough to know that the Trojan myth was the prevalent one.

8St. Mark the Evangelist was said to have founded the Church in Aquileia, then went to Venice for one day where he had his vision, before continuing on to Alexandria, where he was martyred. The translation of his relics to Venice occurred in 804. On their importance in Venice, see Wills, *Venice*, pp. 235–252.

9"I liberi Troiani . . . pervernerunt ad quandam tunbam, ubi nunc Venetiarum civitas est constructa, et deliberantes infra se de stacione loci, qui erat labilis et ab omni exemptus dominio, diposuerunt ibi ipsorum construere mansiones" (Marco, *Codex Marco*, ll. 3-6). I cite Marco from Carile, "Aspetti della cronachistica," pp. 121–122. I thank Nancy Priori for her assistance in translating Marco.

10Carile, "Aspetti della cronachistica," p. 91.

Troy may be assumed. The "deliberation" of the group recalls the eloquence operative in the construction of Troy, related by Orpheus, and so too its paradigmatic civility. For the Trojan colonizers civility is shown again through the decision, made through language, to build their new city. The Trojan value of liberty is also implied, which is revealed in the reasoning behind their decision to choose the marshes as their new home since they are "free from all rule." And lastly, the fact that they are arrivals in a new world hints of the Virgilian legacy of the destiny, and hence, legitimacy of future universalist and imperialist designs. We could then perhaps surmise, in agreement with recent scholarship, that this foundational legend essentially served these two ideological purposes: to instill civic values and to encourage imperialist attitudes. Looking further, however, we shall see that this latter interpretation does not find support in Marco's constellation of the myth, for he pointedly refutes association with Rome and its empire and thus distances himself from the predominant use of Trojan pedigree as a flag of imperialist destiny.

First of all, Marco defines the liberty of this Trojan band in strict contrast to the obstacles and difficulties the Trojans have overcome. He disallows the Trojans the simple acquisition of a natural freedom that is given to all living creatures at birth. Nor does he award them divinely ordained freedom. Instead, Marco equates Trojan liberty with human accomplishment, and thus wholly endows it with civic qualities of virtue, nobility, and civility. This point is elaborated by the following scene of the settlement. In marked juxtaposition to the aggressive, predestined colonization of Rome by Aeneas, in Venice the Trojans were to have arrived to empty lands where they themselves decided to build a city. An independent attitude, instead of an imperialist one, is emphasized in an extra detail: "furthermore, they readied part of their ship to convey loads of earth and timber to build up the area and they built homes of these same materials."[11] Not only did they build their own city, but they constructed the very ground upon which it would be built. Such a characterization of the Trojan founding of Venice testifies to particularly Venetian attributes. First, the importance of human organization is shown at work in the selection of the site. Next, since the free Trojans did not enter the area in violence by conquering a native people, but built their city anew on an uninhabited marsh, their very arrival announces the peaceful nature of this group. Consequently, they all helped build their own city, suggesting them to be

---

[11]"Paraverunt autem partem sui navigii ut, ad amplificacionem tunbe <onera?> terrarum et lignamina deportantent, hedifficavereuntque domos pre mansionibus eorundem" (Marco, *Codex Marco*, ll. 7–10).

resourceful, equal, unified, and, significantly, autochthonous. If they did not spring from the ground as it were, they came from their piling up of fresh earth and wood. Last, Trojan blood did not mix, as did Roman blood, with a conquered people, so the free Trojan line in Venice was not to be tainted with a subjugated populace. Following this line of logic, in Venice neither the arriving group nor any original (non-existent) inhabitants were to suffer either the loss of their customs or their sovereignty. In short, the settlers were demonstrably independent and were to continue in Venice to be free from all rule, *ab omni exemptus dominio*.

In addition, we should note that Marco steps out from the earlier medieval tradition when he credits a band of unnamed Trojans with having founded Venice. Other chroniclers, notably da Canal and Giovanni Decano, attest to Antenor as the city's legendary founder. Marco does not ignore this tradition but his Antenor enters the scene once the location has been found, the city built. Marco's refinement upon this part of the legend is telling. Rather than robbing the Venetians of an identifiable hero, the use of an anonymous group as the city's original founders enhances the Trojan establishment of Venetian liberty within the organization of the site. Here the act of collective settlement broadens the particular configuration of Trojan liberty in the Venetian lagoon. We have already seen how the physical site fortifies their freedom from outside rule. Now the plurality and equality of the original band is demonstrated, since they together were responsible for the construction of the city and thus are free from an internal domination, as in the form of monarchical power. Even though Antenor's preeminence is suggested since he was later elected to be their ruler, the fact that he does not stay, withdrawing instead to the mainland, makes his function in the story questionable. We should note, furthermore, that Antenor had decided to leave the islands because they were so crowded with diverse groups of Trojans who had flocked to the shores. This suggests that even though the Trojans had chosen him to be their king, the conditions that were already set, that is the abundance of free and various peoples, did not leave the space required for proper monarchical authority.

The composition of the Trojan colonizers in Venice can be understood even more acutely as an attribute of original Venetian liberty when Marco contrasts it not only to the single hero-founder of Padua, but also to the founder of Rome. This marks Venice's espousal of liberty as extending beyond the connections of equality, unity, and plurality, for it simultaneously shapes the city's own foundational myth in distinct opposition to imperialism. Two final points, which concern the timing of the Trojans' arrival, will offer further proof of an anti-imperialist perspective in Venice. As I mentioned above, Marco does not simply overlook the tradition that holds Antenor as the supposed founder. When he reports instead that

Antenor first arrived in Castello, then came to Padua after Venice had already been settled by other Trojans,[12] he effectively denies Antenor the role of founder of Venice. He further contrasts Antenor with the anonymous colonizers of Venice so as to underscore the significance of the Trojan band. Antenor is described as a refugee who had remained with the Greeks against his will for approximately five years. Forced confinement clearly labels him as being one less-than-free since he had lost, even if temporarily, a portion of his autonomy. On the other hand, Marco records that the Trojan band arrived at the Venetian mud-flats immediately after the fall of Troy. The implication here is straightforward. Whereas Antenor, hero though he was, had in fact been forced to relinquish his liberty, the group of Trojans enacted their own destiny of freedom. Taking a different tack, Marco makes another comparison. Deftly he no longer challenges the hero Antenor, but instead challenges the hero Aeneas in his own founding of Rome. This gesture finds support in the literary tradition, as Virgil relates Aeneas's laments about Antenor's more timely arrival in Padua,[13] and the Trojan band, according to Marco, even preceded Antenor. Marco elaborates further by remarking that Rome, founded by Romulus and Remus, must therefore follow the construction in the lagoons, relegating Rome to an origin 454 years less ancient than that of Venice.[14] This gives temporal primacy to the Venetian foundation as well, and therefore lays claim to a Venetian authority surpassing that of Rome.[15]

In short, the medieval configuration of the Trojan foundation of Venice was a specifically anti-monarchical, anti-imperialist and anti-Roman myth. Instead of echoing Aeneas' foundation of Rome, it challenged it, and so too Rome's authority, on the grounds of primacy. Similarly, Venice ranked itself superior to imperialist qualities by eschewing the single-hero founder model of Trojan origins. Constructing a specifically Venetian version of Trojan nobility in that pluralistic, consensual, and civil manner in which the city was founded, Marco espoused Trojan values of liberty and peace. Far from using the Trojan myth to support expansionist programs of empire, programs which Venice certainly did have, the medieval chroniclers underlined the Trojan characteristic of freedom, accomplished, shared, and instituted by the founders of the city. The inherited liberty of the Trojans from within the walled city is earned anew by the Trojan settlers of the Venetian marshes. It is enacted

---

[12]Marco, *Codex Marco*, ll. 35-36.

[13]Virgil, *Aeneid*, 1.338-348.

[14]Marco, *Codex Marco*, ll. 42-44.

[15]Carile, "Aspetti della cronachistica," p. 91. Carile has already indicated the anti-Roman implications in this passage.

personally through their communal settling of the marshes; it is instituted in the non-violent construction and foundation of the city out of uninhabited lands. Thus their sense of liberty encompasses freedom from outside subjugation, parity within the group, and peaceful social stability.

This version of the Trojan arrival into the lagoon differs, though, from da Canal's on one major point, namely Antenor's being the city's single founder. At this point I cannot make a claim as to which version had greater purchase during the thirteenth century; however, the later chronicles of the fourteenth century seem to be derived from the same documentary source from which Marco's version draws.[16] In some way, then, Marco's account must have resonated with the most profoundly felt characteristics of Venetian society in the late Middle Ages. It is my contention that it continued to do so well into the sixteenth century since it also finds an echo in the famed Renaissance "Myth of Venice." That the values of nobility, plurality, and liberty were to remain constants bears witness to this resonance since it reflects the dual function of myth: to draw on past record to explain the present and also to indicate consistent strategies of action for the future by shaping present attitudes. In the case of a city, individual attitudes translate into a *forma mentis* that directs a coherent mode of reacting to change, struggle, and the unforeseen in the course of history.[17] In Marco's version of the Trojan foundational myth, we may be able to see myth operating accordingly, that is, as part of a larger historiographical construction which provides an explanatory framework for guiding later developments in Venetian spirit as well as in foreign states' consideration of the city. It is in this larger constructive function of myth that I believe clues may be found regarding the disappearance of the Trojan settlers from Venetian histories.

II

In the fourteenth century the ennobling but pagan association with Troy fell to the wayside, while the Christian myths gained favour. Instead of recounting the arrival of original settlers, now chroniclers started the tale with the Hunnic invasion of Italy, which identified *Veneti* as good Christians escaping the pagan threat of Attila.[18] In some cases, the myth began on an even stronger Christian note, taking as its start the third phase of the originary myth, in the vision of St. Mark the Evangelist.

---

[16]Carile, *Le origini*, p. 110.

[17]Attitudes about the city can also be created outside it, of course, so that a reputation earned through myth can direct not only how a city reacts, but also how it is reacted to.

[18]Carile, "Una 'vita di Attila.'"

Andrea Dandolo, who dominates the historiography of the fourteenth century, exemplifies this new phase of a Christian originary myth in 1360 as his *Cronica Venetiarium* begins with the narrative of St. Mark, which remains the focal point of the originary myth of the chronicle.[19] The fleeting references to the Hunnic and Trojan components, respectively, seem only to bring more relief to the pivotal role of the St. Mark legend, adumbrating the Trojan legend in particular to such a degree as if to offer it a merely perfunctory salute.[20] This may occur as a result of negative logic insofar as the Trojan contribution was deemed too fantastic and romantic to be included in a serious historical work. But also, the benefits of the St. Mark myth being a Christian one became more desirable at a time when Venice was turning its attention to the West, and was affronting "inland rulers who were obstructive or predatory about the passage of goods to and from Venice through their territory."[21] Venice felt provoked to protect its commercial routes in this Catholic land, and this coincides with increased emphasis on the Catholic identification with Mark, in order to demonstrate divine protection and to endow Venice with its own religious authority. Thus, the legend of St. Mark was efficacious in a way that the Trojan legend could not be. The earlier peaceful pluralistic settling of the Venetian marshes provided Venice with a mythological balance with which to contest Rome's greatness and that city's political destiny, and thus to stress Venice's own political liberty and autonomy from the Roman empire. But as the source of Roman power was now coming from divine institution, the authority emanating from Rome was Catholic. The legend of St. Mark would allow Venice to emphasize its religious autonomy by providing it with divine institution, with Mark operating as a ballast to Peter's authority in Rome.

As the legend moves into the Renaissance, Venice moves under the influence of the great European powers, and the city's claims to political independence become less and less tenable. This shift in the European balance of power resulted from a decrease in the concentration of power in dominant structures, like the Church, to a widespread increase of power in various monarchies (Spanish, French, English, United Provinces, Sweden, the Hapsburgs of Austria). The *Serenissima*, however, was left out of this happy group. Venice just did not have the military resources necessary to be an imposing figure in this new European order. These shifts seem to

---

[19]Arnaldi, "Andrea Dandolo doge-cronista."

[20]Dandolo, "Chronica per extensum descripta," pp. 59-60; Carile, "Aspetti della cronachista," p. 122.

[21]Chambers, *The Imperial Age of Venice*, p. 54.

coincide with developments in the city's historiography, where a more secular presentation of Venice's self-image was taking shape.

We know this in the famed "Myth of Venice." Two major contributions to this are Bernardo Giustiniani's *De origine urbis Venetiarum* (1493) and Gasparo Contarini's *De magistratibus et republica Venetorum* (1531). Theirs were two fundamental, yet vastly different histories of Venice: one a history of origins and the other a contemporary municipal history. Despite these formal differences of composition and subject matter, they are both pivotal representations of Venice's changing attitudes towards antiquity. Giustiniani's work gave the most complete rendition of Venetian origins in historiography, and had ready reception throughout Europe's cultured circles.[22] And Contarini's text became a standard in the political literature on Venice, and its wide distribution in the form of many translations and reprints gave way to its becoming a model of Venice abroad.

Giustiniani begins his work by setting forth a humanist objective and methodology. His aims will include attending to the *lacuna* created by the recent histories that, desiring to distance themselves from the pagan and romantic associations, had obfuscated the Trojan part of the foundation myth. His motivation stems from humanist recognition and a patriotic sense of duty to possess a whole knowledge of his city, which must be informed, naturally, by an account of its beginnings. He further clarifies that his methodology will be predicated on circumspection and criticism, and therefore his treatment of remote history, which deals with obscure, distant, and controversial matters, will be guided by the factor of probability. In short, we have a declaration of historiographical purpose and method. On the one side, history has a responsibility to provide complete knowledge of a place, necessitating, therefore, a history of origins so as to perfect a knowledge of place. And, on the other side, he avows the criterion of credibility in directing that research. Thus he resumes the story of Venice's foundation from its very beginnings, by considering both of its originary myths—the Trojan and the less popular Gallican one. For the Trojan settlement, he reverts back to the Antenor myth, recalling Livy (*Ab urbe condita*, I, i) who had recounted that the "Eneti" from Paphlagonia, under Antenor's leadership, had arrived at the lagoons and settled there, giving

---

[22]Marcantonio Sabellico's *Rerum venetarum,* published in 1487, was commissioned by the Venetian government, and was more popular than Giustiniani's (Fortini Brown, *Venice and Antiquity*, pp. 163-164), but it points to the same model of civic government, not to Roman empire. Even though Venetian conquests are celebrated, its superiority to Rome is declared against Roman-style imperialism, witnessed by Venetian "sanità di leggi, di equità di giustizia and di bontà" (Sabellico, *Le istorie vinitiane*, p. 3r).

them their name "Eneti." He confirms this account by citing other authors of the same opinion (Marcus Cato, Cornelius Nepos, Quintus Curtius). He then returns to the Gallican foundation of Venice. In similar fashion, he supports this version by various other authorities (Gaius Julius Caesar, Diodorus Siculus and others). The next phase is important, for he argues that in each case the original settlers were of the most ancient origin, which at least establishes the essential tie to antiquity and so authority. Further, since both accounts have been accepted by worthy authors, he sees no reason to dispute one or the other but opts for a reconciliation of the diverse legends. But, for all that, the contours of the early settlement remain quite vague.

After this rough sketch of the probable origins of Venice, he turns to the St. Mark legend and constructs a more specific identity for Venice. He uses the Catholic legend in order to make an overt comparison with, or rather repudiation of, the Roman Empire. The difference between the two cities, he says, stems from God's omnipotence and his condemnation of all that aspires to immortality to mortality instead. In this way, the rise of Roman imperium was naturally followed by its destruction by barbarous nations, which had plundered Italy for almost 400 years. Venetians, on the other hand, "excellent for piety and religion," chased out of their homeland or having suffered long ordeals, preferred to stay with their wives and children. And then, mentioning both the relics of St. Mark, which have acted as an augury to the city, and also the prolonged time and great labour with which the Venetians built their city, he explains their stable, harmonious and free state. The contrast Giustiniani makes here has little to do with the myth of St. Mark. Rather, Marcian protection is a mere signal of truths that a historical comparison with the fall of the Roman empire and the enduring Venetian peace will prove. He uses history to make evident that violent beginnings will have violent ends, and that, therefore, the slow, organic model of Venice is to be preferred for its more durable, and so more perfect nature. Divine protection is shown in the result. Of course, this ushers in another phase in Venetian myth-making which will depend on the deictic figuring of contemporary reality so as to assert Venetian supremacy as a model state: the Myth of Venice.

★   ★   ★

Gasparo Contarini was to write the contemporary history *par excellence* through which the Republic of Venice would shine as the epitome of justice, unity, and most of all stability, and here the Myth of Venice enjoyed its fullest expression. His *De magistratibus et republica Venetorum,* written in 1531, shows this enviable perfection issuing forth from the balanced organization of the state readily visible in its mixed government, which incorporated three systems of rule. The doge represents monarchical power, the patriciate through the Senate oligarchical power, and the *popolo*, in the *Maggior Consiglio*, the democratic voice. It is, in a nutshell, an argument for superlative civic dynamics as the natural outcome of equality in the institutions of power, and the reality of sixteenth-century Venice was proclaimed to verify this.[23] Together with this discussion of contemporary political structures, however, Contarini, like Giustiniani before him, does not overlook the legendary tales but refers to the ancient past in a way that suits his purpose. This entails taking a measured step away from the legend in its unverifiable form, while maintaining the connection, in vaguer terms, by means of artfully creating credibility in a circuitously construed logic.

As for the originary myths themselves, Contarini makes swift mention of only the Attila phase. He thus bypasses the whole problem of the identification of the early settlers, Trojan or otherwise. This is evidence of a new circumspection introduced by a newly stringent methodology. The political theorist now should derive the elements of this historical narrative from some sort of proof, for example, in artifacts or a lack thereof. Proof now surpasses probability, and hence detail-laden tales about ancient history are no longer acceptable. Consequently, establishing ties to Troy is simply not possible. He manages, nevertheless, to make some suggestions about ancestry, which he does, ingeniously, by proceeding on the basis of the very absence of artifacts. We see this, for example, when he makes a claim for nobility by indicating that "the nobility of the Venetians is linked to their ancestors for their consenting desire to establish, honour and amplify their country, without having the least regard of their own private glory or commodity."[24] The absence of monuments celebrating Venetian heroes of the past substantiates their own absence of ambition and so gives the historical background to the noble humility of sixteenth-century Venetians and their consequent values of wisdom and honesty.[25] This is one of a very few comments he makes about their ancestry. Yet it is significant that in all cases they remain an anonymous community. Like Marco's group of Trojan settlers, Contarini's founders also serve to shape an anti-single-founder myth. Pluralism in ancient organization

---

[23]Given the concentration of power in the patriciate, as Paul Grendler has demonstrated, the notion that power was equally and effectively shared in Venetian government, as its political theorists suggested, is doubtful. In this light, Contarini's historiographical method would seem more reliant on the idea of proof, rather than proof itself, so that myth-creation is shown to have become newly dependent on only the suggestion of proximity, that is veracity. Grendler, "The Leaders of the Venetian State," pp. 35–85.

[24]English translations of Contarini are taken from Contarini, *The Commonwealth and Government of Venice*, p. 15.

[25]Contarini, *The Commonwealth and Government of Venice*, pp. 6, 17.

is similarly implied as crowning the modern mixed government with ancient authority. Thus pluralism is evinced first by the absence of monuments indicative of the native humility and principles of equality among the group and as a causal force in creating the present esteem for honesty and wisdom. It is likewise implied as an early structural trait by the communal nature of the founding group, which finds its echo in the felicitous three-layered system of government in the Republic.

Values of harmony and liberty are likewise positioned in age-old traditions. Contarini indicates that the contemporary mixed government of Venice, and the city's objectives for peace, had roots in the early institutions of Venice, since these ordered the whole life and exercise of the citizens to virtue and the maintenance of civil concord. These civic accomplishments are proved by what they have left to posterity, namely, a cohesive and strong society. The survival of the attack from the League of Cambrai provided evidence of the reality of this in that good laws led to the unity necessary for the ultimate defense of the Republic, and therefore its longevity. The League, formed in December 1508, comprising the forces of Pope Julius II, Emperor Maximilian I, Louis XII of France, and Ferdinand of Aragon, could not have been a more formidable aggressor. Though they did wrest some recent land acquisitions from Venice in 1509, the fact that they were not able to defeat Venice itself was taken to be tantamount to a demonstration of Venetian unity, a result of the city's perfect government.

Since Venice had, in fact, maintained its independence as a result of the incredibly unified and determined defense by urban and peasant forces on the mainland, the city was still able to assert good government as cause of its eternal freedom.[26] Furthermore, and perhaps of more explicit contrast with the League, Venetian values of good government, such as harmony, virtue, and liberty, are favourably compared to imperialist and universalist goals, like the glories of war, à la Rome in antiquity. The chief point for Contarini in this case is that Venetian greatness has no need to reach so far back in time, especially to uncertain, unverifiable myths, in order to establish itself. Venice's greatness was established, visible, well known and, as he argues, to be found in the city's perfect government. He does not hesitate to underline this idea. He says: "the order of its citizens—the true reason, form and matter of

---

[26]On the League, see Chambers, *The Imperial Age of Venice,* pp. 61ff. Gilbert, "Venice in the Crisis of the League of Cambrai," pp. 274–292, indicates that the crisis of the League itself was felt to be due to the moral corruption of the Venetians and thus necessitated a renewed association with their distinguished ancestry. Logan, *Culture and Society,* pp. 4–5, points to Venice's survival of the League's onslaught as stimulating Venice to vaunt the enduring nature of its liberty.

commonwealths—is where [Venice] seems to shine and surpass states of all time . . . for it is apparent many states have exceeded Venice in greatness of Empire and state, military discipline and glory yet none can compare with her institutions and laws, prudently decreed to establish a happy and prosperous felicity."[27]

Such well being is also the responsibility of the state to preserve. In this endeavour the view of military involvement goes beyond the neutral casting. While force must be part of the Republic's composition, aggression and war can prove to be pernicious to felicity because of the damage they do to the nature of the citizenry.[28] In this vein he expressly praises Venice for having a mercenary army and so themselves not fighting, as fighting would alter the citizenry's peaceful and freedom-loving spirit upon which the city is founded—here in explicit contrast to Rome, "instituta ad bellum." An inherently non-violent people, reminiscent of the peaceful Trojan settlers of Marco, continues to be valued in the Renaissance, and the same anti-Roman theme is constituted yet again as an anti-imperialist one. An organic conception of the state unfolds that considers the peace-minded spirit of the city-dwellers to be the primary factor in creating and preserving the Republic's success. The politics must be directed so as to mold the public spirit in a form most conducive to peace and harmony. Within the city, just laws and a balanced order of power foster relationships of equality, whereas beyond its shores, exclusion from the practice of war prevents violent natures from contaminating the spirit of equality with the warring spirit of domination. Local concerns, in antithesis to imperialist prerogatives, continue to be privileged throughout, as the work then dissects the divisions of power in the Venetian government and celebrates their objectives of promoting and inspiring virtue and nobility in their citizenry.

III

If the invocation of Trojan lineage was an anti-imperialist, anti-Roman myth in the Middle Ages, and if through the course of the Renaissance other renditions of this theme occurred through the invocation of St. Mark, through the indication of the ideal, local myth in the political order of the city, what is the connection to the actual empire building of the *Serenissima*? It is significant that Venice began its maritime power in the eleventh century as a defensive force that would protect trading routes in the Adriatic. And its exemptions in Romania were granted already in 1082 by the Golden

---

[27]Contarini, *The Commonwealth and Government of Venice,* p. 5.
[28]Gaeta, "L'idea di Venezia," pp. 639-640.

Bull for having assisted the Byzantine Empire against the Normans.[29] In any event, the Venetian relationship with its maritime colonies was mainly one of commercial exploitation, pursued through winning certain privileges. The business of trade, not universalizing aspiration, was at the forefront of Venice's early expansion into the East.[30] The city's role in the Fourth Crusade and its victory over Constantinople in 1204 intensified its trading ambitions in the East since, besides the looting, the Crusade was used to gain and protect important trading posts. Inland colonization too was essentially commercially motivated, as it was prompted by hostility toward the Venetian flow of merchandise through mainland routes (after 1380).[31] The fall of Constantinople to the Turks in 1453 signalled the erosion of Venice's maritime empire. When the French invaded Italy in 1494, the city's mainland dominion began to recede as well, and a few years later it was decisively, though temporarily, chopped back by the League of Cambrai in 1509. In short, two particular features distinguish the Venetian Empire: its period, waxing in the twelfth century and waning in the Renaissance, and its objectives, primarily its trading privileges rather than any universalizing goal.

I would argue that these features of the empire help to explain both the use and the discontinuance of the Trojan myth in the evolution of Venetian historiography. First of all, Venice did not need an imperialist myth in the Middle Ages because it already had an empire. Its sea fleets had made their naval power felt from the twelfth century on, and even more so after the Fourth Crusade in 1204. Secondly, despite the undeniable use of naval power in these conquests, the trajectory was largely a protectionist one so as to guarantee trading routes. Thus if privilege and protection were the objectives of Venetian expansion, an imperialist myth would have served badly since it would be in opposition to the method and goals of its maritime empire. Moreover, it is exactly because of the existence and configuration of its colonies that a Trojan myth claiming an inheritance of stability and liberty would have benefited Venice, since the city clearly did not need to build power as much as protect it and guarantee its continuation. Venice instead needed consensus at home and acceptance abroad so as to ensure the maintenance of commercial interests. Only with its sea and land empires both receding in the early 1500s did Venice at last need to protect itself. At that point the city turned the anti-imperialist myth of Trojan origins into

[29]Lane, *Venice*, p. 68. Romania included the Greek peninsula, the Aegean islands, and all the neighbouring land which had been a part of the Byzantine Empire.

[30]Lane, *Venice,* pp. 31–85.

[31]Chambers, *The Imperial Age of Venice,* p. 54.

an ennobling myth of just, virtuous, and wise ancestry in which to ground the political myth of her ideal, mixed, and most of all stable government.

The production of various myths at various times must indicate a connection to the changes in the realities the Republic was facing, so that at one time it favoured fabulous inventions of origins, while later, it favoured constructions more apparently informed by reason or legal structures. Several strong arguments, however, have been made that observe, in Venetian self-fashioning, a desire to picture the city as an empire-building nation. Though by no means neglecting the historiographic branch of identity production, these works are rooted in the visual representation of the city. Edward Muir made his signal contribution with a discussion of art and pageantry being used with a political function by the patriciate to justify expansion or reflect their own political interests.[32] In a compelling investigation of the Eastern influences in Venetian architecture during the Renaissance, Deborah Howard observes a Turkish fashioning of identity in architecture, together with an imperialist and specifically Roman identity.[33] Garry Wills too has made a strong case for imperialism in Venetian self-expression by looking at "history *through* art, the art *through* history," seeming to suggest art as a mirror to the actual, historical self-perception of the city.[34] Patricia Fortini Brown, in a veritable tour de force of Venice's relationship to the past, has used medals, illuminated manuscripts, costumes, frescoes, portraits, architecture and histories, to offer a multifaceted view of Venetian identity. She also finds evidence of imperialist designs in Venetian self-fashioning in the Renaissance from both Trojan and Roman sources.[35]

Surely the striking differences reflect certain self-conscious presentations of Venetian identity, so it appears that the pageantal, artistic, architectural, and historiographic productions exemplify the changing faces of Venice because they were each to fulfill different ideological objectives. If, as Muir explains,

---

[32]Muir, "Images of Power."

[33]Howard, *Venice and the East,* pp. xiv, 3.

[34]Wills, *Venice Lion City*, p. 20.

[35]In *Venice and Antiquity*, Fortini Brown's interpretation of Marco (p. 25) as an imperialist and her (qualified) attribution of the commission of the illuminated manuscript *Historia Troiana* to Andrea Dandolo (p. 41) are especially interesting. The first is suggested by the "prophecy, *ex post facto*" of the Fourth Crusade from the Emperor Constantine, who was to have predicted the destruction of Byzantium, making it, in Marco's view, a divinely sanctioned crusade. But as I argue, the fact or the acceptance of Venetian participation in the Fourth Crusade does not inspire imperialism already accomplished as much as protectionism, through defense, needing to be done. As for Dandolo, if he did commission the illuminated manuscript *Historia Troiana,* at any rate he gives the Trojan legend a bare mention in his own chronicle: it seems he personifies my thesis that the faces of Venetian self-image differed according to different means of expression.

pageantry was the language of the patrician class, and as Fortini Brown notes, art a private language and architecture a public one, we should read these not necessarily in dialogue with each other, but more explicitly in contrast. In this expressive mosaic, historiography seems to declare itself an international language. From the chronicles written in Latin or French because they were supposed to speak to all of Europe (da Canal is explicit about this) to the later histories and treatises, translated and widely distributed throughout the Continent, historical accounts of Venice have the particular privilege of reaching beyond its physical domain. Furthermore, the vocabularies of these languages are sufficiently different so as to direct particular articulations. Could realism in Venetian historiography insist on abandoning mythical beginnings in a way that realism in painting would not? Could a Roman heritage evoked in medals and portraiture reflect individual aspirations that civic histories could not allow? Could claims to empire in historical and political treatises, distributed throughout Europe, be taken seriously at a time when Venice was undeniably losing its own?

★   ★   ★

In the historiography of Venice, the Trojan foundation myth was valued for its connotations of nobility, liberty, and peace, and reached its peak in the Middle Ages. As Venice progressed in time, suffering with the rest of Italy the crises of independence, especially in the early 1500s, and as humanism erected more stringent criteria for historiographical accuracy, legendary tales could no longer effectively instill and heighten Venetian patriotism. The desire to account for one's origins persisted in Giustiniani, though he relegated the Trojan myth to the possible but unknowable. A generation later, Contarini treated the myth as irrelevant, while he maintained its values of liberty, peace, and plurality, transforming them in the myth of the enduring, free, and perfect government. Here, as Contarini indicates, demonstrable points of Venetian success reflected the greatness of these values in his own day, so that it was simply more pragmatic to underscore that Venice's model government fostered the principles of democracy, security, and liberty, impelling virtue in its citizenry, rather than to insist that these values were the heritage of the uncertain, if celebrated and exalted origin of Troy.

The Venetian use of the Trojan myth was different from the rest of Europe, since the city had modelled itself chiefly on its characteristic of liberty, whereas countries such as England and France, and perhaps others, used the Trojan myth to identify with their imperialist destinies, so as to affirm their own expansionist agendas as divinely ordained. The main difference in these two uses of the Trojan myth is the perspective of time. Countries who desired to increase their dominion had to initiate a new mandate and therefore were looking towards the future. For this, the myth of Troy was indispensable since the link with Trojan ancestors created a tradition of imperialism which gave credence to otherwise fledgling imperialist states. This interpretation of the Trojan myth would have been invented in order to galvanize a people towards action in the future, namely colonization. In an opposite vein, Venice actually articulated what had been occurring in history because basically the city aspired to maintain itself as it was. Thus the use of the Trojan myth in Venice looked to the present, asserting the mythical origin in order to project the city's continuation.

WORKS CITED

Arnaldi, Girolamo. "Andrea Dandolo doge-cronista." *La storiografia veneziana fino al secolo XVI: aspetti e problemi*. Ed. Antonio Pertusi. Florence: Olschki, 1970. 127–268.

Carile, Antonio. "Aspetti della cronachistica veneziana nei secoli xiii-xiv" and "Appendice." *La storiografia veneziana fino al secolo XVI: aspetti e problemi*. Ed. Agostino Pertusi. Florence: Olschki, 1970. 75–126.

Carile, Antonio. *Le origini di Venezia*. Ed. A. Carile and G. Fedalto. Bologna: Pàtron, 1978.

Carile, Antonio. "Una 'vita di Attila' a Venezia nel XV secolo." *Venezia e Ungheria nel Rinascimento*. Ed. Vittorio Branca. Florence: Olschki, 1973. 369–396.

Chambers, David. *The Imperial Age of Venice, 1380-1580*. New York: Harcourt Brace Jovanovich, 1970.

Contarini, Gasparo. *The Commonwealth and Government of Venice*. Trans. Lewes Lewkenor. London, 1599. New York: Da Capo, 1969.

da Canal, Martin. *Archivio Storico Italiano* 8 (1845): 338.

Dandolo, Andrea. "Chronica per extensum descripta." *Raccolta degli Storici Italiani dal Cinquecento al Millecinquecento*. Ed. Ester Pastorello. Vol. 12, Part 1. Bologna: Zanichelli, 1938. 1–327.

Fortini Brown, Patricia. *Venice and Antiquity: The Venetian Sense of the Past*. New Haven: Yale University Press, 1996.

Gaeta, Franco. "L'idea di Venezia." *Storia della cultura veneta. Dal primo Quattrocento al Concilio di Trento*. Ed. Girolamo Arnaldi and Manlio Pastore Stocchi. Series III, Vol. 3. Vicenza: Neri Pozza, 1982. 565–641.

Gilbert, Felix. "Venice in the Crisis of the League of Cambrai." *Renaissance Venice*. Ed. John Hale. London: Faber, 1973. 274–292.

Giustiniani, Bernardo. *De origine Venetiarum rebusque eius ab ipsa ad quadringentesimum usque annum gestis historia*. Venice, 1493.

Grendler, Paul. "The Leaders of the Venetian State, 1540–1609: A Prosopographical Analysis." *Studi Veneziani* 19 (1990): 35–85.

Hay, Denys. *Europe: The Emergence of an Idea*. Edinburgh: Edinburgh University Press, 1957.

Howard, Deborah. *Venice and the East: The Impact of the Islamic World on Venetian Architecture 1100–1500*. New Haven: Yale University Press, 2000.

Lane, Frederic C. *Venice: A Maritime Republic*. Baltimore: Johns Hopkins University Press, 1973.

Marco. *Codex Marco*. It. XI, 124. (6802). ff. 4v–7r. Rpt. in Antonio Carile. "Aspetti della cronachistica veneziana nei secoli xiii–xiv" and "Appendice." *La storiografia veneziana fino al secolo XVI: aspetti e problemi*. 75–126.

Muir, Edward. *Civic Ritual in Renaissance Venice*. Princeton: Princeton University Press, 1981.

Muir, Edward. "Images of Power, Art and Pageantry in Renaissance Venice." *American Historical Review* 84 (1979): 16–52.

Sabellico, Marcantonio. *Le istorie vinitiane*. Venice, 1544.

Virgil. *The Aeneid of Virgil*. Trans. Allen Mandelbaum. Berkeley and Los Angeles: University of California Press, 1971.

Wills, Garry. *Venice Lion City: The Religion of Empire*. New York: Simon and Schuster, 2001.

Yates, Frances A. *Astraea: The Imperial Theme in the Sixteenth Century*. London: Routledge, 1975.

Rhetoric,
Translatio Imperii,
and Trojan Legacy

Smiting High Culture in the "Fondement": The Seege of Troye *as Medieval Burlesque*

PAMELA LUFF TROYER

Three of the four extant manuscripts of the fourteenth-century Middle English romance known as *The Seege or Batayle of Troye* include a number of peculiar adaptations of events leading up to the destruction of the ancient city. One of the most eccentric re-tellings of scenes from the larger Trojan story is the judgment of Paris, in which Paris, asleep under a tree after having been separated from his hunting companions, is awakened by "ffoure ladies of eluene land"[1] preposterously named Jubiter, Saturnus, Mercurius, and Venus. The mysterious ladies request that Alisaunder Parys decide which of them should be awarded a golden orb inscribed with the incendiary phrase "Þe faireste wommon of al / Schal haue + welde þis riche bal" (ll. 519–520). It is no surprise that Paris chooses Venus, but, contrary to the traditional outcome of the judgment, Parys' initial reward is not the acquisition of the most beautiful woman in the world but instead the privilege of leading Priam's navy in an attack against the Greeks. Helen is a secondary prize.

The judgment is not the only quirky scene in this metrical romance. Looking across the narrative we find many oddities, such as Achilles stabbing Hector in the buttocks as the latter leans over to pick up a shiny helmet, and Paris and his henchmen slaying Achilles by slashing at the soles of his feet. Close enough to other versions of the Trojan myth but different enough so that they attract attention, these scenes suggest that the *Seege* composer did not simply err in his redaction, but consciously tinkered with parts of the tale to create a narrative that suited his particular audiences. Essentially he compressed much of the story in order to foreground certain handpicked events from the matter available to him, so as to demonstrate in facetious, comic terms that the Trojans were agents of their own downfall. The episodes taking pride of place in his narrative are the judgment of Paris, the deaths of Hector and Achilles, the betrayal of the Trojans by Aeneas and Antenor, and

---

[1] *The Seege or Batayle of Troye,* ed. Barnicle, line 508. Subsequent citations of *The Seege* refer to Barnicle's edition of Lincoln's Inn 150 unless noted otherwise.

the two accounts of childhood: Hecuba's dream of Paris' role in the destruction of Troy, which moves her to send him to live with shepherds, and Thetis' fear that Achilles will die in war, which inspires her to have him masquerade as a girl in a foreign court. While all of these events are understood now to be part of the traditional matter of Troy, they do not appear together, nor are they presented in the same way, in any of the extant manuscripts considered to be sources for the *Seege*.

The Seege or Batayle of Troye exists in four manuscripts, each comprising more than 2,000 lines of rhymed couplets. Lincoln's Inn 150, Egerton 2862, and Arundel XXII were transcribed in the late fourteenth century. A fourth, Harley 525, was transcribed in the first half of the fifteenth century. In the Harley manuscript most of the anomalous incidents present in the older versions were brought into closer alignment with traditional knowledge of the story. For instance, the goddesses are presented as Juno, Pallas, and Venus; and Achilles is merely slain by Paris, not stabbed in the soles of his feet by Paris and twenty men. When Mary Barnicle set out to prepare *The Seege of Troye* for publication, the Early English Text Society intended for her to edit only Harley 525 because it was judged to be the more "accurate." But after examining the manuscripts, she felt that Harley did not adequately reflect the story the composer had invented. Accordingly she presented all four texts in her 1927 edition, leaving questions of accuracy to the reader.[2]

Over the last century, scholars have had a variety of reactions to the idiosyncrasies of the *Seege* story, especially the Celtic flavor of the judgment of Paris as it is presented in the three early manuscripts. Until recently, discussion of the *Seege* has been focused on determining the composer's sources. Barnicle carefully recorded correspondences between the *Seege* and several classical and medieval iterations of the Troy myth: Ovid's *Heroides,* Virgil's *Aeneid,* the works of Statius and Hyginius, Dares' *De Excidio Troiae Historia,* Dictys' *Ephemeridos de Historia Belli Troiani,* Benoit de Sainte-Maure's *Roman de Troie,* Konrad von Wurzburg's Middle High German *Der Trojanishe Krieg,* the Old Bulgarian *Trojanska Prica,* the Old Norse *Trójumanna Saga,* and the Irish *Togail Troí.*[3] In the first lines of the poem, the author himself claims Dares as his source, but he includes scenes not to be found in *De Excidio Troiae Historia.* Barnicle even considered the hypothesis of the existence of a lost *Roman de Troie,* but decided that in the case of the *Seege* the theory of "universal servile copying" had been pushed too far and that the *Seege* was an invention, not a facsimile:

---

[2]Barnicle, *The Seege,* Preface.
[3]Barnicle, *The Seege,* pp. lvi. ff. Brent Miles discusses *Togail Troí* above, 81–96.

> It is well to allow to literary men a little latitude in the handling of traditional material and not to postulate a hypothetical, contracted source whenever the dérivé omits a detail, and a hypothetical expanded source whenever the dérivé refurbishes the shabby skirt of tradition with a new ruffle. lxxiv

Nevertheless, contradicting her own willingness to allow a composer latitude in adding "a new ruffle," Barnicle attributes the unusually named goddesses to "ignorance on the part of the redactor,"[4] instead of entertaining the possibility that the author intentionally altered the "shabby skirt" for comic effect.

Barnicle's recommendation against the pursuit of an expanded *Roman de Troie* did not discourage her contemporary, E. Bagby Atwood, from his quest to find an ultimate source for the *Seege*. Intrigued by the close similarities among four medieval-European vernacular versions of the Troy legend,[5] Atwood hypothesized the existence of an ur-text. His efforts were rewarded by his discovery of MS Rawlinson D893, which he edited as the *Excidium Troie* (*ET*). In his introduction he postulated that the *ET* was ultimately traceable to a now-lost classical Latin chronicle adapted over time into a late-medieval Latin textbook.[6] However, despite the close and sustained correspondences between *ET* and the *Seege*, neither *ET* nor the three other cognate vernacular texts include scenes such as the four female elves with odd names or Hector's fatal fixation on the sparkly helmet. After considering likely source material for the *Seege* poet's eccentric account of the judgment and finding none available, Atwood concluded that "the author of the *Seege* had read a fuller version of the tale probably based on the *Excidium* or partly on it, in which occur a great many dramatic speeches, especially those of the three (four) [*sic*] goddesses."[7] In the end he was driven to imagining that there might have been yet another expanded source.

Later scholars have dismissed the *Seege* as the work of a careless provincial minstrel, or at least one who did not have access to detailed versions of the Trojan legend. Derek Pearsall categorized the *Seege* as belonging to a stage in the development of the romance that was "like a backwash from the first surge of romance-writing, third-rate fumbling in an enfeebled tradition when the new points of growth are elsewhere."[8] Pearsall also noted that the Harley scribe, in his later manuscript, corrected what Pearsall described as "the gross errors of the text"[9] present in Lincoln's Inn, Egerton, and Arundel. With an

---

[4]Barnicle, *The Seege*, pp. lxviii–lxix, n6.

[5]The *Seege, Der Trojanische Krieg, Trójumanna Saga,* and *Trojanska Prica.*

[6]Atwood, "The Rawlinson *Excidium Troie*," pp. 389–390.

[7]Atwood, "The Judgment of Paris," p. 353.

[8]Pearsall, *Middle English Romance*, p. 104.

[9]Pearsall, *Middle English Romance*, p. 93.

equally dismissive tone, C. David Benson concluded that while "the *Seege or Batayle* might be entertainment for the common folk, its crude, unlearned approach disqualified it from claiming the attention of any serious audience."[10]

Instead of scoffing at "the gross errors of the text," I would explain them as instances of the Bakhtinian transformation of official culture into the carnivalesque. They are a conscious burlesque of the characters of the Trojan drama—an unusually irreverent and base treatment of a noble tragedy by a minstrel comedian. In the carnival of the *Seege,* dignity is supplanted by narcissism, and combat is presented as a series of pratfalls. Further, we can look to Aron Gurevich who, finding Bakhtin's binary of *carnival-popular* v. *ecclesiastical-serious* oversimplified, redefines our under-standing of the phenomenon in which popular culture co-opts high culture:

> Carnival is a distinctive correlate of the serious culture present in it: it penetrates its substance and "lowers it" for a short while, but not essentially. This "lowering" assumes neither denial nor disregard, but a temporary overcoming of it through an inclusive inversion. The semantics of carnival are not external and extraneous with respect to official culture; rather, to a great degree they draw their elements from it.[11]

Although Gurevich formulated his theories of interdependence between high and low culture by examining ecclesiastical texts specifically, we know that official culture comprises more than religious writings. Venerated histories—"serious" histories—are another legitimated form of educated culture. A great potential for humor can be found in a "lowering" of the great saga of Troy "for a short while, but not essentially." And this is what I think the *Seege* accomplishes by presenting the members of an ancient royal family as comically dim-witted, selfish, and greedy—in other words, portraying them ironically as stereotypes of characters with low-culture status.

In this way the *Seege* composer stands in opposition to writers of medieval history such as Guido delle Colonne who, in his *Historia Destructionis Troiae,* freely rebukes his characters for their unconscionable behavior.[12] Guido plays the moralizing narrator, inserting his own didactic commentary as if he were a disappointed parent.[13] Conversely, the *Seege* composer does not convey a cautionary tale but rather laughs at his own characters' faults. He has produced

---

[10]Benson, *History of Troy,* p. 134.

[11]Gurevich, *Medieval Popular Culture,* p. 180.

[12]The *Historia* was widely available in the fourteenth century.

[13]Guido frequently digresses in order to pass judgment on his characters. In Book Three, for instance, he scathingly rebukes Jason for his poor treatment of Medea, asking rhetorically, "What lack of shame made you dare to mock the bond of your oath so that you, defiled by the disgrace of ingratitude, might deceive a credulous young girl?" (*Historia,* p. 23).

an entertaining oral performance, not a didactic written history.[14] Andrew Taylor reminds us that while the minstrel figure can be exalted as "the guarantor of cultural continuity and of authenticity," medieval poets and manuscript illuminators often portray him as a "chaotic figure," one who is a "source of corruption: corruption of morals through low song and dirty jokes, corruption of truth through rumour-mongering and flattering, corruption of text through oral transmission."[15] I would add that the minstrel was in part a creation of his audience and its conceptions of entertainment. What the Seege suggests about its composer is that he wrote for an audience that enjoyed a good laugh at the expense of that which was supposedly not corrupt: idealized conceptions of Christian morality, the self-serious narcissism of the nobility, and the textual transmissions of histories held in high regard by the educated elite. The Lincoln Inn's *Seege* is in fact less akin to the histories of Troy from which it gets its material than to farces such as the *Tournament of Tottenham*, wherein two suitors armed with kitchen utensils "joust" for the miller's daughter.[16]

A READING OF THE *SEEGE*

In all four extant manuscripts of the *Seege of Troye*, the story is divided into ten battles preceded by an introduction and completed by a brief conclusion. The battles repeat several motifs: an insult answered by a call to arms, an assault on fearful townspeople, a clash between noble warriors, thrashing of swords, burial of the dead. Six odd episodes protrude from the relatively even and predictable narrative surface of the *Seege*, corresponding to classical sources but exhibiting striking differences. These scenes are strewn seemingly randomly across the tapestry of the narrative. The judgment of Paris occurs in the midst of the section reserved for the third battle, Hector meets his end as part of the seventh battle, and Paris ambushes Achilles in the ninth. Aeneas and Antenor's escapades form a major portion of the climax, which appears after the last of the ten demarcated battles, and their defection nearly concludes the tale. These four episodes, combined with two digressions about portents of doom and the childhoods of Paris and Achilles, conduct the current of the composer's humorous presentation of royal inefficacy.

Taking the four scenes in the order of their appearance in the narrative, we begin the discussion with the fateful beauty contest, which is crucial to

---

[14]The text of the *Seege* has significant indications of oral performance. See Bradbury, *Writing Aloud,* ch. 3, and McGillivray, *Memorization.* Moreover, because of its odd size (13 x 30 cm) and its inclusion of romances and *Piers Plowman*, Barnicle believed the Lincoln's Inn manuscript to be a minstrel book.

[15]Taylor, *Textual Situations*, pp. 71, 72.

[16]Sands, *Middle English Verse Romances,* pp. 313–322.

the narrative because Paris' decision there is the tale's central motivation. Even though in most versions it is clear that Paris decides the contest on the basis of truth—he truly believes Venus to be the most beautiful—he is still manipulated by the gods, a feature that the composer exploited for its comic potential. In the pagan world of Troy, divinity itself authorizes moral disaster, so that even Paris, a supposed wise man, is reduced by his goddesses to a laughingstock.

In the Lincoln's Inn *Seege of Troye,* Alisaunder Parys enters the story in earnest as Priam is preparing his navy to rescue Usine from the Greeks. Priam has chosen Hector to lead the mission, but Paris wants the position. In order to convince Priam to let him command the expedition, Paris tells his father of a mysterious incident from his youth, one that should persuade Priam that Paris is the man for the job. "Herkeneþ, fadir, to my spelle," he begins, "And of a wounder y shal þe telle" (ll. 483–484). Once, Paris says, while on a hunting party with his friends, a mist rose up, separating him from his companions. Exhausted from searching for them, he fell asleep beneath a tree. While he slept, a curious group of "ffour elven ladies" entered the glade and found there a golden ball with an engraving: "Þe fairesst wommon of al / Schal have + welde þis riche bal" (ll. 519–520). During their argument over the ball, the names of the four so-called "susteris" (l. 534) are revealed to be Saturnus, Jubiter, Mercurius, and Venus. Venus is the first to spy the slumbering "knyȝt," suggest he settle the dispute, and awaken him.

Presumably sensing his father's incredulity, Paris pauses to assert his veracity: "'ffadir,' saide Paris, 'þus hit was'" (l. 539). He proceeds to explain that each sister offered him a bribe. Saturnus tempted him with being the "rycheste man / þat lyueþ under god alone" (ll. 555–556), but Paris, presumably accutely aware of his father's interest in the reply, claimed that he had all he needed: "And y þouȝte ich was riche ynouȝ þo / What schold y wiþ more richesse do?" (ll. 563–564). Mercurius offers "streynþe and myȝt" (l. 567), and once again Paris rejects the gift: "Me þouȝte y was strong ynouȝ þo. / What schold y wiþ more streynþe do?" (l. 577–578). Jubiter claims she will make Parys the fairest; not unexpectedly, the youth is already convinced he could do with no more beauty. Finally Venus claims she can bring Paris the love of "alle folk" and "alle wymmen þat þe seon wiþ syȝt / schole þe love wiþ al heore myȝt" (ll. 592–594).

Of course the choice is predetermined by the powerful tradition of the Trojan war story—Paris must choose Venus. But note that in the Lincoln's Inn version she has not yet offered him the most beautiful woman in the world for his wife. Before she offers that reward she demonstrates her gratitude by telling Paris he should ask his father to allow him to lead the ships to Greece, where he will also find the fairest lady to be his wife. Priam accepts the incident as a sign and places Paris in charge of the troops; thus, in early extant texts of the *Seege*, Helen and her abduction is a romantic afterthought, an addendum to Paris' manipulation of Priam. Troy will burn because Priam has fallen for his son's tale.

I read Paris' account of the incongruous forest episode as a consciously contrived comic interlude by a composer who is fully aware of the traditional story line. He has after all claimed Dares as his source, and while he may cite Dares only to legitimize his own work, he has included many details common to *De Exidio Troiae Historia* in which Dares writes of three goddesses named Juno, Pallas Athena, and Venus. Earlier in the *Seege* itself, Jupiter is referred to as "þe false god, sire Jubiter" (l. 326), not "goddess" or "dame," and while it is true that in classical sources of the tale, Saturn, Mercury, and Jupiter all play important roles, it still seems unlikely that the composer would have understood them to participate in the pageant. And finally it does not appear as if the minstrel intended the audience to think of them as transvestites. He uniformly refers to them as "susteres" (l. 534), "wymmen" (l. 541), and "ladyes" (ll. E 538, A 541); and two of the three manuscripts use the third-person feminine pronoun of their dialect.[17]

I explain the use of Saturnus, Jubiter, and Mercurius, assigned as they are to female elves, as a way of comically enhancing a pivotal moment in the narrative. By giving the elven ladies the names of male gods, the composer makes them absurd; they are ridiculous figures of ambiguous gender identity, and offer worthless goods. It is probable that audiences for the early versions of the *Seege* were perfectly aware of the traditional version of the story; they may have thought it hilarious that Paris would be intercepted by, and made a pawn of four female elves, three of whom had men's names. Further, medieval rural audiences may have found it amusing, to use a modern analogy, to imagine an immature and sycophantic Paris begging for the keys to his daddy's ships. In that case we could consider the judgment episode as comic relief, inserted to vary the pattern of martial activity: preparation for battle, battle, preparation for battle, battle, and so on.

In fact we might even consider that the *Seege* composer purposefully adapted the episode to recapitulate in an ironic vein a set of Christian

---

[17]Lincoln's Inn 150 uses a West Midland dialectical "heo": "Saturnus þeo eldest þeo bal vp tok / And on þeo letters gon heo loke" (ll. 521–522). Arundel shows signs of East Midland dialect by using "she": "Saturnus sone þat ball gun loke / And anon she vp hit tok" (ll. 521–522). However, the cognate line of the Egerton manuscript employs "he": "Saturnus þe eldest . . . on þe letter gan he lok" (ll. 521–522). Egerton may show that, by pronominalizing Saturnus as "he," the scribe was aware that the *Seege* talked about the name of a god when the traditional story required a goddess, but it could also be that the scribe became confused by copying a manuscript that used "heo."

morality tales, with Paris cast as the spiritual loser. I suggest it may be a mock philosophical digression rehearsing the temptations that Christian men must face and reject in order to achieve moral character. In fact, the questions the elven ladies ask are essentially Boethian ones. Which is better, the story asks: wealth, prestige, power, or love of all men (fame)? As Lady Philosophy proves in her argument to the imprisoned Boethius, none of these is best. Only through the love of God and the commensurate rejection of earthly rewards can come the greatest individual happiness and thus the greatest communal good. The punchline of the gag in *The Seege* is that none of the elven sisters offers Paris this gift; no bribe will redeem him in Christian terms. The *Seege* composer deftly establishes Paris as an unenlightened Boethius, one who is not blessed with the intervention of Lady Philosophy and who can choose only among four equally-bankrupt options. The dramatic irony is that Paris can make only a bad choice and ultimately will choose the worst of the bad choices, with consequences for his entire kingdom. By drawing out the litany of the four questions, the composer provides space for Paris to make a mockery of himself.

Remember that Paris encounters the elven sisters because he falls asleep under a tree. The ladies awaken him, but the suggestion of his *al fresca* slumber calls to mind the convention of the dream vision, of which *The Consolation* is a prototype—Lady Philosophy appears to Boethius in his tormented sleep. Instead of being a physical *state*, dreaming is often presented in medieval literature as a *place* into which the dreamer enters and in which any dream may confront him or her. In *Sir Orfeo*, for example, Heurodis falls asleep under an "ympe-tre" and has a terrifying dream of an encounter with the King of the Fairies, who claims that she must come live with him.[18] Upon waking, she and Orfeo venture to meet the King according to the demands the King has made *in Heurodis' dream*. Despite their "wakefulness," Heurodis is snatched away to a dream/fairy world. In other words, that which happened in a dream had consequences in conscious reality.[19] The *Seege* is analogous to *Sir Orfeo*[20]

---

[18]Dunn and Byrnes, *Middle English Literature*, pp. 216–230.

[19]This formula appears in Chaucer in, for instance, *The Book of the Duchess* and *The House of Fame*, where narrators fall asleep and are "met" by dreams: "y fil aslepe, and therwith even / Me mette so ynly swete a sweven" (*Book of the Duchess*, p. 333, ll. 275–276).

[20]Sir Orfeo's maternal grandfather is King Juno. This use of a goddess' name for a masculine figure could lead us to believe that medieval audiences from the geographical area in which the poem was produced had expected gender identity to be topsy-turvy in magical kingdoms. The extant manuscript of *Sir Orfeo* is dated to the same period as the composition of *The Seege* and is copied in the East Midland dialect prevalent in both the Egerton and Arundel versions; this evidence could reinforce my argument that the

in that its poet explores the potential of the liminal space beween conscious reality and the dream world, doing so in order to delight his audience with an unexpected adaptation of the goddesses and their questions, to make fun of Priam's gullibility, and to allude to Paris' failure in terms of a standard test of Christian morality.

My reading of the judgment of Paris as it appears in *The Seege or Batayle of Troye* is reinforced and supported by later events in the text. Another of the composer's surprising and idiosyncratic adaptations of the Trojan story is the final battle between Hector and Achilles during which an exhausted and demoralized Hector makes the sudden and shocking decision to run away. He mounts his horse, flees from the battlefield, and has the possibility of escape but for one impediment: lying directly in his path is a sparkling helmet "al by-set wiþ preciouse stones" (l. 1490). The sight of the glittering object so distracts Hector that he forgets his flight, brings his horse to an abrupt halt, and leans over to gain a closer view. This unfortunate position provides the fast-advancing Achilles with the opportunity of a lifetime. Achilles aims his spear and smites Hector, lethally, "yn at the fondement" (l. 1500).

We can find the basic elements of this version of the story in other Troy narratives—for instance, in Guido's translation of Benoit, Hector injures Achilles in the groin (168). Returning to the battlefield after attending to the wound, Achilles sees that Hector has slung his shield over his shoulder in order to drag a Greek victim from his companions. Seizing the opportunity for revenge, he spears Hector in the abdomen. The mention of groin and abdomen could put the composer in mind of the "fondement," but the *Seege* version is clearly something new. Dares' account claims that Achilles attacks Hector when he sees him stripping the rich armor from another Greek soldier. Dictys' account varies entirely by stating that Hector is killed in an ambush as his greeting party goes to meet Penthesilea, queen of the Amazons (3.15). Whatever the sources, it seems likely that the *Seege* composer and a succeeding generation of minstrels intentionally misunderstood the detail of Hector's demise in order to provoke their audiences to laughter, not deep thought.

The death of the hero of the Greeks is similarly inglorious. Although versions of the death of Achilles going back to the *Iliad* prescribe that Paris will murder Achilles at the temple where Achilles meets Poluxene, the *Seege* treats this murder in a unique way, emphasizing the Trojan royal family's lack of integrity. In the *Seege*, Achilles' proposal of marriage to Priam's daughter is rejected by Priam himself because he refuses to give her to the enemy. But Priam's wife (she is never named as Hecuba in the *Seege*) considers it a good idea to trade their daughter for "perpetuel pes" (l. 1564), a ruse for which

---

Seege poet did not simply err in naming his goddesses for gods but did so for effect.

Priam eventually falls. Then she and Paris set about plotting Achilles' death. Luring him to the temple under false pretenses, Paris ambushes him with a complement of a hundred "men of armes of gret renoun" (l. 1677).

But even with the combined brawn of a hundred henchmen, Alisaunder Parys cannot easily defeat the Greek with the enchanted iron-clad skin. Achilles slays eighty members of the retinue before Paris and the twenty remaining Trojans

> . . . putten Achilles doun to grounde
> And under his feet þey ʒaf him wounde
> Wiþ sweord and long knyf.
> Þus þey raften him his lyf. 1752–1755

Paris, already marked as comically inane because of his barely believable experience with the goddesses and his short-sighted behavior in the abduction of Elayne, defeats a worthy opponent by carving up his feet while twenty Trojans hold him down. A minstrel performing this scene for comic effect would have a great deal of material to work with: an enraged and duplicitous Trojan queen; a craven son who is goaded by his mother; and a great hero felled by wounds to his feet.

The three scenes described above communicate the parodic humiliation of the Trojan royals: Paris is the dupe of four elves of confused identity who offer bad advice; Hector gets a spear up the arse; and Achilles is slain through his feet in a plot created by Priam's cadging, vengeful wife and his foolish son. What more can happen to burlesque the Trojans? The ultimate scene of damnation comes at the tale's conclusion. Aged and demoralized, Priam admits to his reduced power and diminished vigor and calls his barons to finish the fight for him. At this crucial point in the battle, two important knights forsake their people:

> Þan onswerde a baroun, a faytour,
> Sir antynor, a foul traitour.[21]
> "Lord," he saide, "we schulen out gon
> And awreke ʒow of ʒoure foon."
> Þo wente Antynor ful good pas
> To anoþir traitour, Eneas.
> "Eneas," he saide, "what to rede?
> ʒef we gon to bataile, we arn dede;
> And ʒef we dwelle stille and defende þeo toun,
> ffor honger we schal falle adoun.

---

[21]The Egerton manuscript describes the treachery as "falseness": "Antwere goþ forþ with falsnesse / To anoþer Traytour þat hight Enyas" (E ll. 1878–1880).

> ffor-þy at nyȝt we wole wende out
> To þeo kyng of grece þat is stout
> And bidde him graunte lyme and lyf
> And saue ows boþe child and wyf
> And we wolen Troye to him ȝeilde.
> Better so is þen dye in feilde. 1872–1889

Portraying Aeneas and Antenor as utterly deficient of courage and knightly resolve, this passage makes clear that Troy will fall because of the weakness of its ruling class. Further impressing the audience with the magnitude of Trojan false heartedness, the *Seege* composer describes the duplicitous behavior of Antenor and Aeneas, who set about comforting and reassuring the very townspeople they are about to betray:

> Apon þe morwe þey wente vp and doun
> And comforteden þeo ost ouer al þe toun
> And beden þe folk wiþ al heore myȝt
> Kepe wel þe wardes þat ilke nyȝt. 1920–1923

Even more pathetic than deceiving the townspeople is the fact that the traitors cruelly dupe their own king, whom they deride as "stout" (with the Middle English meaning of *proud* and *haughty*). They bid Priam to make himself "mury wiþ-owte kare," promising to hold the city safe against the enemy; and after lulling him and the townspeople into a falsely secure sleep, the traitors sneak to the gates, open them for the Greeks, and flee with their families, never to be heard from again.

The *Seege* makes it clear that the cost is high for the salvation of Aeneas' and Antenor's families. Sisters and sons, mothers and fathers, children in their cradles, the Greeks slay every Trojan in their path until they have massacred "ten hundred þousand men and mo" (l. 1979). They hack into "peces small" Priam, the queen, and her maidens (l. 2012); no baron is spared for ransom. In light of the comedy present in other *Seege* episodes, we can recognize the intended hyperbole of this one: two melodramatic villains lull foolish townspeople to sleep, outwit a witless king, and leave the town in a state of exaggerated destruction.

The basic elements of the bloody climax of the *Seege* are not new. Medieval redactions include the deal Antenor and Aeneas make with the Greeks but describe it in various ways. Dictys of Crete provides a justification for Aeneas' defection: he can no longer bear Alexander's desecration of the gods' shrines. This explanation ultimately derives from Homer's *Iliad*, which characterizes Aeneas as showing marked piety toward the gods who help him. The *Iliad* also includes the prophecy that Aeneas' descendents will rule over the Trojans (20.307ff.), a detail which prescribes that, whatever the circumstances, Aeneas must escape the sack of Troy. Dictys does not condemn Aeneas and Antenor as traitors; they are simply the cleverest of the Trojan nobles, all of whom "plot sedition against the princes and Priam" (4.22), and the real blame lies with Helen. Of course we expect Dictys, whose sentiments lie with the Greeks, to view the traitors favorably since it is they who arrange for the Greeks to enter the city,[22] but it is surprising that Dares, speaking for the Trojans, also sympathizes with the men who sell out his city. Dares has it that Antenor and Aeneas argue calmly and sensibly in favor of a peace treaty and, while many other nobles and even the people prefer the peace plan as an alternative to certain annihilation, Priam doubts his advisors' loyalty and plots their deaths (1.37–38).

Guido condemns everyone equally. From the beginning of *Historia,* it is a foregone conclusion that Priam's initial act of war will lead to the destruction of Troy, a decision in which Priam, Antenor, and Aeneas are all involved. When Aeneas and Antenor suggest surrender to the Greeks, Priam reminds them that their false counsel was the impetus for the war, and it follows that Priam no longer trusts his chief advisors: "Now after the slaughter of all my sons and after so many losses and setbacks, you rise up brazenly in council to ask me to sue for peace to the Greeks, who have finally ruined me so wickedly and so cruelly?" (29.136–39). The peace plan is too little, too late for a people divided in purpose by an unjustifiable war and the toll it has taken. Aeneas and Antenor are not particularly singled out for approbation. Instead, Guido recites a proverb from the common people: "only young agreements are good, that is, those which are made in the beginnings, before the parties are wearied by losses, expenses, and hardships" (29.42–45).

In contrast to these other accounts known to have existed when the *Seege* was written, the *Seege* itself offers no explanation for Antenor and Aeneas' treachery, nor does it attempt to justify their decisions. By leaving the townspeople, the aged king, and the women and children of Priam's family to be massacred, Antenor and Aeneas have defiled all codes of moral and knightly conduct. This ending reinforces my point that the *Seege or Batayle of Troye* is a story of a group of people who are their own worst enemies. It is not hard to imagine that as a performing minstrel described Aeneas and Antenor skulking around in the night, lying to everyone with

---

[22]How Aeneas and Antenor allow the Greeks to invade the city varies from narrative to narrative. In Dictys the Greeks build a wooden horse so large that the Trojans must dismantle parts of the walls to let it through (5.9); there are no warriors in the belly, and the widened opening is unsecured. Dares reports that the two traitors merely unlock the gate (one decorated with a carving of a horse's head) and raise a torch as a signal (1.40). Guido has the Greeks offering a horse of bronze filled with warriors, for which parts of the walls must be demolished (30.80 ff.).

whom they came in contact, he would bond with the audience over the feeling they shared: the Trojans deserved it.

I conclude my argument by glancing at two more *Seege* episodes that stand out from the martial activity that marks the rhythm of the poem—the digressions about Achilles' and Paris' childhoods. Bradbury speculates that the *Seege* composer may have created some "errors" in order to "cultivate structural parallels," and provides an excellent description of how these two episodes demonstrate a medieval fascination with the "male-Cinderella" plot.[23] Building on her points, I claim that the composer meant to capitalize on the juxtaposition of these two events in order to reinforce the contrast between the moral fibre of Achilles on the one hand and the dissolution of Paris on the other, a man who is made of weaker, anti-heroic, in fact, antic, stuff. While Achilles' boyhood arms him with a warrior's strength (literally, as his skin is magically treated to become impenetrable, figuratively, as it demonstrates his natural inclination toward the rules of honorable conduct), Paris' early life is that of a spoiled son of a privileged family. Even though his mother outfits him in the garb of a swain, he encounters the goddesses only after becoming lost from his aristocratic hunting party.

Just as the *Seege* presents Paris' youthful encounter with the elven sisters in terms of fantastical pagan otherworldliness, it also presents Achilles' childhood[24] as influenced by magical happenings. Dame Tetis, his mother, practices "nygremancy" by dipping Achilles in the "water of helle" so that his skin becomes hard as flint (ll. 1344–1345). She does this in reaction to a warning she reads in "the firmament" that Achilles will be killed in battle. Through these embellishments it is probable that the composer gratified his audiences' fascination with the pagan occult. But they also suggest that Achilles and Paris are to be viewed as opposites. Traditionally, Hector, not Paris, is Achilles' adversarial equal, but since the *Seege* composer treats Hector with such ridicule, we can no longer consider him as a suitable opponent. Instead, the composer replaces Hector with Paris, which reinforces the burlesque tone of the piece and defines Paris as an ironic contrapositive to Achilles. Paris is not noble; he is a sneaky cheater. After all, what glory is to be found in spearing a man through the soles of his feet?

This reading of the *Seege* has at least two interesting ramifications. First, it treats ironically the widespread adoption of Geoffrey of Monmouth's genealogy tracing the British back to the vanquished but noble Trojans. The *Seege* presents a tribe who, because of dishonorable and witless behavior, is not the type of historical ancestor from which medieval English people

---

[23]Bradbury, *Writing Aloud*, pp. 120ff.

[24]See Atwood, "The Story of Achilles in the *Seege of Troye*."

would want to be descended. Second, the presentation of certain scenes in the *Seege* is surprising because it depicts the Trojan disaster as the responsibility of the comically inept and pathetically short-sighted members of the House of Laemadon, whereas classical and early medieval versions blame the destruction of Troy, in large part, on the cruel and capricious gods.

We must consider that the *Seege* was neither meant to justify the noble heritage of the English nor to explain the ways of gods to men; instead it is probable that it was part of the program of a traveling minstrel show and was meant to entertain its audience with the humor implicit in lowering grave events and self-serious characters to the level of farcical happenings among selfish fools. The *Seege* can be read as a facetiously unorthodox version of a history venerated by high culture that features a family of incompetent leaders who disregard one another's advice, make ignoble choices, and ultimately destroy their own world.[25]

WORKS CITED

Atwood, E. Bagby. "The Judgment of Paris in the *Seege of Troye*." *PMLA* 57 (1942): 343–353.

Atwood, E. Bagby. "The Rawlinson *Excidium Troie*: A Study of Source Problems in Mediaeval Troy Literature." *Speculum* 9 (1934): 379–404.

Atwood, E. Bagby. "The Story of Achilles in the *Seege of Troye*." *Studies in Philology* 39 (1942): 489–501.

Benson, C. David. *The History of Troy in Middle English Literature: Guido delle Colonne's* Historia Destructionis Troiae *in Medieval England*. Woodbridge: D. S. Brewer, 1980.

Bradbury, Nancy Mason. *Writing Aloud: Storytelling in Late Medieval England*. Urbana: University of Illinois Press, 1998.

Chaucer, Geoffrey. *The Riverside Chaucer*. Ed. Larry D. Benson. Boston: Houghton Mifflin, 1987.

Dunn, Charles W. and Edward T. Byrnes, eds. *Middle English Literature*. New York: Garland, 1990.

Frazer, R. M., Jr., ed. and trans. *The Trojan War: The Chronicles of Dictys of Crete and Dares the Phrygian*. Bloomington: Indiana University Press, 1966.

Guddat-Figge, Gisela. *Catalogue of Manuscripts Containing Middle English Romances*. Munich: Fink, 1976.

Guido delle Colonne. *Historia Destructionis Troiae*. Ed. and trans. Mary Elizabeth Meek. Bloomington: Indiana University Press, 1974.

Gurevich, Aron. *Medieval Popular Culture: Problems of Belief and Perception*. Trans. János M. Bak and Paul A. Hollingsworth. Cambridge: Cambridge University Press, 1988.

---

[25] I wish to thank Dr. Alexandra Hennessey Olsen for encouraging me in this project.

McGillivray, Murray. *Memorization in the Transmission of the Middle English Romances.* New York: Garland, 1990.

Pearsall, Derek. "The Development of Middle English Romance." *Mediaeval Studies* 27 (1965): 91–116.

Sands, Donald B., ed. *Middle English Verse Romances.* New York: Holt, Rinehart and Winston, 1966.

The Seege or Batayle of Troye. Ed. Mary Elizabeth Barnicle. Early English Text Society os 172. 1927. Rpt. London: Oxford University Press, 1954.

Taylor, Andrew. *Textual Situations: Three Medieval Manuscripts and Their Readers.* Philadelphia: University of Pennsylvania Press, 2002.

Imagining the Masculine:
Christine de Pizan's Hector, Prince of Troy

LORNA JANE ABRAY

From the beginning of her career as a writer (c. 1399) Christine de Pizan mined the tales of Troy for warnings to her own generation about the perils of war and masculine violence.[1] Convinced that the French nobility were descended from the Trojan prince Hector, Christine found in this ancient warrior inspiration for imagining the masculine in French aristocratic society. Hector serves as one of the focal points of her reflections on chivalry, the rearing of sons, good lordship, and eventually the gendering of governance. Hector appears in her texts sometimes as a self-destructive fool driven by greed and bravado, the type of son who would not listen, would not learn, would not mature, and would not survive. Elsewhere, Christine gives her audience a version of Hector more in keeping with the masculine ideal of fifteenth-century chivalry, portraying a darling destroyed by fate, but this Hector is still a flawed hero, whose death either paralyzed or lured to their destruction those who survived him. Even in the more laudatory texts, the doomed prince calls to mind the spectre of chivalry incompletely mastered. In Christine's view, ill-mastered chivalry means untempered masculinity, and evokes the threat of power in the hands of men whose physical maturation has not extracted them from a mire of childish and adolescent values. Such men's access to power threatened to exact a terrible price in her contemporaries' own lives: a kingdom-ruining holocaust comparable to the fiery destruction of their supposed ancestral home of Troy.[2] Hector to Christine was as often anti-hero as hero, as

---

[1]Christine has recently been given justice as a political writer who examines the public sphere. See for example Krynen, *Idéal du prince* and *L'empire du roi*; Quilligan, *Allegory of Female Authority*; Hindman, *Christine de Pizan's* "Epistre Othéa"; and Forhan, *The Political Theory of Christine de Pizan.*

[2]While my reading of these passages is concerned with public affairs, Christine's readers would readily have recognized a commentary on marital and sexual politics in her use of Hector, and a meditation on households at risk from untempered male strength, most notably in the passages dealing with Hecuba's grief and Hector's reluctance to trust

unworthy as worthy. His legend epitomized a politics quite contrary to her own, a politics that came wrapped in a dangerous glamour for the powerful men about her. Christine imagined Hector's story as a cautionary tale, deploying her imagined Hectors to break the hold of bravado on her male contemporaries' imagined masculine ideal.

Since Christine de Pizan usually enters discussions of gender as a speaker of myths and truths about women, and a defender of the female sex, it may seem strange to look to her for commentary on masculinity at the dawn of the French Renaissance. Our own generation knows her first, and still best, as the author of the *Book of the City of Ladies*, that extraordinary revamping of Boccaccio, refutation of the clerical misogynist tradition, and universal western history of women.[3] Christine's life can be summarized in ways that embed her in female and feminine contexts: widow, femme sole, single mother, first professional woman of letters, mother of a daughter; she retired into a community of women and, late in life, issued a swan song, a 1429 poem in praise of the—at that moment—victorious Joan of Arc.[4] In this feminine, even feminist version of Christine's life and oeuvre, however, we lose track of the men who mattered to her.[5] She was the loving, admiring daughter of a father who in her own account bulks larger in her life than does her mother.[6] She had two younger brothers. She was, by her own acknowledgment, the happy wife of a wonderful husband, whose death devastated her. As well as a daughter, she bore two sons, one of whom died young, the other of whom, Jean, grew up to marry and enter royal service, before he, like his father, abandoned his mother and wife by dying prematurely. As a widow, she felt herself cheated by opportunistic men who were feeding on her late husband's wealth, but she also forged productive and supportive alliances with other men, including Jean Gerson, her ally in

Andromache. For a comprehensive recent reading of Christine's works on sexual politics, see Brown-Grant, *Christine de Pizan and the Moral Defence of Women*.

   [3]Christine, *City of Ladies*. Particularly noteworthy among the commentaries is Quilligan, *Allegory of Female Authority*.

   [4]Christine, *Ditié de Jehanne d'Arc*. The standard biography is Willard, *Christine de Pizan*.

   [5]Willard, *Christine de Pizan*, provides ample evidence of the masculine worlds in which Christine flourished, but these perspectives have not always resonated for late twentieth-century historians and literary critics reading Christine. A somewhat anachronistic debate continues as to whether Christine was a feminist: see Brown-Grant, *Christine de Pizan and the Moral Defence of Women*, esp. p. 3 and Hindman, *Christine de Pizan's "Epistre Othéa,"* pp. xiii–xvii.

   [6]Christine, *Mutacion*, ll. 51–1029, *Christine's Vision*, pp. 108–128. Thomas de Pizan belongs exactly where King places him, in the ranks of fathers who encouraged their daughters' intellectual aspirations (*Women of the Renaissance*, pp. 184–185).

the quarrels of the *Roman de la Rose*. She shaped her public persona in masculine circles: the scriptorium where she worked with male intellectuals and craftsmen, the court where she mingled with noblemen; however important to her were other women's responses to her work, she also sought entrée for her texts in masculine places: the boys' schoolroom, the privy council chamber, the warriors' discussions of strategy and tactics, and those most private places of masculine self-appraisal, where a man measured himself against his culture's standards of manhood. Both real men and the attributes of manhood, good as well as bad, were constants in Christine's life as a writer. Her writings included approving references to men who ruled wisely in public or in the domestic realm.[7] In particular she wrote at length and with great admiration of the *Deeds and Good Customs of* [her late sovereign] *the Wise King Charles V*, whom she considered to be a model of true aristocratic masculinity. Given all this, it is perhaps less surprising to find her repeatedly brooding over the figure of one of the great male heroes of antiquity, Hector, prince of the royal house of Troy.

Troy mattered to Christine. She knew that her aristocratic audience cared about the Trojan Wars, and they would listen with fascination as the ancient tragic tales were reborn in modern guise in chivalric art and letters. Although she recommended the Trojan tales to her own teen-aged son, Jean, should he want to read about battles, she was, however, already beginning to develop an anti-Trojan stance by 1400/01.[8] Christine knew the matter of Troy particularly through a French-language compilation of historical information, the *Histoire ancienne jusqu'à César*, a new tool then just beginning its long Renaissance career.[9] Episodes from the Trojan conflict and its echoing aftermath—which in Christine's view included the founding of the royal house of France—figured in many of her works: *The Long Road of Learning* (1402/03), *Charles V* (1404), *Christine's Vision* (1405), the *Book of the Body Politic* (1406) and the *Book of the Deeds of Arms and Chivalry* (1410).[10] The affairs of the doomed city resonated particularly

---

[7]Christine, *City of Ladies*, pp. 52–53 on the husband of Queen Zenobia; on the rhetorician Quintus Hortensius, pp. 153–154.

[8]Christine, "Les enseignemens moraux," p. 39; Kellogg, "Christine de Pizan," pp. 109–111, on Christine's emerging anti-Troy stance. Some of Othea's warnings to Hector are anticipated in comments to her own son, "Les enseignemens moraux," pp. 29 and 36, on greed, covering one's back in battle, and listening to the advice of a good wife.

[9]Meyer, "Les premières," p. x. For Christine's sources in general, see Willard, *Christine de Pizan*, pp. 92, 112–113, 119–120. Solente compares specific passages about Hector in the *Histoire ancienne* and in Christine's versions: see *Mutacion*, 1: xxx–xcviii.

[10]Christine, *An Edition of Christine de Pisan's* Livre du Chemin de lonc Estude, ll. 1296–1300, 3222–3230, 3513–3639. *Charles* V, pp. 46, 47, 149, 156, 178. *Christine's*

strongly in three of her early works: the *Epistle of the Goddess Othea to Hector* (1399), the *Book of the Mutability of Fortune* (c. 1400–1403), and the *Book of the City of Ladies* (1405).[11] Each of these three works allowed Christine to imagine a Prince Hector, and to measure him against her ideas of manhood, lordship and chivalry.

Chivalry mattered as well to Christine. This is hardly surprising in a writer pursuing the patronage of the houses of Valois, Anjou, Berry, Burgundy and Orléans. Her writing career began with love poetry for what we could loosely call the aristocratic market, and the sexual politics of aristocratic life provided themes for her prose works as well. *Christine's Long Road of Learning* took her into medieval lawyers' writings on the law of war, as well as into the Roman Vegetius' work on the art of war, which she translated as the *Book of the Deeds of Arms and of Chivalry*. Christine wrote repeatedly about the lore and values of Christian chivalry, partly because the subject interested her patrons and partly because chivalry appealed to her as a productive self-discipline for the men of courtly circles, one which could bring aristocratic boys to temperate manhood, provide women with protection against otherwise unfettered male violence, and regulate the carnage war inflicted on whole societies.[12] She was certainly no pacifist but her concern was always to confine violence to just causes, and to the minimal imposition of force. When the early Renaissance carried Christine into print and across the Channel, it was conduct books for aspirant knights and military works for adult warriors that issued from the presses.[13] The most popular of all her works in the Renaissance was a strange mirror for princes capitalizing on the brave name of Hector.[14]

The trope of Hector mattered deeply to Christine. Early in the fourteenth century Jean de Longuyon had launched the Nine Worthies as models for knighthood: Hector figured there along with Alexander and Julius Caesar as an example of pagan virtue, and the cult was popular in French ducal and royal circles in the late fourteenth and early fifteenth centuries.[15] Christine insisted on the Trojan prince's tight link to France,

---

Vision, pp. 79–80. Christine, *Le Livre du corps de Policie*, pp. 48–49. *The Book of Deeds of Arms and of Chivalry*, pp. 137 and 141.

[11] Christine, *Epistre Othea*, *Mutacion*, ll. 14059–18244; *City of Ladies*, pp. 47–51, 106–107, 188–189, 204.

[12] See example, Christine, *Livre du Chemin de lonc Estude*, pp. 218–235.

[13] Willard, *Christine de Pizan*, pp. 214–217; Christine, Introd. to *Book of Deeds*.

[14] Christine, *Epistre Othea*, pp. 28–29 and 87–101 on the manuscripts, pp. 11–12 on Renaissance editions in France and England.

[15] In Languyon's version there were three Worthies from the Old Law (Joshua, David, and Judas Maccabeus), three pagan Worthies, and three more from the New Law (Arthur,

making him the father of Francion, founder of the French royal line.[16] She recognized that her cultural circle thought of him as a heroic warrior, a man of prowess and renown, the most perfect knight ever born, the hero whose loss devastated his city and his cause, as the *Mutacion de Fortune* tells us.[17] Christine there recorded Hector's epitaph: "Here lies Hector, the strong, the proud, the flower of all chivalry."[18] From the *Book of the City of Ladies* we learn that Hector was "one of the bravest men in the world, and the one who most excelled in all graces"; in this work, too, she has Penthesilea, Queen of the Amazons, extol him, "O, flower and excellence of the world's knighthood, summit, height, and consummation of all valor. . . ."[19] And surely this is how her audience would have expected Christine to portray the worthy founder of the royal house of her adopted country. But it seems she could not sustain a focus on Hector, the model of aristocratic manhood. Instead, aside from the short set pieces just quoted, her audience gets other images of Hector—an immature Hector, a reckless adult Hector, even an embalmed Hector.

Christine's first Hector is not a man at all but a boy, quite a different creature. He is a fifteen year old—not the manly hero of the Trojan wars, but someone marked out by his age as immature both physically and socially. Late medieval and early Renaissance theorizing of the "ages of man" had not settled into a single, consistent version of the trajectory to manhood.[20]

Charlemagne, and Godfrey of Bouillon, the crusader conqueror of Jerusalem). See Keen, *Chivalry*, pp. 121–124. Around 1402, Louis d'Orléans' castle at Coucy included representations of the Nine in a council chamber adjacent to the hall (Warner, *Joan of Arc*, p. 208). The Worthies could be used, as Christine's contemporary Eustace Deschamps did, as a means of criticizing the sad state of contemporary chivalry in a world no longer worthy of the presence of such heroes, "Contre les vices du temps." Christine can use Hector as a reproach to lords of her day, for example in a short reference in *Le Livre du corps de Policie*, pp. 48–49, where Hector's liberality with those he defeats is contrasted with the destructive behaviour of present day lords of war, who descend on those they defeat like "famished dogs." Her larger Hector project, developed through many works, is fundamentally critical of the Worthy himself. I do not agree with Kellogg that Christine creates a New Hector, revivified by Christian lessons ("Christine de Pizan as Chivalric Mythographer," pp. 111–112).

[16] Her clearest statement of the Trojan descent of the French kings is in *Charles V*, pp. 46–47. Other versions of the origins of France made Francion a nephew rather than a grandson of Priam. On the Trojan connection of the French, see Krynen, *Idéal du prince*, pp. 246–248 and Beaune, *Naissance de la nation France*, pp. 19–21.

[17] Christine, *Mutacion*, ll. 14924 and 14929–14930.

[18] Christine, *Mutacion*, ll. 16641–16642.

[19] Christine, *Book of the City of Ladies*, pp. 48–49.

[20] Some of the available models are discussed in Taddei, "*Puerizia, adolescenza* and *giovinezza.*" See also the suggestive passage in Marchello-Nizia, "Courtly Chivalry," pp. 139–143.

Christine had her own sense of when manhood began, and hers was a scheme that postponed maturity until about twenty-five. Hector, at fifteen, would have long left infancy behind, and was on the cusp of boyhood and youth, but was not a man. Indeed, his humours placed him in an odd physiological situation, where his male heat struggled against a moistness that was, humorally speaking, a hallmark of stereotypical womanhood; an adolescent male, in Christine's view, was an immature being, careening out of control, lacking the rational control of the body that signaled, at last, the beginnings of maturity.[21] Christine's account of humoral development makes the male adolescent a "defective man," a not-man.[22]

We meet this first unmanly Hector in Christine's letter from the imaginary goddess Othea to an equally imaginary adolescent Hector, and neither of these characters acquires much human reality in the course of the text.[23] Othea, Christine tells us, is the allegory of human wisdom; Hector is not explicitly allegorized, but if he were, he would be Youthful Rashness in its masculine mode. The manuscript revolves around Othea's lessons, intended to guide young Hector to masculine, knightly, and spiritual maturity. Having a female figure guide the aspirant knight is no innovation. Chrétien de Troyes had used Percival's mother in this role, and both Huon de Bordeaux and Beaudous, son of Gawain, were prepared for knighthood by their mothers.[24] In divinizing her mentor figure and alter ego Christine may not be so much writing vaingloriously as taking pains to separate this text from an earlier one, the "Enseignemens moraux," explicitly written for her son Jean, Hector's exact contemporary in age.[25]

---

[21]Christine, *Charles V*, pp. 52–59. Here Christine acknowledges a debt to Aristotle but, as was her habit in dealing with classical authority, she takes only what she wants from the master. True maturity, she says later (p. 61), begins in a man's fifties. Perhaps not coincidentally, this is the very age when men's and women's humoral balances are brought together, for men cool as they age, and women dry. For a general account of humoral physiology and temperament, see Lindemann, *Medicine and Society*.

[22]By linking adulthood to rational control of the body, Christine opens the way for a description of maturation that allows women as well as men to escape from a "defective" mode into full adulthood.

[23]In addition to Christine's *Epistre Othea*, *Epistle*, *Letter of Othea to Hector*, see Hindman, *Christine de Pizan's "Epistre Othéa"*; Kellogg, "Pizan as Chivalric Mythographer"; Krueger, "Christine's Anxious Lessons"; Wolfthal, "'Douleur sur toutes autres'"; and Brown-Grant, *Christine de Pizan and the Moral Defence of Women*.

[24]Christine, *Epistle*, pp. xvii–xviii. A generation later Antoine de la Sale imagines a more ambiguous, because eroticized, female mentor in *Jehan de Saintré*, a work which provides a program of moral instruction reminiscent of the *Epistre Othea*.

[25]Christine, "Les enseignemens moraux," pp. 24–44. Hindman sees the text aligning Louis of Orléans and other princes with Hector, so that living Frenchmen fulfil the

In the *Epistre Othea*, Christine chooses to use Hector's name in her title, but never gives her audience a worthy figure for its attention, and indeed does not demand that her audience attend much to the boy. The first thing auditors and readers learn about this Hector—his age—is virtually all they ever learn of him in the *Othea*. In this text Christine displays not the Worthy, but an unformed male creature just entering the dangerous passage through puberty, needing to negotiate his way to control over his body. This Hector is caught in a time of maximal male vulnerability. He needs to learn to temper his nature, control his hot flashes, learn constancy, firmness, and piety, and become devoted to justice. Through this maturation process he emerges from his knightly apprenticeship as a true man. But that is a masculine future that this Hector would not reach, and in this text the audience never encounters him as anything but the unformed juvenile, the unrealized man, the male at a stage of life where he is still, like a woman in common Aristotelian parlance, an imperfect man. His goddess mentor knows, of course, that he would not get her lessons right; the pessimism about pedagogy running through this text is very deep—nurture has no power strong enough to divert fate.[26]

Although she knows her lessons would be wasted, Hector's Goddess-Mentor is conscientious in providing her pupil with a miniature encyclopedia of things to be mastered on the road to masculine adulthood; the *Othea* takes the form of a letter of one hundred lessons written in verse. Each of the verse texts comes with a prose gloss, reading the text as advice to an aspirant knight, and with an allegory, also in prose, rendering the text into something edifying for the Christian soul, predictably likened here to a crusader struggling against the diabolical enemy.[27] Othea moves through both spiritual and temporal information: the planets, astrology, the metals, the humours, the cardinal virtues, the theological virtues, the seven deadly sins, the creed, the commandments, Ovidian fables, Trojan tales, some quite ordinary advice to male youth (do not waste your time hunting or going into trances over music; avoid Venus; accept wise counsel; hate traitors; play chess . . .).[28] The work is colourful and fast-moving (not least because it is jerky and superficial) and leaves readers or auditors no time at all to think

---

allegory (*Christine de Pizan's* "Epistre Othea," p. xx).

[26]Krueger finds this to be generally true of Christine's works ("Christine's Anxious Lessons," p. 18).

[27]Hindman's reading downplays the allegorical rendering of the text in favour of a strictly political one based on text and gloss.

[28]Christine, *Epistre Othea*, on hunting: pp. 288–291, 295–297; on music, pp. 293–294; on the perils of love, pp. 213–214, 253–254, 278–280, 286–287, 302–304, 318–319; on wise counsel, pp. 308–309; on traitors, pp. 314–315; on chess, pp. 317–318.

about what the "real" Prince Hector might have been like as a young man. Christine's juvenile Hector, the recipient of Othea's attentions, is smothered by Christine's texts and their apparatus—he is simply mute in the face of all this erudition and wisdom, silenced by instruction in worldly lore, Christian fundamentals, chastity, and obedience. This is no chivalric *Bildungsroman* documenting the growing strength of a prince en route to the status of a flower of chivalry. Hector's silence is another marker of his "not-man" status in this version of the prince of Troy.

The *Epistle of Othea* is not a text from which Hector ever bursts forth into manhood. Instead the manuscript comes to a sudden end. The wandering structure of the first eighty-seven texts quickens with stroboscopic warnings to Hector about the futile death that awaits him if he does not master his lessons. The silent adolescent comes to his end without ever speaking, without having learned his lessons, comes to death *because* he has not learned his lessons. The text shimmers with maternal fury with this boy who will not learn, and aches with maternal vulnerability for this soon to be lost son: in Scene 88, Othea warns Hector to listen to what his wife will tell him—Andromache will tell him not to fight Achilles.[29] And in Scene 90, the goddess says bluntly, "Hector, you are going to die because you don't listen to your father." Priam, too, will try to dissuade his foolhardy son.[30] Then the divine warnings pour out, jumbling chronology: don't go unarmed into battle, don't covet Polyboetes' armour—Hector of course is killed when Achilles jumps him from behind as Hector stoops to loot Polyboetes' corpse—don't make pacts with your enemies, don't take up arms thoughtlessly, learn from your future, learn from what will happen after your death—until finally the goddess catapults Hector hundreds of years past his death to hold up to him the example of Caesar Augustus, who did listen to the Cumean Sibyl and was rewarded with a vision of Jesus in Mary's arms.[31] By the time that vision took place, rash, stubborn, prideful Hector was long dead.

Christine herself obviously did not find this first Hector exhaustively satisfying, since she would soon imagine the Prince of Troy again, this time in a more straightforward vehicle, *Mutacion*, a long poem rehearsing the mutations of Fortune. In this second sustained treatment of the Trojan hero, Christine presents a more glorious adult Hector, who falls on his enemies "like a lion running after his prey," slaughtering so many Greeks that only the fall of night saves their army from extinction, going on to triumph over

---

[29]Christine, *Epistre Othea*, pp. 324–326.
[30]Christine, *Epistre Othea*, pp. 327–328.
[31]Christine, *Epistre Othea*, pp. 328–341.

Achilles' beloved Patroclus.[32] Here, seemingly, her audience finally gets from her a tale of the admirable hero whose blood coursed through the veins of the nobles of present day France. Here, surely, Christine delivers to them the masculine idol, Hector *prince* of Troy, adult, man among men, leagues beyond the moral twitterings of some imaginary wise woman. Christine did try to sustain this imaginary Hector—at least, this time out, his foreknown death is blamed on Achilles' unchivalrous attack rather than on his own rashness, and readers and listeners do not have to mortify their enthusiasm for Hector with unseemly images of a vainglorious, unarmed fool whose lust for booty blinds him to the danger roaring up from behind to smash the greedy life out of his body. Except the text tricks those who are expecting the Worthy. This second Hector may be unchivalrously attacked, but Christine's audience is not allowed to draw conclusions appropriate to a chivalrous life. Once again, Hector ends up being blamed, and for the same fault: stupid pride, failure to heed the warning of a female voice—Andromache's. Great Hector is afraid he will be thought cowardly if he heeds prudent advice coming from a woman.[33] Like the adolescent Hector of the *Othea*, the Hector of the *Mutacion* cannot resist Polyboetes' fancy armour and so this second Hector also dies fruitlessly, in this case with mourners crowding behind with "ahistorical" speed to bring home his body and organize the funeral.[34]

By the time she wrote the *Mutacion*, Christine was explicitly bored with the story of Troy—"to tell it at length would be wearisome" she remarked there, even though she quickly acknowledged that the story was pleasant, true, remarkable, and demonstrative of her main theme, how Fortune constantly changed human triumph into defeat. But at least the tale of Troy, and more particularly Hector's death, was an excuse to talk about Amazons, since Hector's martial prowess lured Queen Penthesilea to Troy. Penthesilea was always shadowing Hector in Christine's accounts, and she

---

[32]Christine, *Mutacion*, ll. 15493 for the quotation; ll. 15519–15521 for nightfall; ll. 15607–15611 for the death of Patroclus. In "Hector and Penthesilea," Brownlee underlines the emotional involvement Christine displays with both Penthesilea and Hector.

[33]Christine, *Mutacion*, ll. 16248–16276.

[34]True to her principal source, the *Histoire ancienne*, Christine omits the grisly story of Achilles dragging Hector's body behind his chariot round the walls of Troy. Arguably, as the mother of a living son, she cannot bear this image, nor even the attenuated image of the dead Hector of whom Virgil's Aeneas dreamt, "filthy with dust and blood," although the threat of such a ghastly ruin of one's own body should be one of her high cards in the war against mismanaged masculine bellicosity. Virgil, *Aeneid*, p. 59. It is not certain whether Christine read the *Aeneid*: see Willard, *Christine de Pizan*, p. 101. She is directly concerned in the *Mutacion* with the grief mothers feel for sons destroyed in war, the grief she used to explain the founding of the Amazon kingdom (ll. 13532–13612).

claimed centre stage when Christine presented her third Hector, in part one of the *City of Ladies*.[35]

Christine's third Hector is a macabre figure, a dangerous idol of false chivalry. After the mute adolescent, after the mortally proud adult, in this third Hector Christine's audience confronts the corpse of the hero. This time Hector is dead from the start, gorgeously entombed by his grief-stricken parents, Queen Hecuba and King Priam, looking "as though he were completely alive, holding an unsheathed sword in his hand, and his proud countenance still seem[ing] to threaten the Greeks."[36] The remaining Trojans revere him "with the same honour reserved for one of their gods."[37] This Hector has already become a Worthy, an inspiration. His glamorous corpse is all that is left for Penthesilea to meet when she reaches Troy, the city to which she has been drawn by Hector's martial renown. And glamorous the corpse is, bewitching her to her own death. The sight of Hector's corpse plunges the brave Amazon into grief, from which she rallies to vow revenge. Penthesilea takes to the field at the head of her female troops, fights gloriously—"She had fought so much that a single day would hardly have been long enough for Hector to match her"—but in the end, cornered and outnumbered, she grows exhausted. Unlike Hector, she meets her death head on: "[the Greeks] smashed through all her armour and struck off a large quarter of her helmet. Pyrrhus [Achilles' son] was there, and seeing her bare head with its blond hair, dealt her such a great blow that he split open her head and brain. So died the brave Penthesilea, a terrible loss to the Trojans and a profound sorrow for all her land . . . and rightly so, for afterward a woman of her calibre never again ruled over the Amazons."[38] The dead Hector could inspire great deeds, but in the end they were, like his own, futile. Already, almost in his own lifetime, Christine's imagined Hector has become an unworthy Worthy. Those who would follow him would do well, she hinted, to think not just on *his* end, but on Queen Penthesilea's too.

What are we to make of these Hectors: the mute inglorious juvenile, the proud adult who is at fault in his own destruction, and the corpse who enters history and continues thence to cloud the minds of the living with false ideals of chivalry, leading warriors in particular to "glorious" deaths that leave unprotected and leaderless the very people the chivalrous male aristocrat should have succoured and served? That is, in fact, exactly the

[35]Christine, *City of Ladies*, pp. 47–51.
[36]Christine, *City of Ladies*, pp. 48–49.
[37]Christine, *City of Ladies*, p. 49.
[38]Christine, *City of Ladies*, pp. 50–51.

lesson Christine wanted her readers, including her male readers, to draw from her telling of the Trojan tales and the sad ends of Prince Hector. Hector represented to her not the flowering of chivalry but an instance of its failure to discipline boys into men.

It is important to linger on this. The cult of the Nine Worthies held up Hector as a model of aristocratic masculinity. This Christine rejected, for to her Hector was an inappropriate figure to include in the chivalric pantheon. Her Hector was unmanly because he had failed to master the lessons of self-control and had, therefore, remained mired in adolescence; Othea's lessons were always wasted and Christine's contemporaries could never hope to encounter a manly Hector in her portraits of him. Christine felt no compunction about underlining the unmanliness of the Prince of Troy, presenting him as she did not just as an immature adult, but also as a mute adolescent who speaks no lesson to his beholder, and then as a silent corpse whose unspoken lesson is only this: follow me to your destruction, and the destruction of all you hold dear. Christine portrayed him as not-man because that is how she saw him, a flawed antique male whom she refused to imagine as a masculine hero for her own day. Yet she could not get away from the unworthy worthy, because he was so glamorous, apparently becoming ever more appealing through the popularizing of ancient history and the related cult of the Nine Worthies. What the antique Hector stood for is antithetical to Christine's own politics of chivalry and good lordship, so she belittled him and unmanned him.[39] Then, having set him up as not-man, she could address the powerful men in her audience, the nobles whose task it was to govern France while its nominal king, Charles VI, was incompetent to do so.

Remember that Hector was the father of Francion, founder of the royal house of France, and that by Christine's day, all the major French families had invented Trojan genealogies for themselves. When Christine was writing these stories of Hector, her beloved France was badly adrift, its king experiencing bouts of madness, its queen unable or unwilling to exercise a moderating force on the ambitions of the dukes of Orléans and Burgundy. At the level of the kingdom, Hector stood for force, for the use of physical power to settle disputes. The last thing Christine wanted to see was the triumph of the immature masculinity of the bellicose, reckless Hector. Hector was prepared to take extraordinary risks in the hope of maximizing his personal glory and wealth, but what he did toward that end opened the way to the destruction of his kingdom. If the nobility of France—including

---

[39]Hector is also a poor fit for Christine's vision of ideal masculinity within the household, but space constraints prevent my developing that theme.

Christine's own patrons to whom some of these works are addressed—chose Hector as their inspiration, France, like Troy, would remain trapped in a cyclic history where both individuals and generations would be ground down, flung up, and ground down again by Fortune's wheel.[40] Follow his lead, Christine suggested, and the dukes would destroy France, laying it open to partition and perhaps even to foreign conquest. Although Agincourt was still well in the future when Christine was writing, she feared just such a catastrophe. Christine was desperate to turn France toward more wholesome political channels, desperate to protect it from those clamouring for a strong man to supplant a weak king and a weak queen. She worked to preempt the fatal emergence of a new Hector.[41]

Christine admired strong men and had no quarrel with warfare in support of a just cause.[42] In the *Deeds and Good Customs of the Wise King Charles V*, written after the *Othea* and the *Mutacion de Fortune* but before the *Book of the City of Ladies*, she developed a political vision of a strong king, a truly chivalrous hero, a real man. She found her Worthy not in ancient, pagan Troy but in Christian France and living memory. Charles V, whom she knew personally, emerged in her writings as a rounded version of masculine maturity. Charles had nothing of Hector's physical prowess and battlefield triumphs, for after his coronation he had contracted a disease which left him prone to fever, and with a swollen right hand that could no longer control sword or lance. Despite bodily infirmities that kept him from the wars, Charles was a great success as a military leader—he appointed an able constable, Bertrand du Guesclin, who flawlessly executed his king's plans on the battlefield. In Christine's judgment, as a military leader Charles was the best king since Charlemagne.[43] Nevertheless, she refused to privilege Charles' military success in her overall assessment of his legacy. Having consulted chronicles and interviewed witnesses, she concluded that Charles was "a real philosopher and man of high virtue," whose merits resided in three qualities: "nobility of heart, chivalry, and wisdom," a phrase that neatly bracketed the one area where physical strength might have counted

---

[40]Christianity, of course, is the only force in Christine's world that can overpower Fortune's cycles (Kellogg, "Christine de Pizan as Chivalric Mythographer," p. 111).

[41]For a discussion of Christine's drive to use artistic creation politically (including a critique of the chivalric myths of her time), see Forhan, *The Political Theory of Christine de Pizan*, pp. 17–18.

[42]Consider both Christine's glee at Joan of Arc's success and her efforts to popularize Vegetius' military wisdom for her generation in *Ditié de Jehanne d'Arc* and *The Book of Deeds of Arms and of Chivalry*.

[43]Christine, *Charles V*, pp. 125–126, where Christine discusses the king's illness and sums up her assessment of his martial prowess.

between two where it did not.[44] Among his meritorious (and chivalric) qualities, Christine insisted on Charles' respect for sexual decorum.[45] Just once does she compare Charles to Hector: both men are able to attract the support of the noblemen of their time, who flock to serve them.[46] This was a portrait of mature manhood and Christine found little reason to remember her anti-hero Hector as she painted it. Charles, who always cared for the people whose welfare had been entrusted to him, exemplified for her the admirable masculine leader.[47]

By contrast, Christine wanted no truck with the kind of political power Hector carried, a falsely masculine power based on the strength of the male body. The very thing that made Hector glamorous to those besotted with martial success, his physical prowess, was a category Christine would have liked to see removed from models of governance. She was explicit about this in the *Book of the City of Ladies*. Here we find a certain, much remarked-upon essentialism in a comment Lady Reason makes early in the narrative: "God has similarly ordained men and women to serve Him in different offices . . . each in their ordained task, and to each sex has given a fitting and appropriate nature and inclination to fulfill their offices."[48] This sounds very much like anatomically based differences in character and vocation. Yet elsewhere—in the *Mutacion de Fortune*—Christine could be cavalier about the instability of sexual anatomy, recounting several sex changes, some from Ovid, but also one she claimed to have from her own experience, for she asserted that she had emerged, physically, from the catastrophe of her young husband's death as a man.[49] In *Christine's Vision*, anatomical sex was a last-minute addition to a new life.[50] Good Christian that she was, Christine believed that the essence of a human being was spiritual, not physical.[51] The things that mattered in establishing fitness to rule transcended sexual anatomy, and the virtues and vices of rulers were the same in either sex. Faithful to these ideas, Lady Reason thus continued

---

[44]Christine, *Charles V*, p. 44.

[45]Christine, *Charles V*, pp. 93–95, and p. 116, where the defence of women is announced as a goal of chivalry.

[46]Christine, *Charles V*, p. 178.

[47]Christine, *Charles V*, p. 116, where the point of chivalry is defined as "maintenir et défendre le bien de tous," and p. 117, where Vegetius is quoted as defining chivalry as "protéger et défendre le prince, le clergé, les femmes et le menu peuple."

[48]Christine, *Book of the City of Ladies*, p. 31.

[49]Christine, *Mutacion*, ll. 1025–1400. Walters reads this sex change through the hagiographic tradition, drawing on Perpetua's autobiography, in "Metamorphoses of the Self."

[50]Christine, *Christine's Vision*.

[51]Christine, *Mutacion*, ll. 670–679.

her musings on physical strength by acknowledging that "God gives men strong and hardy bodies," and women weak ones, but the consequences that flow from this difference in accidents—for they certainly were not differences in substance for Christine—were not very important for governance. Physical weakness might save women from acting on some temptations to commit cruelty and crime, but strength fitted men not for governance, but for law enforcement. And Lady Reason was quite categoric that law enforcement was a mere exercise of constraint, to be distinguished from true governance, a point she illustrated by a lengthy catalogue of capable female governors. Physical strength, the only thing from the repertoire of worthy masculine traits that Hector was consistently allowed in Christine's versions of him, was no guarantor of the virtues needed in a wise ruler: love of peace, love of justice, prudence, and temperance. The one thing Christine's passage identifies as masculine, physical strength, was not even an exclusively male attribute for her, as the regular deployment of the Amazons in Christine's version of the Troy story should remind us. Indeed, in her last known work, Christine celebrated the extraordinary, divinely granted, physical strength of the female Worthy, Joan of Arc, who, she declared, excelled Hector.[52] Physical strength was a *sine qua non* of knighthood, but it was neither an exclusive nor a necessary attribute of manhood and good overlordship, as her contemporaries could easily see from the reign of Charles V, the physically weak man who was France's exemplary fourteenth-century king.

As a young woman, Christine had learned from Charles V that physical strength was in no way necessary to true manhood. Towards the close of her life, she reveled in an extraordinary set of martial events that demonstrated her Lord's confirmation of her belief that physical strength could arise in either sex and that violence in a just cause was legitimate. Much of her political writing drew on her experience of Charles V and prepared her audience for the revelation that was Joan. Between Charles and Joan fell the deadly, distracting cult of Hector. By undermining Hector, unmanning him, stressing the unheroic circumstance of his death (jumped from behind while looting a dead body), by presenting him as a silent juvenile or a corpse, Christine struck at one of the most powerful images in her culture, that of manhood conceived in terms of physical strength. By doing so she sought to advance her grand

---

[52]Christine, *Ditié de Jehanne d'Arc*. On Joan as female worthy, see Warner, *Joan of Arc*, pp. 207–209. Joan's excellence resides in the goodness of her cause. Hector's cause, the defence of Troy, was too connected with thoughtless lust for Christine to call it just. Although Penthesilea stalked Hector through Christine's retellings of the Troy story, she was in the end not much better a role model than was he. Joan of Arc is the true Worthy.

political project: safeguarding the monarchy and thus peace in the realm. Christine spoke of Hector not to praise him, but to bury him, to close the door on his elaborate tomb before his awe-inspiring corpse betrayed yet more of the living to their doom. Troy to her, like original sin, was a poisoned inheritance and Hector just another old Adam to be transcended.

WORKS CITED

Beaune, Colette. *Naissance de la nation France*. Paris: Gallimard, 1985.

Brown-Grant, Rosalind. *Christine de Pizan and the Moral Defence of Women: Reading Beyond Gender*. Cambridge: Cambridge University Press, 1999.

Brownlee, Kevin. "Hector and Penthesilea in the *Livre de la Mutacion de Fortune*: Christine de Pizan and the Politics of Myth." *Une femme de lettres au moyen âge: Études autour de Christine de Pizan*. Ed. Liliane Dulac and Bernard Ribémont. Orléans: Paradigme, 1995. 69–82.

Christine de Pizan. *Book of the City of Ladies*. Trans. Earl Jeffrey Richards. New York: Persea, 1982.

Christine de Pizan. *The Book of Deeds of Arms and of Chivalry*. Ed. Charity Canon Willard. Trans. Sumner Willard. University Park: Pennsylvania State University Press, 1999.

Christine de Pizan. *Christine de Pizan's Letter of Othea to Hector*. Ed. and trans. Jane Chance. 1990. Rpt. Cambridge: D. S. Brewer, 1997.

Christine de Pizan. *Christine's Vision*. Trans. Glenda K. McLeod. New York: Garland, 1993.

Christine de Pizan. *Ditié de Jehanne d'Arc*. Ed. Angus J. Kennedy and Keith Varty. Oxford: Society for the Study of Medieval Languages and Literature, 1977.

Christine de Pizan. *An Edition of Christine de Pisan's* "Livre du Chemin de lonc Estude." Ed. Patricia Bonin Eargle. Ph.D. diss., University of Georgia, 1973.

Christine de Pizan. "Les enseignemens moraux." *Oeuvres poétiques de Christine de Pisan*. Ed. Maurice Roy. 1896. Rpt. London: Johnson, 1975. 27–44.

Christine de Pizan. *The Epistle of Othea to Hector: A* "Lytel Bibell of Knyghthod" *edited from the Harleian manuscript 838*. Ed. James D. Gordon. Philadelphia: University of Pennsylvania Press, 1942.

Christine de Pizan. *Epistre Othea, Edition critique*. Ed. Gabriella Parussa. Geneva: Droz, 1999.

Christine de Pizan. *Livre du Chemin de lonc Estude*. See Eargle.

Christine de Pizan. *Le Livre du corps de Policie*. Ed. Robert H. Lucas. Geneva: Droz, 1967.

Christine de Pizan. *Le Livre de la Mutacion de Fortune*. Ed. Suzanne Solente. 4 vols. Paris: Société des anciens textes français, 1959–1964.

Christine de Pizan. *Le Livre des faits et bonnes moeurs du roi Charles V le Sage*. Ed. Eric Hicks and Thérèse Moreau. Paris: Stock, 1997.

Deschamps, Eustace. "Contre les vices du temps." *Oeuvres complètes*. Ed. Marquis de Queux de Saint-Hilaire. 1878. Rpt. London: Johnson, 1996. 86–87.

Forhan, Kate Langdon. *The Political Theory of Christine de Pizan*. Burlington: Ashgate, 2002.

Hindman, Sandra L. *Christine de Pizan's* "Epistre Othéa": *Painting and Politics at the Court of Charles VI*. Toronto: Pontifical Institute for Mediaeval Studies, 1986.

Keen, Maurice. *Chivalry*. New Haven and London: Yale University Press, 1984.

Kellogg, Judith L. "Christine de Pizan as Chivalric Mythographer: *L'Epistre Othea*." *The Mythographic Art: Classical Fable and the Rise of the Vernacular in Early France and England*. Ed. Jane Chance. Gainesville: University of Florida Press, 1990. 100–124.

King, Margaret. *Women of the Renaissance*. Chicago: University of Chicago Press, 1991.

Krueger, Robert. "Christine's Anxious Lessons: Gender, Moralizing and the Social Order from the *Enseignemens* to the *Avision*." *Christine de Pizan and the Categories of Difference*. Ed. Marilynn Desmond. Minneapolis: University of Minnesota Press, 1998. 16–40.

Krynen, Jacques. *Idéal du prince et pouvoir royal en France à la fin du Moyen Age, 1380–1440: étude de la littérature politique du temps*. Paris: Éditions A. et J. Picard, 1981.

Krynen, Jacques. *L'Empire du roi: idées et croyances politiques en France, XIIIe –Xve siècle*. Paris: Gallimard, 1993.

La Sale, Antoine de. *Jehan de Saintré*. Ed. Jean Misrahi and Charles A. Knudson. Geneva: Droz, 1965.

Lindemann, Mary. *Medicine and Society in Early Modern Europe*. Cambridge: Cambridge University Press, 1999.

Marchello-Nizia, Christiane. "Courtly Chivalry." *Ancient and Medieval Rites of Passage*. Ed. Giovanni Levi and Jean-Claude Schmitt. Trans. Camille Naish. Cambridge: Harvard University Press, 1977. 120–172.

Meyer, Paul. "Les premières compilations françaises d'histoire ancienne: I. *Les Faits des Romans ou Livre de César*. II. *Histoire ancienne jusqu'à César*." *Romania* 14 (1885): 1–81.

Quilligan, Maureen. *The Allegory of Female Authority: Christine de Pizan's* Cité des Dames. Ithaca: Cornell University Press, 1991.

Taddei, Ilaria. "*Puerizia, adolescenza* and *giovinezza*: Images and Conceptions of Youth in Florentine Society During the Renaissance." *The Premodern Teenager: Youth in Society 1150–1650*. Ed. Konrad Eisenbichler. Toronto: Centre for Reformation and Renaissance Studies, 2002. 15–26.

Virgil. *The Aeneid*. Trans. W. F. Jackson Knight. Harmondsworth: Penguin, 1956.

Walters, Lori. "Metamorphoses of the Self: Christine de Pizan, the Saint's Life, and Perpetua." *Sur le chemin de longue étude: Actes du colloque d'Orléans, Juillet 1995*. Ed. Bernard Ribémont. Paris: Honoré Champion, 1998. 158–181.

Warner, Marina. *Joan of Arc: The Image of Female Heroism*. Harmondsworth: Penguin, 1981.

Willard, Charity Cannon. *Christine de Pizan, Her Life and Works*. New York: Persea, 1984.

Wolfthal, Diane. "'Douleur sur toutes autres': Revisualising the Rape Script in the *Epistre Othea* and the *Cité des Dames*." *Christine de Pisan and the Categories of Difference*. Ed. Marilynn Desmond. Minneapolis: University of Minnesota Press, 1998. 41–70.

La Troade *de Garnier:*
destins malheureux et exemples héroïques

STÉPHANIE BÉLANGER

La Troade de Robert Garnier, publiée en 1579, quelques années après le massacre de la Saint-Barthélemy, met en scène l'horreur des guerres et les injustices perpétuées par les puissants. Dans sa dédicace à l'archevêque de Bourges[1], le dramaturge insiste sur l'actualité du sujet qu'il a choisi de traiter:

> Je scay qu'il n'est genre de poëmes moins agréable que cestuy-cy, qui ne représente que les malheurs lamentables des princes, avec les saccagemens des peuples. Mais aussi les passions de tels sujets nous sont jà si ordinaires, que les exemples anciens nous devront doresnavant servir de consolation en nos particuliers et domestiques encombres [. . .].[2]

En s'inspirant de la tragédie de la défaite des Troyens devant les Achéens, le dramaturge semble vouloir donner un sens aux massacres de victimes innocentes en les présentant comme autant de sacrifices offerts aux dieux dans l'espoir d'obtenir réparation d'un tort.

La Troade, on l'a souvent répété, présente un véritable chapelet de misères et de sacrifices, mais on ne semble pas avoir relevé en quoi toute cette violence peut « servir de consolation ». Comme il sera ici démontré, les pièces écrites au tournant du XVIe siècle héritent de ces discours contradictoires qui expriment à la fois le désir d'en finir avec la violence, la peur de l'autre, le besoin d'expliquer la guerre par des forces surnaturelles qu'on qualifie d'infernales. La souffrance est alors perçue comme un châtiment divin, l'existence comme un monde à sacrifier en vue d'une vie meilleure.

Ce n'est pas un hasard si l'historien Denis Crouzet, dans un ouvrage consacré à la violence des guerres de Religion[3], choisit précisément la *Troade*

---

[1]Dans l'édition de Paris par Patisson en 1579, la dédicace, presque en tous points identique à celle citée ici à partir de l'édition de Pinvert (1923), s'adresse au révérend père Regnaud de Beaune, plutôt qu'à l'archevêque de Bourges. Le passage cité ici est identique dans les deux dédicaces.

[2]Garnier, *La Troade,* p. 1.

[3]Je renvoie ici à l'ouvrage de Denis Crouzet, *Les guerriers de Dieu.*

afin d'illustrer l'étendue de la vision eschatologique de cette période. Il semble que le dramaturge ait choisi les pires épisodes des conséquences de la guerre de Troie. Cette pièce réunit tous les fantasmes apocalyptiques qui peuvent avoir marqué les Français ayant survécu à cette longue période des guerres de religion. Garnier, à l'imitation surtout de Sénèque, y multiplie les signes, les apparitions surnaturelles, les vengeances injustifiées, les victimes innocentes sacrifiées au bûcher de tyrans cruels.

Pour adoucir les peines que produisent les guerres de religion, Garnier ne propose pas simplement d'illustrer les pires exemples de souffrances et d'injustice: il cherche, et c'est ce que je démontrerai dans les pages qui vont suivre, à convaincre son lecteur et son spectateur qu'en dépit de son insistance sur les horreurs de la guerre, subsiste pourtant l'espoir que les dieux écouteront les justes, que les victimes seront un jour glorifiées, que la justice sera, de façon ultime, rétribuée.

JUGEMENT DE DIEU

Dès le premier acte de *La Troade*, Garnier dénonce l'impiété des Argolides qui leur attirera la colère divine. Après avoir énuméré toutes les atrocités dont elle a été témoin pendant la guerre, Hécube, mère d'Hector, aperçoit un messager des princes ennemis s'approcher. D'emblée, elle lui demande si l'on veut sacrifier les captives, « Faire couler le sang sur ces moiteuses rives »[4]. Elle explique que cette réflexion lui est venue à l'esprit en observant des bateaux ennemis, « regorgeant de butins »[5] et ne pouvant, sans danger, être chargés du corps de ces femmes. Ce sacrifice ne servirait ni à remercier les dieux de leur victoire, ni à couronner leur victoire, mais il aurait pour fin mercantile de se débarrasser d'un butin lourd et qui rapporte peu, explique Hécube. Elle a cependant mal calculé leur perfidie: le gain matériel n'est pas le seul auquel ils aspirent. Elles pourront être amenées avec le butin de guerre et leur servir de concubines. Affligée, la mère d'Hector s'imagine voir partir ses filles l'une après l'autre, offertes comme esclaves aux bourreaux de leur frère, de leur père, ou de leur mari.

Cassandre est la première à partir. La prophétesse de malheur tient pourtant le discours le plus optimiste de toute la pièce. Elle voit dans son « fatal mariage »[6] une occasion de réjouissance, car elle pourra aisément tirer vengeance d'Agamemnon. Ainsi, contrairement à Hector, son frère, et à

---

[4]Garnier, *La Troade, Œuvres*, t. 2, 1, p. 16 (les actes ne sont pas divisés en scènes dans cette pièce).

[5]Garnier, *La Troade*, 1, p. 16.

[6]Garnier, *La Troade*, 1, p. 17.

Priam, son père, qui sont morts pleurés et chéris par leur épouse Andromaque et Hécube, ce roi, de même que Phyrre [Pyrrhus], fils du défunt Achille, mourront sous les « mots injurieux »[7] de leurs proches. Au-delà de ce constat face aux circonstances de la mort des belligérants, la guerre de Troie, loin d'être une pure catastrophe, explique la prophétesse, est une *felix culpa*, car grâce à elle, les Troyens seront à jamais considérés comme ceux qui se sont légitimement défendus:

> Toute guerre est cruelle, et personne ne doit
> L'entreprendre jamais, sinon avecques droit;
> Mais si pour sa défense et juste et nécessaire
> Par les armes il faut repousser l'adversaire,
> C'est honneur de mourir la pique dans le poing
> Pour sa ville, et l'avoir de sa vertu tesmoing.[8]

Contrairement aux Grecs qui ont injustement entrepris cette guerre, les Troyens verront leur nom vénéré par la postérité, car ils se sont défendus *in extremis*. S'ils ont perdu, c'est moins faute de vaillance qu'en raison de la perfidie de leurs ennemis. Si la guerre n'avait pas eu lieu, explique-t-elle, les Troyens n'auraient pas eu la chance de prouver leur vaillance, de voir « louangés » leurs efforts, « glorifié » leur nom et même celui d'Hector qui, sans la guerre, « au tombeau [aurait été] esteint »[9]. Ces propos de Cassandre mettent en évidence un trait bien caractéristique de la guerre juste: ses principes, jamais respectés par les plus grandes puissances, servent à assurer, dans le meilleur des cas, la victoire morale des plus faibles. Plus l'ennemi est perfide, plus le juste paraît supérieur dans ses principes. Ainsi, bien que le premier, Achille, remporte la victoire, la postérité s'assure que l'autre, Hector, aura, tout de même, la satisfaction de voir chantés ses efforts.

Le mythe de l'origine troyenne de la France est très présent pendant l'Ancien Régime. On pourrait toutefois se demander pour quelle raison la France considère Hector comme un héros, lui qui n'a pas fait très bonne figure dans la bataille contre Achille. Plusieurs dramaturges français ont d'ailleurs débattu cette question. L'enseignement de l'*Hector* de Montchrestien, par exemple, repose sur ce passage de l'*Iliade* où Hector, conscient que la mort est proche, choisit, plutôt que la fuite, de mourir de façon à ce la postérité se souvienne de lui: « Pourtant, ne périssons pas sans courage, ni sans gloire, mais après quelque grand exploit, qui passe même à la postérité »[10].

---

[7]Garnier, *La Troade*, 1, p. 20.
[8]Garnier, *La Troade*, 1, p. 22.
[9]Garnier, *La Troade*, 1, p. 22.
[10]Homère, *Iliade*, 22, 286–328.

Cette idée maîtresse valorise un aspect bien particulier de la guerre: Hector préfère mourir les armes à la main, ce qui lui assurerait une gloire pérenne, que de fuir la mort et de jouir d'une vie longue et paisible, après laquelle il enterrerait sa gloire. La mort d'Hector pose cependant le problème de la glorification d'Achille, personnage qui, pour Garnier, Montchrestien et plusieurs penseurs de cette époque, est trop cruel pour être ainsi vénéré. Nul besoin d'être rempli d'une « ardeur sauvage », comme on lit souvent dans l'*Iliade*; pour être héroïque, pense-t-on au tournant du XVIe siècle, il suffit d'être courageux. Un homme qui fracasse les membres de l'ennemi qu'il vient de tuer en le tirant sauvagement derrière son char est considéré comme une créature monstrueuse. La manière dont cette action est inter-prétée chez Garnier, ainsi, comme il sera démontré plus bas, que chez Montchrestien, qui a traité du même sujet quelques années plus tard, témoigne d'une conception spécifique de l'héroïsme, qui est propre aux auteurs et aux penseurs du tournant du XVIe siècle[11]. S'il est animé d'une ardeur propre aux plus grands héros, Achille ne peut cependant être loué pour avoir accompli une action aussi inhumaine. Les Français du tournant du XVIe siècle ont une conception bien précise, dont cette pièce en est une des illustrations, des valeurs morales de leur société et ils tentent toujours de montrer, dans leurs pièces, les modèles d'hommes à imiter pour leur sentiment d'humanité et ceux qu'il ne faut observer qu'en guise d'exemple négatif. Montchrestien tente de résoudre ce problème moral auquel il fait face dans le récit d'Homère en transformant complètement l'histoire. Il ne se contente pas de représenter les héros antiques et leurs exploits: il réinvente les récits des Anciens pour mieux édifier ses spectateurs. Ainsi, il embellit le récit de la mort d'Hector. Pour ce faire, il choisit de représenter Achille tel un homme lâche et malhonnête qui tue Hector d'un coup d'épée dans le dos. L'*Iliade* est pourtant bien claire à ce sujet: les deux ennemis s'affrontent face à face, l'arme à la main – c'est même Achille qui sera plus tard outragé par un traître assassinat. Mais pour Montchrestien, il ne peut être logique qu'Achille inflige un tel traitement à un cadavre s'il n'est pas

---

[11]Déchirer la chaire ou, même, désirer dévorer un être comme le fait Achille vis-à-vis d'Hector, sont des actes dont sont témoins les Français ayant vécu pendant les guerres de religion. Loin d'être considérés, comme c'est le cas dans l'*Iliade*, comme des actes héroïques (telle qu'en témoigne l'héroïsation d'Achille), il s'agit plutôt d'actes condam-nables. Plusieurs écrits, outre les tragédies, en portent le témoignage et interprètent ces actions comme un acte barbare, comme la manifestation du mal, voire, comme un châtiment divin. Voir Burel, *Mémoires*, p. 20–22, 48, 520; L'Estoile, *Journal*, p. 155, 248, 321; Pasquier, *Écrits politiques*, p. 40–41; pour les études critiques, voir surtout Crouzet, *Les guerriers de Dieu*, p. 38–39, 46; et Garrisson, *Guerre civile et compromis*, p. 237.

fondamentalement un lâche. C'est pourquoi il lui fait d'abord tuer son ennemi tel un traître.

Ce choix du dramaturge peut être interprété comme une réaction aux guerres de son époque, où les cruautés et les actes barbares commis sans justification apparente se multiplient. Montchrestien cherche peut-être à s'assurer lui aussi, ne fût-ce que dans le monde idéalisé des tragédies, qu'il existe une certaine forme de justice et de respect humain. Pour s'en convaincre, il choisit de laisser le premier rang à Hector et de lui octroyer le fleuron de la victoire sans entacher sa bravoure par les exploits d'autres grands belligérants, surtout si leurs actions peuvent sembler cruelles. Selon le dramaturge, c'est là que réside l'essence même de toute bataille. Le mythe des guerres effectuées selon les règles du code de l'honneur – noblesse d'âme, mort glorieuse – se trouvant ainsi confirmé, la mort du héros peut inspirer les futurs belligérants français. Les guerriers doivent accepter de sacrifier leur vie, sachant que la postérité les fera naître une seconde fois, rappelle le chœur à Hector, dans la pièce de Montchrestien, ce à quoi le héros renchérit:

> Dites plus que le bruit acquis à leur valeur
> Fait naistre une autre vie en la mort de la leur.[12]

Hector est mort les armes à la main pour que sa gloire ainsi obtenue au prix du sang donne un sens à sa vie. Elle est le gage, en ce tournant du XVIe siècle, de la perpétuation de la culture de la guerre – telle qu'elle existait, jadis, chez les Anciens, dit-on, après avoir remanié leurs histoires.

C'est sans doute dans le but d'attirer l'attention sur la perfidie des Argolides que Garnier insiste sur ces propos de Cassandre. Au plus clair de sa défaite, à partir du moment où il se bat vaillamment pour la défense légitime de sa patrie, Hector incarne la victoire des justes sur les impies et le désir glorieux de parvenir à l'immortalité. Chaque fois que les auteurs du tournant du XVIe siècle font le récit de sa mort, ainsi que de celle de tous ses concitoyens[13], ils insistent sur les conditions dans lesquelles il guerroie. La mort d'Hector prouve, en dépit des apparences, que ce sont toujours les bons qui, sur une échelle du temps et des valeurs qui dépasse la contingence de la vie humaine, remportent la palme de la gloire.

Dans cette optique, pour les dramaturges du tournant du XVIe siècle, Hector, à l'instar des Troyens, est la preuve ultime qu'il existe une justice ici-bas. En mettant à l'épreuve la valeur des justes, les bourreaux envoyés

---

[12]Montchrestien, *Hector, Les tragédies*, 3, p. 35 (il n'y a pas de division de scènes dans cette pièce).

[13]Sauf celle d'Énée qui, en fondant Rome, vengera la défaite tout en préservant le sang troyen.

par les dieux jouent eux aussi leur rôle: sans le cruel Achille, le nom fameux d'Hector « n'eus vaguant par l'air aux étoiles atteint »[14]; grâce à l'arrogance et à la cruauté des Grecs, le triste sort des Troyens peut être raconté et servir d'illustre exemple.

BIENHEUREUSES VICTIMES

Gagner une guerre, toujours dans ce même raisonnement logique qui fait des victimes des héros, c'est plus que remporter une bataille: c'est donner au perdant l'impression qu'il est supérieur à son bourreau. Au moindre signe de courage ou de générosité qu'il manifeste à sa mort, il fait paraître l'arbitraire du sort. Pour les dramaturges du tournant du XVIe siècle, les Troyens ne perdent pas tout, puisqu'ils montrent, par la manière dont ils acceptent la mort, une générosité qui laisse présupposer qu'ils auraient aussi bien pu être du côté des vainqueurs. Semblable au récit de la mort des femmes dans les *Lacènes* de Montchrestien, celui des malheurs des Troyennes dans la pièce de Garnier exemplifie la générosité de ce peuple. Ainsi, lorsqu'au deuxième acte, Andromaque défie Ulysse en s'offrant d'elle-même à la torture, elle rappelle l'attitude d'Hector devant Achille – du moins tel que le représentent les dramaturges français: brave jusqu'au dernier souffle – et lui prouve que la victoire des Troyens n'est pas définitive. Elle lui rappelle, au fond, qu'il a bien raison d'avoir peur d'Astyanax, fils d'Hector. Courageuse jusqu'à l'extrémité de ses malheurs, Andromaque dit à Ulysse:

> De fer rouge de feu traversez-moy le sein,
> Versez dans ma poitrine et la soif et la faim;
> Bourrelez-moy le corps de flammes rougissantes;
> Faites-moy consommer en des prisons puantes;
> Tenaillez, tirassez, tronçonnez-moy le corps,
> Genez-moi de tourmens, donnez-moy mille morts:
> Bref, ce qu'eurent jamais tous les tyrans d'envie
> Pour contenter leur rage, exercez sur ma vie.[15]

Si la torture même n'est pas une menace pour cette héroïne qui ne désire rien de plus que de mourir, quelle arme reste-t-il à Ulysse ? Or Andromaque n'est pas victorieuse sur tous les points. Ulysse, à force de ruse, est parvenu à trouver ce pour quoi elle est encore en vie, ce pour quoi elle est prête à combattre, telle une « guerrière », comme elle le dit, et mourir: « pour

---

[14]Garnier, *La Troade*, 1, p. 22.
[15]Garnier, *La Troade*, 2, p. 38.

défendre / De son défunct espoux la scépulchrale cendre »[16]. Cette scène où, épouse, elle se trouve sur le point de voir, pour la deuxième fois, le corps de son mari profané et où, mère, elle est tout près de recueillir les membres broyés de son fils précipité du haut d'une falaise, est du plus noble pathétique. Soutenue tant bien que mal par Hécube, Andromaque entend le récit des malheurs de son petit Astyanax:

> Son corps est tout froissé, tout moulu, écaché,
> Rompu, brisé, gachy, démembré, détaché;
> Sa teste par morceaux, la cervelle sortie;
> En bref vous ne verrez une seule partie
> Qui n'ait les os broyez plus menu que le grain
> Qu'on farine au moulin pour le tourner en pain:
> Si qu'il ne semble plus qu'une difforme masse
> Confuse de tout poinct, sans trait d'humaine face
> Ny d'humaine figure, et puis le sang, qui l'oinct,
> Fait qu'en levant un membre on ne le cognoist point.[17]

Cette énumération fait apparaître un corps d'enfant d'abord morcelé puis broyé, mouliné et, enfin, dépouillé de tout trait humain. Plusieurs critiques ont dénoncé l'emploi de la comparaison entre l'état de la cervelle et le pain que l'on broie[18]. Si elle ne semble pas parvenir à sublimer l'horreur par un langage soi-disant élevé, elle est cependant chargée de sens pour les contemporains de Garnier qui ont vu des cadavres d'enfants à qui on broyait, sinon la cervelle, du moins les os pour en faire de la farine, tel qu'on peut le lire, par exemple, chez d'Aubignac, Burel ou chez Léry[19]. La France de

---

[16]Garnier, *La Troade*, 2, p. 43.

[17]Garnier, *La Troade*, 3, p. 78.

[18]Voir, par exemple, Holyoake, *A Critical Study*, p. 286: « seems particularly infelicitous ».

[19]La famine est en effet extraordinaire et pousse souvent les citoyens à commettre des actes qui peuvent être surprenants pour les témoins de l'époque. Voir, par exemple, le cas de cette famille dont parle d'Augigné: « En fin le suif n'estant plus que pour les plus riches, ils firent du pain de paille haschee et d'ardoize, y meslant du fumier de chevaux: et tout ce qu'ils pensoyent avoir quelque suc » (Aubigné, *Histoire universelle*, 4, 6, chap. 12, p. 41). Voir aussi ce témoignage de Léry, *Histoire mémorable du Siège de Sancerre (1573)*: « Et certes m'estant acheminé prés le lieu de leur demeurance, et ayant veu l'os, et le rest de la teste de ceste pauvre fille, curé, et rongé, et les oreille mangées, ayant veu aussi la langue cuite, espesse d'un doigt qu'ils estoyent prests à manger, quand ils furent *surpris*: les deux cuisses, les jambes et pieds dans une chaudiere avec *vinaigre, espices et sel*, prest à cuire et mettre sur le feu [...] » (*in* Nakam, *Au lendemain de la Saint-Barthélemy. Guerre civile et famine,* p. 290). Ce qui est frappant, dans cet extrait, est que la famille Potard, surprise de cannibalisme, a apparemment reçu « aumosne d'un potage d'herbe et du vin » le jour même (*Au lendemain de la Saint-Barthélemy,* p. 292).

Garnier a, elle aussi, son « Iliade de maux »[20], comme il le dit dans sa pièce. Les désastres de la guerre de Troie sont, dans le contexte des guerres de religion, une réalité pour les Français de la seconde moitié du XVIe siècle.

Juste avant d'écouter avec Andromaque le récit des massacres de son petit-fils, Hécube s'apitoie sur celui des noces funèbres de sa fille Polyxène. La reine troyenne est presque une personnification de la France pleurant les victimes innocentes des guerres civiles. Elle est le personnage central, le pivot autour duquel les catastrophes s'accumulent. Si Hécube est anéantie par les malheurs qu'elle a soufferts injustement, les enfants, eux, font preuve de « magnanimité »[21] et se rendent au trépas courageusement et sans hésitation. Le noble fils d'Hector refuse qu'on le touche et se précipite lui-même depuis la dernière muraille de Troie encore debout. En prenant ainsi en charge sa propre mort, il emporte avec lui, dans l'Hadès, son honneur et enlève à l'ennemi la satisfaction de subjuguer son âme en faisant périr son corps. De même, la vierge Polyxène refuse qu'on la soutienne. Au moment de mourir, elle se laisse choir sur la tombe d'Achille et s'assure, comme le rappelle un messager, de conserver sa pudeur. Avant qu'on lui tranche la gorge, elle découvre pourtant sa poitrine « avec ses mammelettes / S'enflant également, comme rondes pommettes »[22]. Cette gorge qu'elle déploie sous les yeux des guerriers ennemis, eux-mêmes éplorés devant ce sacrifice qu'ils considèrent comme « cruel »[23], est une autre manifestation de cette volonté de prendre en charge sa propre mort. Pour Nicole Loraux, qui a étudié la représentation de la mort des femmes dans les tragédies, le geste de Polyxène imite celui les guerriers: alors que la pendaison est généralement l'option féminine du suicide, Polyxène choisit le glaive et s'approprie ainsi une mort considérée comme plus virile[24]. Mais outre cette appropriation sexuée de la mort, je crois que sa fonction, du moins dans la pièce de Garnier, est surtout de montrer, par la description de cette gorge gonflée d'orgueil, une manifestation de la jeunesse, de la beauté, de la vie face à la mort. La vierge Polyxène, en affichant sa féminité, montre qu'elle est bien en vie en dépit du sort, que c'est « libre »[25] et détachée de toute peur, de toute contrainte,

---

[20]Garnier, *La Troade*, 2, p. 86.

[21]Garnier, *La Troade*, 3, p. 66 et p. 67.

[22]Garnier, *La Troade*, 4, p. 84.

[23]Garnier, *La Troade*, 4, p. 85.

[24]Loraux, *Façons tragiques de tuer une femme*, p. 43, p. 97 et *passim*. Voir surtout ce passage où elle analyse la représentation de Polyxène dans les tragédies grecques et romaines: « Polyxène pouvait bien offrir sa poitrine comme un guerrier, l'armée des Grecs n'y voyait que le dévoilement par une vierge de ses seins de femme » (p. 97).

[25]Garnier, *La Troade*, 4, p. 84.

de tout attachement à sa destinée, qu'elle s'en va, avec la fierté d'une « fille de roy » aux « rives stygianes »[26].

JUSTE VENGEANCE

Après avoir entendu les récits de la mort sacrificielle de sa fille et de son petit-fils, Hécube ne voit plus qu'une solution, si elle veut, à son tour, mourir sans tout perdre. Elle n'a plus qu'une seule arme contre un ennemi aussi cruel: le maudire en implorant les dieux afin qu'ils la vengent:

> Puisse, pour nous venger de vos lasches parjures,
> Neptun vous travailler d'horribles avantures
> Par ses ondes voguant ! [. . .]
> . . . .
> Que la femme, l'espoux, le fils la mère tue;
> Que l'on se plonge au cœur une lame pointue
> Et l'autre par les eaux vagabonde exilé
> Cherchant nouveau séjour sous un ciel reculé [. . .][27]

Ses imprécations témoignent de son refus d'accepter le destin tel qu'il s'impose à elle. Agir autrement serait avouer la victoire des bourreaux sur les victimes, des impies sur les justes. Or, tout ce sang royal n'est pas répandu en vain: les dieux écouteront sa plainte et exauceront ses vœux. Outre le fait qu'il s'agisse là d'un simple lieu commun, le discours d'une victime prévoyant les malheurs de son ennemi vainqueur a surtout pour rôle ici de rappeler que, sur une échelle du temps qui dépasse la vie humaine, la justice finit toujours par triompher[28]. Les malheurs de Troie dépassent ainsi les larmes d'Hécube et des quelques survivantes des ruines de la ville anéantie, pour devenir l'histoire des aléas du destin des grandes nations. Le récit de la défaite de Troie, c'est aussi celui de la chute d'Athènes lors des guerres du Péloponnèse, de la chute de Sparte lors des guerres contre Thèbes, de la mise à sac de cette ville par Alexandre le Grand, de la chute de Rome envahie par les barbares; les malheurs de Troie, ce sont ceux de toutes les victimes, les larmes répandues par les survivantes désormais esclaves, c'est un cri de douleur que tous tendent à exprimer devant les affres de l'existence.

Aussi violent soit-il, le geste des Troyennes perçant de leurs aiguilles les yeux de Polymestor, au dernier acte, constitue un premier pas vers une rétribution divine. L'outrage reçu est souvent vengé dans le sang, et la voix

---

[26]Garnier, *La Troade*, 4, p. 84.

[27]Garnier, *La Troade*, 4, p. 86.

[28]Voir, par exemple, Bowers, *Elizabethan Revenge*, p. 263–264 et *passim*, tout particulièrement ses conclusions qui ouvrent sur le théâtre en général pendant cette époque.

d'Agamemnon, approuvant ce geste barbare, annonce en quelque sorte le destin qui l'attend. Polymestor a beau vouloir « manger son cœur », « d'ongles et de dents » déchirer « son sein », « ses boyaux infects » arracher de sa « main »[29], Hécube a raison d'agir ainsi, explique Agamemnon: « Il ne vous faut plaindre, ains avec patience / La peine supporter de vostre propre offense »[30], dit-il à son allié. Bien qu'Hécube en veuille aux dieux de lui avoir fait subir un tel sort, les derniers vers du poème, prononcés par cette héroïne, comportent le mot d'espoir. En faisant allusion à l'attitude d'Agamemnon, elle affirme: « Et m'allaite d'espoir que quelques-uns encor / Pourront estre punis comme Polymestor »[31].

CONCLUSION

Garnier n'est pas le seul à composer une *Troade*. Bien qu'il ne s'agisse pas de l'un des thèmes les plus repris en France, il fascine tout de même les dramaturges jusqu'à la moitié du XVIIe siècle. Plusieurs éléments peuvent expliquer ce phénomène. S'il est peu souvent adapté, c'est qu'il ne satisfait pas à la poétique dramatique qui impose progressivement la règle d'unité d'action. Sallabery tente sa chance en choisissant Agamemnon comme personnage central à partir duquel les événements s'enchaînent. Il n'obtient pas des résultats beaucoup plus convaincants que Garnier, du moins sur le plan de la poétique. De plus, il est fort difficile de respecter les bienséances, étant donné l'extrême violence que l'on y raconte, quoique ce soit le plus souvent de manière indirecte, par l'entremise d'un messager. Le type de discours contenu dans cette pièce ne survit d'ailleurs pas au classicisme. À l'époque de Garnier, pourtant, un tel sujet a encore de bonnes chances de toucher les spectateurs, puisqu'il jouit d'une certaine crédibilité par sa vraisemblance. Les ruines dont chacun est témoin autour de lui, les assassinats et les erreurs de ceux qui ont pour mandat de protéger leurs citoyens, les maladies épidémiques, les famines et les massacres que les citoyens subissent ou propagent impunément, voilà ce dont Garnier veut parler.

En s'en remettant à la ruine de Troie comme paradigme servant à illustrer les guerres qui déchirent la France, le dramaturge montre les malheurs intimes avec un certain recul[32]. C'est ce qui rend possible la représentation de tels sujets dans les tragédies humanistes de la Renaissance. Garnier ne se contente pas d'offrir aux siens une occasion de s'apitoyer sur

---

[29]Garnier, *La Troade*, 5, p. 99.
[30]Garnier, *La Troade*, 5, p. 101.
[31]Garnier, *La Troade*, 5, p. 103.
[32]Voir Jacoby, *Wild Justice*, p. 20.

leur sort en projetant sur l'Antiquité leurs propres malheurs. Il leur rappelle, dans sa dédicace, que les « extrêmes calamitez » sont un mal nécessaire, causé par « l'ire du grand Dieu ou par l'inévitable malignité d'une secrette influence des astres »[33]. C'est dans la ruine que naissent les grands empires. C'est dans les ruines de Troie qu'a pu naître Rome. C'est grâce à l'effondrement de « l'orgueilleux empire romain » qu'a pu naître la « très-florissante Monarchie » française[34]. Aussi bien dire, c'est dans le sang des guerres de religion que la France peut se régénérer. Ses jours meilleurs sont à venir. Pour le dramaturge, un règne de calamités ne conduit pas nécessairement à une ère de paix, mais de ses ruines peut naître un autre royaume ou la régénération du même. L'injustice se commet dans le sang et elle est punie par le sang. De même, les grands royaumes naissent dans la violence et s'effondrent ensuite en un fracas immense qui engloutit, dans ses ruines, princes et manants. La rétribution divine est une promesse de justice qui ne peut être réalisée qu'au prix du sacrifice de plusieurs vies. Les spectateurs du temps de Garnier ne sont pas insensibles au concept de sacrifice, de rétribution divine et de promesse lointaine d'un monde meilleur[35]. Ils peuvent assez aisément transposer les bases de leur foi sur l'histoire du monde qui semble suivre, au temps des guerres de religion, des lois qui ne ressemblent en rien à celles auxquelles notre société est aujourd'hui soumise. Les critiques attribuent volontiers à Garnier et aux auteurs humanistes, un caractère archaïque et violent[36], alors qu'en fait ils sont tout simplement modernes, sensibles à une échelle de valeurs propre à leur époque.

BIBLIOGRAPHIE

Aubigné, Agrippa d'. *Histoire universelle*. Éd. de Genève, 1626 avec variantes de la 1ère éd., 1616–1620. T. 4, liv. 4 et 7. Éd. André Thierry. Genève: Droz, 1987.

Bono, Barbara J. *Literary Transvaluation. From Vergilian Epic to Shakespearean Tragicomedy*. Berkeley and Los Angeles: University of California Press, 1984.

Bowers, Fredson. *Elizabethan Revenge Tragedy, 1587–1642*. Princeton: Princeton University Press, 1940.

Burel, Jean. *Mémoires de Jean Burel, journal du Puy à l'époque des guerres de religion*. 1586. D'après l'éd. d'Augustin Chassaing, 1875. Nouv. éd. augm. Saint-Vidal: Centre d'étude de la Vallée de la Borne, 1983.

---

[33]Garnier, *La Troade*, p. 1.

[34]Garnier, *La Troade*, p. 1.

[35]Voir Bono, *Literary Transvaluation*, p. 40, qui voit, dans le théâtre humaniste, la transposition des mythes judéo-chrétiens dans les mythes néo-platoniciens de promesse d'un monde meilleur.

[36]Voir, par exemple, Holyoake, *A Critical Study*, p. 286.

Crouzet, Denis. *Les guerriers de Dieu. La violence du temps des troubles de religion. Vers 1525–vers 1610.* 2 t. Seyssel: Champ Vallon, 1990.

Garnier, Robert. *Œuvres complètes. Théâtre et poésies.* 2 t. Éd. Lucien Pinvert. Paris: Librairie Garnier Frères, 1923.

Garnier, Robert. *La Troade: tragédie.* Éd. Jean-Dominique Beaudin. Paris: Champion, 1999.

Garrisson, Janine. *Guerre civile et compromis. 1559–1598.* Paris: Seuil, 1991.

Holyoake, John. *A Critical Study of the Tragedies of Robert Garnier, 1545–90.* New York: Peter Lang, 1987.

Homère. *Iliade.* Éd. et trad. P. Mazon et al. 4 t. Paris: CUF, 1937–1938.

Jacoby, Susan. *Wild Justice.* New York: Harper & Row, 1983.

L'Estoile, Pierre de. *Journal de L'Estoile pour le règne de Henri III (1574–1589).* 10e éd. par Louis-Raymond Lefèvre. Paris: Gallimard, 1943.

Loraux, Nicole. *Façons tragiques de tuer une femme.* Paris: Hachette, 1985.

Montchrestien, Antoine de. *Les tragédies de Montchrestien.* Nouv. éd. d'après l'éd. de 1604 [qui ressemble à celle de 1601, plus *Hector*] avec notice et commentaire par Petit de Julleville. Paris: Plon, 1891.

Nakam, Géralde, éd. *Au lendemain de la Saint-Barthélemy. Guerre civile et famine. Histoire mémorable du Siège de Sancerre* (1573; de Jean de Léry). Paris: Éditions Anthropos, 1975.

Pasquier, Étienne. *Écrits politiques.* 1561–1615. Éd. D. Thickett. Genève: Droz, 1966.

"What's Hecuba to him . . .": Trojan Heroes and Rhetorical Selves in Shakespeare's Hamlet

ANDREW HISCOCK

First the scholler shal learne the precepts concerning the divers sorts of arguments in the first part of Logike, (for without them Rhetorike cannot be well understood) then shall followe the tropes and figures in the first part of Rhetorike, wherein he shall employ the sixth part of his studie, and all the rest in learning and handling good authors: as are Tullies *Offices*, his *Orations*, Caesars *Commentaries*, Virgils *Aeneid*, Ovids *Metamorphosis*, and Horace . . . . And by this time he must observe in authors all the use of the Artes, as not only the words and phrases, not only the examples of the arguments; but also the axiome, wherein every argument is disposed; the syllogisme, whereby it is concluded; the method of the whole treatise, and the passages, whereby the parts are joyned together . . . .

And so let him take in hand the exercise of all these three Artes at once in making somewhat of his owne, first by imitation . . . .[1]

The pre-eminent status of classical writing both in the theory and practice of early modern education has long been appreciated. Here in *The Education of Children* (1588) the schoolmaster William Kempe illustrates how study programmes for Elizabethan pupils should be organised in the first instance around the work of Roman writers (Greek being reserved for the older and/or more able boys). Under this fairly typical educational regime, pupils were to be drilled in translation exercises, recitation and rhetorical analysis for six days a week, thirty-six weeks of the year. The identification of rhetorical *topoi*, a facility for translation of classical scenes and passages into the vernacular, the performative skills of declamation, these were all familiar, formative practices learned in the Tudor school environment and would have been understood as such by a large proportion of the educated members of audiences in early modern playhouses. When the pupil had gone some way to mastering the foundations of the arts of grammar, logic

---

[1]Kempe, *The Education of Children*, G2v–G3r.

and rhetoric, Kempe advises, "then let him have a like theame to prosecute with the same artificiall instruments, that he findeth in his author."[2] In other words, let him exploit the skills and knowledge learned intensively in the company of classical writers and translate them according to the demands of the present.

Such "artificiall instruments," gained as a result of continual cycles of translation, paraphrase, analysis and rote-learning, clearly did not distress early modern teachers in the same way that they have appalled some modern educationalists. In *The Arte of Englishe Poesie* (1589), George Puttenham argued that

> Man also in all his actions that be not altogether naturall, but are gotten by study and discipline or exercise, as to daunce by measures, to sing by note, to play on the lute, and such like, it is a praise to be said an artificiall dauncer, singer, & player on instruments, because they be not exactly knowne or done, but by rules & precepts or teaching of schoolemasters.[3]

Naturally, this raises a question regarding how the necessary stored knowledge was to be retrieved when the occasion demanded. One solution for the business of public speaking was proposed by the classical exponents of rhetoric. Roman writers such as Cicero, Quintilian and the author of the *Rhetorica Ad Herennium*, for example, had advocated the exercise of memory through the mental imaging of a complex architectural structure in which every room would contain a piece of relevant information. As Quintilian writes,

> And all the labour of which I have so far spoken will be in vain unless all the other departments be co-ordinated by the animating principle of memory. For our whole education depends upon memory, and we shall receive instruction all in vain if all we hear slips from us . . . . Indeed it is not without good reason that memory has been called the treasure-house of eloquence . . . . Some place is chosen of the largest possible extent and characterised by the utmost possible variety, such as a spacious house divided into a number of rooms . . . . The first thought is placed, as it were, in the forecourt; the second, let us say, in the living room; the remainder are placed in due order . . . . As soon as the memory of the facts requires to be revived, all these places are visited in turn and the various deposits are demanded from their custodians . . . . We require, therefore, places, real or imaginary, and images or symbols, which we must, of course, invent for ourselves.[4]

---

[2]Kempe, *The Education of Children*, G3r.

[3]Puttenham, *The Arte of English Poesie*, p. 310.

[4]See Quintilian, *The Institutio Oratoria of Quintilian*, bk. XI, pp. 213, 221, 223.

The orator would thus allow his (and it would be *his*—the gender expectations surrounding rhetorical expertise are widely in evidence throughout classical and early modern writing) mind's eye to navigate through the house as his argument unfolded, visiting each chamber in sequence.[5] Such spatial theories were to prove enormously influential across Europe throughout the early modern period. However, if Roman theorists concentrated upon the oratorical experience requisite for success in the *civitas*, Christian theologians, at least as far back as St. Augustine, had recognized the significance of memory and the skills of public performance in coming to understand some of the mysteries of spiritual interiority. Augustine is often seen to conceive of memory in spatial terms: "Great is the power of memory . . . . See the broad plains and caves and caverns of my memory."[6] From the perspective of this Church Father, memory is frequently linked to the gaining of self-knowledge and ethical understanding, and indeed to spiritual commitment. In *De Trinitate*, for example, Augustine envisaged an analogue to the Holy Trinity in memory, understanding and will—"these three are one, one life, one mind, one essence."[7] However, throughout the development of all these various philosophical traditions, the stress returns regularly to the notion of translating learned knowledge into significant human action, and this emphasis continued throughout the sixteenth and seventeenth centuries. Indeed, in a marginal note to his reading matter Gabriel Harvey recorded that "He that woold be thowght A Man, or seeme anything worth; must be A great Dooer, or A Great Speaker: He is a Cipher, & but a peakegoose, that is nether of both . . . ."[8]

In the early modern period there is evidence of a renewed interest, most especially in humanist circles, in the faculty of memory as a creative resource, a necessary attribute for successful civic service and also as a strategic power which might underpin the human endeavour to bridge the gap with an heroic, classical past. Erasmus, for example, placed great value on the selective training of memory as a crucial activity for the aspiring scholar. In particular, he focused attention upon the productive use of memory whereby memorised data was

---

[5]With reference to gender expectations, here is Quintilian's *Institutio Oratoria*: "What use is it if we employ a lofty tone in cases of trivial import, a slight and refined style in cases of great moment . . . ? Such incongruities are as unbecoming as it is for men to wear necklaces and pearls and flowing raiment which are the natural adornments of women, or for women to robe themselves in the garb of triumph, than which there can be conceived no more majestic raiment" (bk. XI, pp. 155–157).

[6]Augustine, *Confessions*, bk. X, xvii (26), p. 194.

[7]Augustine, *On The Holy Trinity*, bk. X, ch. 11, in Schaff, *A Select Library of the Nicene and Post-Nicene Fathers*, vol. III, p. 143.

[8]Marginal comment by Harvey in a volume by Ramus. Cited in Kintgern, *Reading in Tudor England*, pp. 75–76.

deployed by the student to convince his audience of the legitimacy of the argument or action. In an independent letter in *De Conscribendi Epistolis*, Erasmus offered the following advice: "Some people's primary and almost sole anxiety is to learn things by heart, word for word. I do not approve of this as it involves much work and is practically useless . . . . But if there is some saying, maxim, old proverb, anecdote, story, apt comparison, or anything that strikes you as being phrased with brevity, point, or in some other clever way, consider it a treasure to be stored carefully in the mind for use and imitation."[9] Later in the century, in the *Pandectae locorum communium*, John Foxe enquired, "what can poets, what can historians, what can rhetoricians, and orators . . . provide by their art without memory, or by their memory without noting the places?"[10] Moreover, George Puttenham is once again notable in his contention that "There is nothing in man of all the potential parts of his mind (reason and will except) more noble or more necessary to the active life then memory . . . ."[11] In a host of different ways the cultural fascination with rhetorical prowess which dated back centuries had a considerable influence on early modern concepts of artistic creativity, civic and spiritual undertakings and, indeed, the image of the intellectual for contemporaries. Unsurprisingly, this cultural climate encouraged expectations that the well-exercised memory would be indispensable for successful social intervention.

Hamlet, of course, returns obsessively to the subject of memory. This is true whether we consider the 1603 First Quarto:

> The Tragicall Historie of HAMLET *Prince of Denmarke*. As it hath beene diuerse times acted by his Highnesse seruants in the Cittie of London: as also in the two Vniuersities of Cambridge and Oxford, and else-where at London

or the 1604 Second Quarto:

> The Tragicall Historie of HAMLET, *Prince of Denmarke*. Newly imprinted and enlarged to almost as much againe as it was, according to the true and perfect Coppie

or the version in the 1623 Folio where we are presented with a text entitled simply,

> THE TRAGEDIE OF HAMLET, Prince of Denmarke.[12]

---

[9]Cited in Kintgern, *Reading in Tudor England*, pp. 24–25.

[10]Foxe, *Pandectae locorum communium,* A3v. Cited in Rechtien, "John Foxe's Comprehensive Collection," p. 86.

[11]Opening of chapter xix of "the First Booke." See Puttenham, *The Arte of English Poesie*, p. 54.

[12]Henceforth, line references to *Hamlet* relate to the following editions: FQ—*Hamlet*

In all of these versions, the Danish court culture at Elsinore is finely attuned to the political and psychological dangers which acts of memory may pose. It is all too apparent to the new political ascendancy that to re-*member* is to reconnect with an alternative matrix of political power, an alternative existential space of legitimacy. In the First Quarto, for example, the recently crowned Claudius remonstrates with the fatherless hero for what he deems to be his disproportionate grief: "Therefore cease laments, / It is a fault gainst heauen, fault gainst the dead, / A fault against nature . . . " (FQ 2.44–45).[13] In the Second Quarto and 1623 Folio, Gertrude is even more energetic in her rejection of the fruits of memory, viewing them as having destructive, corrosive effects: "Do not for euer with thy veyled lids / Seeke for thy Noble Father in the dust . . . " (SQ & F I.ii.70–71). Hamlet's decision through word, deed and attire, it should be noted, to stage public rituals of memory is a direct threat to the regime in the way that it constantly reminds the assembled company of the contrasting authority of Old Hamlet's governance.

At the beginning of the early modern period, despite an enduring sense of isolation both from his contemporary culture and the classical past, Petrarch had confided in his letters that "I am happier with the dead than the living . . . ."[14] In this sentiment Petrarch is not unrepresentative of succeeding generations of early modern intellectuals across Europe. Interestingly, by the beginning of the seventeenth century Ben Jonson was envisaging a dynamic engagement with the classical heritage whereby the literary forefathers of Rome and Greece were still viewed as an inevitable *point de départ* but should not be seen as having exhausted all forms of textual creativity. He confided in his commonplace book *Timber or Discoveries* that, "I Know *Nothing* can conduce more to letters, then to examine the writings of the *Ancients*, and not to rest in their sole[.] Authority, to take all upon trust from them . . . . For to all the observations of the *Ancients*, wee have our owne experience, which, if wee will use, and apply, wee have better means to pronounce. It is true they open'd the gates, and made the way that went before us; but as Guides, not Commanders."[15] The mind of Shakespeare's prince is also exercised by this cultural drive to re-engage with the

---

First Quarto is the edition by Irace; SQ—*Hamlet* Second Quarto is to *Hamlet Second Quarto 1604–5*, Shakespeare Quarto Facsimiles; and F—*Hamlet* in the 1623 Folio is to Bertram and Kliman, *Three-Text Hamlet*.

[13]In the Second Quarto (I.ii.87–117) and the 1623 Folio (I.ii.87–117), Claudius is more prolix, combining his advice with an announcement of Hamlet as heir to the Danish throne.

[14]Cited in Greene, *The Light in Troy*, p. 8.

[15]Jonson, *Discoveries*, pp. 10–11.

textual landscapes of classical writing and to exploit them for present demands. Rendered profoundly anxious by the *doings* of Danish patriarchs past and present, Hamlet turns back almost effortlessly in his first encounter with the players to a *locus amœnus* for the intellectual elite of early modern Europe: the sack of Troy.

Virgil's epic dealing with this theme had been a source of consuming interest for British scholars throughout the preceding century.[16] Gavin Douglas had translated the *Aeneid* into 'Scottis' at the turn of the sixteenth century (*Eneados*, pub. 1553); and, conversant with this earlier endeavour, Henry Howard, Earl of Surrey, had 'englished' books II and IV of Virgil's epic into blank verse (published for the first time together in 1557). In this latter translation, Surrey offers his reader a Pyrrhus "rejoysing in his dartes, with glittering armes; / Like to the adder with venimous herbes fed" (II.607–8).[17] Another notable translation in the second half of the sixteenth century is that by Thomas Phaer—and this would appear to have been known to Christopher Marlowe.[18] However, it is interesting that the figure of Pyrrhus, seeking to avenge the death of his father Achilles, is not given extensive emphasis in Virgil's epic or in the work of subsequent translators. It is only as the century draws to a close that such an image appears to hold particular attractions for Shakespeare and his contemporaries. In his early narrative poem, *The Rape of Lucrece* (1594), Shakespeare had given his reader a foretaste of a central character deciphering the Fall of Troy, deploying it as a narrative space for exploring personal and political trauma. Gabriel Harvey was inclined to bring both Shakespeare's *Hamlet* and *The Rape of Lucrece* together, finding that they both contained that which might "please the wiser sort."[19] Certainly the texts share important thematic interests, such as unwarranted usurpation ("Why should the worm intrude the maiden bud? / Or hateful cuckoos hatch in sparrows' nests?" 848–849), human degeneracy ("But no perfection is so absolute / That some impurity doth not pollute," 853–854), and resistance to what are perceived as the forces

---

[16]Richardson finds a decisive change in British cultural responses to the Trojan narrative to be marked in Caxton's *Recuyell of the Historyes of Troye* (1474), particularly in its departure from earlier medieval celebrations of virtue and chivalry during the siege in favour of Caxton's emphasis upon human loss and moral conclusions (*The Legends of Troy*, p. 26).

[17]Line references are to the text as it appears in Jones, *Henry Howard, Earl of Surrey: Poems*.

[18]For discussion of Marlowe's acquaintance with Phaer's translation, see Thomas and Tydeman, *Christopher Marlowe*, p. 18. Phaer finished translating the first nine books in 1560. The task was completed by Thomas Twyne in 1573.

[19]Munro, *The Shakespeare Allusion-Book*, vol. I, p. 56.

of destiny ("O this dread night, wouldst thou one hour come back, / I could prevent this storm, and shun my wrack." 965–966).[20] When the violated Lucrece scans a "skilful painting" of the Trojan siege ("To find a face where all distress is stelled" [1444]), she, like Hamlet, finds kinship with the anguish of Hecuba. Rather than concerning herself primarily with the wounded Priam, "bleeding under Pyrrhus' proud foot" (1449), she "shaped her sorrow to the beldam's woes . . . " (1458). This Roman matron, whom Colin Burrow has recently found (like so many readers before him) to be "astonishingly, unstoppably, all-but endlessly eloquent," finds consolation through giving voice to the silenced Hecuba: "I'll tune thy woes with my lamenting tongue, / And drop sweet balm in Priam's painted wound, / And rail on Pyrrhus that hath done him wrong . . ." (1468–1470).[21] Here, in a poem which has already compared Tarquin to the duplicitous Synon (1534–1540), we discover the heroine struggling to formulate a form of interiority through selective readings of the Fall of Troy—a narrative which for generations of European intellectuals had stood as a secular pendant text to that of the Fall from Grace in Eden.[22]

The Tale of Troy (pub. 1589) is one of George Peele's earliest known texts, and it is in this poem that we discover the Greek prince, "whose bloodie mind and murdring rage, / Nor awe of Gods, nor reverence of age, / Coulde temper from a deede so tyrannous . . . ." A little further on, the reader learns that Pyrrhus "Hath hent this aged Priam by the hake, / Like Butcher bent to sley . . . / The mightie king of Troy, / With cruell yron this cursed Greekish boy / Rids of his life" (ll. 440–452).[23] One of Marlowe's earliest dramas, *Dido, Queen of Carthage*, also offers in Aeneas' narration a stirring image of Pyrrhus (Neoptolemus) emerging from the "entrails" of the wooden horse followed by "a thousand Grecians more": 'Kill! Kill!' they cried": "At last came Pyrrhus, fell and full of ire, / His harness dropping blood, and on his spear / The

---

[20]Line references to *The Rape of Lucrece* are taken from *The Oxford Shakespeare: The Complete Sonnets and Poems*.

[21]Burrow, *The Oxford Shakespeare*, p. 51. See also John Kerrigan's restrained comment that "the complaint against Time and Opportunity which Lucrece utters on Tarquin's departure is by any measure remarkable" ("Shakespeare's Poems," p. 71).

[22]Burrow argues that "A single book would have given Shakespeare a grasp of all these variant versions of the story. This was Paulus Marsus's edition of Ovid's *Fasti*, which was frequently reprinted in the sixteenth century. There are strong grounds for believing Shakespeare knew this version. Before the rape of Lucretia, Ovid's Tarquin pretends to the Gabii that he has been cast out by his family. He then betrays the tribe who have taken him in. At this point both Marsus and his fellow commentator Constantius compare Tarquin to Sinon" (Burrow, *The Oxford Shakespeare,* pp. 48–49).

[23]Line references are taken from the text as it appears in *The Life and Minor Works of George Peele*, ed. Horne.

mangled head of Priam's youngest son . . . ."[24] At this key moment in the narrative, Marlowe appears keen to embellish his sources, providing graphic details of physical torments which will ultimately serve to counterbalance the psychological traumas being prepared for the dénouement. In this extended evocation of Priam's death, Polites' head is now speared, Hecuba becomes witch-like,[25] and the king is butchered in a seemingly improvised and gruesome ritual:

ÆNEAS:	O, let me live, great Neoptolemus!
	Not mov'd at all, but smiling at his tears,
	This butcher, whilst his hands were yet held up,
	Treading upon his breast, strook off his hands.
DIDO:	O, end, Æneas! I can hear no more.
ÆNEAS:	At which the frantic queen leap'd on his face,
	And in his eyelids hanging by the nails,
	A little while prolong'd her husband's life.
	At last the soldiers pull'd her by the heels,
	And swung her howling in the empty air,
	Which sent an echo to the wounded king: . . . .
	Then from the navel to the throat at once
	He ripp'd old Priam, at whose latter gasp
	Jove's marble statue gan to bend the brow,
	As loathing Pyrrhus for this wicked act.
	Yet he, undaunted, took his father's flag,
	And dipp'd it in the old king's chill-cold blood,
	And then in triumph ran into the streets,
	Through which he could not pass for slaughter'd men;
	So, leaning on his sword, he stood stone still,
	Viewing the fire wherewith rich Ilion burnt.

II.i.239–249, 255–264

It is also worthy of note that in *The Second Part of the Iron Age* (pub. 1632), for example, Thomas Heywood (unlike his predecessors) chooses to bring the whole scene onto a crowded stage: "*King* Priam *discovered kneeling* at the Altar, *with him.* Hecuba, Polixena, Andromache, Astianax: to *them enter* Pyrrhus, *and all the Greeks,* Pyrrhus *killing* Polytes Priams sonne *before the Altar*" (III.i.)[26] Indeed, Heywood's audience is left in doubt that a *grand spectacle* awaits them:

---

[24]Marlowe, *The Tragedy of Dido, Queen of Carthage*, II.i.183–215. Subsequent line references to *Dido* are to Steane's edition.

[25]It is in Ovid's *Metamorphoses* that Hecuba attacks King Polymestor, who has murdered her youngest and last son. I am indebted to Thomas and Tydeman, *Christopher Marlowe*, p. 58.

[26]The edition of *The Second Part of the Iron Age* [printed 1632] I refer to is in Heywood,

PYRRHUS: Still let your voyces to hye Heauen aspire
            For *Pyrhus* vengeance, murdring steele and fire.
ALL THE LADIES: Oh, oh.   III.i.

After carefully matching each of the Trojan women with her executioner in the shape of various Greek princes, Pyrrhus allows the theatrical fireworks to continue as he turns his attention to the remaining victims:

ASTIANAX: Where shall I hide me?
PYRRHUS: So nimble *Hectors* bastard?
            My father slew thy father, I the sonne:
            Thus will I tosse thy carkas upon hie,
            The brat aboue his fathers fame shall flie.
            He tosseth him about his head and kills him.
SYNON: No, somewhat doth remayne,
            Alarum still, the people's not all slaine,
            Let not one soule survive.
PYRRHUS: Then Trumpets Sound Till burning *Troy* in Troian blood
            be drown'd.   *Exeunt.* III.i.

On turning to Elsinore, the mental reflex on Hamlet's part to repeat (quite literally on this occasion) an account of the bloodlust of the avenging Pyrrhus should not surprise the audience, for Shakespeare's dramatic world appears wholly given over to cycles of repetition of one kind or another. Gertrude, the failed Hecuba in her son's eyes, has "sinned" in marrying twice; Claudius tries to kill two different members of the royal family; Hamlet himself kills two patriarchs; there are two grief-stricken avengers eventually in Elsinore in Laertes and Hamlet himself; and, of course, we find the visiting company offering two entertainments to the court in the dumbshow and the play proper. This proliferation of duplicating narratives may link to a wider sense of this culture's dissatisfaction in its relations with the past. Indeed, it is tempting to conjecture that we are being presented with a society locked into a relentless cycle of human experience, mourning for a lost integrity.

As this scene with the players unfolds, the narration is begun and begun again, interrupted and revised; and it becomes increasingly apparent at this famously metatheatrical moment that Hamlet, as a seasoned theatre-goer with a profound knowledge of dramatic production, repeatedly conceives of his own persona as revenger according to modes of theatricality. Rosencrantz quips that the dour prince will give but "lenten entertainment" to the players when they arrive (F II.ii.316). In the event, Hamlet certainly

The Dramatic Works of Thomas Heywood, vol. 3. See pp. 390–394.

resolves upon grim festivities for whom he considers to be the newly-instituted mock king.

If *The Murther of Gonzago* is concerned with the *mimesis* of revenge, explicitly creating in the darker purpose of Lucianus (nephew to the Player King) a lens through which to consider recent actions at Elsinore, in the staging of Troy the audience is given an intimation of this in the *diegesis* of revenge. Both are invitations to interrogate the ethical base of this culture. The frictional energies generated between these two modes excite the mind of the prince. William Hazlitt famously proposed at the turn of the nineteenth century that Hamlet's "ruling passion is to think, not to act: and any vague pretext that flatters this propensity instantly diverts him from his previous purposes."[27] If we choose in this way to discount any performative dimension to Hamlet's speech acts and to liken them to displacement exercises, such a scene with the players could be viewed as apotropaic, a way of keeping death at bay. However, Shakespeare's tragedy in general may be encouraging us to collapse the boundaries between *doing* and *telling* in order to diversify our understanding of cultural intervention.

Whatever the evocation of Troy offers, for example, it clearly offers the prince the possibility of empowerment. Through the power to narrate, or *to govern the narration of others*, Hamlet secures (albeit provisionally) a mode of control and interrogation. From the perspective of the audience, the narrative of Troy which Hamlet summons up from his memory becomes the most recent in a sequence of meditations on possible courses of action. Whether Hamlet is reflecting upon the conflicting cultural identities of Fortinbras, Horatio, Laertes, Osric or Pyrrhus, these must be seen as experiments in narrative spaces from which possible selves may be recuperated: "Examples gross as earth exhort me: / Witness this army of such mass and charge, / Led by a delicate and tender prince" (4.4.47). Temporarily thwarted in his search for role models in the present, in Troy Hamlet is exploring textual personae which cannot be remembered, only recited. Moreover, whatever translations Hamlet accomplishes in his movements back and forth from biological to textual fathers in the murders of Priam and Gonzago, such acts should be studied with early modern expectations of translation in mind: being viewed not as examples of slavish replication, but as creative acts of self-definition: fresh narratives which convert and extend the source material, engaging fully with their new cultural home *and* offering the audience the opportunity to take the measure of the translator

---

[27]Howe, *The Complete Works of William Hazlitt*, p. 235.

himself. In this context, Ben Jonson's observations in his commonplace book *Discoveries* prove once again instructive:

> Indeed, things, wrote with labour, deserve to be so read, and will last their Age. The third requisite in our Poet, or Maker, is Imitation, to be able to convert substance of Riches of another Poet, to his owne use. To make choise of one excellent man above the rest, and so to follow him, till he grow very hee; or so like him, as the Copie may be mistaken for the Principall. Not, as a Creature, that swallowes what it takes in, crude, raw, or undigested; but, that feeds with an Appetite, and hath a Stomacke to concoct, devide, and turne all into nourishment. Not, to imitate servilely, as Horace saith, and catch at vices, for vertue, but to draw forth out of the best, and choisest flowers, with the Bee, and turne all into Honey, worke it into one relish, and savour: make our imitation sweet: observe, how the best writers have imitated, and follow them.[28]

In the prince's first encounter with the players at Elsinore, the audience witnesses the competing ambitions of those present to perform. Putting to one side Polonius' claims to theatre experience, it is Hamlet who initially seizes the opportunity to prove his credentials as an actor. However, the prince does not bring even this act of narration to a close and so the audience is left to consider once again his *potential* for action rather than his powers of closure.

> The rugged *Pyrrhus*, he whose Sable Armes
> Blacke as his purpose, did the night resemble
> When he lay couched in the Ominous Horse,
> Hath now this dread and blacke Complexion smear'd
> With Heraldry more dismall: Head to foote
> Now is he to take Geulles, horridly Trick'd
> With blood of Fathers, Mothers, Daughters, Sonnes,
> Bak'd and impasted with the parching streets,
> That lend a tyrannous, and damned light
> To their vilde Murthers, roasted in wrath and fire,
> And thus o're-sized with coagulate gore,
> Vvith eyes like Carbuncles, the hellish *Pyrrhus*
> Old Grandsire *Priam* seekes.
>
> POLONIUS: Fore God, my Lord, well spoken, with good accent, and good discretion.
>
> F II.ii.452–467

At this point, with the memorial recovery of Troy by Hamlet, Shakespeare's play offers an arresting opposition between the pursuit of the *vita activa* and

---

[28]See fragment 130 *Poesis* in Jonson, *Discoveries: A Critical Edition*, pp. 124–125.

the *vita contemplativa*. The tremendous image of Pyrrhus' ruthless dynamism renders him the most frightening of all the avengers in this play, exposed as an indiscriminate killer in a manner keenly in contrast to Laertes, Hamlet and indeed Fortinbras. Whether this black, infernal Pyrrhus emerges as a version of Claudius for the audience or a would-be Hamlet with an inky cloak, clearly the awe-inspiring demonic figure of the murdering Greek prince is being controlled in this dramatic fragment through reduction to a stereotype of evil. The relentless demonisation of the "dread," "blacke," "hellish" Pyrrhus in Hamlet's speech serves to diminish any Virgilian notion of heroic rage relating to the killing of Achilles, his father. Instead, the emphasis falls upon responses of alarm and disgust, but these are responses which Hamlet himself must master if he is to adopt effectively the role of revenger, whether it be as stage performer:

> 'Tis now the verie witching time of night,
> When Churchyards yawne, and Hell it selfe breaths out
> Contagion to this world. Now could I drink hot blood,
> And do such bitter businesse as the day
> Would quake to looke on. F III.ii.388–392

or as man of action:

> This man shall set me packing:
> Ile lugge the Guts into the Neighbour roome,
> Mother goodnight. F III.iv.211–213

Having fully digested the collapse of Trojan patriarchy as the blade of the "painted tyrant" strikes at "the milkie head of the Reuerend Priam," Hamlet is now eager to turn to an angle of vision other than that of victim and aggressor: "Say on; come to Hecuba." Identifying all too closely with the "inobled" (F II.ii.502) or "mobled" (SQ II.ii.524) queen, the prince hungers for an account of her emotional trauma—a trauma which subsequently he is determined to compel upon his mother when he decides to "speake Daggers to her, but vse none . . . " (F III.ii.396). What is significant in this context is Hamlet's irrepressible and, from the point of view of speedy revenge, debilitating drive to narrativise his situation. It may be that in the competition for attention on stage between onlookers and performers, "Th'obseru'd of all Obseruers" (F III.i.154), as Ophelia frames him, is losing control of his own rhetorical selves. Nonetheless, in his quest for viable identities might not the prince be stimulated most of all in this scene by the role of the Senecan *nuntius* in the form of Aeneas? The attractions of such a figure are experienced by characters elsewhere in the Shakespearean canon, most notably in a play which directly precedes *Hamlet*. In *Julius*

Caesar, Cassius aspires to heroic stature by comparing his endeavours with those of the Trojan prince:

> I, as Aeneas, our great ancestor,
> Did from the flames of Troy upon his shoulder
> The old Anchises bear, so from the wave of Tiber
> Did I the tired Caesar. And this man
> Is now become a god, and Cassius is
> A wretched creature, and must bend his body
> If Caesar carelessly but nod on him. I.ii.111–117[29]

Both Cassius and Hamlet are concerned in their different ways to equal, indeed to surpass, the achievements of those who have gone before them both historically and textually. In the "rotten state" of Denmark, Hamlet also feels himself challenged to recreate political heroism in spite of the violence which is his inheritance. Are Hamlet's strategic powers of memory excited by the situation of the fugitive prince in Carthage who is trapped within the narrative space of others? Alternatively, in this scene does the audience remember the classical icon of filial piety (a sentiment articulated mostly through violence in Shakespeare's tragedy) who, as we learn in *2 Henry VI*, "did . . . old Anchises bear" out of burning Troy (V.ii.62)? At this point, should we not also be mindful of the false Aeneas who abandons queen Dido? Whatever the case, as this scene progresses Hamlet finds himself displaced on stage by the Player's interventions and compelled to assume the role of auditor, like the Carthaginian queen, and spectator, like the Trojan one.

The interpretative crises presented in this short scene give insight into the difficulty of Hamlet's endeavour to endow the past with superior meaning and authority. As we move from Pyrrhus to Priam and then to Hecuba, back and forth from Hamlet, to Polonius and then to the Player, the competing narratives force Hamlet to acknowledge that any given tale may be amended and retold by the interested parties and that loss can be understood in a multitude of ways, especially by those who subsequently seek to legitimise their cultural power. With limited and partial knowledge, Hamlet, the Player and Polonius try to summon up the myths of an ancient city. With limited and partial knowledge, Pyrrhus, Priam and Hecuba reformulate the burden which the past places upon them. And with limited and partial knowledge, Shakespeare's audience is endeavouring to reconstitute imaginatively the power struggles that unfolded during the reign of Old Hamlet.

---

[29]Line references to *Julius Caesar* and *2 Henry VI* are taken from *The Arden Shakespeare Complete Works*.

In this context, it is sobering to be reminded of Augustine's claim in the *Confessions* that the past does not exist, there is only our strategic re-*membering* of it: "When a true narrative of the past is related, the memory produces not the actual events which have passed away but words conceived from images of them, which they fixed in the mind like imprints as they passed through the senses. Thus my boyhood, which is no longer, lies in past time which is no longer . . . . [N]either future nor past exists . . . . The present considering the past is the memory, the present considering the present is immediate awareness, the present considering the future is expectation."[30] Having been haunted throughout the play by a painful awareness of human impermanence, the dying Hamlet insists once again upon another's powers of closure, upon another's ability to re-member the past:

> But let it be: *Horatio*, I am dead,
> Thou liu'st, report me and my causes right
> To the vnsatisfied . . . .
> If thou did'st euer hold me in thy heart,
> Absent thee from felicitie awhile,
> And in this harsh world draw thy breath in paine,
> To tell my Storie.   F V.ii.338–340, 346–349

WORKS CITED

Augustine. *Confessions*. Trans. Henry Chadwick. Oxford: Oxford University Press, 1998.

Greene, Thomas M. *The Light in Troy: Imitation and Discovery in Renaissance Poetry*. New Haven: Yale University Press, 1982.

Hazlitt, William. *Complete Works*. Ed. P.P. Howe. London: J.M. Dent, 1930.

Heywood, Thomas. *The Dramatic Works of Thomas Heywood now first collected with illustrative notes and a Memoir of the Author in six volumes*. Vol. 3. London: John Pearson, 1874.

Jonson, Ben. *Discoveries: A Critical Edition*. Ed. Maurice Castelain. Paris: Hachette, 1906.

Kempe, William. *The Education of Children*. London, 1588.

Kerrigan, John. "Shakespeare's Poems." *The Cambridge Companion to Shakespeare*. Ed. Margreta de Grazia and Stanley Wells. Cambridge: Cambridge University Press, 2001. 65–81.

Kintgern, Eugene R. *Reading in Tudor England*. Pittsburgh: University of Pittsburgh Press, 1996.

Marlowe, Christopher. *Christopher Marlowe: The Complete Plays*. Ed. J.B. Steane. 1969. Rpt. Harmondsworth: Penguin, 1980.

---

[30]Augustine, *Confessions*, bk. XI, xviii(23), xx (26), pp. 234, 235.

Munro, John, ed. *The Shakespeare Allusion-Book*. Originally compiled C. M. Ingleby *et al.* Re-edited and reissued with preface by E.K. Chambers. 2 vols. London: Humphrey Milford and Oxford University Press, 1932.

Peele, George. *The Life and Minor Works of George Peele*. Ed. David H. Horne. New Haven: Yale University Press, 1952.

Puttenham, George. *The Arte of English Poesie*. Ed. Edward Arber. Westminster: Constable, 1895.

Quintilian. *The Institutio Oratoria of Quintilian*. Trans. H.E. Butler. London and Cambridge, Mass.: Heinemann and Harvard University Press, 1936.

Rechtien, John G. "John Foxe's Comprehensive Collection of Commonplaces: A Renaissance Memory System for Students and Theologians." *Sixteenth Century Journal* 9 (1978): 83–89.

Richardson, Mark Lewis. *The Legends of Troy in the English Renaissance: A Study in Decadent Literature*. Ph.D. diss. Emory University, 1980.

Schaff, Philip, ed. *A Select Library of the Nicene and Post-Nicene Fathers of the Christian Church*. Vol. III. Edinburgh and Grand Rapids: Clark and Eerdmans, 1993.

Shakespeare, William. *The Arden Shakespeare Complete Works*. Ed. Richard Proudfoot, Ann Thompson and David Scott Kastan. Rpt. London: Arden Shakespeare, 2001.

Shakespeare, William. *The First Quarto of Hamlet*. Ed. Kathleen O. Irace. Cambridge: Cambridge University Press, 1998.

Shakespeare, William. *Hamlet Second Quarto 1604–5*. Shakespeare Quarto Facsimiles No. 4. Oxford: Clarendon, 1964.

Shakespeare, William. *The Oxford Shakespeare: The Complete Sonnets and Poems*. Ed. Colin Burrow. Oxford: Oxford University Press, 2002.

Shakespeare, William. *The Three-Text Hamlet*. Ed. Paul Bertram and Bernice W. Kliman. New York: AMS, 1991.

Surrey, Henry Howard, Earl of. *Poems*. Ed. Emrys Jones. Oxford: Clarendon, 1964.

Thomas, Vivien and William Tydeman, ed. *Christopher Marlowe: The Plays and their Sources*. London: Routledge, 1994.

Embracing Troy: Surrey's Aeneid

STEPHEN GUY-BRAY

For my part I am lost in the admiration of it: I contemn the World, when I think on it, and my self when I Translate it.[1]

Never will there be another language like Latin, never again will precision and beauty and clarity be so epitomized. Our modern languages are altogether too wordy; look at any bilingual edition: on the left the spare, measured Latin phrases, the sculptured lines, on the right the full page, the traffic jam, the jumble of words, blathering chaos.[2]

In 1554 John Day published the Earl of Surrey's translation of book four of the *Aeneid*; Richard Tottel published a somewhat different version of this poem as well as Surrey's translation of book two in 1557. These poems would have struck contemporary readers as unusual because they were written in metrically regular and non-alliterative verse without rhyme—what we now, following Thomas Nashe, call blank verse. Nashe himself appears to have meant the term as an insult. Apprehensive that this form, which had never before been used in English, would put off readers, Day made a pitch for it in the title he provided: *The fourth boke of Virgill, intreating of the love betwene Aeneas & Dido, translated into English, and drawne into a straunge metre by Henrye late Earle of Surrey, worthy to be embraced.* In his title, however, Tottel saw no need to anticipate objections: *Certain Bokes of Virgiles Aenaeis turned into English meter by the right honorable lorde, Henry Earle of Surrey.*[3] Exactly what Tottel meant by "English meter" is hard to understand, unless we are to think that he is referring only to the rhythm of Surrey's lines, most of which are five-stress lines of the sort with which

---

[1]Dryden, "Dedication," in *The Works of John Dryden*, vol. 5, p. 335. Dryden's reference is to *Aeneid,* VIII.364–365: "aude, hospes, contemnere opes et te quoque dignum / finge deo" [dare, o guest, to despise riches and to make yourself equal to the god]. Out of respect for Dryden, I shall not quote his version, which is surely one of the least successful passages in his translation.

[2]Nooteboom, *The Following Story*, p. 11.

[3]Both these titles are quoted in Surrey, *Poems*, p. 132. All quotations from the poems of Surrey will appear in parentheses in the text by line number.

English readers of his day would have been familiar and which later readers recognize as iambic pentameter.[4] But unrhymed verse, or at least unrhymed verse without alliteration and obviously of high cultural cachet, would have seemed unusual to English readers in 1557: Sackville and Norton's *Gorboduc*, the first English play to be written in blank verse, was still four years in the future and the convention of using blank verse for drama was not the norm until the 1580s; Thomas Campion's *Observations on the Art of English Poesie*, with its attack on rhyme, did not appear until 1602; and when Milton published the first version of *Paradise Lost* in 1667 the use of blank verse for non-dramatic poetry was still considered "straunge."

As we look back now, of course, Tottel's characterization appears prophetic: blank verse did in fact become the quintessential "English meter," first in drama and then in poetry. We could even say that blank verse is doubly English since it is not only the standard form for much of the greatest poetry in the language but it is also a form that has historically been more dominant in English than in other European languages, although it was used in both Italian and French before Surrey's translations. We thus feel closer to Tottel's statement than to Day's: we see blank verse as typical of English poetry from the beginning of the sixteenth century until the end of the nineteenth century and we find it hard to imagine it as being strange in any way. This, it seems to me, is precisely the problem with our attempts to assess what it is that Surrey is doing in his translations from the *Aeneid*. In his excellent article on the subject, Stephen Merriam Foley has pointed out that "[m]aking Surrey's unrhymed line the origin of forms and properties that follow it tends to obscure its relation to the texts that define the scene of its own writing."[5] Since the end of the sixteenth century and the efforts by Elizabethan writers to construct a glorious English literary tradition, the primary approach to Surrey and his poetry has been to consider them as origins, often to the exclusion of other considerations. That is, Surrey's poetry has been more frequently studied for what it can tell people about later English poetry than for what it can tell us about earlier poetry or, indeed, for its own merits. Although the situation is changing (particularly in critical discussions), I would say that both Surrey and Sir Thomas Wyatt are primarily used in literary histories and in teaching in order to break up what would otherwise be presented as a vast emptiness between Chaucer and Shakespeare.

---

[4]For an interesting discussion of Surrey's experiments with what would become the standard English metre, see Cooper, "Iambic Pentameter," pp. 343–349.

[5]Foley, "not-blank-verse," p. 153. In this section of his article, Foley goes so far as to object to the use of the term "blank verse" and to the description of Surrey as the first classical poet in English. See pp. 151–153.

Questions of the periodization and narrativization of English literary history seem inevitably to arise in discussions of Surrey and his poetry (although usually implicitly, as the standard narrative of English poetic development is typically accepted without comment), but the question of how we evaluate the past has implications beyond those concerning Surrey and his reputation. Our propensity to approach the past through what happened afterwards—and primarily through ourselves—is also the problem with our attempts to categorize the time in which he wrote. The term "Renaissance," the former word for the period, has given way to "early modern," admittedly an altogether more glamourous term. A particularly clear account of the reason for this change in terminology is provided by Leah S. Marcus:

> We are moving away from interpreting the period as a time of re-naissance, cultural rebirth, the reawakening of an earlier era conceived of as (in some sense) classic; we are coming to view the period more in terms of elements repeated thereafter, those features of the ages that appear to us precursors of our own twentieth century, the modern, the postmodern.[6]

The first point to make is that from an intellectual point of view, there is clearly no reason to prefer to interpret a period through the future over interpreting it through the past: it could more plausibly be argued that the reverse is true. In addition, the advantage of using "Renaissance" was that the word could at least be taken to suggest that the sixteenth and seventeenth centuries were connected with the past, even if the emphasis was almost always on the "naissance" rather than on the "Re." In contrast, one function of the term "early modern" appears to be to separate the sixteenth and seventeenth centuries from the past and to provide support for the teleologi-cally-oriented literary history that prevails, now more than ever, in the field of English studies: the sort of thinking that is called "Whig history," although discredited in History departments, is still firmly entrenched in English departments.

As I have suggested, one of the results of this change in terminology from "Renaissance" to "early modern" is that we tend to read Surrey through what came after him. His ideas about what Troy means are presumed to be the same as, or at least to resemble, the ideas about what Troy means that we are familiar with from Spenser and others; his technical innovations are valued insofar as they lead us to Shakespeare or Sidney or Marlowe. What further complicates the situation is that we tend to compare Surrey's translation with that of Gavin Douglas, which was written perhaps

---

[6]Marcus, "Renaissance," p. 41.

two or three decades earlier.[7] Although Douglas' version was only available in manuscript in Surrey's lifetime, there is no doubt that Surrey made use of it. The question of how we should regard this use has been extensively debated, with some critics almost going so far as to regard Surrey as a plagiarist. For instance, in her 1963 edition of his translations of Virgil (and this is still the only free-standing edition of these poems), Florence Ridley italicises everything that she considers Surrey to have taken from Douglas. Ridley's edition continues to influence critical thinking about Surrey, but not everyone sees the issue in the same way. The most sensible comment comes from O.B. Hardison, Jr: "Surrey consulted Douglas as one might consult a Loeb translation today to check the quality of his own work and to pick up any ideas Douglas might have to offer."[8]

I would argue that the unprejudiced reader will be more struck by the many differences between the two translations, the most obvious of which are that Douglas writes in Scots, that he chooses to write in rhyming couplets, and that he gives his *Eneados* a structure that will probably remind most modern readers of Chaucer. Because of these things, the comparisons between the translations have tended to result in the perception of Douglas' version as medieval, while Surrey's use of blank verse has been seen as an innovative move that began as a response to the blank verse produced in Italian at about the same time by writers like Alamanni and Trissino and especially Liburnio, whose 1534 translation of the *Aeneid* was in blank verse. Surrey would certainly have been aware of Alamanni's work and of French experiments in blank verse,[9] but I feel that the virtually unanimous decision to consider this trend in European prosody as a bold step forward comes from a desire to see the first half of the sixteenth century as the beginning of a new age and perhaps even the beginning of modernity. It is curious that so many critical discussions of early sixteenth-century England continue to rely on unexamined notions about "the spirit of the age." In this case, the critical insistence on the shift from "Renaissance" to "early modern" obscures the fact that the belief that a desire to be different swept Europe from about 1400 on remains unchallenged as something everybody "knows" about history.

---

[7]For two of the best comparisons, see Bawcutt, "Douglas and Surrey" and Hager, "British Virgil." Bawcutt's analysis is especially interesting as she takes into account the manuscripts of Virgil available to his translators.

[8]Hardison, "Tudor Humanism," p. 100. The comparison is apt, but should not be taken as an endorsement of the Loeb Classical Library.

[9]Surrey may even have met Alamanni at the court of Francis I in the winter of 1532–1533. See Sessions, *Henry Howard*, pp. 93–94.

My argument in this paper is not that we cannot find a difference between the Middle Ages and the Renaissance, but rather that the new departure we seem to want to find is better represented by Douglas' translation than by Surrey's. As I see it, Douglas' version is actually a more forward-looking poem than Surrey's. By translating not only the language but also the form, it is Douglas who really makes it new. His *Eneados* is a distinctively sixteenth-century poem, one that in all its aspects builds on the author's own national poetic traditions, while Surrey's translation represents a retrograde step, and his decision not to use rhyme should not be considered in isolation. As Hardison has pointed out, Surrey tries always to return to the original:

> [A]long with enjambment and the verse paragraph came the opportunity—at times the necessity—to vary the expression through devices used only infrequently in the poetry of Chaucer and the translation of the *Aeneid* into couplets by Gavin Douglas. These devices . . . appear in Surrey's translation as corollaries of his verse form: suspension, inversion, parenthesis, substitution, counterpoint of syntactical against metrical rhythms and moveable caesura.[10]

Only what would seem to be a deep-seated psychological need to see the sixteenth and seventeenth centuries as progressive and forward looking—a need that is more prevalent among those who say early modern than it is among those who say Renaissance—has prevented us from seeing that Surrey's use of blank verse is really, to use an oxymoron, a conservative innovation. Surrey's blank verse has been very useful to literary historians, who have tended to use it to reinforce chronological divisions and, specifically, to make Milton's choice of that form for *Paradise Lost* seem less strange. This standard history of blank verse in English ignores the fact that Surrey's example was not followed. As I have pointed out, not only was Milton apparently unaware of Surrey's translations, but Surrey is not mentioned by Campion in *Observations in the Art of English Poesie*, even though Campion does present the first half of the sixteenth century as a time in which there was a great renewal of classical learning.

Rather than being the beginning of something, then, Surrey is the end of something. Andrew Hiscock has aptly described Surrey's work as "poetic dialogues with the past";[11] I would stress that they are dialogues with the

---

10Hardison, "Blank Verse Before Milton," pp. 54–55. My analysis is indebted to Hardison's work on Surrey's blank verse, which is unlikely to be surpassed. As well, see Hardison's "Tudor Humanism" and *Prosody and Purpose*, pp. 127–147. For a somewhat different analysis, see Foley, "not-blank-verse," pp. 155–160.

11Hiscock, "'To Seek the Place,'" p. 37. Hiscock's main interest is in the importance

past rather than—and perhaps even instead of—with the present or with the future. Surrey's focus on the past should lead us to reconsider our sense of what the legend of Troy might have meant for him.[12] The best way to begin this reconsideration is with the obvious question that, to my knowledge, has hardly ever been asked: why did Surrey only translate books two and four? Of course, as Surrey was only twenty-nine or thirty when he was executed and as he had had a very busy life, it is not surprising that he did not find the time to translate all of Virgil's epic, but why those two books?[13] Why not books one and two? I think the answer lies in the subject of those books: each is concerned with the end of a civilization. The second book is Aeneas' own narrative of the destruction of Troy and the death of almost all the members of the Trojan royal family; the fourth tells the story of the love between Aeneas and Dido and ends with the suicide of the latter after she has vowed eternal war between Carthage and Rome:

> Our costes to them contrary be for aye,
> I crave of God, and our streames to their fluddes,
> Armes unto armes, and offspring of eche race
> With mortal warr eche other may fordoe. 840–843

This vow led to the Punic Wars and ultimately to Carthage's total destruction less than a century before Virgil's birth.

In choosing to translate those parts of the *Aeneid* that deal with destruction, Surrey is making a comment on the nature of the poem as a whole, and I want to look briefly at this question before considering Surrey's translation. The *Aeneid* is often taken to be a triumphant narrative, but it is not. Readers make the poem triumphant by adding their own knowledge of the successes of the Roman empire, as Virgil must have assumed they would. But although this power is alluded to several times in the poem, most notably in the conversation in Hades between Aeneas and Anchises in the sixth book and in the description of the site of Rome in the eighth book, Virgil does not show it. What we do get from the *Aeneid* is a succession of deaths, most of them the deaths of beautiful young men. Aeneas never receives any compensation either for the tragic losses he relates in the second book or for the losses that will fill the second half of the poem. This is not to say that compensation, or rather consolation, is not one of

---

of Surrey's poetry to Henrician politics.

[12]For an intriguing situation of Surrey's theory and practice of translation in the context of his life, see Sessions, *Henry Howard*, pp. 260–287.

[13]For a very brief discussion of the question, see Richardson, "Humanistic Intent," p. 215.

the poem's major themes, but that the consolation is always deferred. To illustrate this I want to look briefly at two famous passages from the first book, in which Aeneas and the few men he has left find themselves shipwrecked and starving on the coast of Africa. In the first, Aeneas offers two consoling thoughts: "o passi grauiora, dabit deus his quoque finem" [what's past was worse, God will put an end to this as well], and "forsan et haec olim meminisse iuuabit" [perhaps one day it will be pleasant to remember even this].[14] These passages are often quoted out of context as examples of consolatory discourse. Of the first, we could say that the story of the poem turns out to be a narrative in which the gods end one form of suffering only to expose Aeneas and his (rapidly dwindling) followers to another. Of the second, that forsan it will, forsan it will not; like the happiness of the new Troy in Latium, this moment never arrives within the narrative, which famously ends with the death of Turnus on the battlefield. This death does assure Aeneas' victory, but neither the victory itself nor the establishment of a Trojan kingdom in Italy is ever represented.

In the second passage, Aeneas and Achates have reached the walls of Carthage and seen the paintings of the fall of Troy. As so many similar scenes of ecphrasis in classical literature do, this passage might seem to suggest that human suffering can be transformed into a work of art that will provide consolation. That, at any rate, is what Aeneas thinks:

> "sunt hic etiam sua praemia laudi,
> sunt lacrimae rerum et mentem mortalia tangunt.
> solue metus; feret haec aliquam tibi fama salutem."
> sic ait atque animum pictura pascit inani
> multa gemens, largoque umectat flumine uultum
>
> [Here indeed are the rewards of praise, here are tears for things. Dispel your fear: this fame may bring some good fortune. Thus he spoke and fed his soul on the empty picture, groaning deeply, with streaming tears covering his face]. I.461–465

The consolation here is aesthetic and will be felt by other people, as Virgil's juxtaposition of Aeneas' consoling remark with the description of his sorrow suggests. Whatever the future may bring, what we see in the narrative present is that the very accuracy and excellence of the work of art causes immediate sorrow. Consolation is both deferred from the poem's present and displaced from the poem's characters. As Surrey must have realized, the

---

[14]Virgil, *Aeneid*, I.199 and 203. Subsequent references to Virgil are to the edition cited and will appear in parentheses in the text. The translations of Virgil not by Surrey or Douglas are my own.

Aeneid does not offer consolation but rather a view of life in which, as Aeneas says over the corpse of Pallas: "nos alias hinc ad lacrimas eadem horrida belli / fata uocant" [the same dreadful fates of war call me hence to other tears (XI.96–97)].

The sense of memory as painful is of course explicitly the subject of the beginning of Book II, from the moment when everyone stares expectantly at Aeneas to his weary and reluctant "incipiam" [I shall begin] at the beginning of the thirteenth line. A comparison of Douglas' handling of this passage with Surrey's reveals the very different translating strategies. The comparison is admittedly somewhat unfair in this case, as Douglas' version of this famous passage is well below his usual standard, although the sorts of things he does are typical of his work throughout. Here is his version of the first three lines:

> Thai cessit all at anis incontinent,
> With mowthis clois, and visage takand tent.
> Prince Eneas, frome the hie bed, with that,
> Into his seige riall quhar he sat,
> Begouth and said: Thi desyir, lady, is
> Renewing of ontellable sorow, I wis.[15]

Douglas has consistently padded the lines in order to achieve rhymes, as in "with that / he sat." While "he sat" is probably necessary to fill out the sense of "inde" [thence] in the original, "with that" is superfluous. His rhyming "is" with "I wis" is unfortunate, and it is especially noticeable because "I wis" has no equivalent in the original. Douglas also resorts to padding to fill out the line, as both "I wis" and the fifth line of this passage demonstrate. In the latter case, the Latin "sic orsus" [thus began] does not require filling out, and the double verb "Begouth and said" is clearly present only for metrical reasons.

The result of Douglas' strategies is a version that is much longer than the original. For instance, in this passage Douglas takes twenty-four lines to translate twelve lines and one word of Virgil; the overall difference in number of lines between his *Eneados* and Virgil's *Aeneid* is staggering even without including the line count for Douglas' thirteenth book. In contrast, Surrey's version has more lines than Virgil's but almost the same number of syllables, given the difference between pentameters and hexameters. Fur-

---

[15]Douglas, *Poetical Works*, vol. 2, First Buik, Cap.XII, p. 65. I am citing Douglas's work by book, chapter, and page numbers. Subsequent references to this work will appear in parentheses in the text. For reasons best known to himself, Douglas moved the introduction from the beginning of the second book to the end of the first.

thermore, Surrey is clearly attempting to reproduce the movement of Latin syntax. Consider Virgil's "et iam nox umida caelo / praecipitat suadentque cadentia sidera somnos" (II.8–9). Douglas takes three lines to translate this:

> And now the hewin ourquhelmis the donk nycht,
> Quhen the declining of the sternis brycht
> To sleip and rest perswades our appetite. First Buik, Cap.XII, p. 66

Translating "umida" as "donk" is, I think, a good change as it intensifies the gloom of the passage, but I feel that Douglas' other decisions are less good. He has restructured the phrase in order to give it a syntax that is customary in his own language. He has also expanded it by adding adjectives—the stars are now "brycht"—and, as in his translation of the first two lines of the book, he has used a double verb: the stars persuade us both to sleep and to rest.

What should strike anyone comparing the translations is that Surrey's version has fewer syllables than the original: "And loe, moist night now from the welkin falles, / And sterres declining counsel us to rest" (12–13). Surrey reduces one and a half dactylic hexameters to two iambic pentameters. He also manages to imitate the Latin syntax (to reproduce it exactly would not be possible), and his use of rhythm in this passage is a reasonable approximation of Virgil's elaborate patterning. In general—and this is true of his strategy throughout his translation—Surrey interferes less than Douglas. For instance, the verb in line nine of the original (suadentque) has no object. In both Scots and English one is required, but while Douglas supplies "our appetite" to fill out the line and to set up a rhyme with "plesour and delite," a pair of nouns for Virgil's single "amor," Surrey merely adds "us." The only thing in Surrey's version that is not in the original is "loe." In his version, Surrey fails to match Virgil, but who could? After all, the original is arguably one of the greatest passages in a poem filled with great passages. What Surrey does manage to do is both translate the sense and convey something of Virgil's particular brilliance. As a translator, Surrey continually demonstrates his belief that form and content should not be considered separately, if, indeed, they can be distinguished at all. On the other hand, Douglas takes what may seem to us to be extraordinary liberties with Virgil. Whatever we may think of the merits of one translation or another, it should be clear that Douglas' freedom with the text—the desire to remake the *Aeneid* and to recast it into the context of his own native poetic tradition that he demonstrates throughout his poem—is precisely the sort of refashioning of the classical heritage that we are most likely to consider as indicative of the advent of modernity.

At times, Surrey is almost as bold as Douglas, although usually in the direction of even greater concision than the original. Some of his changes to passages are accompanied by an adherence to the Latin syntax that make his translation hard to follow; in fact, it has often been remarked that many passages in his translation are obscure without a knowledge of the original. We can find examples of both these tendencies in the passage I quoted above in which Dido prays for eternal enmity between Carthage and Rome (lines 840 to 843 of Surrey's version of Book IV). Here is the original: "litora litoribus contraria, fluctibus undas / imprecor, arma armis: pugnent ipsique nepotes" (IV.628–629). The first part of this passage, up to the colon after "armis," is controlled by the single verb "imprecor," and the syntax is conveyed by word endings. This sort of verbal economy is simply impossible to reproduce in English, which may explain Marlowe's decision to leave it in Latin in his *Dido, Queene of Carthage*, one of the few works that can be seen to have been influenced by Surrey's translations.[16] Surrey's attempt to reproduce Virgil's effects in English in his version of this passage, and, in particular, his refusal to supply enough verbs, makes his version hard to follow. He does add the verb phrase "be for aye" to his translation of the first of these lines in order to clarify the sense, but his version would obviously have benefited from another equivalent (or two) for "imprecor." Furthermore, Surrey's decisions to move his translation of Virgil's first verb towards the beginning of the passage and to move his translation of the second verb to the end of the passage result in the impression that Dido craves of God the "offspring of eche race."

At the same time that he tries to adhere to Latin syntax, however, Surrey adds a good deal, and this makes his handling of this passage unusual in the context of his translation as a whole. For instance, he translates "imprecor" as "I crave of God," which is considerably stronger. Not only does Virgil not specify a god, but the connotations of "imprecor" are rather more dignified than the desperation implied by "crave." Surrey's most important change in this passage is to "pugnent ipsique nepotes," which means simply "may their descendants themselves fight." Surrey renders this as "offspring of eche race / With mortal warr eche other may fordoe." His changes emphasize the mutual nature of the conflict and specify the outcome.[17] Virgil's Dido is obviously unaware of what will happen and asks

---

[16]Marlowe, *Dido, Queene of Carthage*, V.i.310–311. Marlowe's decision to put several lines of Virgil into his play without translating them may result from a conscious strategy.

[17]I also think that to translate "nepotes" as "offspring" is to increase the pathos of the situation, as the English noun is normally used to refer to children, while the Latin one means descendants of any age.

only for a long-lasting conflict; in having his Dido ask for a "mortal" war and in his choice of the verb "fordoe" [annihilate] Surrey makes his Dido more savage. He also—and I think this is the crucial effect of his expansion—hints at the fact that although Rome won the Punic Wars, it too was eventually destroyed. I think we could say of Surrey's version of this passage what Andrew Hiscock has said of Surrey's biblical translations: "in the bleakest moments of these texts, the very notion of human memory, indeed human meaning, is not only interrogated but collapses into a nihilistic despair."[18] What we can learn from this is that when Surrey does treat Virgil with the sort of freedom that is a standard aspect of Douglas' translation he does so to emphasize the power of the past over the present; a power that it appears is never a power for good. The return to the past does not result in a new beginning or a transformation that will lead to modernity but rather to an ending.

My second example from Book II is the passage in which Aeneas' recounting of the Trojan decision to bring the wooden horse within the walls leads him to burst into an apostrophe to his lost city:

> o patria, o diuum domus Ilium et incluta bello
> moenia Dardanidum! quater ipso in limine portae
> substitit atque utero sonitum quater arma dedere;
> instamus tamen immemores caecique furore
> et monstrum infelix sacrata sistimus in arce. II.241–245

As before, a comparison of the original with Douglas' and Surrey's translations shows how much padding Douglas includes. Parts of his rendering, which the marginal note identifies as an "Exclamacyon," are excellent, particularly his version of the ending: "Quhill that myschancy monstir, quentlie bet, / Amyd the hallowit temple wp was set" (Second Buik, Cap.IV, p. 82). Still, although I think that "myschancy monster" is a happy choice and "quentlie bet," for which there is no equivalent in the original, is a nice touch, his decision to fill out the line and find a rhyme for Troy by saying that the city was "full of joy" is a very bad idea indeed. Furthermore, his translation has many more syllables than the original. As so often, the greater length is due to Douglas' fondness for pairs of verbs and for additional adjectives, which leads him into still more expansiveness: once he has said that the gate [portae] is "wyde," he has no choice but to add the adverb of time "that ilk tyde" to provide a rhyme.

Surrey's version, as in his translation of lines eight and nine of Book II, has fewer syllables than the original:

---

[18]Hiscock, "'To Seek the Place,'" p. 40.

O native land! Ilion! and of the goddes
The mansion place! O warrlik walles of Troy!
Fowr times it stopt in th'entrie of our gate,
Fowr times the harnesse clattred in the womb.
But we goe on, unsound of memorie,
And blinded eke by rage persever still.
This fatal monster in the fane we place. 304–310

Most of the syllables are saved in his very successful handling of the apostrophe. Surrey's treatment of the last line of the passage is particularly good. First of all, Virgil connects the conclusion of this passage—the action that results in the fall of Troy—to the preceding lines by using "et"; Surrey's grammatical separation of this line emphasizes it effectively. The two salient stylistic features of the last line of the original are the collocation "infelix sacrata" (which is jarring because the former word has religious connotations in Latin) and the alliteration of "sacrata" and "sistimus." I would argue that "sistimus" is especially emphasized because three of the four conjugated verbs in the original are derived from *sto, stare, steti, statum*. Surrey does not reproduce this verbal connection (indeed, I do not see how he could have), but he does find an English version for the other effects I have mentioned in the alliteration of "fatal" and "fane" and he does reproduce the four "a" sounds of Virgil's line.[19]

There is, however, a problem with Surrey's translation, although I think this particular problem is actually productive for him. In the original, Aeneas characterizes the Trojans as "immemores." In context, this clearly means that they are heedless of the sounds of weapons from the belly of the horse: that is, they do not remember these sounds even though they have just heard them. Douglas translates the word as "forgetting" but adds "this" for clarity as the range of meaning of the English or Scots "forgetting" is narrower than that of the Latin "immemores." Surrey translates the word as "unsound of memorie." The meaning of this phrase is unclear without reference to the original and the use of "memorie" would appear to be an example of a linguistic false friend. I would like to argue that it is instead a deliberate inaccuracy, one that recalls (or anticipates—the order of composition of Surrey's works is not clear) a similar inaccuracy in his use of Petrarch in "O happy dames." In two lines of that poem (the poem as a whole is not a translation), the source is Petrarch's sonnet 189, which begins "Passa la nave mia colma d'oblio."[20] Wyatt translates this correctly as "My galley

---

[19]For an excellent analysis of Surrey's attempts to reproduce Virgil's sound effects, see Oras, "Surrey's Technique of Phonetic Echoes."

[20]Petrarch, *Canzoniere,* 189.1.

charged with forgetfulness,"[21] but the speaker in Surrey's "O happy dames" says that his or her lover sails "In ship, freight with rememberance / Of thoughtes and pleasures past" (ll. 8–9).[22] Surrey would probably have been pleased that this line was remembered by Shakespeare: "When to the sessions of sweet silent thought / I summon up remembrance of things past,"[23] a passage that was itself remembered, fittingly enough, by Charles Scott Moncrieff when he was looking for a title for his translation of the most famous treatment of memory in modern literature.

In the case of his translation of the passage from the *Aeneid*, Surrey changes a comment in which a group of people is said to be heedless in a particular situation to a general characterization of that group. In the case of "O happy dames," Surrey reverses the meaning of an image in order to focus attention on the question of the relation of memory to attention itself. Both these changes should be understood as paradigmatic. Surrey's alterations point to his preoccupation with the role of memory; furthermore, to do a translation is already to deal with this theme, as translation is really just a kind of memory. In discussions of the role of the Trojan legend in sixteenth and seventeenth century England, the usual assumption has been that while it may be painful to remember the fall of Troy in the short term, in the long term the memory of pain will lead to present happiness and that Troy is a precedent for England only in a good way. Surrey, I think, is not so sure, and this would be a good time to remember that just as the glory that was Rome lies beyond the boundaries of the *Aeneid*, so too almost everything that is normally considered remarkable about Renaissance England comes after Surrey's execution in January 1547.

Instead of using Troy as a way to make optimistic predictions about English advances, then, Surrey tends to use it as a way to foreground the pain of memory. One final example will suffice. In "So crewell prison," his poem about his imprisonment at Windsor Castle, Surrey makes at least two references to Troy.[24] When he reflects at the beginning of the poem upon his former happiness growing up at Windsor Castle with the Duke of Richmond, he says that they grew up "In greater feast then Priams sonnes

[21] Wyatt, *The Complete Poems,* sonnet XIX.1.

[22] The usual assumption is that "O happy dames" has a female speaker, perhaps even the Countess of Surrey. As there is no textual warrant for this assumption, I have chosen to write "his or her." For a discussion of this assumption and of the poem's authorship, see Goldberg, "The Female Pen."

[23] Shakespeare, *The Riverside Shakespeare,* sonnet XXX.1–2.

[24] A further allusion can be found in Surrey's use of the planctum Troili from Chaucer's *Troilus and Criseyde.* For a fuller analysis of "So crewell prison," see my *Homoerotic Space,* pp. 103–117.

of Troye" (l. 4). The emphasis here is obviously on Troy as a symbol of the transience of human happiness and prosperity, rather than as the beginnings of Roman—and English—power. Throughout the poem, Surrey contrasts present sorrow with former happiness, and at the end he says "And with remembraunce of the greater greif, / To bannishe the lesse I fynde my chief relief" (ll. 53–54). This couplet is not so much a translation of "O passi grauiora, dabit deus his quoque finem" as a response to it or even a refutation of it. There is no mention in Surrey's version of a god or of any end to sorrow. Instead, the most that can be hoped for is that some sorrows will be less painful than others.

Throughout his poems, Surrey returns to the pain and dangers of memory, and for this reason his translations from the *Aeneid* should be seen as central to his work. Although the story of Troy has typically been thought to offer a picture of memory as a necessary step, however painful, toward a glorious future, Surrey sees it as a story about the perils of memory. This reading of the *Aeneid* is partial in both senses, since Surrey translated only books II and IV. I suggested earlier that to read these books out of context—insofar as that is possible with such a famous poem—emphasizes both the destruction of Troy that is the subject of book II and the destruction of Carthage for which book IV supplies the rationale. Reading these books out of context also obviously emphasizes memory and even links memory and destruction. The famous scene of Aeneas at the depiction of the fall of Troy on the walls of Carthage can be taken to suggest that memory can become art and that the resulting art is consolatory, and this is how Aeneas takes it, but such a reading of the scene is also partial. The representation of the walls of Troy is a decoration, but also a prediction, since Carthage too will be utterly destroyed. Leah S. Marcus says that "*Renaissance* is optimistic, upbeat—rebirth and renewal are marvelous ideas."[25] While this may often be true, in this context we should note that Aeneas begins his narrative of the fall of Troy with the words that Surrey translates as "O quene, it is thy wil / I shold renew a woe can not be told." In an excellent discussion of Surrey's "Dyvers thy death doo dyverslye bemone," the sonnet on Wyatt's death, James Simpson says that "[t]he classical past . . . is itself metaphorically revived only to constitute the time of loss,"[26] and I see this as typical of Surrey's poetry as a whole. For him, renewal is painful and there is no sense that to tell grief will lessen it, that memory is in any way therapeutic. We should read these two representations of the fall of Troy, one pictorial and one verbal, in the first book of the *Aeneid* as suggesting

---

[25]Marcus, "Renaissance," p. 43.
[26]Simpson, "Breaking the Vacuum," p. 327.

that remembering and renewing woe are synonymous throughout the *Aeneid*, and surely this was one of the poem's attractions for Surrey.[27] It has always seemed to me that Surrey's alteration of the scene in which the Trojans, "unsound of memorie," drag the wooden horse into the temple results in a passage that can be read allegorically. The Trojan horse is a figure for memory: we desire memory because we tend to think of it as offering consolation in difficult times, but it may actually contain something that will be fatal to us.

WORKS CITED

Bawcutt, Priscilla. "Douglas and Surrey: Translators of Virgil." *Essays and Studies* 27 (1974): 52–67.

Cooper, John R. "Iambic Pentameter in the Lyrics of Surrey and Sidney." *Meter, Rhythm and Performance—Metrum, Rhythmus, Performanz*. Ed. Christoph Küper. Frankfurt: Peter Lang, 2002. 343–354.

Douglas, Gavin. *The Poetical Works*. 1874. Ed. John Small. Vol. 2. Hildesheim: Georg Olms, 1970.

Dryden, John. "Dedication of the Æneis to the Lord Marquess of Normanby." *The Works of John Dryden*. Ed. William Frost. Vol. 5. Berkeley and Los Angeles: University of California Press, 1987. 267–341.

Foley, Stephen Merriam. "not-blank-verse: Surrey's *Aeneid* Translations and the Prehistory of a Form." *Poets and Critics Read Vergil*. Ed. Sarah Spence. Vol. 5. New Haven: Yale University Press, 2001. 149–171.

Goldberg, Jonathan. "The Female Pen: Writing as a Woman." *Language Machines: Technologies of Literary and Cultural Production*. Ed. Jeffrey Masten, Peter Stallybrass, and Nancy J. Vickers. London: Routledge, 1997. 17–38.

Guy-Bray, Stephen. *Homoerotic Space: The Poetics of Loss in Renaissance Literature*. Toronto: University of Toronto Press, 2002.

Hager, Alan. "British Virgil: Four Renaissance Disguises of the Laocoön Passage of Book 2 of the *Aeneid*." *Studies in English Literature* 22 (1982): 21–38.

Hardison, O.B., Jr. "Blank Verse Before Milton." *Studies in Philology* 81 (1984): 253–274. Rpt. in Kinney, ed., *Poetics and Praxis*. 47–63.

Hardison, O.B., Jr. *Prosody and Purpose in the English Renaissance*. Baltimore: Johns Hopkins University Press, 1989.

Hardison, O.B., Jr. "Tudor Humanism and Surrey's Translation of the *Aeneid*." *Studies in Philology* 83 (1986): 237–260. Rpt. in Kinney, ed., *Poetics and Praxis*. 97–114.

Hiscock, Andrew. "'To Seek the Place Where I Myself Had Lost': Acts of Memory in the Poetry of Henry Howard, Earl of Surrey." *The Anatomy of Tudor Literature: Proceedings of the First International Conference of the Tudor Symposium*. Ed. Mike Pincombe. Aldershot: Ashgate, 2001. 34–43.

---

[27] For the argument that the crucial aspect of Virgil's poetry for Surrey was the concept of "labor," see Sessions, "Surrey's Wyatt."

Kinney, Arthur F., ed. *Poetics and Praxis, Understanding and Imagination: The Collected Essays of O.B. Hardison, Jr.* Athens: University of Georgia Press, 1997.

Marcus, Leah S. "Renaissance / Early Modern Studies." *Redrawing the Boundaries: The Transformation of English and American Literary Studies.* Ed. Stephen Greenblatt and Giles Gunn. New York: MLA, 1992. 41–63.

Marlowe, Christopher. *Dido Queene of Carthage. The Complete Works of Christopher Marlowe.* Ed. Fredson Bowers. Vol. 1. Cambridge: Cambridge University Press, 1973.

Nooteboom, Cees. *The Following Story.* Trans. Ina Rilke. New York: Harcourt Brace, 1994.

Oras, Ants. "Surrey's Technique of Phonetic Echoes: A Method and its Background." *JEGP* 50 (1951): 289–308.

Petrarch. *Canzoniere.* Ed. Gianfranco Contini. Turin: Einaudi, 1979.

Richardson, David A. "Humanistic Intent in Surrey's *Aeneid.*" *English Literary Renaissance* 6 (1976): 204–219.

Sessions, W.A. "Surrey's Wyatt: Autumn 1542 and the New Poet." *Rethinking the Henrician Era: Essays on Early Tudor Texts and Contexts.* Ed. Peter C. Herman. Urbana: University of Illinois Press, 1994. 168–192.

Sessions, W.A. *Henry Howard, the Poet Earl of Surrey: A Life.* Oxford: Oxford University Press, 1999.

Shakespeare, William. *The Riverside Shakespeare.* Ed. G. Blakemore Evans. Boston: Houghton Mifflin, 1974.

Simpson, James. "Breaking the Vacuum: Ricardian and Henrician Ovidianism." *Journal of Medieval and Early Modern Studies* 29 (1999): 325–355.

Surrey, Henry Howard, Earl of. *The Aeneid of Henry Howard, Earl of Surrey.* Ed. Florence Ridley. Berkeley and Los Angeles: University of California Press, 1963.

Surrey, Henry Howard, Earl of. *Poems.* Ed. Emrys Jones. Oxford: Clarendon, 1964.

Virgil. *Opera.* Ed. R.A.B. Mynors. Oxford: Clarendon, 1969.

Wyatt, Sir Thomas. *Sir Thomas Wyatt: The Complete Poems.* Ed. R.A. Rebholz. New Haven: Yale University Press, 1978.

Appropriating Troy: Ekphrasis in Shakespeare's The Rape of Lucrece

CHRISTOPHER JOHNSON

In his *Méditation troisième*, Descartes observes, "les idées sont en moi comme des tableaux, ou des images, qui peuvent à la vérité facilement déchoir de la perfection des choses dont elles ont été tirées."[1] The analogy suggests the problematic importance of the visual imagination in the creation of new ideas in the early modern period. Indeed, Descartes' struggle with the deceit inherent in verbal rhetoric and the visual imagination is one of the hallmarks of his epistemological revolution—again and again he raises the specter of an evil genius, or a "Dieu qui soit trompeur," plying him with illusory ideas. In this sense, Descartes recalls Plato, who, in the *Phaedrus*, casts the relation between word and image in a manner that echoes throughout the Renaissance:

> You know, Phaedrus, that's the strange thing about writing, which makes it truly analogous to painting. The painter's products stand before us as though they were alive, but if you question them, they maintain a most majestic silence. It is the same with written words; they seem to talk to you as if they were intelligent, but if you ask them anything about what they say, from a desire to be instructed, they go on telling you the same thing forever.[2]

Plato's indictment here of the deceitful "silence" of word and image impels Sidney to devote a good part of his "A Defence of Poetry" (1595) to refuting it. The main goal of the "Defence" is to rework the Horatian commonplace *ut pictura poiesis*: "Poesy . . . is an art of imitation, for so Aristotle termeth it in his *mimesis*, that is to say, a representing, counterfeiting, or figuring forth—to speak metaphorically, a speaking picture—with this end, to teach and delight."[3] Likewise, in 1605, Francis Bacon stresses the visual and heuristic power of poetry when he observes that poetry "was ever thought to have some participation of divineness, because it doth raise and erect the

---

[1]Descartes, *Les méditations*, p. 440.
[2]Plato, *Phaedrus*, p. 521.
[3]Sidney, *Defence of Poetry*, p. 345.

mind, by submitting the shows of things to the desires of the mind."[4] Yet these "shows," Bacon elsewhere makes clear, also have their dangers: "It seems to me that Pygmalion's frenzy is a good emblem or portraiture of this vanity: for words are but images of matter; and except they have life of reason and invention, to fall in love with them is all one as to fall in love with a picture."[5]

It is in this ambivalent context that I would like to situate the following reading of the so-called Trojan ekphrasis in Shakespeare's 1594 epyllion, *The Rape of Lucrece*. This ekphrasis, I will argue, is the vehicle of a sophisticated, mannerist commentary on the "conceit deceitful"[6] nature of visual and verbal representation, a commentary that at once looks back to classical and Renaissance precedents even as it forces the reader to question the nature of Shakespearean mimesis. Literally, a "speaking-out," ekphrasis, or the verbal description of a visual, usually an artistic object, was a favorite figure in early modern English literature: Marlowe, Chapman, Spenser, Marvell, and Milton all use it to great effect. An "ornamental digression that refuses to be merely ornamental," ekphrasis often provides a "rival narra- tive" that sets image and word at odds, partially because the static, spatial nature of the image tends to forestall the passage of narrative time.[7] Ekphrasis in this way may become the site/sight of complicated conceptual and emotional play. The mimesis of a mimesis, ekphrasis generally suspends narrative time and flow, as the reader's attention is redirected towards a physical object whose connection with the narrative, at first glance, is only ornamental. Yet, inevitably, what the reader sees is already mediated by the poem's larger context. Often, moreover, the visual object is mediated by the Aristotelian convention that views it as passive and therefore feminine.[8] Subject to the masculine, controlling gaze, the imagined artwork struggles to find its own, digressive voice.

Written early in Shakespeare's career, while the theaters were closed due to the plague ravaging London, *The Rape of Lucrece* is Shakespeare's most theatrical poem. Long dismissed by neo-classical critics as excessively rhetorical, recent post-structuralist criticism has begun taking its tropes

---

[4]Bacon, *Advancement of Learning*, pp. 461–462.

[5]Bacon, *Advancement of Learning*, p. 460.

[6]Shakespeare, *The Rape of Lucrece*, l. 1423. Subsequent citations will appear in the text.

[7]Heffernan, *Museum of Words*, pp. 3–7.

[8]Heffernan notes: "The contest [ekphrasis] stages is often powerfully gendered: the expression of a duel between male and female gazes, the voice of male speech striving to control a female image that is both alluring and threatening, of male narrative striving to overcome the fixating impact of beauty poised in space" (*Museum of Words,* p. 3).

more seriously, to paraphrase Katharine Eisaman Maus.[9] This is not to say, of course, that the nature of readerly *jouissance* vis-à-vis the poem has remained unchanged from what the Earl of Southampton, to whom the poem is dedicated, must have experienced reading this narrative of nearly 1900 lines. The original reception of the poem, on the contrary, can be summarized in the observation of the Elizabethan wit and scholar Gabriel Harvey, that "Lucrece, and his tragedie of Hamlet . . . have it in them to please the wiser sort."[10] This suggests a moral if not also a political reading of the poem and drama. Our own pleasures, I would suggest, result in part from Shakespeare's self-conscious interrogation in both texts of the nature and possibility of representation. In the case of *Lucrece*, as Maus, Coppélia Kahn, and Joel Fineman have variously argued, Shakespeare forces the reader to constantly interrogate the eidetic, epistemological, and subjective aspects of his language.[11] In other words, the pleasures that *Lucrece* still affords have little to do with its uniformly bleak theme, its misogynist common-places, or its largely "feudal" world view.[12] Nor can we recreate the degree to which the historical figures and motifs in the poem were ubiquitous in the visual and print culture of the late sixteenth century. Instead, as Maus argues, we tend to focus on the poem's moral ambiguities, its rhetorical complexities, and its "acute and profoundly uneasy self-consciousness about poetic technique and resources" which mirror our own post-structuralist relation to language.[13]

This uneasiness, I would show, is most acute in the Trojan ekphrasis, the episode that, along with Lucrece's suicide, dominates the poem's second half. Here the pleasures of the text derive from the vivid, metapoetic manner that Shakespeare fashions a self for Lucrece out of the depths of her despair. Angrily declaring after the rape, "For me, I am the mistress of my fate" (1069), Lucrece has yet, though, to really exercise her agency. Such agency, along with a new form of self-awareness, are most poignantly explored during the 216-line ekphrasis in which Lucrece, waiting for her husband to return, gazes upon the painting of Troy's fall. Forced to struggle with the "deceit" (1507) inherent in art even as she searches for the means to express her grief, shame, and outrage, Lucrece learns that identity is more perfor-mative than rhetorical, and that art and the (historical) content that it

---

[9]Maus, "Taking Tropes Seriously," pp. 66–82.

[10]Quoted in Maus, "Taking Tropes Seriously," p. 66.

[11]Kahn, "The Rape in Shakespeare's *Lucrece*," pp. 45–72; Fineman, "Shakespeare's Will," pp. 25–76.

[12]Lanham, *The Motives of Eloquence*, p. 97.

[13]Maus, "Taking Tropes Seriously," p. 82.

contains may be obstacles to, as well as prompts for such self-discovery. In these ways, *Lucrece* prepares the way for that dynamic, subjective interiority which will come to dominate the great tragedies like *Hamlet*. Furthermore, the Trojan ekphrasis also suggests that the "lacrimae rerum," with which Virgilian ekphrasis memorably epitomizes the fall of Troy, no longer could be assuaged in the waning years of Elizabeth's *Troynovant*. Thus, even as it reanimates a poetic figure that classical poets self-consciously used to link the fate of Troy with reflections on the nature of art, it heralds the advent of a mannerist aesthetic that charts the limits of mimesis and the illusions of history.

While antiquity's most famous ekphrasis is Homer's cosmographic description of Achilles' shield in Book 18 of the *Iliad*, it is doubtful that Shakespeare, in the 1590's, knew the *Iliad* save in digest form.[14] Nonetheless, because it served as the immediate model for Virgil, to whom I will turn presently, and because it links the figure of ekphrasis to the fate of Troy, Homer's description of the shield deserves brief consideration. After Hector kills Patroclus and strips him of Achilles' borrowed armor, the nymph Thetis beseeches Hephaestus to forge new armor for her son. The shield Hephaestus crafts produces "wonder," *to thauma*, but it also becomes an object of *admiratio* in the long history of the poem's reception. In 1598, the same year that he completed the first seven books of his *Iliad* translation, George Chapman published separately "Achilles' Shield," a version of the events in book 18 cast in rhymed decasyllabic verse rather than in his infamous fourteeners. In his dedication, Chapman admires Homer's ekphrasis:

> . . . nothing can be imagined more full of soule and humaine extraction; for what is here prefigurde by our miraculous Artist but the universall world, which being so spatious and almost unmeasurable, one circlet of a shield representes and imbraceth? In it heaven turnes, the starres shine, the earth is enflowred, the sea swelles and rageth, Citties are built—one in the happinesse and sweetnesse of peace, the other in open warre and the terrors of ambush, etc. And all these so lively proposde as not without reason many in times past have believed that all these thinges have in them a kind of voluntarie motion, even as those Tripodes of Vulcan and that Daedalian Venus *autokineteos* . . . for so are all things here described by our divenest Poet, as if they consisted not of hard and solid mettals but of a truely living and moving soule.[15]

---

[14]"At present, there is no conclusive evidence that Shakspere knew the *Iliad* directly in any form before the edition of Chapman's translation in 1610." Baldwin, *William Shakespere's Small Latine*, vol. 2, p. 660.

[15]Chapman, "To the most honored Earle, Earle Marshall," p. 543.

The shield, to borrow Aristotle's terminology, has both *enargeia* (vividness) and *energeia* (actuality). Further, Homer self-consciously draws the reader's attention to the shield's material; a fence is made out of tin and the "black earth forged from gold." Thus even as Homer describes what the shield represents and what it means to his hero—it heightens his already solipsistic anger—he focuses on the means of representation.

Virgil's ekphrasis depicting the epic events of the Trojan War on the walls of Dido's temple of the *Aeneid* provides the formal model for Shakespeare's ekphrasis.[16] In book one, Aeneas and his men, who have fled from the ruins of their native Troy and just survived Neptune's wrath on the high seas, land on the shores of Dido's newly established kingdom. Seeking a temporary haven, they are uncertain how they will be received. Shrouded in a cloud of mist by their protectress, Venus, they are able to approach the centre of the city and the temple precincts without being seen. They, however, are all eyes; they marvel at the newly raised walls, the deeply dug harbor, and the immense columns which will adorn the theater's stage ("immanisque columnas / rupibus excidunt, scaenis decora alta futuris" [*Aen.*, 1:428–429]). Above all, though, they feast their gaze on the spectacular murals adorning a temple to Juno. Balancing a description of the painted walls of Juno's temple in newly founded Carthage with the portrayal of Aeneas' astonished, grieving reaction to the artwork, Virgil thus gives his hero the opportunity to reconsider the meaning of Troy's fall:

> hoc primum in luco nova res oblata timorem
> leniit, hic primum Aeneas sperare salutem
> ausus et adflictus melius confidere rebus. *Aen.*, 1.450–452
> [First in this grove did a strange sight appear to him and allay his fears; here first did Aeneas dare to hope for safety and put surer trust in shattered fortunes.]

As the repetition of "primum" suggests, this site/sight is crucial to Aeneas' understanding of his fate. Yet the actual experience of looking at the artwork proves to be more conflicted than "sperare" and "confidere" at first suggest:

> namque sub ingenti lustrat dum singula templo,
> reginam opperiens, dum, quae fortuna sit urbi,
> artificumque manus inter se operumque laborem

16The main classical sources of the Lucrece story are in Livy, *Ab urbe condita* (bk. 1), which William Painter translated as *The Palace of Pleasure* (1566). While this is largely a political reading of the myth, Ovid's *Fasti* (2.721–852) provides a more sentimental one. However, the ekphrasis is absent from both sources. See Baldwin, *On the Literary Genetics*. Baldwin concludes that Shakespeare uses principally Virgil and Ovid for the ekphrasis, *Aeneid* (1.456–655; 2.76) for the form, and Ovid for much of the content.

miratur, videt Iliacas ex ordine pugnas
bellaque iam fama totum vulgata per orbem,
Atridas Priamumque et saevum ambobus Achillem.
constitit et lacrimans, "quis iam locus," inquit, "Achate,
quae regio in terris nostri non plena laboris?
en Priamus! sunt hic etiam sua praemia laudi,
sunt lacrimae rerum et mentem mortalia tangunt.
solve metus; feret haec aliquam tibi fama salutem." *Aen.*, 1.453–463
[For while beneath the mighty temple, awaiting the queen, he scans each
object, while he marvels at the city's fortune, the handicraft of the several
artists and the work of their toil, he sees in due order the battles of Ilium, the
warfare now known by fame throughout the world, the sons of Atreus, and
Priam, and Achilles, fierce in his wrath against both. He stopped and weeping
cried: "What land, Achates, what tract on earth is now not full of our sorrow?
Lo, Priam! Here, too, virtue has its due rewards; here, too, there are tears for
misfortune and mortal sorrows touch the heart. Dismiss thy fears; this fame
will bring thee some salvation.]

The exemplary viewer, Aeneas reacts with *admiratio* and *pathos*. Weeping
["lacrimans"], he literally mimics the "lacrimae rerum" of the murals. Still,
neither "fama totum volgata per orbem" nor the more ambiguous promise
of "aliquam salutem" is enough to completely assuage the pain of seeing his
friends and enemies suddenly and unexpectedly re-presented. Although the
murals are but "empty images" ["pictura . . . inani"], they wet Aeneas' face
with a "long river" ["largoque . . . flumine"] of tears and fill his chest with
a "deep groan" ["ingentum gemitum"].[17]

Detailing six different scenes from the Trojan War, the subsequent
verses show indeed that these "miranda" or wonders, for all their heuristic
and emotional force, are not able to redeem Priam's grief, nor curb Achilles'
savagery, nor, most importantly, prevent Aeneas himself from becoming
another city's doom. For as soon as Aeneas turns his attention from the
murals where, among other figures, the doomed Amazon warrior Penthesilea rages, Virgil resumes the main narrative by having Dido naively
welcome the Trojans whose divinely ordained fate will be her downfall.
Michael Putnam, in his subtle, far-reaching study of Virgilian ekphrasis, thus
argues that the epic's six ekphrases are synecdoches of the entire narrative;
they "have much to teach the reader about the poem as a whole."[18] Yet
because their form and content also disrupt the narrative and its heroic,

---

[17]Servius, glossing *pictura inani*, suggests that the murals lack substance: "inani
epitheton est picturae . . . quia caret corporum quae imitatur plenitudine" (*Servii
Grammatici*, vol. 1, p. 149).

[18]Putnam, *Virgil's Epic Designs*, p. 2.

imperial claims, Putnam reads the ekphrases as undermining inherited notions of epic. More problematically still, Virgil never really resolves the rival claims of visual and verbal representation enacted in these ekphrases. For instance, how the reader regards the ekphrastic object is often at odds with how the protagonists experience the artwork.[19] Gazing at the Trojan murals, Aeneas reacts with grief and admiration; his appropriation of the artwork depends on personal experience. Readers, meanwhile, can afford more objectivity, even as they revel in Virgil's skillful hexameters that seem to defy spatial and temporal verisimilitude. When Aeneas views the ekphrastic shield crafted by Vulcan in book eight, he rejoices in the shield's depiction of history, but he remains "ignarus" of its meaning. As Putnam asks, "Does he rejoice, though he is ignorant, because, were he to find out the meaning of the whole, it would give him pleasure to contemplate the future when image would become reality? Or does he rejoice only because he remains uninitiated into any deeper meaning behind superficial brilliance . . . ?"[20] In his attempt to resolve or at least describe such ambiguity, Putnam reads the ekphrasis against the entire poem and its ambivalent celebration of empire. In terms of the literary history of ekphrasis, however, we marvel at the shield, but our *admiratio* derives also from Virgil's outbidding of Homer's shield and the manner in which he urges us to read an imagined visual object as if it were also a linguistic object.[21]

Even to a greater degree than Virgil, Shakespeare employs ekphrasis as a vehicle for metapoetic reflection on the nature and value of art. While the same concerns about perception, morality, and mimesis also dominate Shakespeare's ekphrasis, the lessons learned from Lucrece's experience of ekphrasis are far more subjective than Aeneas'. Shakespeare undermines the exemplarity of Troy's fall in a manner that at once recalls Virgil's ambiva-

---

[19]After Homer and Virgil, ekphrasis, especially in the epic, became a self-conscious form of literary *imitatio*. When Milton, for instance, describes Satan's shield as "massy, large and round" (*Paradise Lost*, 1.285) and then compares it to the moon that Galileo sees from his telescope, we are meant to see also the ekphrastic weapons of Homer, Virgil, Lucan, and Ariosto.

[20]Putnam, *Virgil's Epic Designs*, p. 153. In the twelfth century, Bernard Silvestris, in his *Commentary*, reads Aeneas' conflicted reaction to Dido's murals as a stage in the allegorical education of the hero: "We understand his eyes as the senses, some of which are true, some of which are false; just as there is a right eye and a left one, so too we know certain senses are true and others false. We understand the pictures to be temporal goods (*bona temporalis*), which are called pictures because they are not good but seem so" (p. 13). By the epic's end, however, Bernard holds that Aeneas has learnt to read and to act without being distracted by temporal things.

[21]In the *Aeneid* (6.34), where Daedalus' artwork is ekphrastically described, *legere* clearly means both to scan a picture and decipher a text.

lence—not to mention Spenser's imitation of that ambivalence in *The Faerie Queene*—and outdoes it. His ekphrasis is a conflicted site/sight of literary, historical, and psychological appropriation—or what the German hermeneuticists call *Aneignung*. Looking at the painting of Troy's calamity, Lucrece learns to appropriate the experiences of others, even as Shakespeare portrays the disjunctive violence inherent in the *Troynovant* tradition which helped shape his political and, according to Heather James, his theatrical culture.[22]

The prefatory "Argument" outlines the main narrative events of *The Rape of Lucrece*: "Sextus Tarquinius, being inflamed with Lucrece's beauty . . . treacherously stealeth into her chamber, violently ravished her, and early in the morning speedeth away . . . [her husband, father and two companions and friends having returned] and finding Lucrece attired in mourning habit demanded the cause of her sorrow. She first taking an oath of them for her revenge, revealed the actor and whole manner of his dealing, and withal suddenly stabbed herself."[23] Rewriting this narrative, Joel Fineman reads *Lucrece* as an exploration of what happens to the subject after the "poetry of praise" and "idealizing, unitary, visionary speech" is no longer tenable.[24] To this I would add, reductively, that the principal actors in the poem are not Lucrece or Tarquin, but their eyes. Eyes—Tarquin's, Lucrece's, our own—are the subject of constant amplification, puns, and conceits. Shakespeare overdetermines the process of seeing and the ideal of identity until they seem to collapse from the rhetorical and cognitive weight they are forced to bear. Near the beginning of the poem, for example, the narrator baldly declares: "Beauty itself doth of itself persuade / The eyes of men without an orator" (29–30). Unable, seemingly, to help himself, Tarquin's "greedy eye-balls" (368), his "cockatrice' dead-killing eye" (540), and his "burning eye" (435) shape and distort experience. He makes a *blasón* out of the sleeping Lucrece which, in turn, leads to an excess of Petrarchan commonplaces and various sophistic, self-serving conclusions such as when he declares to Lucrece: "The fault is thine / For those thine eyes betray thee unto mine" (482–483).

Meanwhile, Lucrece does her own seeing. She begins her education in visual semiotics rather naively: "Thou look'st not like deceit," she tells Tarquin, "do not deceive me" (585). And just as Shakespeare will soon prove to be a reader of Troy's fall, he makes Lucrece a reader of history's exempla. She warns Tarquin: "This deed will make thee only loved for fear . . . For princes are the glass, the school, the book / Where subjects' eyes do learn, do read, do look" (610, 615–616). Aware of history's "spectacle" (631), Lucrece already

---

[22]James, *Shakespeare's Troy*, pp. 9, 30–41.

[23]There is some debate as to whether Shakespeare actually wrote the *Argument*.

[24]Fineman, "Shakespeare's Will," pp. 27, 29.

sees her plight as a future exemplum. After the rape, this spectacle is further exaggerated in Lucrece's elaborate lamentations against "Time" and "Opportunity." Her apostrophes ably express the extremity of her grief and, paradoxically, her increasing awareness of language's insufficiency. Yet out of "this helpless smoke of words" (1027), Lucrece is still able to embrace the Renaissance ideal of eloquence and declare, "My tongue shall utter all; mine eyes, like sluices, / As from a mountain spring that feeds a dale / Shall gush pure streams to purge my impure tale" (1076–1078). Such a contradictory stance is due in part to how Shakespeare deconstructs the act of seeing. The self-knowledge gained through sight is problematic, and "So with herself is she in mutiny" (1153).

Still, rhetorical considerations aside, part of this confusion results from the imagery adopted to represent Lucrece's gender. Recasting the metaphor of god the artificer, Shakespeare asserts:

> For men have marble, women waxen minds,
> And therefore are they formed as marble will.
> The weak oppressed, th'impression of strange kinds
> Is formed in them by force, by fraud, or skill.
> Then call them not the authors of their ill,
>   No more than wax shall be accounted evil
>   Wherein is stamped the semblance of a devil. 1240–1246

Here Lucrece is refused, as the exemplary woman, both authority and responsibility; the imagery suggests that her will is a mere artifice. The question, then, is whether Lucrece becomes in any way an author of her own "ill" by the end of the poem.

Part of her authority, I think, is grounded in literary history; *Lucrece* was written in the same year as the gaudy, sanguinary *Titus Andronicus*. In this early play, Shakespeare, depending on the recently revived conventions of Senecan tragedy, gruesomely paints Titus' revenge for his daughter's rape and mutilation. Bereft of hands and tongue, Lavinia is unable to speak the name of her assailants; she instead inscribes the crime and the criminals' names in the sand with a staff held in her mouth. This recalls the case of Philomela who, as Ovid recounts in the *Metamorphoses*, was raped by King Tereus, her sister's husband. Loudly declaiming for justice, Philomela is killed and dismembered by Tereus; later transformed into a nightingale, she continues to denounce her rapist in non-verbal song until she takes vengeance.[25] Shakespeare, in turn, has Lucrece, after her rape and before she encounters the Trojan painting, compare herself to Philomela. Evoking

---

[25]See Newman, "'And Let Mild Women,'" p. 310.

her predecessor, Lucrece folds the Ovidean myth into a strikingly violent, visual image:

> "And whiles against a thorn thou bear'st thy part
> To keep thy sharp woes waking, wretched I,
> To imitate thee well, against my heart
> Will fix a sharp knife to affright mine eye . . . ." 1135–1138

The punning conceit—"I" and "eye"—explicitly conflates the act of seeing and the attempt to fashion a sense of self, while the artifice of the actor becomes essential to Lucrece's "part" in the poem. If the knife with which Lucrece will eventually take her life seems to be no more than a prop here, the violence of seeing would upstage the sexual violence she has just suffered. Caught in the strictures of mimesis, she ostentatiously "[h]olds disputation with each thing she views" (1101).

Such *imitatio* is also inextricably bound up with the poetics of *enargeia*. Shakespeare makes this explicit when he interpolates this dictum just before the ekphrasis:

> To see sad sights moves more than hear them told,
> For then the eye interprets to the ear
> The heavy motion that it doth behold,
> When every part a part of woe doth bear. 1324–1327

At first glance, the proclamation of the supreme virtues of vividness would seem to be out of place in a long narrative poem. Also, given how Lucrece's experience impeaches the worth of visual appearance, and given the poem's intense rhetoricity, the eye would seem to be a poor judge either for the reader or for the poem's protagonists. With the ekphrasis, however, Shakespeare gives "the eye of mind" (1426), as he later puts it, the task of interpretation. By presenting the Trojan painting as an irrefutable object, as a thing-in-the-world, this eye comes to belong to the reader as well as Lucrece and Shakespeare. Indeed, after Lucrece fortuitously finds the "skilful painting" (1367) we hear nothing of her for ten stanzas. She is replaced by the reader whom Shakespeare now addresses directly. Why, though, does the poet at this crucial juncture ignore Lucrece's immediate plight and instead begin to address abstract questions concerning representation? Does this not confirm, as Richard Lanham argues, that her grief is more "rhetorical" than real?[26]

Initially, the motivation for the ekphrasis seems clear. The painted Greeks are described as besieging Troy "[f]or Helen's rape the city to

---

[26]Lanham, *Motives of Eloquence*, p. 104.

destroy" (1369). In this way, Lucrece's interior struggles are made to have broader historical importance. Trojan history is pictured as a natural extension of Roman history—and both are implicitly naturalized in Elizabethan England. This is accomplished in part by the way the ekphrasis adopts a peculiar, almost aorist present tense:

> There might you see the labouring pioneer
> Begrimed with sweat and smearèd all with dust,
> And from the towers of Troy there would appear
> The very eyes of men through loop-holes thrust,
> Gazing upon the Greeks with little lust.
>> Such sweet observance in this work was had
>> That one might see those far-off eyes look sad. 1380–1386

The dynamics of the painting might, anachronistically, be labeled cinematic or cartoonish. As we gaze at it, work is being done and peeping eyes suddenly appear; in a subsequent stanza all the action is cast into present participles and we experience "triumphing . . . bearing . . . marching . . . trembling" (1388–1391). The painting has *energeia* as well as *enargeia*. Its "observance" or verisimilitude has initially a cathartic effect. The painter's "art / of physiognomy" (1394–1395) makes us "quake and tremble" (1393) at the suffering of the sight of "heartless peasants" (1392).

This interplay of message and medium leads, though, to a further digression in which Shakespeare becomes concerned with the painter's technique for its own sake:

> Some high, some low, the painter was so nice.
>> The scalps of many, almost hid behind,
>> To jump up higher seemed, to mock the mind.
> Here one man's hand leaned on another's head,
> His nose being shadowed by his neighbour's ear;
> . . . .
> For much imaginary work was there;
> Conceit deceitful, so compact, so kind,
> That for Achilles' image stood his spear
> Gripped in an armèd hand; himself behind
> Was left unseen save to the eye of mind;
>> A hand, a foot, a face, a leg, a head,
>> Stood for the whole to be imaginèd. 1412–1416; 1422–1428

With this, Shakespeare replaces the "whole" of Troy with the fragments of the human body. Doing to the epic tradition what he does to the Petrarchan in sonnet 130 ("My mistress' eyes are nothing like the sun") where the conventions of visual description are similarly parodied, this *blasón manqué* replaces the objective ideal of proportionality with a radically subjective perspectivism. (Given the history of ekphrasis, it is a curious twist that Shakespeare focuses on Achilles' spear rather than his shield.) It also historicizes Troy's fall, making it into a domestic object much like the prints and tapestries of classical subjects which, as Sasha Roberts shows, were not only ubiquitous in the homes of the Elizabethan elite, but, she argues, were also the potential source of numerous literary ekphrases.[27]

Nancy Vickers has argued that in the first half of *Lucrece*, Shakespeare examines "the limits—indeed the dangers—of inherited, insufficient, descriptive rhetoric."[28] Concentrating on how the "male imagination" contests and possesses the site/sight of the female body, Vickers strangely ignores, however, how the Trojan ekphrasis undermines this fantasy of possession, a fantasy, which as René Girard has shown, may be regarded as the central desire motivating the mimetic act.[29] Thus as one considers alternately Shakespeare and Lucrece in the role of art critic, it is important to examine what is at stake for each. The poet, I think, would master and at the same time subvert a *topos* that since Homer had become a requisite site/sight of metapoetic meditation on the nature of mimesis.

In contrast with Spenser's ekphrases, which are generally employed to celebrate the *Troynovant* myth, Shakespeare's is far less interested in the moral and historical trappings of allegory.[30] Also, the necessity of reconciling the claims of art and nature which dominates Spenser's poetics, is, to be blunt, less compelling to Shakespeare than having the freedom to play with their competing, contradictory claims. Likewise, Shakespeare's famous inability to resist a pun, or his Senecan penchant for piling up corpses on the stage, mocks the notion that art must follow the transparent dictates of an orderly, measured vision of nature. Thus, if the mimetic ideal of

---

[27]Roberts, "Historicizing Ekphrasis," pp. 103–124, notes the ubiquity of Lucrece in Renaissance art, citing Titian's "Tarquin and Lucrece" and "Lucretia," Veronese's "Lucretia," and the "Lucrecia Romana" by a follower of Cranach. Also relevant are the engravings by the likes of Heinrich Goltzius and Agostino Veneziano which represented the whole or a part of the story. These engravings, in turn, were often reproduced as prints that were readily available in the art markets of the major European cities. Another material, visual analogue which suggests itself are the twelve magnificent trompe l'oeil murals depicting scenes from the history of Troy in the Château d'Oiron. Painted by Noël Jallier around 1550, the so-called *Galerie du Grande Écuyer* is precisely the kind of scene that Shakespeare imagines his anachronistic Lucrece viewing. See Guillaume, *La Galerie du Grande Écuyer*.

[28]Vickers, "'The blazon of sweet beauty's best,'" p. 96.

[29]Girard, *Deceit, Desire, and the Novel, Violence and the Sacred*, and *"To Double Business Bound."*

[30]On Spenserian ekphrasis and Virgil, see Watkins, "'Neither of idle shewes,'" pp. 345–363.

"proportion poeticall" championed by Shakespeare's contemporary, George Puttenham—an ideal grounded in Aristotelian notions of decorum, nature, and intelligibility—is abandoned in the Trojan ekphrasis, then it appears that the reader, as well as Lucrece, will inevitably be deceived. How, moreover, are we to value the classical tradition in this ekphrasis, if the archetypal epic hero, Achilles, is eclipsed by a mere spear? By refusing to describe or anatomize in any conventional sense, Shakespeare conveys the experience of seeing rather than providing us with any visual essence. Art, at best, presents but a synecdoche or a fragment of reality or history. And if the imagination is encouraged to reestablish a lost, perhaps illusory, unity, it also must, at least in the painter's case, be branded as "Conceit deceitful." The "universall" artistic ideal Chapman celebrates in *Achilles' Shield* has been undermined with Virgilian ambivalence.

No wonder, then, that the painter effectively becomes an actor in the poem. Lucrece searches the painting for "a face where all distress is stelled . . . Till she despairing Hecuba beheld / Staring on Priam's wounds with her old eyes" (1444, 1447–1448). As Shakespeare conflates Hecuba's grief with Lucrece's, he almost seems to envy the painter's skill: "In her the painter had anatomized / Time's ruin, beauty's wreck, and grim care's reign" (1450–1451). Such a dense, metaphysical portrait is a visual impossibility; when we read: "[h]er blue blood changed to black in every vein" (1454), we recall the *autokinesis* Chapman found in Homer's shield. But even this dynamic image of Hecuba is not enough for Lucrece; the painter is reproached for doing Hecuba "wrong / To give her so much grief, and not a tongue" (1462–1463). Thus prompted, Lucrece begins to read the painting like a discarded script, or, to recall Shakespeare's earlier marble-wax analogy, the painting becomes her marble and Lucrece, eschewing passivity, now claims the prerogatives of the male imagination:

> . . . feelingly she weeps Troy's painted woes;
> For sorrow, like a heavy hanging bell
> Once set on ringing, with his own weight goes;
> Then little strength rings out the doleful knell.
> So Lucrece, set a-work, sad tales doth tell
>   To pencilled pensiveness and coloured sorrow.
>   She lends them words, and she their looks doth borrow. 1492–1498

The incongruity of such impromptu thespianism aside, it is consistent with the notion that knowledge is a form of self-representation as well as a kind of memory—Lucrece recalls both her knowledge of Troy's history and her own experience. That such representation strains the limits of verisimilitude and dramatic logic does not lessen its epistemological value. Lucrece is figured both as an object, a tintinabulating bell, and as dramatist-actor reshaping her own sorrow. Shakespeare would have her play Hecuba: "On this sad shadow Lucrece spends her eyes, / And shapes her sorrow to the beldame's woes" (1457–1458). Moving then from mimicry to action, Lucrece promises Hecuba, "I'll tune thy woes with my lamenting tongue / . . . And with my knife scratch out the angry eyes / Of all the Greeks" (1465, 1469–1470). Reversing also her initial identification with Helen, she exclaims: "Show me the strumpet that began this stir, / That with my nails her beauty I may tear" (1471–1472). Such "iconophobia" signals a subtler stance toward the mimetic object and, implicitly, the Trojan tradition.[31] It depends less on the psychological motivations that Lucrece might have than Shakespeare's desire to replace the reader with his protagonist turned actress and art critic. Before the ekphrasis, the language of sight was over-determined and its ability to signify deceit and the uncertainties of subjectivity was unreliable. Now, however, the language of action is presented as a direct, unambiguous expression of what Bacon calls the "desires of the mind."

To act here is ultimately an extreme form of reading. Seeing her private thoughts mirrored in the public, historic spectacle of the painting, Lucrece learns to appropriate the artwork, the visual text for her own ends. She becomes, in short, an author "of her own ill," though not in the way that Shakespeare a few hundred lines before had claimed was impossible for a woman, but rather in the sense that Wolfgang Iser calls "esthetic."[32] If the esthetic is "the realization accomplished by the reader," the reader gains such insight by navigating between a subjective reality and the objective illusions proffered by a text.[33] If Lucrece simply misreads or misprisons the Troy painting by taking its mimetic illusions too seriously, then, judged from the standpoint of the text's absolute authority or from the desire to have consistency of interpretation, this would confirm her inability to see the world or her role in it. But if the mimetic ideal, the poetics of *enargeia*, has already been undermined by the poet himself, to say nothing of the heroine's own experience, then Lucrece's complicated, confused response to the painting signals an important critique of the "ideality of vision."[34]

It is in this latter sense that Lucrece, nicely abstracting the plight she and Hecuba share, interrogates the nexus between self and world: "Why should the private pleasure of someone / Become the public plague of many moe?" (1478–1479) This question not only bears on the perfidy of Tarquin and Paris, but also paves the way for the complex dialectic of interiority and

---

[31] Heffernan, *Museum of Words*, pp. 79–80.
[32] Iser, "The Reading Process," p. 956.
[33] Iser, "The Reading Process," p. 956.
[34] Fineman, "Shakespeare's Will," p. 59.

exteriority which will power Shakespeare's tragedies. As if rehearsing such a dynamic, Shakespeare has Lucrece play both audience and actor when "[s]he throws her eyes about the painting round" (1499) until she encounters the image of Sinon, the artificer of the Trojan horse. "In him," the narrator tells us, "the painter laboured with his skill / To hide deceit" (1506–1507). Sinon's "mild image" (1520) is at odds with his words, which "like wildfire burnt the shining glory / Of rich-built Ilion, that the skies were sorry, / And little stars shot from their fixèd places" (1523–1525). Such hyperbolic sympathy between language and world sets the stage for Lucrece's abrupt realization of the disjunction between sight and the world. I say realization, but the manner in which Lucrece sees through the painter's "deceit" has a chaotic, almost chiasmic quality so that we glimpse the heuristic turmoil of thought itself:

> This picture she advisedly perused,
> And chid the painter for his wondrous skill,
> Saying some shape in Sinon's was abused,
> So fair a form lodged not a mind so ill;
> And still on him she gazed, and gazing still,
>   Such signs of truth in his plain face she spied
>   That she concludes the picture was belied.
> "It cannot be," quoth she, "that so much guile"—
> She would have said "can lurk in such a look",
> But Tarquin's shape came in her mind the while,
> And from her tongue "can lurk" from "cannot" took.
> "It cannot be" she in that sense forsook,
>   And turned it thus: "It cannot be, I find,
>   But such a face should bear a wicked mind." 1527–1540

As Lucrece discovers the truth of the painting, she also discovers something of her own ability to reason and the role she has been playing. Looking at Sinon's face, she sees Tarquin's face repeated. But a species of metaphysics is also at work in her gaze. She sees, to paraphrase Lévinas' phenomenology of the visage, the infinity of otherness and difference, as well as the necessity of making a moral judgment vis-à-vis the other.[35] Yet if ethics and sight are indistinguishable here, Lucrece's intuitive judgment, the syntax suggests, does not depend on received notions of religion or even gender commonplaces. Instead, her verdict is like the ekphrasis itself, synecdochal and experiental. "[C]an" must substitute for "cannot," and seeing is thinking. Thus concerning Sinon, she concludes: "As Priam him did cherish, / So did I Tarquin, so my Troy did perish" (1546–1547). This analogy of body with city, as the rest of the poem will prove, is a fatal one.

---

[35]See Lévinas, *Totalité et infini*, pp. 203–242.

The body politic and the Trojan myth have been rescaled, feminized, and raped. Art has proved to be immoral and, her analogy notwithstanding, incomprehensible. This explains, perhaps, why Lucrece turns to paradox in the remaining stanzas chronicling her gaze. "Look, look . . ." she urges herself (1548), and us, as Sinon's crocodile tears turn into "balls of quenchless fire" (1554) burning Troy. Experienced now in the abyss separating appearance and reality, Lucrece desires another species of "unity" (1558), the unity of self-knowledge and action. At first, this is vicarious:

> She tears the senseless Sinon with her nails,
> Comparing him to that unhappy guest
> Whose deed hath made herself herself detest. 1564–1566

The repetition of the personal pronoun paves the way for other repetitions. "Fool, fool" she calls herself, only to have Shakespeare conclude that her "woe" is only somewhat mitigated by the fact that others have suffered too: "It easeth some, though none it ever cured, / To think their dolour others have endured" (1581–1582).

How then does such a dictum help us to interpret Lucrece's subsequent suicide and the manner in which her dead body becomes the public spectacle that prompts the Romans to overthrow Tarquin's uncle, the tyrant, and establish the Republic? In other words, is Lucrece's experience looking at the Troy painting transferable to our own experience of reading the poem? At first blush, the answer would seem to be no. Arguably, too much historical distance, too many epistemological barriers separate us from Shakespeare, to say nothing of his creation, Lucrece. Still, from the reader's standpoint the ekphrasis has shown mimesis to be more than a morally suspect illusion. By blurring the boundaries between visual and verbal representation, between private and public rhetoric, and finally, between the roles of poet, character, and reader, the ekphrasis precludes the adoption of any absolute standpoint. This dynamic also helps create a space for self-consciousness, and thus, I would argue, the kind of extreme subjectivity with which Shakespeare will later endow the likes of Hamlet and Lear. To borrow from Schiller, the ekphrasis reveals a poet writing in both the naive and sentimental modes. Along with Lucrece we accept the illusion created by the painting even as we learn to question it. We also, inevitably, have the same experience with the entire poem. In this way, Shakespeare's narrative threatens to enact a hermeneutic circle.

But in his essay "Appropriation," Paul Ricoeur offers us a possible escape from this circle.[36] The reader who appropriates seeks the opposite of the

---

[36]Ricoeur, "Appropriation," pp. 182–196.

timeless objectification of a text's meaning. To appropriate, as the German *Aneignung* suggests, is to subject the text to the play, desires, and needs of the self. At the same time, as a dialectical concept and as an "event," appropriation is also a "letting-go" which universalizes a text's meaning.[37] If Lucrece can turn her back on the painting and reenter the stream of time and action, the same possibility exists for the reader. Of course, there is often great violence inherent in the act of appropriation. Nowhere is this symbolized more vividly than in one of Shakespeare's models, Ovid's *Metamorphoses*. There Minerva destroys an ekphrastic tapestry woven by her would-be rival Arachne and which, significantly, depicts the gods' deceit and sexual violence:

> Non illud Pallas, non illud carpere Livor
> possit opus: doluit successu flava virago
> et rupit pictas, caelestia crimina, vestes,
> utque Cytoriaco radium de monte tenebat,
> ter quater Idmoniae frontem percussit Arachnes.
> non tulit infelix laqueoque animosa ligavit
> guttura 6.129–136
> [Not Pallas, nor Envy himself, could find a flaw in that work. The golden-haired goddess was indignant at her success, and rent the embroidered web with its heavenly crimes; and as she held a shuttle of Cytorian boxwood, thrice and again she struck Idmonian Arachne's head. The wretched girl could not endure it, and put a noose about her bold neck.]

With characteristic irony, Ovid insists here on the artwork's materiality as the weaving shuttle becomes a weapon. But it also is transformed into a voice, a voice heard in texts as diverse as Sophocles' and Shakespeare's. Thus while the tapestry is, at least in Minerva's biased eyes, a lying text, for us latter-day readers, the woven pictures ["pictas . . . vestes"] symbolize that endless intertextuality which informs literature and history.

Perhaps the most compelling intertextual trace to be read in *The Rape of Lucrece*, however, points to a later tragedy. Shakespeare looks back to Lucrece's gaze when he has Hamlet, after one of the players recites a speech for him, play the drama critic:

> O, what a rogue and peasant slave am I!
> Is it not monstrous that this player here,
> But in a fiction, in a dream of passion,
> Could force his soul so to his whole conceit
> That from her working all his visage wanned,
> Tears in his eyes, distraction in 's aspect,
> A broken voice, and his whole function suiting

---

[37] Ricoeur, "Appropriation," p. 191.

> With forms to his conceit? And all for nothing.
> For Hecuba!
> What's Hecuba to him, or he to Hecuba,
> That he should weep for her?   2.2.527–537

Here, as readers of *Lucrece*, we see the critical commonplace of the divorce between Hamlet's words and action cast in a new, albeit retrospective light. Both have suffered unspeakable crimes, and both turn to art as a means to comprehend their plight. That both turn also to the example of Hecuba confirms not only the force of her example, but also how vivid and yet ultimately problematic art can be as a means of self-discovery. Like the player, Lucrece has affected what Hamlet still cannot—she has married "forms" to her "conceits." In the poem, Hecuba repeats Lucrece's grief and yet the limits of *enargeia* prompt Shakespeare to supplement it with all the means available to the orator and dramatist. Hamlet, in turn, uses the speech about Hecuba and Priam, together with *The Mousetrap*, to repeat his uncle's crime, make them visible to other protagonists and render them more tangible to his own imagination, if not understanding. The player's feeling for Hecuba increases Hamlet's awareness of the gap between art and life. Hamlet becomes "monstrous" to himself; he becomes, that is, a poor imitation of art imitating life. Tempted to turn to "self-slaughter" as a remedy for this monstrosity, he nevertheless refuses Lucrece's fateful decision.

As Robert Weimann reminds us, Shakespeare has Hamlet declare various neo-classical precepts concerning mimetic decorum while in practice his hero rants, puns, and dissembles as if he would eschew all "representational logic."[38] Weimann observes:

> Hamlet, through his own histrionic knowledge and activity, is both a product of mimesis, an object of mimetic appropriation to his audience in the theater of the world and an agent of mimesis, a *Subjekt* of appropriation, i.e. one who attempts to assimilate a theatrical situation . . . in the world of his own theater.[39]

Could not the same be said of Lucrece, save for the caveat that her theater of mimesis and history is instead a private gallery open only to her, the reader, and Shakespeare? The solipsism that some have seen in her suicide may also be read as the rehearsal or repetition of the rape, but this time it is achieved, at least, on her own terms. As the ekphrasis and its momentary suspension of time fade from view, all that remains for Lucrece is the ability to act. Having become a "fool" in her own eyes, Lucrece makes a picture

---

38 Weimann, "Mimesis in *Hamlet*," p. 286.
39 Weimann, "Mimesis in *Hamlet*," p. 288.

speak only to discover that its mocking language was already her own. This realization or "appropriation" reminds me of Hamlet contemplating Yorick's skull. Like Lucrece's self-conscious, tragic encounter with the painting, Hamlet considers the skull, as Horatio puts it, "too curiously." Nevertheless, the examples of Lucrece and Hamlet appear to give the lie to Ernst Gombrich's insight in *Art and Illusion*: "though we may be intellectually aware of the fact that any given experience *must* be an illusion, we cannot, strictly speaking, watch ourselves having an illusion."[40]

WORKS CITED

Bacon, Francis. *The Advancement of Learning*. Excerpted in *English Renaissance Literary Criticism*. Ed. Brian Vickers. Oxford: Clarendon, 1999. 457–469.

Baldwin, T. W. *On the Literary Genetics of Shakespeare's Poems and Sonnets*. Urbana: University of Illinois Press, 1950.

Baldwin, T. W. *William Shakespere's Small Latine & Less Greeke*. 2 vols. Urbana: University of Illinois Press, 1944.

Bernard Silvestris. *Commentary on the First Six Books of Virgil's* Aeneid. Trans. Earl G. Schreiber and Thomas E. Maresca. Lincoln: University of Nebraska Press, 1979.

Chapman, George. "Achilles' Shield." *Chapman's Homer: The Iliad, the Odyssey and the Lesser Homerica*. 2 vols. Ed. Allardyce Nicoll. Princeton: Princeton University Press, 1967. 1.543–558.

Descartes, René. *Les méditations. Œuvres philosophiques*. Tome II. Paris: Classiques Garnier, 1996.

Fineman, Joel. "Shakespeare's Will: The Temporality of Rape." *Representations* 20 (1987): 25–76.

Girard, René. *Deceit, Desire, and the Novel*. Trans. Yvonne Freccero. Baltimore: Johns Hopkins University Press, 1965.

Girard, René. *"To Double Business Bound": Essays on Literature, Mimesis, and Anthropology*. Baltimore: Johns Hopkins University Press, 1978.

Girard, René. *Violence and the Sacred*. Trans. Patrick Gregory. Baltimore: Johns Hopkins University Press, 1977.

Guillaume, Jean. *La Galerie du Grande Écuyer: L'Histoire de Troie au Château d'Oiron*. Chauray: Éditions Patrimonies et Medias, 1996.

Heffernan, James F. *Museum of Words: The Poetics of Ekphrasis from Homer to Ashbery*. Chicago: University of Chicago Press, 1993.

Iser, Wolfgang. "The Reading Process: A Phenomenological Approach." 1974. Rpt. in *The Critical Tradition: Classic Texts and Contemporary Trends*. Ed. David Richter. Boston: Bedford, 1998. 956–967.

James, Heather. *Shakespeare's Troy: Drama, Politics, and the Translation of Empire*. Cambridge: Cambridge University Press, 1997.

Kahn, Coppélia. "The Rape in Shakespeare's *Lucrece*." *Shakespeare Studies* 9 (1976): 45–72.

---

[40]Quoted in Iser, "The Reading Process," p. 963.

Lanham, Richard. *The Motives of Eloquence: Literary Rhetoric in the Renaissance*. New Haven: Yale University Press, 1976.

Lévinas, Emmanuel. *Totalité et infini: essai sur l'extériorité*. Paris: Livre de poche, 1990.

Maus, Katharine Eisaman. "Taking Tropes Seriously: Language and Violence in Shakespeare's *Rape of Lucrece*." *Shakespeare Quarterly* 37 (1986): 66–82.

Milton, John. *Paradise Lost*. Ed. Scott Elledge. New York: Norton, 1993.

Newman, Jane. "'And Let Mild Women to Him Lose Their Mildness': Philomela, Female Violence, and Shakespeare's *The Rape of Lucrece*." *Shakespeare Quarterly* 45 (1994): 304–326.

Ovid. *Fasti*. Trans. J. G. Frazer. Cambridge: Harvard University Press, 1969.

Ovid. *Metamorphoses I–VII*. Trans. F. J. Miller. Cambridge: Harvard University Press, 1999.

Plato. *Phaedrus*. *The Collected Dialogues of Plato*. Trans. R. Hackforth. Princeton: Princeton University Press, 1985. 475–525.

Putnam, Michael C. J. *Virgil's Epic Designs: Ekphrasis in the* Aeneid. New Haven: Yale University Press, 1998.

Ricoeur, Paul. "Appropriation." *Hermeneutics and the Human Sciences*. Trans. John B. Thompson. Cambridge: Cambridge University Press, 1981. 182–196.

Roberts, Sasha. "Historicizing Ekphrasis: Gender, Textiles, and Shakespeare's *Lucrece*." *Pictures into Words: Theoretical and Descriptive Approaches to Ekphrasis*. Ed. Valerie Robillard and Els Jongeneel. Amsterdam: VU University Press, 1998. 103–124.

Servius. *Servii Grammatici qui feruntur in Vergilii carmina commentarii*. Ed. Georg Thilo and Hermann Hagen. 2 vols. Hildesheim: Georg Olms, 1986.

Shakespeare, William. *The Rape of Lucrece*. *The Norton Shakespeare*. Gen. ed. Stephen Greenblatt. New York: Norton, 1997. 641–682.

Sidney, Philip. "A Defence of Poetry." *English Renaissance Literary Criticism*. Ed. Brian Vickers. Oxford: Clarendon, 1999. 336–391.

Vickers, Nancy. "'The blazon of sweet beauty's best': Shakespeare's *Lucrece*." *Shakespeare and the Question of Theory*. Ed. Patricia Parker and Geoffrey Hartman. New York: Methuen, 1985. 95–115.

Virgil. *Eclogues, Georgics, Aeneid I–VI*. Trans. H. R. Fairclough. Cambridge: Harvard University Press, 1994.

Watkins, John. "'Neither of idle shewes, nor of false charmes aghast': Transformations of Virgilian Ekphrasis in Chaucer and Spenser." *Journal of Medieval and Renaissance Studies* 23 (1993): 345–363.

Weimann, Robert. "Mimesis in *Hamlet*." *Shakespeare and the Question of Theory*. Ed. Patricia Parker and Geoffrey Hartman. New York: Methuen, 1985. 275–291.

Exemplarity

in

Troynovant

Slanderous Troys: Between Fame and Rumor

READING TROY AS OBSOLETE IN EPIC

During the Renaissance it was customary for European royal houses to boast the prestige of a Trojan ancestry. Virtually every European country claimed to have been founded by an exiled hero from Troy: Italy by Aeneas, France by Francus, Portugal by the sons of Lusus, Britain by Brutus, and so forth. A primary aim of the genre of dynastic epic in the Renaissance was to trace carefully the Trojan ancestry of the royal house being celebrated. Within this ideological framework, veneration of and piety towards the old, fallen Troy were axiomatic: the poignancy of the fallen Troy was deeply embedded in the cultural imaginary of dynastic epic, even as it recounted a Trojan *renovatio*.

Edmund Spenser's *The Faerie Queene* (1590–1596), true to the generic formula of dynastic epic, celebrates the presumed Trojan ancestry of Queen Elizabeth I. Spenser's epic presents Elizabeth's England as "Troynovant," founded by the Trojan exile Brutus and miraculously arising as a New Troy from the ashes of the old. To adduce one piece of visual evidence of Elizabethan England as "Troynovant," a famous 1569 portrait of Elizabeth at Hampton Court recasts Paris' disastrous awarding of the apple to Venus over Juno and Minerva. In this portrait, Elizabeth awards the apple to herself as a glorious sublation of the three competing goddesses, Juno, Minerva, and Venus. Elizabeth's imperial glory and wisdom redeem the inflammatory, short-sighted "judgement" of Paris and pave the way for England as a new Troy.[1]

But in Book III, Canto ix of *The Faerie Queene* the archetypal adulterer Paris, as a kind of Trojan "return of the repressed," comes back to haunt Spenser's epic in the figure of Paridell, a libidinal faerie knight in the Ovidian mold, sporting the image of a "burning hart . . . on his breast" and flaunting an impiety toward the fallen Troy.[2] This episode arguably consti-

---

[1]On the Hampton Court painting, see Montrose, "Gifts and Reasons," pp. 433–461.

[2]Spenser, *The Faerie Queene*, III.viii.45. Subsequent citations of the poem refer to Hamilton's edition.

tutes the most fraught return to the story of a fallen Troy in all of Renaissance epic. I say "fraught" because the episode opens with Paridell's address, as disruptive as it is seemingly preposterous, to the fallen Troy: "What boots it boast thy glorious descent, / And fetch from heauen thy great Genealogie . . . ?" (III.ix.33). This taunt places his interlocutor Britomart (the woman warrior destined to become a dynastic spouse for Britain's version of the New Troy, and a key figure for Elizabeth herself) on the defensive and, in light of the ideological aims of dynastic epic, under unaccustomed pressure to preserve the good name of Aeneas, Brutus, and Troy itself from Paridell's strategic slander.

My argument's starting point is its insistence that we should not underestimate the significance of Spenser's pointed reference to Paridell as *The Faerie Queene*'s paradigmatic "learned louer" (III.x.6). I propose that Spenser may be offering Paridell's extensive reading (and, one presumes, his knowledge of literary history) as nothing less than a key interpretive clue for this episode. Because he plays no role in the formation of Troynovant, Paridell, to be sure, carries with him the taint of obsolescence. But although Paridell may be a cultural dead end, he is also the "*learned* louer." As I argue, Paridell's erudition exercises its own kind of *ad hoc* subversive power at Malbecco's banquet table; and it necessarily reflects Spenser's own capacity to recall any number of mytho-historical accounts of Troy that would vindicate the faerie knight's insistence on Troy as "now nought, but an idle name," creaking under the ideological burden of propping up Renaissance imperial genealogies.[3] In short, as far as Spenser is concerned, it may be the case that obsolete knights can best recognize obsolete legends and Troy, at this point in epic literary history, may be one such legend.

My argument has two parts. First, I will map the complex gender tactics Paridell deploys to undermine Britomart's nostalgia for the fallen Troy. As we shall see, Paridell, the "learned louer," dabbles not only in ancestral genealogies but also, we could say, in Foucauldian genealogies: the cynically erudite Paridell is less interested in stories of a "correct" Trojan genealogy than he is in a genealogy of Troy stories that traffic in "embaste" "of-spring" and call into question an "authentic" history of Troy. Thus Paridell, ensnaring Britomart within the web of his manipulative banter, unsettles Britomart as the episode's reliable historian. Paridell's exchange with Britomart challenges its readers to recognize the strands of literary history running throughout.

---

[3]In this context, one thinks, for example, of such works as Ariosto's fragmentary, cynical *Cinque Canti*, where the enchantress Alcina slanders Charlemagne's ancestors as "a despicable nation that fled from Troy all the way to the deep swamps of the Don" (I, 45–46).

In the second stage of my argument I propose to add Spenser's own beloved precursor Chaucer, particularly his *House of Fame*, to the intertextual weaving of this episode. Mihoko Suzuki has perceptively described the episode as "a locus for Spenser's meditation on his own classical genealogy, his descent from Virgil and Ovid."[4] I would add that Spenser's "classical genealogy" of Virgil and Ovid inevitably intersects with Chaucer (and with Chaucer's own Virgil and Ovid) as his influential predecessor in shaping a vernacular English poetry. Though Ovid's *Heroides* is indeed a key text for Paridell's destabilizing of the authority of Virgilian dynastic epic, I argue that it is the episode's possible echoes of the *House of Fame* (1374–1385), an unsettling critique of the truth content of poetry itself, that presents an equally serious challenge to the "truth" of Troy.[5] This underread text (a text we can imagine Paridell as having read) persistently tests poetic authority in ways that reinforce, not to say justify, Paridell's "bad" Trojan historiography. In the *House of Fame*, the "truth" of the fall of Troy is a highly contested site. Reading the Paridell-Britomart exchange through a Chaucerian lens enables us to perceive Spenser's faerie knight as more than simply obsolete: he is rather *The Faerie Queene*'s powerful embodiment of an already existing counter-discourse of alternative Troys of dubious or contested authority.

In the Britomart-Paridell episode, Britomart and a third knight, Satyrane, are drenched by a storm and forced to take shelter in the swine shed of Malbecco, the miserly, senile husband of the young and beautiful Hellenore. Eventually Malbecco relents and reluctantly admits the knights into his castle. As they sit around Malbecco's banquet table, Paridell launches into praise of his ancestor Paris, in the process slandering Britomart's beloved Troy as "now nought, but an idle name," "buried low" in its ashes, inflicted with a "direfull destinie," its "worthy prayses being blent" by disgrace and an "embaste" "of-spring" (III.ix.33). Even as Paridell defames Troy, he and Hellenore (a Helen-"whore") exchange flirtatious glances, and later he rapes her in what, as any number of critics have pointed out, Spenser clearly intends as a parodic re-enactment of Paris' abduction of Helen as the cause of the Trojan War. Although Britomart demonstrates grace under pressure in her exchanges with Paridell, the episode prompts speculation as to how

---

[4]*Metamorphoses of Helen*, p. 169. Picking up where Roche and O'Connell leave off, Suzuki teases out the episode's echoes of Virgil's *Aeneid* (i.e., the Paridell-Hellenore flirtation as re-enacting the exchange between Dido and Aeneas), written in the service of empire, commingling with echoes of Ovid's *Heroides* (Paris' wooing of Helen, as well as Dido's lament), conceived as an anti-Virgilian critique of empire.

[5]See Watkins, *The Specter of Dido*, p. 165, on Hellenore as "the pitiable Dido" of Chaucer's *Legend of Good Women*.

Elizabeth, as the most prominent of *The Faerie Queene*'s intended readers, might have read Britomart's struggles to fend off Paridell's attacks on her venerable genealogy.

Britomart and Paridell share the same Trojan origins, but the similarities end there. As a latter-day Paris, Paridell is, by definition, excluded from the future heroism and imperial glories of Britain's Troynovant. As Harry Berger rightly argues, Paridell has reached "a cultural dead end," dissipated within "a climate of literary cliché."[6] Paridell is indeed obsolete, but obsolescence is also a return of the repressed that renders him all the more insidious for the ideological framework of Renaissance dynastic epic: he engages in competitive banter with Britomart, in the process calling into question her "correct" Trojan genealogy. In questioning the prestige of Britomart's (and, indeed, all of epic literary history's) beloved Troy, the obsolete Paridell has nothing to lose but some sadistic satisfaction to gain. My essay argues that we must not overlook the possibility that Paridell, though excluded from Troynovant's future, may be Spenser's way of suggesting that the imaginative power of dynastic epic's definitive topos of "the westering of empire" as a New Troy may, by the end of the sixteenth century, have begun to play itself out or, put another way, may itself have reached a cultural dead end.

Before I can argue this possibility, some space clearing is necessary. Previous close readings of this episode have emphasized the moral superiority of the earnest, sincere Britomart over the cynical, decadent Paridell. The unsavory motive behind Paridell's dismissal of Troy's "embaste" "of-spring" is of course his strategy for, in his words, narrating his own lineage "deriue[d] aright" (III.ix.36), a pseudo-genealogy from Paris to Parius to Paridas (all exiled on an island in the Aegean as a geographically perverse "eastering" of Troy)—a narration whose purpose is no deeper than to send an amorous signal to Helen/Hellenore that he is a new Paris preparing to abduct her. Despite the obvious shallowness of his motive, Paridell's apostrophizing praise for his wanton ancestor Paris (as opposed to, say, the heroic Hector or the poignant King Priam, slipping in his own blood) has persisted as a kind of lightning rod for Spenser scholarship, prompting stern critiques of Paridell as an unreliable mytho-historiographer and as perhaps the most outrageous abuser of the tracing of a Trojan genealogy in all of early modern literature. Critics have described Paridell's account of the fall of Troy as "slanted" and "distorted by his own selfish

---

[6]Berger, *Revisionary Play*, p. 156. See also Nohrnberg, who describes Paridell as "still attached to the adulterous cycle of the first Troy" (*The Analogy of* The Faerie Queene, p. 634).

interests."[7] He has been accused of "know[ing] just enough of the past to give a tolerable sort of summary," but as a historian of Troy and a Trojan genealogist, he is at best a "revisionist," obviously favoring his ancestor Paris.[8] Narcissistically invoking his ancestor Paris as "[m]ost famous Worthy of the world" (III.ix.34), Paridell exhibits a "cavalier attitude toward history."[9] Conversely, Britomart is seen as the reliable Trojan historian, whose more sympathetic account of the aftermath of the fall of Troy—her nostalgia for its "one sad night" of destruction (III.ix.39)—evinces a more "dynamic relationship to history," serving to "correct and supplement" Paridell's faulty history.[10] Even though Paridell is the last to speak in this dialogue ("So ended *Paridell*" [III.ix.51]), Britomart's Troy has been, within Spenser scholarship, the episode's "final word" on the glory that was once Troy.[11]

Britomart is, of course, the chief heroine of Spenser's dynastic narrative, and she comes to Malbecco's banquet table fresh from Merlin's prophecy that her future "famous Progenie" will spring from "the auncient *Troian* blood" (III.iii.22). Thus we can understand the usual critical impulse of readers of *The Faerie Queene* to distance Britomart from Paridell's sullied Troy, and to legitimate her piety for, in her words, the "lamentable fall of [this] famous towne, / Which raignd so many yeares victorious" (III.ix.39). After all, to linger over Paridell's slandered Troy would be to take seriously the possibility that Britain's "famous Progenie" of future imperial glory is, to echo Paridell himself, merely another strain of Troy's "embaste" "offspring." For that matter, it would be to threaten the genealogical integrity of no less than Queen Elizabeth's own claim to a prestigious Trojan ancestry.

Nevertheless, it is just such a slow lingering that my essay proposes. Rather than succumbing to the impulse, like an antibody, to surround and contain Paridell-as-infection, I seek to unsettle the received notion of Paridell's representation of Trojan history as outrageously faulty. I am by no means proposing a defense of Paridell's "revisionist" Troy, framed as it is by his tawdry flirtation with Hellenore. But I would suggest that these attacks on Paridell's Trojan counter-knowledge—the sheer ludicrousness of

---

[7]Roche, *The Kindly Flame*, pp. 62, 66.

[8]O'Connell, *Mirror and Veil*, pp. 84, 85.

[9]Suzuki, *Metamorphoses of Helen*, p. 165.

[10]Suzuki, *Metamorphoses of Helen,* p. 179.

[11]These same critics rarely go beyond a moral disparagement of Paridell. Roche berates Paridell for taking no "moral responsibility" for his ancestor Paris (*The Kindly Flame,* p. 63); O'Connell dismisses Paridell as "trivial" (*Mirror and Veil,* p. 72) and a mere "raconteur" (p. 84); Suzuki calls attention to Paridell's "callousness toward suffering" (*Metamorphoses of Helen,* p. 167).

his glorification of his "linage" from Paris to Parius to Paridas—a bit too comfortably presuppose a historical truth for the *fata Troiana*, as well as foreclose on any number of medieval and early modern redactions of the Troy story that positioned the glory of Troy in the precarious divide between fame and rumor. To dismiss Paridell as nothing more than a trivial, unfeeling "raconteur" (see my footnote 11) forecloses on the possibility that Paridell *can* be meaningfully accommodated into *The Faerie Queene*'s allegorical register. Specifically, this faerie knight errant may be Spenser's embodiment of the possibility that no history or genealogy of Troy can be separated from the errancies of its complex literary history.

PARIDELL'S TROY: BETWEEN RHETORIC AND LITERARY HISTORY

That Paridell is "the learned louer" intersects with another crucial characteristic of this knight of the "burning hart . . . on his breast." In this section, I reassess the complex gender dynamics of Paridell's and Britomart's exchange by unearthing what I believe is one of the most astute and overlooked observations as to what, in general, motivates the "louer" Paridell in his sojourns throughout Faerie land. Again, I turn to Harry Berger and in particular his provocative but largely undeveloped claim, made some thirty years ago, that Paridell, more than just a polished Ovidian seducer, seeks to "destroy whatever resistances protect the feminine psyche."[12] Not simply seeking Helens to satisfy his lust, Paridell also looks for opportunities to break women down—to breach their psychic forts, as it were. Expressed in a contemporary idiom, we might say Paridell seeks to destroy women's self-esteem or undermine their sense of well-being *as women*. In such a scheme, Britomart is, to be sure, not an object of Paridell's lustful pursuit of "faire Ladies loue" (III.ix.37), as is Hellenore: rather, because of her very earnestness, she can be more productively viewed as the premeditated target of his sadistic attack on the "feminine psyche"—in Britomart's case, a psyche thoroughly invested in Troy and in her identity as Troynovant's new ruler. Not coincidentally, we are told that Paridell possesses "a kindly pryde / Of gracious speech, and skill his words to frame" (III.ix.32), giving readers the impression that, in the past, Paridell has not been reluctant to deploy this "gracious speech" as a sophisticated verbal assault on the feminine psyche.

Spenser's pointed allusion to Paridell as "the learned louer" necessarily invites us to speculate on what texts the knight has read—particularly works that, in demonstrating a lack of piety for the fallen Troy, could reinforce his efforts to weaken the psychic resistances of Britomart as overinvested in

---

[12]Berger, *Revisionary Play,* p. 162.

the "truth" of Troy. Even before his verbal sparring with Britomart at Malbecco's dinner table, we see evidence of how his wide reading enables his seduction of women. Because of his acquaintance with tales of the miserly cuckold, as in Ovid's *Amores*, *The Romance of the Rose*, and Gascoigne's *The Adventures of Master F.J.*, he easily flirts with Malbecco's wife Hellenore, herself widely read in "that lewd lore" (III.ix.28).[13] At Malbecco's dinner table, his past reading of bawdy fabliaux prompts his strategic decision to place himself on the old husband's blind side between him and Hellenore. And through Paridell's reading of such works as Ovid's *Amores* and the *Heroides*, he knows how to spill his wine on the table and write messages of love to Hellenore in the "dauncing bubbles" (III.ix.30).

When Hellenore invites the three knights sitting at her husband's dinner table, Britomart, Satyrane, and Paridell, to tell after-dinner stories of their "kindred," Paridell immediately reveals his embeddedness in the literary history of the Trojan saga.[14] The further point I wish to tease out here is that Paridell, more than simply the first dinner guest to speak, is the only dinner guest who seemingly recognizes the discursive *potential* of Hellenore's request: he wastes no time in using her invitation to set in motion a complex, intertextual scenario, perceiving Hellenore as both the *Iliad*'s Helen and the *Aeneid*'s Dido, who famously requested a similar account from Aeneas at her banquet table. Had Satyrane or Britomart wished (or, worded differently, had they recognized the literary historical potential of Hellenore's invitation to speak as quickly as Paridell did), they could certainly have spoken of *their* genealogy first, giving this after-dinner replay of the *Aeneid* (not to mention of the *Iliad*) an entirely different narrative outcome.

But it is only Paridell who immediately perceives in Hellenore's invitation to speak an opportunity (a "fit tyde" [III.ix.32]) to shape the story of Troy for his own philandering ends. Paris-Paridell promptly transforms himself into an Aeneas, seizing the discursive opportunity to seduce Hellenore-as-Dido through his narrative. More accurately, Paridell becomes an anti-Aeneas, who opens not with the poignancy but the "glory shent" of a fallen Troy, buried in ashes and "now nought, but an idle name."

Paridell's self-serving allusion to his ancestor Paris as the "[m]ost famous Worthy" (and his perverse neglect to mention the more obvious Hector as an "authentic" Worthy) may be a historical outrage, but it has real consequences for his women listeners, Hellenore and Britomart. Almost

---

[13]For a recent reassessment of Spenser's use of Gascoigne for his depiction of Malbecco as a cuckold, see Hutson, "Spenser and Suspicion," pp. 32–40.

[14]Roche, O'Connell, Berger, and Suzuki all comment on how Paridell's knowledge of literary history fuels his seduction of Hellenore as he plays Aeneas to her Dido.

on cue, Hellenore, willingly playing Dido to Paridell's Aeneas, responds to him by hanging "[v]pon his lips . . . / With vigilant regard" (III.ix.52). At the same time, his allusion to Paris and the "ruefull story" of Troy leaves Britomart "empassiond"—not with Paridell, of course, but with his very mention of Troy's destruction (III.ix.38). For entirely different reasons, then, both Hellenore and Britomart become transfixed by his narration of the Troy story. And we can imagine Paridell, the future success of his seduction of Hellenore all but assured, momentarily choosing to amuse himself not with Hellenore's "vigilant regard," but with Britomart's "empassiond" state of desire to hear more about Troy and, in her words, the "lamentable fall of famous towne."

From Paridell's perspective, the decadent Hellenore predictably participates in the early stages of her eventual rape. But it is also worth noting that the eager, earnest Britomart's deeply emotional reaction to Paridell's opening speech ("What stony hart, that heares thy [Troy's] haplesse fate, / Is not empierst with deepe compassiowne . . . ?" [III.ix.39])—i.e., the sheer *affective* intensity of her "empassiond" investment in the very mention of Troy—is not something Paridell could have predicted. If Berger is right that Paridell seeks opportunities to destroy "whatever resistances protect the feminine psyche," then Britomart's unanticipated desire to hear more of Troy emerges as something Paridell is poised to exploit: this destroyer of feminine psyches could not have scripted the after-dinner conversation any better himself. Observing the "empassiond" Britomart sighing over, in her words, the "*Troian* warres, and *Priams* Citie sackt" (III.ix.38), Paridell realizes, retroactively, that his invocation to Paris has performed some intriguing cultural work on her. In the process of deploying his ancestor Paris as erotic capital in wooing Hellenore as the latter-day Helen, Paridell, intentionally or not, has also succeeded in explicitly offering Paris as an exemplar of great historical provocation for Britomart, as well as inadvertently exposing a breachable wall in her psychic fort.

Critics have argued that Paridell's allusion to Paris as a "Worthy" is the first of many times in this exchange that he tampers with historical truth.[15] To be sure, Paridell's self-serving description of Paris as a "Worthy" does not square with Trojan history (nor, for that matter, with the history of the Nine Worthies). But it may be more productive to judge Paridell's opening gambit not within a historical register (delivered, as it is, to an after-dinner audience) but within a *rhetorical* one. As the "learned louer," Paridell surely knows his rhetoric, particularly the fundamental Ciceronian

---

[15]Suzuki, for example, claims that here especially, Paridell "has withdrawn from the historical process" (*Metamorphoses of Helen,* p. 166).

definition of rhetoric as speech that seeks to persuade. Thus, it is Paridell's deployment of Paris as an *exemplar* that I particularly want to call attention to here. Given the intensity of its effect on Britomart, Paridell's invoking of Paris as an exemplar warrants a brief glance at Timothy Hampton's *Writing from History*, a study of exemplary figures from antiquity and how they functioned as models for action for Renaissance readers. Hampton's study can enable us to interpret Paridell's invoking of Paris as something more complex than the product of a cultural exhaustion. Hampton can help us historicize how Spenser's readers might have evaluated the unfolding gender drama between Paridell and Britomart, i.e., their possible perception that Paridell, more than just a shallow "raconteur," is exerting a carefully calculated *rhetorical* control over Britomart.

Hampton describes the exemplary figure in a Renaissance text as "a marked sign that bears the moral and historical authority of antiquity and engages *the reader in a dialogue with the past* . . . ."[16] When Paridell alludes to Paris as that "[m]ost famous Worthy of the world," he invokes his ancestor (however ironically) with a *gravitas* that is literally exemplary; and there is no reason to disallow Paridell's "most famous Worthy of the world" Paris as just such a "marked sign" of Trojan antiquity—*the* privileged exemplar dictating the direction of this after-dinner dialogue with the past. What Paris (sowing his wild oats with Oenone long before his abduction of Helen) lacks in moral authority, he more than makes up for in his rich associations with *Troianitas*. And he possesses a sufficient historical resonance to plunge Paridell's most ardent listener, Britomart, into a kind of Trojan *trance*. As Hampton observes, "In humanist discussions of exemplarity, it is common to note how exemplars 'inflame' the reader, how they 'incite' or 'animate' [the reader] to imitate them . . . ."[17] Accordingly, Paris' association with Britomart's beloved Troy renders her "empassiond," "empierst," and "sighing soft awhile" (III.ix.38–39)—to be sure, not the sighs of amorousness toward Paridell, but rather the sighs of a felt need to engage with Paridell in a dialogue about her Trojan past, a willingness to embrace the example of Paris as a provisional opportunity to learn more about her Trojan past: "What stony hart, that heares thy hapless fate, / Is not empierst with deepe compassiowne, / And makes ensample of mans wretched state . . . ?" (III.ix.39). Although Paridell's invoking of Paris as an exemplar may be historically perverse, it nevertheless does possess a genuine rhetorical energy that engages Britomart, and offers insight into how effectively Paridell's rhetorical procedures may be fashioning Britomart's responses.

---

[16]Hampton, *Writing from History*, p. 5 (italics mine).
[17]Hampton, *Writing from History*, pp. 4–5.

All of which is to say that this same rhetorical energy also exposes the "empassiond" Britomart as a *desiring* Britomart and, thus, highly vulnerable to Paridell's quest to destroy the feminine psyche. Hampton, expanding on the concept of exemplarity, refers to the "hermeneutic activity" that accompanies any invoking of the exemplar—and this is the point at which Britomart's investment in Troy reveals itself most fully. Hampton defines hermeneutic activity as "the choice of what moment from the past one applies to the present, by definition rooted in the reader's specific sociopolitical context and shaped by particular needs."[18] In such a scheme, Paridell's self-serving apostrophe to Paris as his opening gambit for seducing Hellenore has the unexpected—but eminently exploitable—result of intersecting with Britomart's particular need to engage in a dialogue with her Trojan past, a need rooted in her "specific sociopolitical context" as a dynastic spouse within Britain's founding of a new Troy. (She is, to repeat, fresh from Merlin's prophecy that her "famous progenie" will come "out of the auncient Troian blood.") Thus, she cares not to hear of Paridell's depressing account of "the fieldes of faire *Scamander* strowne" with the carcasses of Trojan soldiers, nor of "*Xanthus* sandy bankes with bloud all ouerflowne" (III.ix.35), but rather to hear of Troy as, in her words, "that nation, from whose race of old / She heard, that she was lineally extract" (III.ix.38). From her perspective in British history, she is interested not in Troy's "idle name," but in its "race of old" as her genealogical link with Troynovant. All too willingly conforming to the framework of Paridell's rhetorical protocols, she desires an exemplar that can even further "inflame," "incite," and "animate" her as she engages with her Trojan past. Thus, *on her sleeve* she wears her desire to hear of the heroism of Aeneas and Britain's own Brutus, who, as founders of subsequent New Troys, she regards as more prestigious counter-exemplars to Paridell's wanton Paris—heroic figures by whom Troy, in Britomart's words, "againe out of her dust was reard" (III.ix.44).

Britomart's desire to engage in a dialogue with her Trojan past signals Paridell that he can breach her psychic fort not only by depicting her "of-spring" as "debaste," but also by foiling her gentle efforts to coax him into offering the after-dinner listeners a more "correct" genealogy of her "auncient Troian blood" via the figures of Aeneas and Brutus. Although Paridell does feed her desire to hear of New Troys, Britomart, caught within the web of Paridell's manipulative banter, fails to get the heroic narratives she anticipates and craves. Thus, he offers not the traditionally "pious" and

---

[18]Hampton, *Writing from History*, p. 17.

heroic Aeneas of Virgil, but rather an aimless Aeneas who "weetlesse[ly] wandered" toward the shores of Africa, guided to Latium not by epic destiny but only by "fatall errour," and regretting his eventual marriage to Lavinia (i.e., "hardly prais[ing] his wedlock good" [III.ix.41–42]).

Britomart then attempts to steer the conversation in the direction of "a third kingdome yet [. . .] to arise / Out of the *Troians* scattered of-spring," i.e., the Albion of Britain's "soueraigne king," the "*Troian Brute*" (III.ix.44).[19] As Hamilton informs us in his editorial notes to this episode, here Britomart implicitly relies on Geoffrey of Monmouth's *Historia regum britanniae* (I, xi, xvii) as she seeks to guide Paridell's discourse toward Brutus' prophetic vision of a *Troia Nova*. But we should also note that Paridell, always learned, counters Britomart with his *own* carefully culled allusions to Geoffrey of Monmouth (I, iii–xv), placing his emphasis on a "wearie wandring" Brutus, driven to Britain by "fatall course"—and, most scandalously, a patricidal, self-exiled Brutus, haunted by the memory of having slain his father Sylvius in a hunting accident "through luckless arrows glaunce" (III.ix.48–49).[20] Throughout this exchange at Malbecco's banquet table, Paridell may be less an irresponsible "revisionist" historian than a knowledgeable *literary* historian—and the most unsettling kind of interlocutor for Britomart, committed, as she is, to the concept of a "correct" history of Troy and its "great Genealogie."

No one may know better than Spenser himself that casual slanderings of Troy have their own tradition within epic literary history. Thus, by way of concluding this section, we need look no further than Spenser's epic predecessor in sixteenth-century Ferrara, Ludovico Ariosto, to understand the extent to which even dynastic epic was, on occasion, inclined to depict Troy as "nought but an idle name." If readers were to come to the Paridell-Britomart exchange having just read Ariosto's *Orlando furioso* (1516–1532), Britomart's attempt to ground Troy in historical "truth" might surely strike them as folly. In Canto 35, Astolfo journeys to the moon to retrieve the lost wits of the lovesick Orlando. What he encounters is a kind of lunar junkyard, testifying to the vanity of human wishes—a random, chaotic landscape of pools of "spilled soup," the "chirrupings" of cicadas,

---

[19]For a reassessment of *The Faerie Queene*'s three key genealogical narratives—i.e. Arthur's reading of the *Briton monuments* in Alma's Castle (II.x), Merlin's prophecy of Britomart's and Arthegall's descendants (III.iii), and Paridell's account of Brutus's arrival in Albion—as "asynchronous," "dividing," and "disordering" revelations, see Ullyot.

[20]Paridell insists he is drawing on "aged *Mnemon*" (III.ix.47) as his source. A reference to Geoffrey of Monmouth's account of Brutus's arrival by "fatall errour" to Albion's shores can also be found in Arthur's reading of the *Briton monuments* in Alma's Castle (II.x.9).

"swollen bladders," "vain projects," the tears of lovers, the ruins of cities (such as Troy?)—and, perhaps most significant, the "tatters of fame," as exemplified by all the gifts given to patrons and avaricious princes and kings. Astolfo's guide and interpreter St. John points out that also scattered amidst this lunar junkyard is nothing less than the truth of all poetry: among the "tatters of fame" are all the poems written for patrons, princes, and kings, including poems endowing their royal houses with the gift of a celebratory Trojan genealogy. Consequently, St. John also emphasizes that the story of Troy itself is implicated in the "lost truth" of poetry:

> Aeneas not so pious, nor so strong
> Achilles was, as they are famed to be;
> Hector was less ferocious; and a throng
> Of heroes could surpass them, but we see
> Their valour and their deeds enhanced in song,
> For their descendants had so lavishly
> Rewarded poets for their eulogies
> With gifts of villas, farm-lands, palaces.[21]

Ariosto's lunar junkyard, then, strewn with the villas, farmlands, and palaces that patrons have lavished on poets, is also littered with the "vain projects" of writing about Troy for these same patrons. If dynastic epic itself is centered on the fraudulent lies of poets, if the poignancy of a fallen Troy is merely the product of self-aggrandizing pacts between writers and their patrons, and if it is patronage and self-interest, not historical truth, that reside at the core of representations of Troy in dynastic epic, then what is Ariosto's own patron Ippolito supposed to conclude as he reads the *Orlando furioso*'s overarching celebration of the Trojan ancestry of the House of Este? What are readers to make of the possibility that the story of Troy itself has been banished to a lunar junkyard of spilled soup and the tears of lovers?

To return to Malbecco's banquet table, there is little difference between St. John's Aeneas "not so pious" and Paridell's "weetlesse[ly] wander[ing]" Aeneas who is so threatening to Britomart. This brief glance at Canto 35 of the *Orlando furioso* is not by way of "justifying" the ways of Paridell to readers of *The Faerie Queene*. Rather, my point is to call attention to how Paridell is in a unique position to predict that Britomart's Troy is similarly destined for the lunar junkyard's scrap heap of "vain projects" and poetic "lost truths." And again, in such a literary historical framework, it makes little sense to label Paridell as a mere "revisionist" historian. He is,

---

[21] Ariosto, *Orlando Furioso*, 35.25. For an ironic reading of Ariosto's "lunar junkyard," see Quint.

rather, the embodiment of epic literary history's own efforts at questioning the "truth" of Troy in poetry.

TROY: BETWEEN FAME AND RUMOR

Chaucer's *House of Fame* features a casual but no less disturbing questioning about poetry's ability to represent the "truth" of the Troy story that is uncannily similar to St. John's claims in the *Orlando furioso*. It is unlikely that Ariosto was familiar with the *House of Fame* but Spenser was. As we have seen, Paridell's exchange with Britomart is highly allusive, continually challenging its readers to recognize the varying strands of literary history running throughout; as I noted earlier, Suzuki has perceptively described the episode as "a locus for Spenser's meditation on his own classical genealogy, his descent from Virgil and Ovid." In this section, I will read the Paridell–Britomart exchange against the grain of Chaucer's *House of Fame*. If Britomart had read the *House of Fame*, she might not have been taken so off guard by Paridell's attacks on Troy.

As epic literary history's most "learned louer," Paridell would surely have read Spenser's own beloved Chaucer, his influential predecessor in shaping an English vernacular poetry. After all, as critics have often noted, in *The Faerie Queene* Spenser lavishly praises his mentor, "Dan *Chaucer*, well of English vndefyled, / On Fames eternall beadroll worthy to be fyled" (IV.ii.32); and in his concluding *Mutabilitie Cantos,* he again singles out Chaucer as nothing less than "[t]he pure well head of Poesie" (VII.vii.9). As Theresa M. Krier eloquently reminds us, "Chaucer is always, for Spenser, the other through whom he may think himself as poet."[22] *The Faerie Queene* is an unceasing "play / With double senses" (III.iv.28); and Spenser's "think[ing] himself as poet" was often a "thinking" of the truth claims of poetry itself—a process that inevitably would have intersected with his special appreciation for, in particular, Chaucer's irony.

In this part of my argument, I contend that we can plausibly identify Chaucer as an influential "other" for Paridell's persistent rumors of an "embaste" Troy in the face of Britomart's desire to hear of the fame of her "famous towne" (III.ix.39). It should be noted that Spenser's praise for his predecessor is not without irony because no one knew better than Chaucer that "[f]ames eternall beadroll" is not all that far removed from rumor's domain. As author of *The Canterbury Tales*, Chaucer is indeed preserved in "fames eternall beadroll," but it is as the author of the lesser known *House of Fame* that Chaucer demonstrates his intimate understanding of the slippages

---

[22]Krier, "Receiving Chaucer in Renaissance England," p. 11.

between fame and rumor, particularly as they accrue around poetic accounts of the story of Troy.

But first, let us turn to the *Iliad* as the "well head" of the story of Troy, and its own ambiguous positioning of Troy between fame and rumor. Imagine Paridell, who likes to tamper with the story of Troy, reading Homer's catalog of the ships bound for Troy in the *Iliad* 2. In the invocation before this catalog, Homer addresses the muses because they are omniscient, while mortals must rely solely on the rumoring "fame" of what happened—on *kleos* (l. 486) as "that which is heard":[23]

> Tell me now, you Muses who have your homes on Olympos,
> For you, who are goddesses, are there, and you know all things,
> And we have heard only the rumor of it and know nothing.
> Who then of those were the chief men and the lords of the Danaans?
> I could not tell over the multitude of them nor name them,
> Not if I had ten tongues and ten mouths . . . .[24]

Homer admits that as a mortal he has heard "only the rumor" of who were in the ships bound for Troy. For that matter, the scholium for the line, "For you, who are goddesses, are there," says that some ancient editors proposed a change to the imperfect ("You were there") to indicate that the muses were present as *witnesses* at Troy.[25] This editorial urge to authorize the muses as authentic eyewitnesses reveals, at the very origin of epic literary history, an underlying anxiety about the reliability of Homer's narration of the Trojan war—the extent to which the *Iliad* may be blurring the distinction between conjecture (*kleos* as "uncertain report") and the truth.

Before turning to the *House of Fame*, though, a brief overview of the "truth" of the Troy story in the Middle Ages is also necessary. Paridell would surely have known that the vexed question of the reliability of Homer's narration of Troy resides at the core of a number of medieval redactions of the Trojan saga. Medieval readers believed that more reliable *"auctoritees"* of the Trojan saga than Homer were two books of Latin prose, the fourth-century *Ephemeris Belli Trojani* by Dictys Cretensis, and Dares Phrygius' sixth-century *De Excidio Trojae Historia*. Dares was particularly favored by medieval readers because, unlike Dictys, who spoke for the Greeks, Dares

---

[23]Although *kleos* generally translates as "renown" or "glory," it can also mean "that which is heard," "far-famed," "talked about all over." For the range of meanings of Homer's *kleos*, see Mackie, *Talking Trojan*, pp. 85–90.

[24]Homer, *The Iliad of Homer*, 2.484–489.

[25]Erbse, *Scolia Graeca in Homeri*. For an account of Milton's interest in Homer's invocation for his invocation to *Paradise Lost*, see Teskey, "Imagining Error in Spenser and Milton," pp. 17–19.

gave the Trojan side and presumably spoke from first-hand knowledge. Six centuries later, Benoit de Sainte-Maure, in his *Roman de Troie* (c. 1160), would assert that Homer's *Iliad* "does not tell the truth, for we know well, beyond any doubt, that he was born a hundred years after the great hosts in battle. No wonder if he errs since he never was there and saw nothing thereof." Dares, who was born in Troy, is generously praised by Benoit: "Never on any account would he refrain from saying and setting forth the truth. Therefore, though he was of the Trojans, he did not on that account show more favour to his own people than he did to the Greeks. He wrote the truth of the story."[26]

What I wish to emphasize here is a certain urgency in Benoit's emphatic praise of Dares for telling the "truth" of the Troy story. This urgency demonstrates that, by the Middle Ages, virtually every representation of Troy was a highly contested site between, on the one hand, the reliability of eyewitness testimony and, on the other—to echo Homer's invocation—"only the rumor" of what transpired during and after the Trojan war. Benoit's urgency masks underlying anxieties about the influence of rumor in shaping the "truth" of Troy's fame.

With this brief literary history from Homer to Benoit, we can now turn to Chaucer's *House of Fame*, where the poet demonstrates an intimate understanding of the slippages between fame and rumor, particularly as they accrue around the story of Troy. As we shall see, the *House of Fame* serves as a useful backdrop—if not an outright source—for Paridell's trafficking in alternative Troys of dubious or contested authenticity.

Not unlike *The Faerie Queene*'s Paridell-Britomart exchange, the *House of Fame* is a highly allusive and self-consciously "bookish" poem, one that we can imagine the "learned" Paridell having read with relish. The unruly, fragmentary *House of Fame* is difficult to summarize. But in its broadest scope, it is a rigorous questioning of the truth content of poetry, leaving its readers to ponder such overwhelming questions as: what is it that grounds the truth claims of poetry? Can poetic authority ever withstand testing? And (in a foreshadowing of the *Orlando furioso*, Canto 35), is the fame a poet bestows true?[27] In the *House of Fame*, over three hundred lines (1520–1868) are devoted to the arbitrary judgments of Fame, who, at one point, is

---

[26]Benoit de Sainte-Maure, *Le Roman de Troie*, in Gordon, ed., pp. 3–4.

[27]In "Authority and the Defense of Fiction," Martin observes that standard Renaissance editions of Chaucer's works (such as Thomas Speght's 1598 edition of The *Works of our Antient and Learned English Poet, Geffrey Chaucer*) "handle the *House of Fame* gingerly, for the *House of Fame* resolves neither itself nor the questions it raises about speaking truly" (p. 40).

depicted as the sister of the blind "dame Fortune" (1547).[28] We could say that the *House of Fame* persistently nudges the concept of *kleos* in the direction of rumor. This is the meaning of fame that Chaucer plays with in his *House of Fame*, where *kleos* as "uncertain report" ("that which is heard," "that which is talked about all over") explicitly intersects with the "truth" of the Trojan saga.

The *House of Fame* opens not in the House of Fame itself but in the Temple of Venus with an exposition on the theme of love. Given that a standard episode of the medieval tale of Troy has Paris abduct Helen from the Temple of Venus, the *House of Fame*'s opening not only signals the Trojan saga as a central preoccupation of the work, but also calls attention to Chaucer's general interest in redactions of the Troy story, even beyond his far more widely read *Troilus and Criseyde*.[29] Eventually, the narrator, "Geffrey," comes across a highly condensed, three hundred fifty-line version of the *Aeneid* written on the temple's walls: the tale of Troy's destruction, Aeneas' escape from the burning city with Anchises and Creusa, his dalliance with and subsequent abandonment of Dido, etc.[30]

But in the midst of narrating Aeneas' journey to the underworld, the narrator curiously loses interest, confessing to his readers that the story

> . . . is longe to telle;
> Which whoso willeth for to knowe,
> He moste rede many a rowe
> On Virgil or on Claudian
> Or Daunte, that hit telle kan. 446–450

With whatever degree of his signature irony, Chaucer lapses into the *topos* of authorial weariness: the narrator signals that if readers want to know more about Aeneas in the underworld, they can read the source Virgil himself—or such authorities on the underworld as Dante or Claudian. The aftermath of the Troy story "is longe to telle," and the narrator readily cedes place to the many authors who have their own versions of its key episodes. Calling further attention to his growing boredom with the story of Troy, the narrator then concludes his already condensed account of the *Aeneid* with

---

[28]All references to Chaucer's *House of Fame* are from *The Works of Geoffrey Chaucer*, ed. Robinson.

[29]Benoit, Guido, Caxton, Lydgate, and Gower all have accounts of Paris abducting Helen from the Temple of Venus. In Dares, Helen is abducted from the isle of Cytherea while sacrificing to Diana at the Temple of Venus.

[30]Here, the "bookishness" of the *House of Fame* is particularly evident, for the Temple of Venus's story of Aeneas and Dido is indebted less to Virgil than to Ovid's legend of Dido in his *Heroides*.

a peremptorily brief seventeen-line summary of the epic's latter six books. The narrator's bored haste can remind us of Paridell's own comically abbreviated two-stanza summary of the *Aeneid* at Malbecco's banquet table. And we can imagine Chaucer's weariness-*topos* as suggesting to Paridell that no single narration of the Trojan saga can sufficiently accommodate its many revisions: in Chaucer's Temple of Venus, the "story" of Troy gives way to the story of how others have told its story.

The Temple of Venus' condensed *Aeneid* foreshadows Chaucer's future references to Troy in the second half of the *House of Fame*, which shifts rather abruptly from love to the vicissitudes of Fame; and almost immediately, Fame is associated with the unreliability of poetic truth. Crowding around the House of Fame, "a castel that stood on high" (l. 1160), are "alle maner of mynstralles, / And gestiours, that tellen tales . . . / Of al that longeth unto Fame" (ll. 1197–1200). This jangling throng of "mynstralles" and "gestiours" demonstrates how Fame can degenerate so quickly into rumor. As Robinson suggests in his editorial notes to the *House of Fame*, Chaucer's "castel on high" is indebted to Ovid's mountain palace where Rumor dwells in the *Metamorphoses*, 12.39–63. Rumor's dwelling is similarly crowded with wandering "presences" who "go far-off to tell / What they have heard, and every story grows, / And each new teller adds to what he hears."[31] In the dwelling place of Ovid's Rumor, there is neither quiet nor "uproar"—rather, "only the subdued / Murmur of little voices, like the murmur / Of sea-waves heard far-off, or the last rumble / Of thunder dying in the cloud." It is a dwelling where, we are told, lies and truth co-exist, "[c]onfused, confusing"—after which Ovid narrates a condensed story of the Greeks' invasion of Troy, leaving readers to judge for themselves the extent to which this version of the Trojan saga is implicated in the "confused" murmur of the House of Rumor, destined to fade like "the last rumble / Of thunder dying in the cloud."

That Chaucer's "castel on high" is a House of *Fame* reminds us, as we have seen, that one translation of fame-as-*kleos* is "uncertain report." We could say, then, that in light of its Ovidian source, Chaucer's bookish House of Fame seems also designed to proffer Troy as vulnerable to "uncertain report." Perhaps remembering his own earlier summary of the *Aeneid* in the Temple of Venus, Chaucer's narrator observes that appearing on the House of Fame's "yren pilers" are many of the celebrated authors who have been "besy for to beare up Troy" (l. 1472), beginning with

---

[31] All citations of Ovid are from *Ovid's Metamorphoses*, trans. Humphries.

> the gret Omer;
> And with him Dares and Tytus [Dictys]
> Before, and eke he Lollius,
> And Guydo eke de Columpnis,
> And Englyssh Gaufride eke, ywis. 1466–1470

Earlier in the Temple of Venus, the narrator, bored by the prospect that the Trojan saga "is longe to telle," readily cedes place to other authors. But in the House of Fame, the authors of the Trojan saga jostle competitively:

> But yet I gan ful well espie,
> Betwex hem was a litil envye.
> Oon seyde that Omere made lyes,
> Feynynge in hys poetries,
> And was to Grekes favorable;
> Therfor held he hyt but fable. 1475–1480

The "subdued [m]urmur of little voices" that constitutes Ovid's Rumor is, in Chaucer's House of Fame, amplified into a not-so-subdued "litil envye." This authorial "envye" refers, of course, to a major objection to Homer by medieval readers discussed earlier—i.e., that the poet had been born too late to be an eyewitness of the events he described, "[f]eynynge in hys poetries." Thus, Homer's own calling on the muses for their perfect knowledge in the *Iliad* 2—his admission that, as a mortal, he has heard "only the rumor" of who were in the Greek ships bound for Troy—has now come back to haunt him in Chaucer's House of Fame, where fame imperceptibly degenerates into rumor, rendering the author of the *Iliad* vulnerable to charges that he has "made lyes."

That Chaucer's bookish House of Fame is indeed a house of *kleos* or "uncertain report" is no better demonstrated than in its memorializing of those who have been "besy for to bere up Troy." The House of Fame's "yren pilers" are exposed in all their structural precariousness as an anxiety of influence—in the form of a "litil envye"—that creates a rift among these celebrated authors (themselves mere "mynstralles" and "gestiours"?) and transforms the *fata Troiana* into a battle of the books. Thus, the House of Fame's "yren pilers," structured as they are on authorial "envye," render medieval legends of the Trojan saga stories of "uncertain report."[32]

----

[32]Further evidence of the dubiousness of those who have been "besy for to beare up Troy" is the possibility noted by Robinson that Chaucer's "Lollius" is most likely the poet's own invention—a seemingly prestigious "Latin" authority and author of the pretended source of *Troilus and Criseyde*, but in fact a *pseudo*-authority to whom only Chaucer ever refers.

To return full circle to Malbecco's banquet table in *The Faerie Queene*, we can now fully appreciate the extent to which this authorial "litil envye" constitutes the contentious space of rumor where Paridell flourishes: it is the intertextual core of his assault on Britomart's psyche. We can imagine Paridell viewing the House of Fame's battle of the Trojan books as an implicit warning for Britomart. One of the lessons of Chaucer's *House of Fame* would seem to be: do not attempt to build your ancestral house on the shifting sands of the narration of the Trojan saga lest you wander errantly into rumor's terrain. This lesson lends a greater legitimacy to Paridell's opening address to Troy itself: "What boots it boast thy glorious descent, / And fetch from heauen thy great Genealogie . . . ?"

Before exiting the *House of Fame*, we should note that also appearing on the House of Fame's pillars is, predictably,

> . . . [t]he Latyn poete, Virgile,
> That bore hath up a longe while
> The fame of Pius Eneas.
> And next hym on a piler was,
> Of coper, Venus clerk, Ovide. 1483–1487

Again returning to Malbecco's banquet table, where echoes of Virgil and Ovid abound, we can recall that it is precisely an account of the fame of a "Pius Aeneas" that Britomart craves from Paridell. But Paridell, having established Hellenore as the banquet's Dido-figure, is determined to retain his status as the banquet's only heroic "Aeneas." So, as we have seen, Paridell offers Britomart a debased Aeneas of "fatall errour" and "weetlesse wandr[ing]"—in the end, "hardly prais[ing] his wedlock good." In short, the "fame" of the Aeneas of "the Latyn poete, Virgile" has eroded to "uncertain report," anticipating the Aeneas "not so pious" of Ariosto's St. John. We should note that the "Englysshe Gaufride" (Geoffrey of Monmouth) is also represented on the House of Fame's shaky authorial pillar. But again, as Paridell may have suspected, the *House of Fame* calls into question any invoking of a Trojan "auctoritee." Britomart's privileging of Geoffrey of Monmouth as a source for her beloved Brutus is fully implicated in the "envye" that destabilizes the House of Fame's pillars. Thus, Paridell can freely counter with a "wearie wandring" and patricidal Brutus, driven to Britain by "fatall course"—a Brutus who, as we have seen, is also recounted in the "Englyssh" Geoffrey of Monmouth (I, iii–xv).

In Chaucer's *House of Fame*, a rigorous questioner of the truth content of poetry, Geoffrey of Monmouth, or the "Englyssh Gaufride," is a decidedly unstable authority for Britomart to invoke as the "truth" of the story of Troy and its aftermath. Chaucer's point is that the chronicles of the "Englyssh Gaufride" perpetuate the "feynyng poetries" that constitute the story of Troy—merely another instance of Ovid's "last rumble of thunder dying in the clouds." In the House of Fame, Troy is indeed "nought, but an idle name." Dissipated within the House of Fame's jangling "mynstralles" and "gestiours," within the Temple of Venus' condensed *Aeneid* narrated in bored haste, within the narrators of the Trojan saga smoldering in "envye" towards one another, Troy finds itself precariously positioned between fame and rumor. Chaucer concludes his catalog of authors with, once again, a note of bored haste: "But hit ful confus matere / Were alle the gestes for to here, / That they of write, or how they highte" (1516–1519). Thus, to read *The Faerie Queene*'s Paridell-Britomart exchange against the grain of the *House of Fame* is to appreciate the full extent of Paridell's awareness that the literary history of Troy has itself dissolved into "ful confus matere." As such, he may be *The Faerie Queene*'s most powerful indication that no history or genealogy of Troy can be separated from the errancies of its complex literary history. Paridell is evidence that the imaginative power of dynastic epic's definitive topos of "the westering of empire" as a New Troy may, by the end of the sixteenth century, have begun to play itself out.

WORKS CITED

Ariosto. *Cinque Canti:Five Cantos.* Trans. Alexander Sheers and David Quint. Berkeley and Los Angeles: University of California Press, 1996.

Ariosto. *The Orlando Furioso.* Trans. Barbara Reynolds. Harmondsworth: Penguin, 1977.

Berger, Harry. *Revisionary Play: Studies in the Spenserian Dynamics.* Intro. Louis A. Montrose. Berkeley and Los Angeles: University of California Press, 1988.

Chaucer, Geoffrey. *The Works of Geoffrey Chaucer.* Ed. F. N. Robinson. 2d ed. Boston: Houghton Mifflin, 1957.

Erbse, Hartmut. *Scolia Graeca in Homeri.* 5 vols. Berlin: Gruyter, 1969–1983.

Gordon, R. K., ed. *The Story of Troilus as Told by Benoit de Sainte-Maure, Giovanni Boccaccio, Geoffrey Chaucer, and Robert Henryson.* New York: Dutton, 1964.

Hampton, Timothy. *Writing From History: The Rhetoric of Exemplarity in Renaissance Literature.* Ithaca: Cornell University Press, 1990.

Homer. *The Iliad of Homer.* Trans. Richard Lattimore. Chicago: University of Chicago Press, 1951.

Hutson, Lorna. "Spenser and Suspicion." *The Spenser Review* 33 (2002): 32–40.

Krier, Theresa M. "Receiving Chaucer in Renaissance England." *Refiguring Chaucer in the Renaissance.* Ed. Theresa M. Krier. Gainesville: University Press of Florida, 1998. 1–18.

Mackie, Hilary. *Talking Trojan: Speech and Community in the Iliad.* New York: Rowman and Littlefield, 1996.

Martin, Carol A. N. "Authority and the Defense of Fiction: Renaissance Poetics and Chaucer's *House of Fame.*" *Refiguring Chaucer in the Renaissance.* Ed. Theresa M. Krier. Gainesville: University Press of Florida, 1998. 40–65.

Montrose, Louis A. "Gifts and Reasons: The Contexts of Peele's *Arraignment of Paris.*" *ELH* 47 (1980): 433–461.

Nohrnberg, James. *The Analogy of* The Faerie Queene. Princeton: Princeton University Press, 1976.

O'Connell, Michael. *Mirror and Veil: The Historical Dimension of Spenser's* Faerie Queene. Chapel Hill: University of North Carolina Press, 1977.

Ovid. *Ovid's Metamorphoses.* Trans. Rolfe Humphries. Bloomington: Indiana University Press, 1964.

Quint, David. "Astolfo's Voyage to the Moon." *Yale Italian Studies* 1 (1977): 398–408. Rpt. in Quint, *Origin and Originality in Renaissance Literature Origin and Originality in Renaissance Literature: Versions of the Source.* New Haven: Yale University Press, 1983.

Roche, Thomas P. *The Kindly Flame: A Study of the Third and Fourth Books of Spenser's* Faerie Queene. Princeton: Princeton University Press, 1964.

Spenser, Edmund. *The Faerie Queene.* Ed. A.C. Hamilton. London: Longman, 1977.

Suzuki, Mihoko. *Metamorphoses of Helen: Authority, Difference, and the Epic.* Ithaca: Cornell University Press, 1989.

Teskey, Gordon. "Imagining Error in Spenser and Milton." *PMLA* 101 (1986): 1–21.

Ullyot, Michael. "'Yet the end is not': The Limits of History in Spenser's *Faerie Queene.*" Paper delivered at the 2001 meeting of the Renaissance Society of America.

Watkins, John. *The Specter of Dido: Spenser and Virgilian Epic.* New Haven: Yale University Press, 1995.

Falling into History:
Trials of Empire in Spenser's Faerie Queene

Rebeca Helfer

Spenser's unfinished epic *The Faerie Queene* ends with a dramatic scene of trial: the Cantos of Mutability, where readers stand witness to Dame Mutability's case against Jove. Challenging his authority on several grounds, Mutability contends that Jove has usurped her rightful reign and rules over heaven and earth illegitimately, because she had had a prior claim on heaven's throne interrupted by Jove when he seized power from her ancestor Saturn. Moreover, she charges, Jove has thereby fashioned himself as a god presiding over *endless* empire. In doing so he has subsequently denied this fall into history, in effect rewriting history as a fiction.

Mutability's prosecution of Jove thus goes beyond issues of eternity, entering into the realm of history. Indeed, Mutability's testimony implies that heaven can wait; in the end, her case concerns earthly matters. When Spenser puts the promise of permanence on trial in the Mutability Cantos, he is recalling earlier trials of history in Books II and III of *The Faerie Queene*, where England's history is told. Timelessness yields to time when we consider Mutability's case in the light of history—that is, when we see the fall of the Golden Age as both prehistory and antecedent to the fall of Troy. This essay moves from Mutability's day in court to the representation of English history in Books II and III, then to a brief view of Ireland, in order to observe Spenser's defense of Mutability's charges: that tales of endless empire make monarchs into gods, allowing them to rewrite history as fiction. Mutability's case, I argue, stands for *The Faerie Queene*'s larger trial of English empire.

I. JOVE ON TRIAL: JUDGING HISTORY IN THE MUTABILITY CANTOS

Spenser begins his courtroom narrative with the trial's verdict, Jove's victory in Nature's court, along with a plaintive invocation to the muses for help. For here, Spenser must sing not of arms and the man, nor of knights and their Faerie Queene, but of "The Gods" themselves. Doubting his poetic ability in the face of this daunting task, Spenser wonders whether his "fraile spirit" can "Lift vp aloft, to tell of heauens King / (Thy soueraine Sire) his fortunate success, / And victory . . . / Which he obtain'd against that *Titanesse*, / That him of heauens Empire sought to dispossesse"—or if "this too high flight" requires "bigger noates to sing" than he can muster.[1] Spenser ultimately overcomes the anxiety of Jove's influence. However, his timid and perhaps disingenuous reluctance suggests that leaving the other-worldly but nevertheless familiar "Faery Land" of the present tense means entering dangerous territory: a place where Jove—and by association, Queen Elizabeth—is charged with building empire upon fictions of perma-nence, with arrogating divinity to the monarchy. Thereby distancing himself from the facts of Mutability's case, Spenser begins the Cantos of Mutability by calling this case a matter of ancient history:

> . . . here falleth fittest to vnfold
> > Her antique race and linage ancient,
> > As I haue found it registred of old,
> > In *Faery* Land mongst records permanent
> > [Mutability] was, to weet, a daughter by descent
> > Of those old *Titans*, that did whylome striue
> > With *Saturnes* sonne for heauens regiment.
> > Whom, though high *Ioue* of kingdome did depriue,
> Yet many of their stemme long after did surviue. Vii.vi.2

Although we learn from the outset that Jove triumphantly preserves his "heauens Empire" from the mutinous Mutability, Spenser skirts the true cause of this struggle. Only when Mutability takes the stand does she articulate—in fact, she repeats—complaints about empire voiced earlier in *The Faerie Queene*'s story of English history.

This case turns on the question of imperial inheritance and Jove's dubious claim to it. Mutability's primary charge, that Jove stole heaven's throne from her Titan ancestor, Saturn, lends an irony to her own rebellion that Spenser coyly makes readers aware of. As the daughter of a Titan, Mutability swears, "I greater am in bloud (whereon I build) / Then all the Gods, though wrongfully from heauen exil'd," then elaborates why: "For *Titan* . . . / Was *Saturnes* elder brother by birth-right." Yet Mutability argues to Jove himself, "by vniust / And guilefull meanes . . . / The younger thrust the elder from his right: / Since which, thou *Ioue*, iniuriously hast held / The Heauens rule from *Titans* sonnes by might" (Vii.vi.26–27). Thus Mutability asserts that Jove did not rightfully inherit heaven's throne, but seized it by force. Not surprisingly, however, Jove gives her little satisfac-

---

[1]Spenser, *The Faerie Queene*, VII.vii.1. Subsequent citations of the poem refer to Hamilton's edition.

tion, maintaining that he in fact "wonne the Empire of the Heauens bright" in accordance with providence: "by eternall doome of Fates decree" (Vii.vi.33). When Mutability later appeals for a trial at Nature's higher court, she restates her case against Jove as a problem of permanence. "Men themselues doe change continually," she says: "From good to bad, from bad to worst of all," and "eeke their minds (which they immortall call) / Still change and vary thoughts, as new occasions fall" (VII.vii.19). Change born of the Golden Age leads to Mutability's overwhelming question:

> Lo, mighty mother, now be iudge and say,
> Whether in all thy creatures more or lesse
> *CHANGE* doth not raign and beare the greatest sway:
> For, who sees not, that *Time* on all doth pray?
> But *Times* do change and moue continually.
> So nothing here long standeth in one stay:
> Wherefore, this lower world who can deny
> But to be subiect still to *Mutabilitie*? VII.vii.47

The world's incessant fall into history is Mutability's evidence of her earthly rule. "Time" marches inexorably forward, preying on all things, just as change exerts itself "continually."

Yet these are not simple assertions of mutability but rather indictments of permanence. At stake in the trial is not only Jove's apparent ruin of the very notion of permanence, but also, tacitly, his subsequent promise to repair the damage to permanence by way of the empire of Rome. As Mutability contends, the record of history itself refutes Jovian claims to endless empire. The Trojan legend, which Spenser adopts as England's myth of origin, describes the movement from ruin to repair: after the fall of Troy, empire and learning migrate westward (to Italy, France, England, even the New World), following a path to Rome's empire charted in Virgil's *Aeneid*. From Troy's ruin, Jove has prophesied in the *Aeneid*, a new Troy will rise and last forever:

> In Italy, [Aeneas] will fight a massive war,
> Beat down fierce armies, then for the people there
> Establish city walls and a way of life . . .
> And call by [Romulus'] name his people Romans.
> For these I set no limits, world or time,
> But make the gift of empire without end.[2]

If "the gift of empire without end" offered Rome eternity, it also endowed its rulers with divinity. As Jove proclaims, "From that comely line / The

---

[2]Virgil, *The Aeneid*, I.355–375. Subsequent citations appear in the text.

Trojan Caesar comes, to circumscribe / Empire with Ocean, fame with heaven's stars" (1.384–386); Jove refers to Julius but implies Augustus too. Descended from the gods, these Roman Caesars inherit empire as much from Jove as from Troy. A later prophecy affirms that Caesar will return the Golden Age to Italy—to its original location. In the underworld, Anchises tells his son Aeneas how "Caesar Augustus, son of the deified / . . . shall bring once again an Age of Gold / To Latium, to the land where Saturn reigned" (6.1064–1067).

This tale of imperial ruin and re-edification mattered in early modern England, critics have long believed, because it was the mytho-historical foundation for new imperium. Writing that "Spenser is the Virgil of the Elizabethan golden age," Frances Yates explains how Christian reinterpretations of Virgil's poetry allowed for England's own golden age, calling it a "complex tissue of Elizabethan imperialism" based upon "the Tudor claim to Trojan descent."[3] Viewed thus, Spenser has long been seen as Elizabethan imperialism's prime champion. From the perspective of early modern Protestant England, of course, Rome's fabled empire had doubtless fallen to ruin—a view motivated as much by politics as by religion. The Trojan legend was nevertheless adapted by poets and monarchs alike, who thereby adopted Trojan genealogies for their own new "empires without end," even if historians increasingly distrusted such tales, even if Christianity said no earthly empire was *without end*.

While this matrix of Trojan myth and Golden Age rhetoric is indeed articulated in *The Faerie Queene*, the extent to which Spenser supports a Virgilian ideology has been subject to growing debate. As David Read writes, critics have traditionally "create[d] a generalized version of 'imperial' Spenser functioning almost independently of his poetic output"; "citations of one or two significant episodes of *The Faerie Queene*," he argues, are often "enough to confirm Spenser's place as the great apologist for an Elizabethan dream of transoceanic monarchy."[4] I am suggesting that *The Faerie Queene* articulates a greater ambivalence toward empire-building, and toward Virgil's cultural legacy as an Elizabethan inheritance than even recent critics have asserted.

Indirectly, through Mutability, Spenser voices doubts about the use and abuse of the Troy legend. Readers will recognize the Jove of the Mutability Cantos as Ovid's, not Virgil's, king of the gods, which matters not least of all because Ovid's *Metamorphoses* obliquely criticizes the *Aeneid*. Ovid frames *Metamorphoses* with two tales—the fall of the Golden Age and the fall of

---

[3]Yates, *Astraea*, pp. 69, 50.
[4]Read, *Temperate Conquests*, p. 12.

Troy—that provide the alpha and omega of history, themselves bracketed by stories of metamorphosis: an originary myth of creation at the beginning, and a doctrine of endless change at the epic's end. Mutability reigns supreme in the *Metamorphoses*, which surveys Jove's all-too-human exploits. The numerous rapes described by Ovid, notably Jove's rape of Europa, depict cultural transmission as a violent endeavor achieved by the use of force and deception, transformation often used for a clear and clearly brutish end.

The differences between how Ovid and Virgil depict Jove's power, and Caesar's, are worth considering. As Ovid tells it, Jove's rebellion ends the Golden Age: "When Saturn fell to the dark Underworld / And Jove reigned upon earth, the silver race / Replaced the gold, inferior . . . in worth."[5] This tale reverses Virgil's story of the Golden Age, which he credits Jove with creating, not destroying. Evander explains to Aeneas that Saturn had brought the Golden Age to Italy after Jove's coup: "Saturn came . . . [as] a fugitive from his lost kingdom," bringing the Golden Age set to return with Caesar Augustus, a once and future emperor (*Aen.* 8.418–425). Significantly, Ovid's Jove, in contrast to Virgil's, makes no promises for Rome's eternity. "If your heart hold fast / My prophecies," Jove ironically predicts, then "Troy shall not wholly fall":

> Now I discern
> A city destined for the Trojan race,
> Greater than any city was of old,
> Or is or shall be. Through the length of years
> Princes shall build her power, until one born
> Of your [Venus'] son's line shall make her sovereign,
> The mistress of the world; and when on earth
> His work is ended, the sky's palaces
> Shall welcome him and heaven shall be his home.[6]

Ovid's Jove promises or prophesies a great deal here, but not "empire without end." This crucial omission underscores the contingency of life and empire that Ovid instead portrays. Rome has a deadline and, perhaps like Aeneas, a new imperial destination after death: "the sky's palaces," a home in heaven. Mutability's case against Jove echoes *Metamorphoses*, calling upon Ovid as a key witness; however, Virgil's Jove also lingers in the court during *The Faerie Queene*'s trials of empire in English history.

---

[5]Ovid, *Metamorphoses*, p. 4. Subsequent citations of the poem refer to the Melville edition.

[6]Ovid, *Metamorphoses*, pp. 364–365.

II. Trying History in *The Faerie Queene*

Seeing Ovid's and Virgil's versions of Jove as being opposed in simple terms in *The Faerie Queene* ignores their complex relationship within English history. In Book III, Spenser ends his three-part story of English history with its ostensible origin: the fall of Troy. In the episode, Spenser examines the relationship between Ovid's and Virgil's tales of empire; in doing so, he gives credence to Mutability's complaint against Jove, intimating that England is building its empire upon fictions of history.

In Book III, the knights Britomart and Paridell offer accounts of the fall of Troy and their Trojan genealogies, accounts that ultimately turn this legendary history into parody. Paridell begins by recounting Troy's ruin: "*Troy*, that art now nought, but an idle name, / And in thine ashes buried low dost lie / Though whilome far much greater then thy fame, / Before that angry Gods, and cruell skye / Vpon thee heapt a direfull destinie" (III.ix.33). "What boots it boast thy glorious descent / And fetch from heauen thy great Genealogie," Paridell asks, "Sith all thy worthy prayses being blent, / Their of-spring hath embaste, and later glory shent" (III.ix.33). Surely Paridell means himself here, since his seduction of his host's wife, Hellenore, debases the cause of Troy's fall through a burlesque re-enactment: a "rape" that casts a willing new Helen in an Ovidian role. Despite demurring, Paridell "boasts" all the same, describing his ancestor's journey from ruined Troy. As Paridell narrates it, when the "stately towres of *Ilion*" were "Brought vnto balefull ruine . . . after *Greekes* did *Priams* realme destroy," his ancestor then "gathred the *Troian* reliques sau'd from flame, / And with them sayling thence, to th'Isle of *Paros* came" (III.ix.34, 36).

The symbolic translation of Troy's ruins for new Troynovants practically defines Virgilian *translatio*. Yet here the movement from cultural ruin to repair apes the *Aeneid*, just as Paridell's parodic re-enactment of Helen's seduction makes light of epic matters. Significantly, though, when Paridell prophesies an imperial destiny for himself and France, he also reminds Britomart of her own. She then chimes in with a revised version of the Trojan family myth for England: "Whenas the noble *Britomart* heard tell / Of *Troian* warres, and *Priams* Citie sackt," she thinks of England, "from whose race of old / She heard, that she was lineally extract: / For noble *Britons* sprong from *Troians* bold, / And *Troynouant* was built of old *Troyes* ashes cold" (III.ix.38).

If this episode is rarely read as an easy assertion of England's imperial identity, the canto is nevertheless seen from a split perspective, with Paridell's version of Virgil taken to be a laughably mindless imitation and Britomart's version of history taken to be a laudable (even redemptive) answer to Paridell's botched effort.[7] Yet Britomart and Paridell only *seem* to offer competing versions of history. Rather, their claims to Trojan genealogies provide an important parallel: both are unreconstructed fictions of Virgil's epic—the divine translation of Troy's ruin into eternal repair. Britomart's genealogy is sprung fully formed. This mythological fantasy describes imperial edification as an immaculate conception, for Troynovant rises out of "old *Troyes* ashes" like the phoenix rising from its ashes into a new life—a fiction of cultural rebirth. When Britomart asks "what to *Aeneas* fell [?]" (III.ix.40), we see that the prototype they duplicate is Virgil's pattern of *translatio imperii*, translating ruin into permanence. Paridell replies with Aeneas' divine pedigree, clarifying how Troy's ruin established Rome's future empire: "*Anchyses* sonne begot of *Venus* faire, / . . . out of the flames for safegard fled, / And with a remnant did to sea repaire" when "At last in *Latium* he did arriue" (III.ix.41–42).

But readers already know this story. Paradoxically, Spenser presents the *Aeneid*'s fiction of history as a kind of cultural commonplace, leaving out the important detail of "endless" empire in order, I believe, to make a point about this very end. With their re-enactments of Virgil's epic verging on farce, Britomart and Paridell's claims to ever-newer Troynovants empty out the essential meaning Virgil gave it: that of permanence. Rather, Paridell simply concludes that "the fates ordaind" Aeneas' conquest of Latium— "Wedlock contract in bloud, and eke in blood / Accomplished, that many deare complaind"—along with violence necessary to achieving this end: Rome (III.ix.42).

Omitting any reference to Rome's eternal "Troynovant" punctuates a clear irony: that this new Troy will also fall. In describing the "second" Troy, Britomart indirectly gestures to reproductions of Jove's imperial fiction as well as to repetitions of history. "There there"—meaning Rome— "The glory of the later world to spring, / And *Troy* againe out of her dust was reard," Britomart predicts, "To sit in second seat of soueraigne king, / Of all the world vnder her governing"; but thinking again of England, she adds hopefully that "a third kingdome yet is to arise / Out of the *Troians* scattered of-spring, / That in all glory and great enterprise, / Both first and second *Troy* shall dare to equalise" (III.ix.44). When Britomart claims that

---

[7]McCabe argues that "for Paridell history forms a repetitive sequence of tragic falls occasioned by wild, undisciplined passion," while "For Britomart, seeking the legitimate creative union of marriage, disaster heralds rebirth and renewal" (*Pillars of Eternity*, p. 185). More emphatically, Parker calls Britomart's rendering of imperial myth wholly superior, writing that her "'Troynovant' is only suggested as the hopeful opposite of the tawdry and reduced 'second Troy' of Paridell, its character the only hoped-for transformation of cultural late-coming into promise, in England, of something genuinely new" (*Inescapable Romance*, p. 77).

England's "third" Troynovant "both first and second *Troy* shall dare to equalise," her national ambitions unintentionally mock their expression, since, after all, this means that like Troy and Rome, England will fall, too.

Britomart unwittingly points to the great lie (but still open secret) of Virgilian *translatio*: the nearly endless replication of new Troys, each of which seeks endless empire. Ironically, though, Paridell confirms Britomart's prophecy of English imperium when he struggles to remember history. "Whilome I heard tell / From aged *Mnemon*," Paridell reflects, "(if I remember right,) / That of the antique *Troian* stocke, there grew / Another plant" and that "far abroad his mighty branches threw, / Into the vtmost Angle of the world he knew" (III.ix.47). Attempting to recollect England's history, which he remembers only as myth, Paridell soon gives up. Instead, he merely gestures to the history, or historiography, he forgot: "A famous history to be enrold / In euerlasting moniments of brasse, / That all the antique Worthies merits far did passe" (III.ix.50).

While Britomart and Paridell unselfconsciously replicate Troynovants and express naive notions of cultural rebirth in Book III, making clear the bankruptcy of their claims to permanence, Spenser has already launched a more serious investigation of the Trojan legend in history in Book II. When Paridell partially repeats what he "heard tell / From aged *Mnemon*," he unwittingly directs readers back to Book II, where Arthur and Guyon read about English history and their places in it: Alma's castle of the soul, where "Mnemon" writes the story of England. By moving England's three part history in a narrative circle, from Book III to Book II and back, Spenser encourages readers to remember what Britomart and Paridell have forgotten: Troy's fall never translates into permanent empire, though the story is repeated as history.

If Book II explores how Trojan genealogies are reproduced throughout English history, how they are used to legitimize conquest in England's past and present, it begins by pondering Spenser's own fictional history. In his story of Elizabeth, his "mighty Soueraine," and indeed of all Tudors, he wonders whether "this famous antique history, / Of some th'aboundance of an idle braine / Will iudged be, and painted forgery, / Rather then matter of iust memory" (II.Proem.1). To defend against this judgment, he qualifies the history to be narrated. "Where is that happy land of Faery, / Which I so much do vaunt, yet no where show [?]" He promises to "vouch antiquities, which no body can know" (II.Proem.1). Comparing England's history to the discovery of old and new worlds, India and Virginia, he justifies his portrait of Faerie Land as one of many "great Regions" until now unknown: a place once thought of as fantasy but later verified as an actual place (II.Proem.2).

For all this praise of Elizabeth, however, Book II's history fractures any ideal image of Tudor monarchy. Indeed, Spenser explicitly questions England's Golden Age in Alma's castle, where Guyon and Arthur read different versions of "aged Mnemon's" historiography, primarily by illustrating the Trojan legend's fraudulent uses throughout England's history. That is, Spenser portrays England's history as an ongoing pattern of ruin and edification. Arthur's history book, *Britons Moniments*, punctures myths of permanence by repeatedly challenging the status of Brutus in England's national destiny. First Arthur attacks the Trojan legend by depicting Brutus' arrival on England's shores not as the work of fate but as an accident, "Driuen by fatall error" (II.x.9). Then he portrays Brutus' legacy as a form of cultural violence. "The second *Brute* . . . / With recompense of euerlasting fame /. . . with his victour sword first opened / The bowels of wide Fraunce, a forlorne Dame, / And taught her first how to be conquered; / Since which, with sundrie spoiles she hath beene ransacked" (II.x.23). The metaphoric rape of culture is repeated throughout *Britons Moniments,* marking the distance between Troy and conquests made in its name. England has built itself upon the spoils of conquest.

There are no monuments in *Britons Moniments*—only endless attempts to make them. Spenser ends Brutus' line by suggesting its dubious uses in "Britons'" genealogy, the reproduction of a Trojan fiction in English history:

> Here ended *Brutus* sacred progenie,
>> Which had seuen hundred yeares this scepter borne,
>> With high renowme, and great felicitie;
>> The noble braunch from th'antique stocke was torne
>> Through discord, and the royall throne forlorne:
>> Thenceforth this Realme was into factions rent,
>> Whilest each of *Brutus* boasted to be borne,
>> That in the end was left no moniment
> Of *Brutus*, nor of Britons glory auncient. II.x.36

As in the *Aeneid*, the implied promise of a Trojan ancestry is the repair of ruin: to gather "this Realme . . . into factions rent," to rebuild the past into a new and endless Troynovant. But the lack of "moniment" implies less that Brutus' golden age left no monuments than that his legend remains historically suspect. Despite the efforts of various unifiers, we read again and again about how "this sad Realme [was] cut into sundry shaires / By such, as claymed themselves *Brutes* rightfull haires" (II.x.37). Nearly every stanza reveals the perpetuation of this genealogical fiction and its divisive effects on England's history. Even the seeming success of "*Lud,*" who "Left of his life most famous memory, / And endlesse moniments of his great good: /

The ruin'd wals he did reædifye / Of *Troynouant*, gainst force of enimy,"
illustrates the fall of yet another Troynovant when Lud's nephew "betrayd
his contrey vnto forreine spoyle"—ironically to Rome's empire
(II.x.46–48).

The promise of a permanent Troynovant is always broken, Spenser
intimates, in history. Instead, a continuing pattern of imperial theft prevails
throughout *Britons Moniments*. As if to emphasize the absence of an "end"
to this history, Arthur's history breaks off suddenly, producing in him a
deeply ironic response. "O how dearly deare / Ought thy remembraunce,
and perpetuall band / Be to thy foster Childe," Arthur proclaims, and "How
brutish is it not to vnderstand, / How much to her we owe, that all vs gave,
/ . . . what euer good we have" (II.x.69). How Brute-ish, indeed, not to
remember history, Spenser reminds readers, and how it is built: not upon
the ruins of Troy but rather upon the ruins made in Troy's name.

Critics often have argued that Guyon's version of history, *Antiquitie of
Faerie Lond*, redeems Arthur's brutal *Britons Moniments*.[8] But far from
depicting England as a golden world, Guyon's *Antiquitie* offers a similar
vision of history translated into fiction:

> Of these a mightie people shortly grew,
>> And puissant kings, which all the world warrayd,
>> And to them selues all Nations did subdew:
>> The first and eldest, which that scepter swayd,
>> Was *Elfin*; him all *India* obayd,
>> And all that now *America* men call:
>> Next him was noble *Elfinan*, who layd
>> *Cleopolis* foundation first of all:
> But *Elfiline* enclosd it with a golden wall. II.x.72

The spoils of India and America, echoing Book II's proem about places
once undreamed of in European philosophy, are Cleopolis' imperial foundation. "Enclosd . . . with a golden wall," Cleopolis' very architecture
suggests how the lust for gold (an ironic Golden Age) motivates history,
even in an obviously fictional form. And as in Arthur's history, Faerie Land
achieves empire through conquest. "With rich spoiles and famous victorie,"
they "did high aduaunce the crowne of *Faery*," the same crown the Faerie
Queene inherits and the basis of her power (II.x.75). These histories clarify

---

[8]O'Connell argues that "it is to this bitter reality of conflict and turmoil [in *Britons
Moniments*] that the Faery chronicle contrasts," that "the important thing about the Faery
chronicle is that it *is* idealization—not flattery, but conscious fictive idealization . . . .
Insofar as Tudor rule approaches the Faery ideal of order, it fulfills the promise of its
'heavenly' genealogy" ("History," pp. 251–252).

the historical basis for Mutability's charge. Imperial leaders call themselves gods to justify re-writing history, fictionalizing endless empire when, in time, ruin never ends.

III. Falls Into History: Mutability on Trial

In returning to Nature's court we may hear echoes of Spenser's complaints in Mutability's argument. Yet Spenser is not a poet of mutability simply because of his fascination with flux. Just as Ovid's *Metamorphoses* places the fall of the Golden Age in relation to the fall of Troy, as bookends of history, so Mutability's trial of Jove needs to be judged in these two contexts. In both cases permanence is a fiction perpetuated in history, a promise perpetually broken. When Mutability challenges Jove's authority vis-à-vis the fall of the Golden Age, she also evokes a vexed portrait of Trojan mythology in English history. Spenser's story of England points readers in a circle, moving from Book III to Book II, then presumably back again, in order to make a point about writing epic after (and in imitation of) Virgil's *Aeneid*: the promise of permanence masks the ruins of war, making empire the gift of the gods, turning history into fiction and monarchs into deities.

Jove's trial thus implicates Tudor divinity and England's imperium. On trial is the question of whether England can justly claim to inherit Trojan fictions of history. Are there precedents for rejecting what seems to be England's birthright? What motives might Spenser have for challenging Virgil's rich, varied legacy in England? In the Cantos of Mutability, through Mutability's case, Spenser himself asks whether Troy's legend truly translates into "English," so to speak, and, if so, at what cost.

After Mutability appeals to Nature, calling Jove "no equall Iudge" of her "desert," she elaborates her initial claim that she deserves heaven's estate by right of birth, demanding a place in heaven by demonstrating Jove's failures on earth (VII.vi.35). Where Jove claims to preside over permanence, she rules over those who, she claims, falsely call themselves gods:

> Then weigh, O soueraigne goddesse, by what right
> These gods do claime the worlds whole souerainty;
> And that is onely dew vnto thy might
> Arrogate to themselues ambitiously:
> As for the gods owne principality,
> Which *Ioue* vsurpes vniustly; that to be
> My heritage, *Ioue's* self cannot deny. VII.vii.16

As Mutability sees it, Jove serves his own ambitions by arrogating power to himself.

Indeed, when Mutability articulates her most serious charges against Jove—that his divinity is fraudulent—we hear echoes of charges that were being made against Elizabeth and other Tudors. Jove defends himself, arguing that the gods themselves control all change within a master plan, but Mutability scorns him openly: "The things / Which we see not how they are mov'd and swayd, / Ye may attribute to your selues as Kings, / And say they by your secret powre are made: / But what we see not, who shall vs perswade?" She concludes, "But were they so, as ye them faine to be . . . / Yet what if I can proue, that euen yee / Your selues are likewise chang'd, and subiect vnto mee?" (VII.vii.49). Mutability throws a trump card on the table when she accuses Jove of a fraudulent identity. Dramatically, she dares Jove to reveal his genealogy, his self-fashioned divinity, goading him to confess that the king of gods is no more than human:

> But you *Dan Ioue*, that only constant are,
>   And King of all the rest, as ye do clame
>   Are you not subiect eeke to this misfare?
>   Then let me aske you this withouten blame,
>   Where were ye borne? some say in *Crete* by name,
>   Others in *Thebes*, and others other-where;
>   But wheresoeuer they comment the same,
>   They all consent that ye begotten were,
> And borne here in this world, ne other can appeare. VII.vii.53

The differing accounts of Jove's birthplace suggest a fictionalized origin that Mutability makes explicit. "Then are ye mortall borne, and thrall to me," she reasons, "since within this wide great *Vniuerse* / Nothing doth firme and permanent appeare" (VII.vii.54–56).

Mutability claims then that she already rules the universe. Despite her undeniably forceful arguments, however, she loses her case. Nature decides in favor of Jove since, as she knows well, even mutability is not without end: if "all things stedfastnes doe hate / And changed be," they "turning to themselues at length againe, / Doe worke their owne perfection so by fate. . . / But time shall come that all shall changed bee, / And from thenceforth, none no more change shall see" (VII.vii.58–59). In essence, Nature denies Mutability with the wakeful trump of doom, recasting this pagan debate in tacitly Christian terms: she argues that time itself is not endless. Yet throughout this trial, readers have seen that Jove must defend himself and can barely do so, while Mutability seeks justice but cannot find it. This alone reveals the earth-bound nature of Nature's court.

Spenser suggests, in other words, that true justice cannot exist in this fallen Golden Age, and that what passes for justice represents the self-justifying fictions of imperial power, both Elizabeth's and Jove's. Certainly

Spenser leaves little doubt that their histories are a matter of "heauenly things": "thou alone, / That art yborne of heauen and heauenly Sire," Spenser tells Elizabeth, "Can tell things doen in heauen so long ygone; / So farre past memory of man that may be knowne" (VII.vii.2). Like the still undiscovered regions of the world, Elizabeth's divine lineage represents an unknowable history that, Spenser implies here, requires an act of faith. The origins of the gods, after all, precede written record, "farre past" mortal memory.

Ironically, of course, Spenser has sought just such proof in the Cantos of Mutability where, by digging in the archive of Faerie Land's ancient history, the past can be made present. Thus if Jove's victory against Mutability stands for Elizabeth's own triumph against time, so Mutability's charges against Jove must also be understood in the context of Tudor rule. These cases are related by a profound questioning of authority: both Jove and Elizabeth stand accused of illegitimate rule and of falsifying their own permanence in history. Historiography reveals repercussions of such fiction, especially Trojan fictions of history, the ongoing fall into history, and ruin, by which an empire achieves conquest.

By questioning England's mythology throughout *The Faerie Queene*, Spenser questions Elizabeth's ability to create a just empire beyond the sheer fiction of doing so. In fact the Mutability Cantos cut to the heart of Elizabeth's personal mythology, thereby allowing her to perform Jove's role and making Virgil safe for the readers of Protestant England. Since late antiquity, Virgil's *Aeneid* and its vision of imperial transmission had been rendered Christian by allegorizing the epic, on the one hand, and, on the other, by interpreting it within the context of Virgil's fourth eclogue, where he writes: "Now is come the last age of the song of Cumae / the great line of the centuries begins anew. / Now the Virgin returns, the reign of Saturn returns . . . / and a golden race will spring up throughout the world."[9] Exploring the mythology that Elizabeth inspired and cultivated, Frances Yates calls Elizabeth "Astraea-Virgo, the just and pious virgin, whose return in the Fourth Eclogue heralds the golden age of empire" and who in England "becomes an imperial virgin."[10]

Virgil's poetry about the Golden Age could be interpreted as Christian prophecy, just as his epic about empire-building could be squared with the cities of Man and God. This conventional wisdom, however, seems suspect in the light of Spenser's several trials in *The Faerie Queene*. At the beginning of Book V's allegory of Justice, Spenser reminds us that the Golden Age has passed and consequently that Astraea has fled earth. "So oft as I with state of

---

[9]Virgil, *Eclogues*, IV.4–7.
[10]Yates, *Astrea*, p. 33.

present time," the poet begins, "The image of the antique world compare . . . / Me seemes the world is runne quite out of square, / From the first point of his appointed sourse, / And being once amisse growes daily wourse and wourse" (V.Proem.1). While lamenting that "the golden age, that first was named, / It's now at earst become a stonie one" (V.Proem.2), Spenser gestures to a still more compelling claim: that Elizabeth's self-fashioned mythology as a new Astraea ruling over England's new Golden Age may also be a broken promise.

Such a challenge may be indicated too in the physical location of the trial, Ireland. Nature's earthly court takes place in "*Arlo-hill,*" in an Ireland that stands perhaps as the test-case for England's claim to eternal empire (VII.vi.36). This "Faery Land" history recounts not only Mutability's trial but also Ireland's ancient history, a time "when *IRELAND* florished in fame / Of wealths and goodnesse, far aboue the rest / Of all that beare the *British* Islands name" (VII.vi.38). Through the trial's location, Spenser hints that despoiled Ireland may stand as much chance as Mutability of receiving justice in the face of England's greatest fiction, a divine imperial genealogy that is destined for endless empire.

★   ★   ★

Turning briefly to *A View of the Present State of Ireland* now I would like to glance at Spenser's critique of Trojan fictions in this dialogue about problems of English empire. While the *View* is clearly a colonial work, and a brutal one at that, critics sometimes map this polemic onto *The Faerie Queene* and thus miss or over-generalize Spenser's complex, contradictory views of England's imperial ambitions.[11] By reading Spenser's epic complaints about empire in *The Faerie Queene* in the context of the *View*, this dialogue may sound less univocal than we frequently hear it to be.

Noting how the Irish sometimes fictionalize their historical origins, Eudoxus charges his interlocutor with bad faith: "You doe very boldly Iren. adventure upon the histories of auncient times, and leane too confidently on those Irish Chronicles which are most fabulous and forged."[12] Because "no

---

[11]As Read argues, "the looming peril at present is that *The Faerie Queene* will be superseded by *A View* as the primary historical document of Spenser's political and ethical vision. Analysis of the poem in the recent Irish studies leans heavily toward the three books added in the 1596 edition and especially to Book 5"; "Spenser's most dedicated thinking about the general problem of English colonialism . . . actually occurs in the 1590 edition and . . . this thinking mainly occurs in Book 2, which seems to have replaced Book 5 as the most under represented section of the poem in current criticism" (*Temperate Conquests*, p. 13).

[12]Spenser, *A View of the Present State of Ireland*, p. 45. Subsequent citations of the *View* refer to this edition.

monument remaines of her beginning and first inhabiting," the Irish, like the English, instead have "only bare traditions of times and remembrances of Bardes, which use to forge and falsifie every thing as they list, to please or displease any man" (p. 45). Such historical lies, Eudoxus tells Irenaeus, are merely conventional. Irenaeus reminds readers that "the Irish doe heerein no otherwise, than our vaine English-men doe in the Tale of Brutus, whom they devise to have first conquered and inhabited this land, it being impossible to proove, that there was ever any such Brutus of Albion or England" (p. 44). Irenaeus adds, "yet there appears among them some reliques of the true antiquitie, though disguised, which a well eyed man may happily discover and finde out" (p. 47). Having read about an Ireland "utterly wasted and defaced, of which the ruines are yet in many places to be seene," we might see Ireland as the location of the return of the repressed, as a part of England's history it chooses to forget (p. 158).

As Willy Maley has observed, critics tend to create two Spensers, one "the humanist" and the other "the colonist, as though these domains did not overlap."[13] In this essay, I have attempted to rethink our view of Spenser as thoroughly divided, as the foremost proponent of English imperialism on the one hand, and as a humanist poet on the other. Both Spensers seem to want England to be a place that remembers ruin. Remembering ruin most obviously means remembering the *fact* of ruin, the eventual ruination of all empires, including England's, and the ruin England can cause in pursuit of empire. Perhaps in the dialogue between "brutish" empire and collective memory we can locate Spenser's endeavors, for he recalls what England has been and what it could be. Eudoxus concludes the View by remembering a promise:

> withall not forgetting, not in the shutting up, to put you in minde of that which you have formerly halfe promised, that hereafter when wee shall meete againe, upon the like good occasion, you will declare unto us those your observations, which you have gathered of the antiquities of Ireland. 161

Ending *The Faerie Queene* with an unfinished canto, Spenser reminds readers that only at the end of time, when fictional gods are exchanged for the "God

---

[13]Maley, *Salvaging Spenser*, p. 73. Lim's reading of the *View* works to achieve such a balance: "the program Spenser proposes for colonizing Ireland in the *View* provides one of the most sustained imperialist articulations in Elizabethan England"; yet "While . . . [Spenser] obviously does not stand alone in holding to such an implacable imperialist policy, his views stand in direct opposition to Elizabeth's own. And it is in Spenser's conflict with the queen concerning the conduct of English foreign policy that we locate a central significance of the *View*" (*Arts of Empire*, p. 143).

of Sabbaoth," will a Golden Age come again—to remain "firmely stayd / Vpon the pillours of Eternity" (VII.viii.2).

WORKS CITED

Fichter, Andrew. *Poets Historical: Dynastic Epic in the Renaissance*. New Haven: Yale University Press, 1982.

Lim, Walter S. H. *The Arts of Empire: The Poetics of Colonialism from Raleigh to Milton*. Newark: University of Delaware Press, 1998.

Maley, Willy. *Salvaging Spenser: Colonialism, Culture, and Identity*. New York: St. Martin's, 1997.

McCabe, Richard. *The Pillars of Eternity: Time and Providence in* The Faerie Queene. Dublin: Irish Academic Press, 1989.

O'Connell, Michael. *Mirror and Veil: The Historical Dimension of Spenser's* Faerie Queene. Chapel Hill: University of North Carolina Press, 1977.

Ovid. *Metamorphoses*. Trans. A. D. Melville. Oxford: Oxford University Press, 1988.

Parker, Patricia. *Inescapable Romance: Studies in the Poetics of a Mode*. Princeton: Princeton University Press, 1979.

Read, David. *Temperate Conquests: Spenser and the Spanish New World*. Detroit: Wayne State University Press, 2000.

Spenser, Edmund. *The Faerie Queene*. Ed. A. C. Hamilton. New York: Longman, 1977.

Spenser, Edmund. *A View of the State of Ireland*. Ed. Andrew Hadfield and Willy Maley. Malden: Blackwell, 1997.

Virgil. *The Aeneid of Virgil*. Trans. Robert Fitzgerald. New York: Vintage, 1990.

Virgil. *Eclogues*. Trans. H. Rushton Fairclough. Loeb Classical Library. Cambridge: Harvard University Press, 1967.

Yates, Frances. *Astraea: The Imperial Theme in the Sixteenth Century*. 1975. Rpt. London: Pimlico, 1993.

According to "the common receiued opinion": Munday's Brute in The Triumphes of Re-United Britannia (1605)

SCOTT SCHOFIELD

Anthony Munday, the English dramatist, pamphleteer, translator, city annalist, draper, and civic pageant-writer, was chosen to devise London's annual Lord Mayor's Show for 1605.[1] The newly elected Mayor for that year was Sir Leonard Holliday, a knight and Merchant Taylor who was welcomed, like his predecessors before him, with a spectacular show through the city's streets. In accordance with tradition, on 29 October 1605 he started his day early, accompanied by representatives of the twelve great London livery companies and other civic worthies. Following a brief land procession, the Mayor boarded a barge that carried him and his entourage up the Thames to Westminster, where he took a ceremonial oath of office. Returning to the Thames, the group taxied by barge back to the city and then proceeded northward by foot toward the Guildhall; after disembarking they stopped at well-known city landmarks to view pageants and listen to speeches. The day ended with a Guildhall dinner and yet another procession to the Mayor's house.[2] Or at least that was the plan.

But all went amiss on 29 October 1605. As foul weather brought the newly appointed Mayor's rite of passage to a halt, the procession was delayed, then completed three days later, on November 1st, All Saints Day. The total costs recorded in the Merchant Taylors' Account Book, including wages and other expenses set aside for the painters and porters, the costumes to clothe the children, fireworks for the ship, drink for the workers, and still more paint for the defaced pageant devices, amounted to £710.2s.5d. for the two days,

---

[1] Title phrase is from Stow, *A Summarie*, p. 8. Munday's literary output amounted to more than 50 printed works and a few plays in manuscript (Branyan, "Anthony Munday," pp. 173–180).

[2] Lancashire discusses the earliest surviving records of the London Lord Mayor pageantry in *London Civic Theatre*, pp. 171–184. Lobanov-Rostovsky, "*The Triumphes of Golde,*" pp. 880–881.

£6 of which Munday received for "printing the books of the speeches in the pageant and the other shows."[3] The whole occasion was thus designed as a magnificent tribute to the Mayor, the livery company of which he was a member, and the city, while also providing a festive communal setting for the throngs of Londoners who filled the streets along the ceremonial route.[4]

By all indications Munday's 1605 show, despite the inclement weather, was well received by the civic authorities; its success may be judged by the fact that in subsequent years Munday was hired to devise more Lord Mayor's Shows (LMS) than any other dramatist involved with the form. This included contemporaries Thomas Middleton, Thomas Dekker, John Webster, and Thomas Heywood.[5] Munday's *Triumphes* incorporates many elements common to English Renaissance civic pageantry. Allegorical and mythical speakers address and perform dramatic exchanges for the Lord Mayor at the various stops. Neptune speaks, for instance, of his trust in the new mayor's ability "to governe justlie and amend each misse,"[6] while other speakers catalogue the long line of famous precedents of the Company, including English kings who were Merchant Taylors (ll. 340–420).

Having said that, there are a few unusual aspects to this printed account. First, in Munday's LMS text the majority of the praise is reserved for the new king, James I, rather than the mayor, Sir Leonard Holliday. Second, Munday chose the legendary Trojan founder of Britain, Brute, as the central exemplary figure for his device. Such a decision would seem only fitting to the highly imaginative nature of English pageantry, with its regular celebration of popular heroes and famous historical persons. Munday had already shown a particular interest in the legendary past, as seen in the stories of romance heroes that he translated and his choice of men such as Robin Hood for his plays. Yet for Munday to choose Brute for his LMS at least implicitly raises important questions about the uses of the past, questions critical to a long-standing debate in English Renaissance historiography. By 1605, the figure of Brute was increasingly dismissed by many of England's most reputable historians and antiquaries, explained away as a hero of the imagination who clouded the serious scholarly labour needed to uncover Britain's origins. In his celebration of Brute, Munday had joined a long line of defenders of the British Trojan

---

³For the Merchant Taylors' account records see Gordon and Robertson, *Collections III*, pp. 68–70, and Withington, *English Pageantry*, vol. 2, pp. 28–29. For an illustrated layout of the route see Manley, *Literature and Culture*, pp. 226–227.

⁴Manley, *Literature and Culture*, pp. 260–293.

⁵Bergeron notes that "Munday was connected in some way with at least fifteen lord mayor's shows during the period 1602–1623" ("Anthony Munday," p. 347).

⁶Munday, *The Triumphes of Re-United Britannia*, l. 467. Subsequent citations are indicated parenthetically.

founder. But his pageant text has less to do with holding on to the tenuous claims of an undocumented past. Brute was a cultural icon connected to what many London chroniclers of the period refer to as the common received opinion. What was at stake here was nothing short of the preservation of an important piece of cultural identity. *Triumphes* stands for a celebration of story as well as of the communities that embrace such tales in both oral and written traditions. This paper will explore the fascinating and at times controversial reception history surrounding the figure at the centre of the Lord Mayor's Show for 1605. In order to do that, we first need to look at the pageant text itself.

★   ★   ★

Recent scholarship of English civic pageantry addresses discrepancies between printed texts and staged events.[7] As we may expect, LMS texts highlight selections from the LMS, providing us with an account of what was heard, what was seen, and why a particular speech or image may have been chosen on the occasion. Part of the text often mirrors a dramatic script, complete with speakers and their lines. But rather than provide us with a documentary recital of the mayor's procession, the LMS text—like other Renaissance occasional verse and prose—offers other related materials, ranging from dedications made to the London civic elite to discourses on the histories of mayors, liveries and the city. As David Bergeron says, these texts "constitute some meta-dramatic event, resembling yet differing from what took place . . . [while] they exhibit a growing self-consciousness as books . . . [that] do not obliterate theatrical performance or displace it so much as they complete it."[8] Details, such as costumes and costs, names of those in the procession, the places where the speeches are spoken, and audience reactions to the pageants are often spared from the account in order to convey the larger theme. Taken as a whole, then, the textual parts form a tribute to the idea that inspired the occasion.

Anthony Munday's *Triumphes* is no exception. While the pageant text provides us with selections from the day's proceedings—offering a detailed sketch of the central pageant and an appended selection of dramatic exchanges—the work opens with an extended framing narrative, a condensed and annotated chronicle account of the legendary Kings of Britain, with special attention given to the Brute myth (ll. 1–106). Munday qualifies his long introduction as a response to another's wishes:

> Because our present conceit, reacheth unto the antiquitie of *Brytaine*,
> which (in many mindes) hath carried as many and variable opinions: I thought
> it not unnecessary, (being thereto earnestly solicited) to speake somewhat
> concerning the estate of this our Countrey, even from the very first originall

[7]Bergeron, "Stuart Civic," pp. 163–183; Smuts, "Occasional Events," pp. 179–198.
[8]Bergeron, "Stuart Civic," pp. 164–165.

until her honourable attaining the name of *Brytannia*, and then lastlye how she became to be called *England*. 1–9

This opening qualification for the subject of the LMS itself affords Munday the ideal authorial position, as he is still able to claim credit for the potential success of the conceit while remaining the mere respondent to another's wishes if all does not go as smoothly as planned. At the least, this seemingly innocent act of solicitation reminds us of the collaborative nature of the occasion as well as the many persons who participated in the composition and printing of what the title page announces as a single-author text.

Munday's pageant was undoubtedly created to please the civic elites who hired him. To stray too far from the City's desires could jeopardize his chances of being hired in future years. Similarly, much as they would with a modern parade, Londoners would have anticipated certain pageants and mythical figures from year to year. For instance, the Albion giants Gog and Magog were regularly stationed as guards to the city gates in English civic pageantry. While they were present in these pageants at least as early as the fifteenth century, they can still be seen in the annual LMS today.[9] In other words, we need to see both the LMS and the LMS text as creations that respond to the interests of London civic leaders and audiences alike, the end product of a complex interaction between various social, economic, and political forces. While the title page to *Triumphes* tells us that the show was "Devised and Written by *A. Mundy*, Cittizen and Draper of London" (p. 2), there were other significant and unrecorded contributions to both the event and the text.

Triumphes begins, as many medieval and Renaissance European chronicles do, with the story of Noah and his three sons populating the four corners of the earth, before turning to the early island rulers Samothes, Albina, and the Saxon Kings. It is Brute and his British descendants, though, who clearly dominate the account. According to the ancient story dating from the ninth century, but expanded and popularized in Geoffrey of Monmouth's account in *Historia Regum Britannie* (c.1136),[10] Brute (or Brutus) was the great-grandson of Aeneas. After inadvertently killing his father, he sought refuge in nearby Greece, where he joined other exiled Trojans. From here, he made his way westward via France to Albion, the prophetic land shown to him in a dream

---

[9]Fairholt, *Gog and Magog*, pp. 28–29. For discussion of the giants in recent shows, see <http://www.lordmayorsshow.org/>.

[10]Extant copies of Geoffrey's *Historia* survive in more than 215 manuscripts. Printed versions appeared in 1508 and 1517, but the History, often in a condensed and revised format, was a staple in the opening chapters of sixteenth-century English chronicles. Along with Higden's *Polychronicon* and the anonymous *Brut*, both of which borrow material from Geoffrey, the *Historia* was arguably the most popular history in medieval English culture. See Crick, *Dissemination*.

by Diana. After landing at Albion, Brute and his Trojan band conquered what was a corrupted land ravaged by giants, united and renamed the adjoining territories "Britain" and the inhabitants "Britons" (both names derived etymologically from Brute), and built the great city Troynovant (London) by the River Thames. This union was short-lived, however, as civil war broke out soon after Brute divided Britain between his three sons, in turn forming England, Scotland and Wales.

In Munday's staged appropriation of the popular story—what he describes as "the whole frame and body of our devise" (l. 105)—a female figure, Britannia, stands atop a triangular mountain representing Britain. Loegria, Cambria, and Albania, the equivalents of England, Wales, and Scotland surround her. As Brute stands beside his sons, Britannia explains how she chose to change her name from Albion to Britain because God consented for Brute to conquer her "virgine honour" (l. 159). This dramatic exchange alludes to the recent dynastic transition from a queen of England to a king of Great Britain. Brute reassures her that he has brought order to this untamed wilderness, while giving her the means to now "raigne as an Imperial lady" (ll. 165–166). Unfortunately, it is Brute's division of the monarchy into three realms, for which Britannia reproves him (l. 168), that eventually leads to division of the kingdom. As the pageant closes, Britannia is restored to her "former Felicity" "by the powerfull vertue of Poesie" (ll. 173–174), first in the image of Henry VII and then in James, both of whom are described as second Brutes. Finally, Brute's three sons deliver up their crowns, and the Thames and other rivers sing paeans to celebrate the miraculous restoration (ll. 188–190). In this device, the ancient golden beginnings of a past Britain resurface in the figure of James.

This familiar story serves as a fitting analogy for celebrating the accession of the new Stuart king, for just as Brute had conquered and brought unity to an ancient land so too had James, as king of Scotland, newly re-united Britain, in theory at least, by ascending the English throne in 1603. In his accession lay the potential for a future peace between England and Scotland, or at least that is how panegyrists like Michael Drayton envisioned it:

> O now reuiue that noble Brittaines name,
> From which at first our ancient honors came,
> Which with both Nations fitly doth agree
> That Scotch and English without difference be,
> And in that place wher feuds were wont to spring
> Let us light Iigs and ioyfull Paeans sing.[11]

Like Drayton, Samuel Daniel also envisioned a British Isle without borders:

---

[11]Drayton, *A Gratulatorie Poem*, B2v.

> Now thou art all great *Brittaine*, and no more,
> No Scot, no English now, nor no debate:
> No Borders but the Ocean, and the Shore,
> No wall of *Adrian* serues to seperate
> Our mutuall loue, nor our obedience,
> All Subjects now to one imperiall Prince.[12]

While Daniel presents a Great Britain founded upon James' arrival, it is Drayton who envisions the transformation as a revival of the ancient British state. As in Munday's pageant, the British union is envisioned as the inevitable solution to a long-standing feud between neighbouring countries. No borders, walls, names or past identities shall prevent the reunion.

A defence of the King's royal descent and the future prosperity of his progeny were common components of dramatic entertainments after James' English succession in 1603. In one sense Anthony Munday was simply capitalizing on the political excitement of the day by alluding to a story that had become a staple in chronicles of the sixteenth century, and more importantly, a story that could be adapted to celebrate the new Stuart dynasty. What did it matter if he blurred the lines between civic and royal celebration, so long as he captivated the crowd?

Much of the creative endorsement for the union of Scotland and England simply incorporated a set of ideas and decisions made by the Crown and articulated in writings by King James himself. In the period immediately following his accession, James had made it his primary goal not only to unite England and Scotland symbolically, but ultimately to unite the political and religious institutions of those two distinct countries. James' desire for union could be seen in the coins that presented him as a Roman-like emperor of Great Britain and in the uniformity of the Book of Common Prayer issued throughout the realm. In fact, in October 1604, James boldly proclaimed himself King of Great Britain, following a House of Commons decision to reject his request for the new title.[13] By 1605 James completely dedicated himself to this issue, and union thus came to dominate everything from parliamentary debates to church sermons. Even certain plays such as Shakespeare's *King Lear* offered a type of counter-analogy for a reunited land, reminding audiences of problems that inevitably arise for a British monarch who divides his kingdom.[14]

---

[12]Daniel, *Panegyrike*, A1r.

[13]Larkin and Hughes, *Stuart Royal Proclamations,* vol. 1: on the King's title see Entry 45, pp. 94–98; on coinage, Entry 47, pp. 99–103; on The Book of Common Prayer, Entry 35, pp. 74–77.

[14]Dutton, *"King Lear, The Triumphs,"* p. 141.

Furthermore, the ancient British kings had been previously adopted as propaganda in medieval and Tudor pageants. Henry VII, for example, had been celebrated "as fulfiller of the prophecy made to Cadwalader," the last of the British kings.[15] When Mary and Philip entered London for coronation in 1554 they encountered the giants Corineus and Gog Magog. The first was Brute's close ally, the second an embodiment of the two giants he subdued.[16] It is not so much that the use of British pre-history was novel to English pageantry by 1605, but that it had never before served so completely for a single pageant: a pageant, we must remember, that was produced to celebrate the inauguration of the mayor and his company. In this sense Munday's pageant is unique.[17] For Munday to choose the British–Trojan myth in 1605 was to choose a historical subject that was increasingly being treated with scepticism by other contemporary seventeenth-century English historians and antiquaries.

Antiquaries like Robert Cotton chose to deal with the controversial British–Trojan past by ignoring it all together. Only two days after the death of Queen Elizabeth, he prepared a detailed genealogy legitimizing James' right to the English throne and his claim to "stile" himself King of Great Britain.[18] That Cotton was responsible for producing the genealogy should not come as a surprise, for he owned the largest private library in England, complete with holdings in Anglo-Saxon and medieval manuscripts, Roman coins, tablets and inscriptions. What is surprising, however, is that the genealogy excludes any mention of Britain's Trojan kings, including Brute, Arthur and Cadwalader. Instead, it relies on the Saxon kings to make the claim, and Roman rather than English sources to substantiate it. English genealogies drawn up in pedigree rolls for English medieval and Renaissance kings—particularly kings like Edward IV, who enjoyed a solid claim to the British line—often included the ancient founders as sources of their pedigree.[19] Furthermore, James had shown his own interest in the British past by promising a beautiful jewel, designed by Nicholas Hilliard, to anyone who could successfully trace his genealogy back to the Trojan Brute. The miniature, later named the Lyte medal, was granted to Henry Lyte in 1610

---

15 Anglo, *Spectacle*, p. 45.

16 Anglo, *Spectacle*, pp. 327–328.

17 Two recent editors of Munday's LMS consider this and other unique features of the text: Dutton, "Introduction," p. 118, and Kinney, "Introduction," pp. 372–373.

18 PRO SP 14/1/3. "A Discourse of the Descent of the King's Majesty from the Saxons." Sharpe suggests the pedigree was prepared at the request of Henry Howard, a proponent of the new Stuart succession (*Sir Robert Cotton*, pp. 114–115).

19 Anglo, *Images*, pp. 40–60. For an earlier version of this chapter, complete with a list of the surviving manuscript rolls, see Anglo, *British History*, pp. 17–48.

for producing the genealogy.[20] Despite ample historical precedent and occasional royal endorsement, however, many scholars such as Cotton chose to ignore this fabled British past.

Other writers rejected the history outright, declaring it a ridiculous fiction. The English recusant Richard Verstegan was one such critic. In his popular work *A Restitvtion of Decayed Intelligence: In antiquities. Concerning the most noble English nation* (1605), he like Cotton looked to the Saxons for the true foundation of both the English past and James' own ancestry. While his study makes allowance for the possibility of a historical figure named Brute, he is critical of the popular story surrounding him, including "his descent from *Troy*, [and] his going into *Greece*, and bringing thence the remnant of the Troyans."[21] In the early sections of Edward Ayscu's *A Historie . . . betweene England and Scotland* (1606; printed 1607), a work which supports James' dream of union, we see one of the most vocal challenges to Britain's Trojan origins. Ayscu offers his boldest pronouncement on the subject at the start of his history:

> To let passe the Fables of *Dioclesian* his Daughters, and of their successors the *Troyans*, vnder the conduct of (I know not what) *Brute*, coyned in some Munkish mint about foure hundred years agone, and generally receaued for currant paiment, during the time wherein ignorance preuailed over the face of the earth, like vnto the palpable darknesse of *Egipt*: I will begin this my History of our famous Island of *Britaine* . . . grounded vpon such proofes . . . [that] shall seeme to come neerest to the truth.[22]

Ayscu does not simply reject these stories as an unreliable source of history but insists on emphasizing what he sees as suspicious associations between the ignorant age that inspired the legends and the "monkish mint" in which they were conceived. In fact, association was arguably the decisive factor for those persons taking sides in the debate.

Cotton's teacher, mentor, and close friend William Camden, who subscribed to an idea of history that depended heavily on extant and reliable sources, approached with caution the myths of England's legendary Trojan origins:

> But as touching those reports of *Brutus*; were they true, certeine, and vndoubted, there is no cause why any man should bestow farther study and

---

[20]For a description of the Lyte medal with photo reprints, see Auerbach, *Nicholas Hilliard*, p. 167; plate 165. For an earlier printed account linking James to Brute and the British line, see Harry, *The genealogy of the High and Mighty Monarch*.

[21]Verstegan, *Restitvtion*, pp. 90–91.

[22]Ayscu, *A Historie contayning*, B1r.

labor in searching out the beginning of the Britains . . . For mine owne part, it is not my intent, I assure you, to discredit and confute that storie which goes of him, for the upholding whereof, (I call *Truth* to record) I have from time to time streined to the heighth, all that little wit of mine. For that were, to strive with the streame and currant of *Time;* and to struggle against an opinion commonly and long since received.[23]

Although Camden may be sceptical, even he was aware of the danger of challenging such a popular legend.[24] Or was he? After leaving the final decision on Brute open to his fellow antiquaries and historians, he proceeds to dismiss the myth point by point. John Speed would offer the same mixed reaction to both the controversy surrounding Brute and how Britain received its name, noting, like Camden, that "the further we follow this entangled thread, the further we are lead into the labyrinth of ambiguity." Despite this moment of insight, Speed, like Camden, could not resist entering the labyrinth in order to dismiss much of what he found.[25]

Amid the ever-growing body of sceptics, there continued to be patriotic support for Brute and his descendants. Much of this support came from sixteenth-century English historians, who reacted against Polydore Vergil's comments on the subject. The Italian humanist who worked under both Henry VII and Henry VIII was not the first to challenge the veracity of Geoffrey of Monmouth's *Historia*—even some of Geoffrey's own contemporaries discredited the myth[26]—but as a foreign historian who challenged the veracity of the popularly held accounts of the British past, he found himself subject to a heavier than usual dose of criticism. Vergil noted that such stories,

in the admiration of the common people[,] (who always more regard novelties than truth) . . . seem to be in heaven, where with a good will I will leave them, thinking it not good to debate the matter with them as touching those feigned trifles.[27]

To discredit a shared historical past was essentially to erase the identity of a people, for these legendary origins, whether true or false, were nonetheless conceived in England and had been popular for four hundred years. To reject the British-Trojan story in the sixteenth century was a seemingly innocent, educated opinion, but to some it represented the endorsement of a foreign, anti-English sentiment. Many antiquaries thus saw it as their duty to retaliate

---

[23]Camden, *Britain*, p. 6.

[24]On Camden's reputation and career see Parry, *Trophies of Time*, pp. 22–48.

[25]Speed, *Historie of Great Britaine*, pp. 6, 20.

[26]The two most notorious twelfth-century English sceptics, William of Newburgh and Gerald of Wales, were historians. Crick, *Dissemination*, p. 2.

[27]Vergil, *Anglica*, quoted in Gransden, *Historical Writing in England*, p. 437.

against Vergil, even as many also acknowledged the quality of his scholarship. The antiquary John Leland blasted Vergil for his bold dismissal of the British history, and so too did the Welsh antiquary Humphrey Llwyd. In the opening of *The Breuiary of Britayne* (1573), a translation of Llwyd's *Commentarioli Brittanicae descriptiois fragmentum* (1572), several dedicatory poems appear for both Twynne and Llwyd. One of the dedicatees, Edward Grant, uses the occasion to celebrate Llwyd's rebuttal:

> By whose endeuour *Polidore*,
> must now surfeace to prate,
> To forge, to lie, and to defame,
> kynge BRVTVS worthy state.[28]

Philip Sidney also defends Llwyd's support for the British myth, after his close friend Hubert Lanquet has sent him a letter criticizing the antiquary's methodology.[29] Such statements attest to the long tradition of support for Brute and the British history throughout the sixteenth century, even though it was clearly losing credibility amongst historians by the end of that century.

In fact, many of the allusions to Brute, whether supportive, dismissive, or indifferent, are regularly connected with the "common" or "vulgar" opinion. Thomas Lanquet opens his 1549 Chronicle this way:

> Brvte, after the vulgar opinion, sonne of Syluius posthumius,
> in this tyme arriued in this Ilande, wherin he begane the fyrst
> to reigne, and named it Britayne, whyche be-fore was called
> Albion, and therin founded the noble citee of London, whan
> he had rei-gned xxiiii yeres, he diuided this wholle empire
> among his thre sonnes.[30]

Grafton's 1570 chronicle begins similarly:

> Brvte after the common opinion of the auncient & most approued wryters
> beyng the Sonne of *Siluius Posthumus* was the fyrste that reig-ned in this
> Realme.[31]

And Stow's 1604 Abridgement announces

> Brute the sonne of Siluius (following, as heretofore, the common receiued
> opini-on).[32]

---

[28]Llwyd, *Breuiary of Britayne*, 2r.
[29]Schwyzer, "'British history,'" p. 13–15.
[30]Lanquet, *An epitome,* fol. 32v.
[31]Grafton, *Abridgement*, p.1.
[32]Stow, *A Summarie*, p. 8.

The sheer frequency of the phrase is tied to the genre itself. Chronicles regularly recycle material, with whole chapters sometimes copied verbatim. While English chroniclers also practice the familiar historical method of citing sources for place-names and dates in the margins of pages, it is this long-standing "common opinion," disseminated through both oral and written traditions, that provides the ultimate qualification for telling the myth. In this sense, "common" signifies the community that embraces the story.[33]

The similarity between Munday's account and those found in earlier chronicles is illustrated down to the choice of word or phrase. Munday's framing narrative, which is reminiscent of such accounts, is complete with printed annotations in the margins, making it an anomaly amongst surviving LMS texts. Interestingly, Munday's scholarly sources (Geoffrey, Leland, Bale and Llwyd) are all English or Welsh historians who champion rather than simply recite British history. One wonders if Munday's LMS text was a response to the now-lost 1604 LMS devised by Ben Jonson. Jonson is notorious for glossing every possible reference in his plays and masques printed during this period, often from Latin editions, and it seems likely that he would have done the same for an LMS text.[34] But as Richard Dutton argues, we should be careful in assigning too much credit to Munday's scholarly practice. The printed marginalia surrounding his text are not the result of careful research, but careful recycling, as it is almost verbatim with that found in Holinshed's *Chronicles*.[35] Still, whether recycled or not, Munday's printed marginalia reinforce his defence of the history and his credibility as a poet-historian.

It is poetry rather than history that allows the ancient past to come to life and be applied to a new historical moment. In Munday's *Triumphes*, Brute even says at one point that his history could only be "raised againe by the powerfull vertue of Poesie" (l. 173). In fact, despite the dominant feeling of scepticism, many English writers described the British history as a necessary piece of cultural identity, and Brute as the ideal exemplar. In his notes to Michael Drayton's *Poly-Olbion* (1612), John Selden for one is openly sceptical of the ancient story, but nevertheless defends Brute as a suitable "Advocat for the muse."[36] In his contribution to the royal entry for

---

[33] *OED*, "common" (7): "that is matter of public talk or knowledge . . . generally known, popular rumour or report."

[34] On the surviving records from 1604, see Gordon and Robertson, *Collections*, pp. 61–68. On *Triumphes* as a response to Jonson's scholarly approach, see Kinney, "Introduction," p. 372.

[35] Dutton, "*King Lear, The Triumphs*," p. 140.

[36] Drayton, *Poly-Olbion*, A2r.

James I, staged in March 1604, Jonson offers a similar explanation when citing a founder for the city:

> Rather then the Citie shuld want a Founder, we choose to
> folowe the receiu'd story of *Brute*, whether fabulous, or true,
> and not altoge-ther vnwarranted in Poetrie: since it is a fauor of Antiquity to
> few cities to let them know their first Authors.[37]

Jonson, in his typical scholarly form, turns to Virgil's *Aeneid* for the classical example. For the scholarly-minded poet it matters less if Brute is "fabulous or true," so long as a classical precedent justifies his inclusion in the day's festivities. Despite Jonson's pedantic method, there is support here for Brute. Even the meticulous scholar was aware of the importance of founding myths to the London community.

But while claims for poetic utility may come to the rescue of sketchy historical figures, they do not explain why Munday would choose this myth, clearly aimed at the new king, also to welcome the incoming mayor. How can a pageant produced for the mayor "so consciously, explicitly, and unrelentingly refer to the sovereign"?[38] The obvious answer lies in the timing. Perhaps the Merchant Taylors responsible for the financing of the day's events saw an opportunity to capitalize on the recent propaganda for the British union. We need to look more closely at the events surrounding the occasion and more carefully at how these shows operated. For instance, an important clue for understanding Munday's 1605 show is found in an LMS text published nearly thirty years later.

After cataloguing the former London mayors who were Clothworkers in the early section of his 1633 Lord Mayor's Show, Thomas Heywood stops to reflect:

> Neyther is it the least Honour to this right Worshipfull Fraternity, that it pleased Royall King Iames, (of sacred memory), besides diuers others of the nobility, to enter into the freedome and brother-hood of this Company.[39]

Looking back some eight years after James' death, Heywood does what any good deviser of a LMS must do: he lists the most recent members to join the Clothworkers' line of prosperity. If there is one common component in any LMS it is this catalogue of honour. The names of past kings, nobility, and civic worthies were often recited orally by a figure representing Fame or Time. The roll call reminded Londoners that that day's new investiture

---

[37]Jonson, *B. Jon: His Part*, B3r, n.C.
[38]Bergeron, "Introduction," p. xiii.
[39]Heywood, *Londini emporia, or Londons mercatura*, A4r–A4v.

relied on the careful preservation of past agreements. In this rite of passage, the mayor is constantly made to participate in a larger process of civic commemoration. He is but the next worthy to occupy Fame's house one day. These shows acknowledge a series of reciprocal agreements, including the pact between the mayor and his company, the mayor and the people, and the city and crown. Each agreement is honoured through an established negotiation with the past.

Again Munday's *Triumphes* is no exception. After different personified Vertues recite the good works of past kings made free by the Merchant Taylors, the figure of Pheme (Fame) interjects with questions for Epimeleia, who has just recorded Henry VII's contributions to the company:

> But sacred Lady, deigne me so much grace,
> As tell me, why that seat is unsupplied,
> Being the most eminent and chiefest place,
> With State, with Crowne and Scepter dignified?

Epimeleia replies:

> Have our discourses (Pheme) let thee know,
> That seaven Kings have borne free brethrens name,
> Of this Societie, and may not time bestow
> An eight, when Heaven shall so appoint the same? 399–406

The dramatic exchange that comes near the end of Munday's show is no less than an attempt to solicit James to become an honourary member of the Merchant Taylors. As James had not made himself free of a company by October 1605, the Merchant Taylors saw fit to try to persuade him to occupy the empty seat in the royal house of fame next to Henry VII, the last English king to have been made free of the company.[40] This sequence of events, along with earlier connections made in *Triumphes* between James and Henry, draws on a central element of James' own self-fashioning, for he insisted that his claim to the English throne depended on his descent from Henry VII himself.

It is in this context that Munday's final dramatic exchanges become clear, for Henry also held a special place in the Merchant Taylor's memory. The only Tudor king to become an honourary member, Henry had been responsible for issuing them a new corporation charter in 1502, which granted them the name they still carry. Prior to Henry's act, the company

---

[40]James was made free of the Clothworkers on 12 June 1607. See Clode, *Early History of the Merchant Taylors*, vol. 1, p. 276. While editors have noted the reference to James, they have overlooked its larger significance.

had used the title "Taylors and Linen Armourers." As a part of the 1502 grant Henry was to be prayed for evermore "as the first Founder of the said Fraternity of St. John the Baptist of Merchant Taylors of London." Furthermore, an annual observance of prayers for the dead was to follow every year thereafter on the eve of St John the Baptist Day to ensure that Henry's generosity would be remembered, particularly his role as a second founder of the company and an instiller of new beginnings.[41] If James were seeking to become a second Henry, then he would need to embrace the Merchant Taylors. What better timing—for on November 5, only four days later, another ceremony was set to move through London's streets—the opening of Parliament.[42]

What could be a more fitting prelude to Parliament than a pageant celebrating James as the restorer of the kingdoms? This would be especially potent considering that the English parliament had been the one major obstacle in James' plans for union in 1604. It is unlikely that James had any direct engagement with the theme for the 1605 LMS, but perhaps the civic authorities that comprised the committee that chose Munday to devise the show sensed a perfect opportunity to please their king. Either way, in the weeks to follow the rumours throughout the kingdom were less about Brute, Troy, and the re-uniting of a kingdom, and more about the near demise of a king and his parliament, for on 5 November 1605, the Gunpowder Plot was discovered. It offered the ultimate anti-climax to the long awaited opening of Parliament. Any memories of the myths of Trojan descent celebrated in the streets of London on November 1st would be overshadowed by a new set of concerns after November 5th.

Munday's pageant questions the ways the poetic imagination relates to the political and historical discourses of early modern London. Munday was chosen on eight subsequent occasions to devise a London LMS, but all of these are somewhat less interesting, as they are clearly written for mayors and not kings. While James would reign for another twenty years, his dream of union would remain unfulfilled. It is here, in this historical picture of a divided kingdom comprised of distinct identities and separate borders, that a more accurate picture of early modern Britain emerges. While the poetic imagination must submit occasionally to the temporality of the historical moment, the printed text has the ability to preserve ideas and inspirations long eradicated by time.

---

[41]Clode, *Early History of the Merchant Taylors*, vol. 1, pp. 37, 347–350.

[42]Larkin and Hughes, *Stuart Royal Proclamations*, vol. 1: Entry 45, pp. 103–104; Entry 54, pp. 117–118.

WORKS CITED

Anglo, Sydney. "The *British History* in Early Tudor Propaganda." *Bulletin of the John Rylands Library* 44 (1961–1962): 17–48.

Anglo, Sydney. *Images of Tudor Kingship*. London: Seaby, 1992.

Anglo, Sydney. *Spectacle, Pageantry, and Early Tudor Policy*. Oxford Warburg Studies. Oxford: Clarendon, 1969.

Auerbach, Erna. *Nicholas Hilliard*. London: Routledge, 1961.

Ayscu, Edward. *A Historie containing the warres . . . and other occurents betweene England and Scotland*. London, 1607.

Bergeron, David M. "Anthony Munday: Pageant Poet to the City of London." *Huntington Library Quarterly* 30 (1967): 345–368.

Bergeron, David. "Stuart Civic Pageants and Textual Performance." *Renaissance Quarterly* 51 (1998): 163–183.

Branyan, Richard H. "Anthony Munday." *Dictionary of Literary Biography (DLB)*. Ed. David A. Richardson. Detroit: Gale (1996). 173–180.

Camden, William. *Britain; or a Chorographicall Description of . . . England*. Trans. Philemon Holland. London, 1610.

Clode, Charles Matthew. *The Early History of the Guild of Merchant Taylors of the Fraternity of St. John the Baptist, London*. 2 vols. London, 1888.

Cotton, Robert. "A Discourse of the Descent of the King's Majesty from the Saxons." PRO SP 14/1/3.

Crick, Julia C. *The Historia Regum Britannie of Geoffrey of Monmouth. Dissemination and Reception in the Later Middle Ages*. Vol. 4. Cambridge: Brewer, 1991.

Daniel, Samuel. *A Panegyrike Congratvlatory to the Kings Maiestie*. London, 1603.

Drayton, Michael. *Poly-Olbion*. London, 1612.

Drayton, Michael. *To the Maiestie of King James. A Gratulatorie Poem*. London, 1603.

Dutton, Richard. "*King Lear, The Triumphs of Reunited Britannia* and 'The Matter of Britain.'" *Literature and History* 12 (1986): 139–151.

Dutton, Richard, ed. "Introduction to *The Triumphs of Reunited Britannia*." *Jacobean Civic Pageants*. Ryburn Renaissance Texts and Studies. Ryburn: Keele University Press, 1995. 117–118.

Fairholt, F.W. *Gog and Magog. The Giants in Guildhall; their Real and Legendary History*. London: Hotton, 1859.

Gordon, D.J. and Jean Robertson, ed. *Collections III: A Calendar of Dramatic Records in the Books of the Livery Companies of London, 1485–1640*. Oxford: Malone Society Reprint, 1954.

Grafton, Richard. *An Abridgement of the Chronicles of Englande*. London, 1570.

Gransden, Antonia. *Historical Writing in England. Vol 2. c. 1307 to the Early Sixteenth Century*. Ithaca: Cornell University Press, 1982.

Harry, George Owen. *The genealogy of the High and Mighty Monarch, James, by the grace of God, King of Great Brittayne*. London, 1604.

Heywood, Thomas. *Londini emporia, or Londons mercatura*. London, 1633.

Jonson, Ben. *B. Jon: His Part of King James his Royall and Magnificent Entertainment through his Honorable Cittie of London, Thurseday the 15 of March 1603*. London, 1604.

Kinney, Arthur F., ed. "Introduction to *The Triumphs of Re-United Britannia.*" *A Companion to Renaissance Drama*. Malden: Blackwell, 2002. 370–373.

Lancashire, Anne. *London Civic Theatre: City Drama and Pageantry from Roman Times to 1558*. Cambridge: Cambridge University Press, 2002.

Lanquet, Thomas. *An epitome of cronicles*. London, 1549.

Larkin, James F. and Paul L. Hughes, ed. *Stuart Royal Proclamations*. 2 vols. Oxford: Clarendon, 1973.

Llwyd, Humphrey. *The Breuiary of Britayne*. Trans. Thomas Twynne. London, 1573.

Lobanov-Rostovsky, Sergei. "*The Triumphes of Golde*: Economic Authority in the Jacobean Lord Mayor's Show." *ELR* 60 (1993): 879–898.

London Lord Mayor's Show. http://www.lordmayorsshow.org.

Manley, Lawrence. *Literature and Culture in Early Modern London*. Cambridge: Cambridge University Press, 1995.

Munday, Anthony. *The Triumphes of Re-United Britannia*. 1605. Rpt. in *Pageants and Entertainments of Anthony Munday*. Ed. David M. Bergeron. New York: Garland, 1985. 1–23.

Parry, Graham. *The Trophies of Time: English Antiquarians of the Seventeenth Century*. Oxford: Oxford University Press, 1995.

Schwyzer, Philip. "British history and 'The British History': the same old story?" *British Identities and English Renaissance Literature*. Ed. David J. Baker and Willy Maley. Cambridge: Cambridge University Press, 2002. 11–23.

Sharpe, Kevin. *Sir Robert Cotton 1586–1631. History and Politics in Early Modern England*. Oxford: Oxford University Press, 1979.

Smuts, R. Malcolm. "Occasional Events, Literary Texts and Historical Interpretations." *Neo-Historicism: Studies in Renaissance Literature, History and Politics*. Ed. Robin Headlam Wells, Glenn Burgess, and Roland Wymer. *Studies in Renaissance Literature*. Vol. 5. Woodbridge: D.S. Brewer, 2002. 179–198.

Speed, John. *The Historie of Great Britaine: Vnder the Conqvests of the Romans, Saxons, Danes and Normans vnto the Raigne of King Iames, of Famous Memorie*. London, 1632.

Stow, John. *A Summarie of the Chronicles of England*. London, 1604.

Verstegan, Richard. *A Restitvtion of Decayed Intelligence: In antiquities. Concerning the most noble and renovvmed English nation*. Antwerp, 1605.

Vergil, Polydore. *The Anglica Historia*. Ed. and trans. Denys Hay. Camden Third Series. Vol. 74. London: Royal Historical Society, 1950.

Withington, Robert. *English Pageantry: An Historical Outline*. 2 vols. Cambridge: Harvard University Press, 1918–1920.

Wright, C.J., ed. *Sir Robert Cotton as Collector: Essays on an Early Stuart Courtier and his Legacy*. London: British Library, 1997.

The Fall of Troynovant:
Exemplarity after the Death of Henry, Prince of Wales

Michael Ullyot

> Hector is dead. There is no more to say.
> Stay yet. —
>
> Shakespeare, *Troilus and Cressida*

In royal entries and plague pamphlets, in history plays and civic pageants, early modern London sometimes wears an ancient guise. "I warrant we haue old hacksters in this great Grandmother of Corporations, Madame *Troynouant*," wrote Thomas Nashe in 1592.[1] His prediction was right: poets and "hacksters" like Thomas Dekker, George Peele, Thomas Middleton, William Herbert, and Henry Petowe praised London as the "Empresse of Cities, Troynouant," "*Troynouant* / That deckes this Thamesis on eyther side," "that all admired towne, / Where thousands still do trauell vp and downe."[2] As travellers thronged the streets of London for King James' coronation entry in 1604, Petowe described the city's lavish displays ("The Synowes of the Cittye Troynouant, / Clad in their richest robes in comely sort"), while Dekker's Genius of London delivered this magnanimous welcome to the king: "our hearts make good, what words doe want, / To bid thee boldly enter *Troynouant*."[3] When James obliged, William Herbert praised his effect on the city: "Mine eyes distill sweete teares, the teares of ioy, / To see *Troyes* issue raigne in new found *Troy*."[4]

These are but a few examples of the practice among early modern writers of presenting London as Troy reborn. It was a selective inheritance of Troy's glory before its fall, necessarily omitting the myth's more caution-

---

[1]Nashe, *Pierce Penilesse*, p. 181.
[2]Dekker, *Nevves from Graues-end*, D4r; Peele, *Decensus Astrææ*, A4r–A4v; Middleton, *Micro-cynicon*, C4v.
[3]Petowe, *Englands Cæsar*, C3v; Dekker, *Magnificent Entertainment*, p. 257.
[4]Herbert, *Prophesie of Cadwallader*, H4v.

ary elements. But everything changed in the early evening hours of Friday, 6 November 1612. An unexpected event made London suddenly resemble Troy in ways it had previously refused to consider:

> May not I liken *London* now to *Troy*
> As she was that same day she lost her *Hector?*
> When proud *Achilles* spoil'd her of her ioy
> (And triumph't on her losses) being victor?[5]

George Wither thus likens the event to Hector's death, an event so decisive for the outcome of the Trojan War that Homer used it to end his *Iliad*. When Hector falls prey to the Myrmidons in Shakespeare's *Troilus and Cressida*, their master Achilles exults, "So, Ilium, fall thou! Now, Troy, sink down! / Here lies thy heart, thy sinews and thy bone."[6] Yet this event wrought none of the literal destruction of Hector's death; unlike Troy, Troynovant was not about to be beset by a wooden horse or burning towers. While the fall of Troy began with dramatic public spectacles which had devastating personal consequences for its citizens, the fall of Troynovant began as a private affair, unknown to those outside a limited circle. Its implications, however, would soon resonate through civic and national spheres.

This event was obviously quite unexpected, for just two years after his creation as Prince of Wales, King James' son Henry had been the subject of both public acclaim and enthusiastic predictions of his future reign. Prince Henry's reputation for temperance and chivalry, his patronage of artists, and his predilection for muscular Protestantism had all inspired predictions of foreign and domestic policies to come—among them, Britain's participation in a pan-European Protestant coalition and a renaissance of arts, architecture, and letters. But late in October 1612, Henry was struck by an illness that would prove to be fatal. He languished on his deathbed in St. James' Palace for twelve days, surrounded by men with good intentions but inadequate medical knowledge. To calm his ravings and convulsions, the prince's physicians administered a cordial which caused him to sweat profusely. When this treatment failed, they "committed the rest into the hands of God, whom it pleased a litle [sic] after, to take from the world this most noble & heroicall soule up to himselfe."[7]

---

[5]Wither, *Prince Henries Obseqvies*, C3r.
[6]Shakespeare, *Troilus and Cressida*, 5.9.11–12.
[7]Mayerne, *Relation of the Sicknes and Death*, F2r.

I

Prince Henry's death made London's revival of Trojan civilization less discriminating than ever. The Troynovant myth relied on a close relationship between the city of London and its public figures, whose re-embodiment of Trojan virtues and claims to Trojan ancestry suffused this new civilization with the spirit of the old. Such was the claim of the poets who praised figures like James and Henry, who would trace their ancestry to Brute and thence to Troy. The roots of Troynovant ran more deeply than Thomas Nashe or William Herbert, of course, beginning in the twelfth century with Geoffrey of Monmouth's historiographic myth of Brute. From this outset, Britain's revival of Troy depended on public figures to embody the virtues of their ancestors in the reconstruction of their fallen city.

Troynovant's reliance on public figures had not abated by the early seventeenth century, but had changed its orientation from building to protecting Brute's city. London sought to emulate Troy's fame while avoiding its fate, by charging figures like Prince Henry with protecting it from destruction by furthering its glory. Henry's future and London's protection were perilously intertwined. In panegyrics, dedications, and other tributes, London's poets compared Henry to a cast of mythical and historical warrior-princes: Hector, Alexander the Great, the Black Prince, Henry VII. Elegies by the likes of Arthur Gorges and William Drummond lamented Henry's lost revival of his Trojan forebears: "A brauer youth, pale *Troy* with trembling walls / Did never see."[8] Just as the loss of these Trojan youths had left Troy vulnerable, the death of Henry reveals Troynovant's over-reliance on individual lives to support its imaginative self-image, which suffers a setback after his death. Prince Henry's story is a matter of life and death, rather than of poetic conventions, whose frailty and contingency reveal that the present occasionally fails to live up to the past. The success or failure of his life is revealed by its degree of resemblance to his exemplars' lives, but this is a contest Henry cannot win. His death does not forever disrupt the use of exemplars, which people need for both goals and warnings. However, this study will reveal that Henry's death exposed the truth behind these idealized images, that even exemplars are vulnerable to shifts of occasion.

To cite an exemplar is to reactivate the past through what Timothy Hampton calls a hermeneutic *applicatio*, an interpretive "application of a text to action in the world," with the aim of influencing one's objects (readers and spectators) in the world. In this application, "a contingent past activity

---

[8]Drummond, *Teares on the death of Meliades*, A3r.

is raised to a momentary universality that makes discernible its value for the present."[9] Exemplarity's present object actualizes this value by putting its ideas into practice, either by undertaking or avoiding a given course of action: distrusting flattering counsellors; upholding chaste love; or fighting foreign wars to quell internal dissent. Alexander Gelley notes that exemplarity's "outward reach to an agency of reception" always has a pragmatic "goal of ethical transformation."[10] Because exemplary biographies deliberately omit details that do not fit their author's purposes, exemplars are represented as living highly-artificial lives in which every action has a didactic purpose.[11] They are misrepresented as masters of their fates, but more importantly, of their reputations—of the laudatory or cautionary lessons they will teach future readers.

This study measures the impact of historical events in London in late 1612 on literary exemplarity, by examining texts written immediately before and after the death of Prince Henry. I advocate the extension of studies of exemplarity from the genres on which critics such as Hampton and Gelley have traditionally concentrated—namely epic, biblical scripture, tragedy, the non-fiction essay, and prose fiction—to include such texts as panegyrics, dedications, and elegies. Rather than distorting past experience by removing its contingency, many of these occasional texts find in this very contingency the neglected lesson of universal variability, of the need to anticipate human vulnerability.

I focus on panegyrics, dedications, and elegies because they dominate literary treatments of the prince immediately before and after his death, and because they contrast so starkly in their uses of mythical and historical exemplars. In life, the tributes and dedications Henry received from the likes of Thomas Dekker, Michael Drayton, William Herbert, and George Chapman express overly optimistic forms of exemplarity. In death, the elegies for Henry by William Drummond of Hawthornden, Arthur Gorges, Thomas Heywood, James Maxwell, George Wither, John Webster and others dismantle the optimistic exemplarity which characterized Henry's lifetime. Finally, John Browne's Latin elegy suggests that Henry's death reveals the vulnerability plaguing his exemplars themselves. By reorienting

---

[9]Hampton, *Writing from History*, p. 11.

[10]Gelley, *Unruly Examples*, p. 3.

[11]Hampton posits biography as the ideal form of exemplary narratives because it depicts virtues prevailing through time, rather than as aberrations (*Writing from History*, p. 26). These biographies succeed in guiding present behaviour only if they are more purposeful than the contingent, meandering lives of their present readers.

exemplarity's *applicatio*, Henry's death reveals (*pace* Hampton) that contingency itself is the most valuable universal lesson.

Elegy is a reluctant genre, whose poets conventionally struggle against the turn of events that occasions it. With its requisite preoccupation with human frailty, elegy lacks the exuberance of panegyric. When Prince Henry died, those writing in his memory could no longer project his glorious future, but were forced to confront this failure in verse. While the more pedestrian elegies for Henry merely express their disbelief and console his mourners, others invert the standard methods of exemplarity. Rather than applying past experiences to present circumstances, an *applicatio* whose distortion is most evident when the present has manifestly failed to re-enact the past, these elegies review past exemplars through the lens of this failure. In these elegies the legacies of the long-departed dead are not always glorious, because of their resemblance to the more recently dead. The reception of Henry's death proves not that the present is inadequate to the past, but that past exemplars are equally vulnerable to shifts of occasion.

II

In the days immediately before Henry's death, the city of London seems to have thought itself exempt from the tragedies of the past. On 29 October 1612, London received its new mayor Sir John Swinnerton with a spectacular Lord Mayor's Show which praised the occasion as worthy of comparison to the past. "This was that day for Antique deeds renown'd," recalled Richard Niccols, when "people, yeare by yeare, with triumph crownd / To honour their elected Magistrate."[12] This year, the allegorical triumphs were provided by Thomas Dekker's *Troia-Noua Triumphans* (*London Triumphing*), whose adherence to the didactic and panegyric conventions of Lord Mayor's Shows did not prevent it from acknowledging its present circumstances and audience.[13] The servant to many masters, Dekker praises the king, the city, the twelve livery companies and specifically the Merchant Taylors, of whom both Swinnerton and Prince Henry had been made free. Civic pageants are for the admiration of common people, Dekker notes, but even "*Princes* themselues take pleasure to behold them." This is a nod to the noble spectators Dekker expected to be present: Prince Henry and the Elector Palatine, Frederick V.[14] Along with the Lord

---

[12]Niccols, *Three Sisters Teares*, B3r. On this customary annual date of Tudor-Stuart mayoral inaugurations, see Manley, *Literature and Culture*, p. 219.

[13]Bergeron describes the occasion of this pageant in "Prince Henry," pp. 113–114. On sources of the iconographical and allegorical elements of English civic pageantry, see Bergeron, "Symbolic Landscape" and "Emblematic Nature."

[14]Dekker, *Troia-Noua Triumphans*, p. 230. Frederick and his entourage were in

Mayor's presence, Prince Henry's spectatorship of *Troia-Noua Triumphans* was essential to realizing the didactic purpose of such a ceremony to *laudando praecipere*, or to teach by praising.[15]

Dekker's four allegorical devices promoted the virtues Prince Henry and Sir John Swinnerton required to protect and preserve Troynovant as a kind of prelapsarian Troy, a glorious civilization before its fall. Following behind the chariot of Neptune and the fort of Furies, the throne of Virtue was presented to Swinnerton supported by the livery companies, "*All* arm'd, *to knit their* Nerues (*in* One) *with* Thine, / *To guard* this new Troy." Dekker's final device "and highest honour," the House of Fame, paid yet another tribute to his own company and to its noblest member.[16] There, alongside Fame herself, "In other seuerall places sit Kings, Princes, and Noble persons, who haue bene free of the *Marchant-tailors*: A perticular roome being reserued for one that represents the person of *Henry* the now [*sic*] Prince of *Wales*."[17] Dekker urges his audience to admire Henry's illustrious ancestors like Henry VII, who grafted the red rose to the white: "*A* Sprig *of which* Branch, (Highest *now but* One) / *Is* Henry Prince of Wales, *followed by none*."[18]

London for his forthcoming marriage to Henry's sister Elizabeth. Dekker praises his livery company, the Merchant Taylors, for assuming the considerable cost of "*Heightning*" this pageant for "our best-to-be-beloued friends, the *Noblest strangers*," and "to do honour to their Prince and Countrey" (Dekker, *Troia-Noua Triumphans*, pp. 230, 231). Werner concludes from this reference to Henry that rather than describing the events of the day (as recorded by an eyewitness), Dekker's account was composed and perhaps even printed beforehand ("A German Eye-witness," p. 253). Hoy argues that "Prince Henry had been invited to attend with his future brother-in-law" (Hoy, *Introductions, Notes, and Commentaries*, vol. III, p. 133).

15Manley, *Literature and Culture*, p. 215.

16Dekker, *Troia-Noua Triumphans*, pp. 236, 240.

17For the honorary membership of the Merchant Taylor's company, see the roll presented to James on Henry's investiture in Clode, *Early History*, vol. I, pp. 292–304; for an account of the ceremony in June 1607, see Birch, *Life of Henry*, G6v–G7v, pp. 92–94. Prince Henry was made free of the company in 1607, with an elaborate entertainment written by Ben Jonson and planned in part by Swinnerton, a second-generation Merchant Taylor since 1589 (Clode, vol. I, p. 263; Heaton and Knowles, "'Entertainment Perfect,'" pp. 593, 595). Thanks to Scott Schofield for bringing this to my attention.

18Dekker, *Troia-Noua Triumphans*, p. 241. As Bergeron notes, references to the union of York and Lancaster recur in civic pageantry from Elizabeth's first royal entry of 1559 to the last Jacobean Lord Mayor's Show of 1624, John Webster's *Monuments of Honor* (*English Civic Pageantry*, p. 173). In his inaugural speech to Parliament, King James sought to surpass the legacy of his ancestor Henry VII, whose "Vnion of these two princely houses is nothing comparable to the Vnion of two ancient & famous Kingdoms," England and Scotland (*Kings Maiesties Speech*, A4v).

Dekker's premise for predicting the prince's future is the genealogical link between Prince Henry and his famous ancestors, more than their shared livery company. The players who impersonate England's past and future kings suggest that Henry's own virtue and fame will resemble what Niccols calls the "Antique deeds renown'd" of his ancestors. These ancestors not only permit his inheritance of the crown, they bequeath to him the virtues necessary to maintain and glorify the kingdom. Henry stands on the verge of a grand and storied future because he is also at the culmination of this overdetermining past. With its assurances that England will prosper if Henry re-enacts the virtues of his ancestors, *Troia-Noua Triumphans* foreshadows the royal entries Dekker might have written for King Henry IX. Its conservatism is essential to royal panegyric, the genre from which civic pageants borrowed most heavily.[19]

This indebtedness is evident from even the limited number of pane-gyrics written in the decade before Henry's death. The Tudor myth exploited throughout the sixteenth century revealed the extent to which the past could be shaped by the present—or more specifically, by the present desire for a genealogical link between Aeneas and Henry VII through Brutus. Genealogies continued to promote various agendas in the next century, when the technique of *laudando praecipere* (teaching by praising) recurred even in self-praise. At his accession, James spoke to parliament of "my descent lineally out of the loynes of *Henrie* the seuenth," both to legitimize his inheritance and to assert his reunion of the kingdoms divided after Brutus.[20] At James' royal entry in March 1604, Michael Drayton found this Tudor family tree too confined for Prince Henry's praise. In his *Paean Trivmphall* Drayton describes "the faire Prince" in both narrative and historical contexts as one "in whom appear'd in glory, / As in th'abridge-ment of some famous story, / Eu'ry rare vertue of each famous King / Since *Norman Williams* happie conquering."[21] Like Dekker's pageant, Drayton's panegyric demands a suspension of disbelief in order to give local events the broad resonance they deserve. Never mind that Henry was scarcely a month past his tenth birthday at the time of this entry; Drayton's subject is no mere child, but the locus of a nation's hopes for a future king worthy of comparisons with his famous ancestors. By emulating the ancestors he

---

[19]On relations between civic entertainments and royal entries, and particularly on the mutual dependence of city and crown, see Manley, *Literature and Culture*, pp. 216–221.

[20] James, *Kings Maiesties Speech*, A4v.

[21]Drayton, *Paean Trivmphall*, A4r–A4v. Drayton's narrative expectations for Henry are clear in this poem, particularly in its closing injunction to "Liue ever mightie, happely, and long, / Liuing admir'd, and dead be highly song" (B3v).

resembles by birth, Henry will earn a comparable reputation—initiating another panegyric cycle for his own descendants.

Panegyric is a self-perpetuating genre, but its motives are not entirely self-serving. By promoting parallels between past exemplary subjects and present objects, it urges those objects toward such civic-minded goals as restoring the greatness of past civilizations. If this public-spirited project demands a little hyperbole, so much the better. As we have seen, in 1604 William Herbert celebrated King James' descent from Trojan stock in *A Prophesie of Cadwallader*: "Mine eyes distill sweete teares, the teares of ioy, / To see *Troyes* issue raigne in new found *Troy*."[22] In Herbert's blear-eyed logic, this city ruled by new Trojans must itself be a new Troy. Such euphoria lasted well into James' reign. In 1609 Thomas Heywood dedicated *Troia Britanica* to one of the king's privy counsellors, Edward, Earl of Worcester, praising king and peers alike:

> Tis fit those Lordes which we from Troy deriue,
> Should in the Fate of Troy remembred be,
> For since their Graund-sire vertues now suruiue,
> And with the Spirits of this Age agree.

Had Homer or Virgil survived, added Heywood, "Rankt next to Troy, our Troy-novant should be, / And next the Troyan Peeres, your places free."[23] Neither panegyrics nor dedications are known for sober assessments of their intended readers or audience. Both have a weakness for literary conventions that cast the living in terms usually reserved for the glorious dead, because they hope to preserve their living reputations for posterity. To this end, their poets suggest that either they or a ready supply of future scribes will gladly turn noble actions into yet more representations.

Many of Henry's elegists express the calamity of his death in precisely these terms, gesturing toward the lost narratives Henry's life would have inspired. The anonymous sonnet sequence *Great Brittans Mourning Garment*, written and printed with impressive speed for the prince's funeral on 7 December, expresses its poet's frustrated expectations for Henry's future in generous terms: "A thousand graces with him buried lie, / A thousand Triumphs, and a thousand loues."[24] Charles Lawson's Latin elegy for the Cambridge memorial volume *Epicedivm Cantabrigiense* compares Henry to an array of exemplars, including Hercules, Alexander, Caesar, Achilles, Hector, and Menelaus. Such lists appear aimless, but their deliberately vague

---

[22] Herbert, *Prophesie of Cadwallader*, H4v.
[23] Heywood, *Troia Britanica*, A3v.
[24] *Great Brittans Mourning Garment*, B1v.

copiousness connotes the full range of Henry's lost virtues. Lawson implies that with adequate time, Henry would have resembled any of these models: "*Illis par animo, si par aetate suisset, / Quid ni fortunâ? Spes satis ampla suit.*" [Had he equaled them in age and in spirit, why not also in fortune? Expectation was sufficiently ample.][25] William Drummond reiterates that misfortune, not weakness, caused Henry's untimely death: "That thou did not attaine these honours spheares, / Through lacke of power it was not, but of yeares."[26]

Exemplarity's paradox lies in its contradictory notions of historical engagement and historical selectiveness, its adoption of either positive or negative lessons from past experiences. Panegyric uses exemplars to impose unrealistic expectations on its present objects, by distorting and denying the true vulnerability of its past subjects. While any deficiencies in the lives and reputations of the "Kings, Princes, and Noble persons" standing alongside Henry in Dekker's House of Fame had long since been eclipsed by the passage of time, Henry's death soon disrupts his smooth transition into the panegyric future Dekker has imagined for him. Few things ruin a good triumph like the spectre of death.[27] *Troia-Noua Triumphans* typifies panegyric's disjunction between reality and its representations by promoting a triumphant image that neither its object nor its audience can sustain. Henry's death nullifies Dekker's implicit promises: that by embodying the virtues of his historical exemplars, he and his subjects will enjoy good fortune under his reign; and that this stable future will be immune to past misfortune so long as Henry embodies these exemplary virtues from the past. His death proves decisively that this conservative genre has no power to conserve.

For Prince Henry's subjects on 29 October 1612, there was no contrast between the player impersonating their prince in the streets of London and the pale figure lying on his deathbed in St. James' Palace. Dekker's undoing owes not to his use of exemplarity as a poetic technique, but merely to his unfortunate timing. The stark contrast between these two Henries exposes the gap between representations of exemplary figures and an underlying reality that is, in this instance, drastically different. This contrast was later noted by Richard Niccols, whose moralizing account of *Troia-Noua Triumphans* is filled with references to wanton excesses, fashionable displays,

---

[25]Lawson, "*Fvneris infandi coram,*" I2r.

[26]Drummond, *Teares on the death of Meliades,* A3r.

[27]The exception is funeral triumphs, designed to defy death's power by inverting their defeat of the dead. Recalling Henry's funeral procession, Wither asks, "What needed all that Cerimonious show?" The answer comes quickly: "it shew'd that though he wanted breath, / Yet he should ride in tryumph ouer death" (*Prince Henries Obseqvies,* D2v).

prodigious eating and drinking, and general idleness among Dekker's audience: "VVith diuers change of fashions and of face, / That stately townes proud streets did ebb and flow." Niccols paraphrases their mood before Henry's death cracks this exemplary façade:

> Let not vaine doubt disturbe our strengthned state,
> Nor feare awake our peace with warres alarm's,
> ....
> Inioy we not the Sonne of such a King
> So faire a branch, which now such fruit doth beare,
> That from such fruit, such hopes already spring,
> That our great Fortunes shake the world with feare?[28]

The wisdom of hindsight allows Niccols to view Dekker's audience with ironic detachment, and to characterize their optimism as presumption. His images of the heady days immediately preceding Henry's death are conventional to elegy, but they underscore the contrast between Dekker's representations and their underlying reality. In this expectant atmosphere, Henry's subjects had little reason to probe beyond what they saw.

Until he withdrew from the public arena only four days before this pageant, Prince Henry had been the very picture of youthful vitality and resilience. At eighteen years of age, two years after being created Prince of Wales, "he was tall and of an high stature," recalled William Haydon, his senior Groom of the Bedchamber, "his body was strong and well proportioned, his shoulders were broad . . . the colour of his face some what swarte and scorched with the sunne."[29] Niccols himself recalls that "Nature in constructure of those parts" of Henry's physical body, "The grace of all good feature gaue to him / In euery Muskle, member, ioynt and limbe."[30] Throughout the sweltering summer of 1612, Henry had tested the limits of his physical endurance. He rode horses for days on end, ate "Oysters both raw and dressed with fire, at euery meale, three or foure dayes in the weeke," and cooled himself with midnight swims in the Thames.[31] When he first complained of a fever, the royal physician Theodore Turquet de Mayerne attributed the illness to excessive and repeated chafing of the blood.[32] In

---

[28]Niccols, *Three Sisters Teares*, B2v, B3v.

[29]Haydon, *Trve Picture*, D4r. I owe the attribution of this 1634 biography to Strong (*Henry*, p. 5).

[30]Niccols, *Three Sisters Teares*, D2v.

[31]Mayerne, *Relation of the Sicknes*, E1r. Henry's predilections flouted his father's quite specific advice in *Basilicon Doron*: "Let all your food bee simple, without composition or sauces; which are more like medecines then meate" (p. 50).

[32]Mayerne's journal, BL Sloane MS. 1679, gives a detailed account of Henry's

early October, Mayerne obliged the prince to rest more frequently at his residence in Richmond Palace. Henry defied his physician's advice, however, continuing to neglect both his health and the dictates of the weather. Only days before Swinnerton's entry as Lord Mayor, the prince played an exhausting outdoor tennis match in which he ignored "the former weake estate of his body" and "looked so wonderfull ill and pale, that all the beholders tooke notice thereof, muttering to one another what they feared."[33] This match was thought to have fatally exacerbated Henry's condition, and on 25 October he finally obeyed his doctor's orders. His condition rapidly deteriorated until he died at eight o'clock on Friday evening, 6 November 1612.[34]

III

When Henry's chaplain Daniel Price lamented in a memorial sermon that the prince "would haue been *subiect* for all pens, and *obiect* for all eies," he was only half right.[35] The literary impact of Henry's death was both immediate and unprecedented. Nearly every active poet in London, Edinburgh, and both universities contributed an elegy to the more than forty memorial anthologies and single-author volumes that were printed or circulated in manuscript.[36] In those prolific days after Henry's demise, any

---

symptoms and physiology; for a summary see Nance, *Turquet de Mayerne*, pp. 171–190. Though Moore concludes that only the pathology of Mayerne's time prevented him from recognizing Henry's illness as enteric fever (*History of the Study of Medicine*, p. 96), retrospective diagnoses are notoriously unreliable. We now know little more about Henry's illness than the English Ambassador to Venice knew in December 1612, when he described it as "a continuous fever that became violent and malignant, refusing to yield to any medicine or remedy" (*Calendar of State Papers-Venice*, p. 464).

[33]Hawkins, *Life and Death*, C3r–C3v. Cornwallis refers to the incident in his *Discourse*: "at tennis play . . . he neither observed moderation, not what appertained to his dignity and person, continuing oftentimes his play for the space of three or four hours, and the same in his shirt . . . . Of this and of his diet, wherein he shewed too much inclination to excessive eating of fruits, he was, as in all other things, content to hear advice, but in these two particulars not to follow it" (pp. 16–17).

[34]Haydon, *Trve Picture*, D4v. The Venetian ambassador erroneously reports the time of death at two hours after midnight on Friday (*Calendar of State Papers-Venice*, p. 448).

[35]Price, *Spiritvall Odovrs*, C4v.

[36]"Posthumous testimonials to the talents and virtues of that very promising Prince, Henry Frederick . . . were so numerous, that a mere enumeration of them would run on to considerable extent," notes Bridges (*Restituta*, vol. III, p. 477). Despite Pigman's appeal in 1985, there is still no comprehensive bibliography of Prince Henry's elegies (*Grief*, p. 143 n.2). For incomplete lists, see Edmond, "Elegies," pp. 146–158; Nichols, *Progresses*, vol. II, pp. 504–512; and Bridges, *Restituta*, vol. IV, p. 172.

reluctance to compose elegies virtually disappeared. Thomas Heywood wrote his *Fvnerall Elegie* "wishing with my soule, I might haue had a more pleasing subiect," while conceding that "since the Heauens haue giuen vs this cause it is a duty to entertaine the occasion, and an vnswerable [*sic*] negligence to omit it."[37] "Never before," observes Dennis Kay, "had so many elegies been written on a single occasion, by such a wide range of practitioners: poets of all kinds, all (or most) religious and political persuasions."[38] The release of a nation's hopes and expectations for its future king required most available outlets of expression, surging forth in sermons, diaries, letters, and thousands of lines of elegies.

Preaching over Henry's body in St. James' chapel, Daniel Price predicted this widespread sorrow: "all the orders and *Companies* . . . of all this *Realme*, from the honourable Counsellour, to him that draweth water, from the man of *grey yeeres*, to the young *child*, shall plentifully water their *cheekes*."[39] "The staines of sorrow are in euery face," George Wither intoned as he witnessed the news take hold.[40] Some years earlier Thomas Dekker had written in his plague pamphlet, *Nevves from Graues-end*, of the imagined impact of a prince's death on a city and its people:

> For Princes death's do euen bespeake
> Millions of liues; when Kingdomes breake,
> People dissolue, and (as with Thunder)
> Cities proud glories rent asunder.[41]

As Dekker had anticipated, Prince Henry's death would have a devastating effect on the language of London's self-image. It brought an abrupt end to many years of anticipation of the "proud glories" to come under his reign, and more immediately, to the city's exemption from the problems of the past. Through these veils of tears, Dekker's *Troia-Noua Triumphans* must have appeared ever more blurred and distant.

The genre suitable to this occasion was diametrically opposite to panegyric, as Thomas Heywood soon suggested: "Had all the world deuis'd one *Tragedy*, / And drawne the proiect from a thousand yeares, / From the spectators could it draw more teares?"[42] Yet Henry's subjects were hardly spectators to the tragedy of Henry, Prince of Wales. Not only had they

[37]Heywood, *Fvnerall Elegie*, A2r.
[38]Kay, *Melodious Tears*, p. 124.
[39]Price, *Teares shed over Abner*, N2r.
[40]Wither, *Prince Henries Obseqvies*, D4r.
[41]Dekker, *Nevves from Graues-end*, D4v.
[42]Heywood, *Fvnerall Elegie*, A4v.

witnessed little of its unfolding, they had invested greater expectations of future glory and civic protection in Henry than in any strutting protagonist—save one. Henry's death did bear a resemblance to one previously staged tragedy cited by Heywood:

> ... as oft-times we see
> (Presented in a lofty buskind stile)
> *Achilles* fall, *Thersites* to scape free,
> The eminent *Hector* on the dead-mans file
> Numbred and rank't, when men more base then he
> Suruiue the battell of lesse worth and stile.
>   So thousands haue suruiu'd these mortall brals,
>   Whil'st amongst millions, standing, *Henry* fals.[43]

That men of "lesse worth and stile" still stand is a testament to Henry's protection, but it is hardly a fitting legacy. Henry lost a decisive battle in the figurative war in which every being struggles for survival, the "mortall brals" his survivors are left to fight. Heywood recalls Hector's death in plays like Shakespeare's *Troilus and Cressida* to draw an adequate response from his fellow citizens: "Not for Him then, but for our selues lament."[44] Such self-concern after the death of a public figure reproduces the mourning for Hector in Troy, whose dependence on its greatest warrior and Priam's heir is so acute that in bemoaning his death, its citizens lament their own.

With Henry protecting Troynovant from Troy's fall, the city's dependence on the prince became as essential to London's future as Hector had been to Troy's. On this scale, Henry's death merely reminded his subjects that both civic and individual exemplars could bequeath both positive and negative legacies. On a more personal scale, however, the effects of his death were more injurious. Heywood drew an emotive parallel between King James and his Trojan forebear:

> ... *Priam*, as it was to thee
> When worthy *Hector*, both the first and last
> Of all *Troyes* hopes, sunke dead; me thinkes I see
> in Royall Iames, thy sorrowes quite surpast,
>   With double anguish, treble passions fired,
>   When he first heard Prince *Henry* was expired.[45]

---

[43]Heywood, *Fvnerall Elegie*, B1r.
[44]Heywood, *Fvnerall Elegie*, C3v.
[45]Heywood, *Fvnerall Elegie*, C2r.

Other elegists echoed this lament. As one wrote of Henry, simply, "thou yᵉ Hector wert of her new Troye."[46] Arthur Gorges extended his sympathy to other members of the royal family, drawing parallels between mourning Trojans and bereft Britons:

> Contemplate but Troyes greife when Hector fell;
> And pensive Priamus and Hecuba;
> Or lovelie Paris how his hart did swell;
> Or the sadd teares of faire Polixena;
>   You may conceipt the woe of Troynovant,
>   Of James, Anne, Charles, Eliza for theire want.
>
> New Troy her Prince, James wayles his Hector heire:
> Anne moanes the prime braunch of her owne selfe gon:
> Charles mournes this losse, which he cannot repaire.
> For what cann value deere affection?
>   But faire Eliza (when she heard the newes)
>   Polixen like all comfort did refuse.[47]

These precedents of familial mourning recognize that exemplars can easily turn cautionary. The meaning of the Troy-narrative has shifted since its recent appearances in panegyrics and dedications. It now warns against relying on an individual, mutable hero like Hector, "the first and last / Of all *Troyes* hopes." For the uneasy spectators of Henry's tragedy, the suffering of these principal characters is difficult to witness.

   Elegists approached the new meaning of Troy with a mix of regret and anticipation. When Thomas Campion suggests that Prince Henry's death surpasses even the death of Priam, his elegy staggers under the weight of an epic subject: "O singing wayle a fate more truely funerall, / Then when with all his sonnes the sire of Troy did fall."[48] Any reader of Virgil will tell you that mourning the death of Priam is a prelude to Troy's resurrection. Yet Campion makes no mention of Aeneas, let alone of his grandson Brutus or of the founding of Rome or Britain. This is because circumstances immediately after Henry's death preclude a triumphant Virgilian narrative of reconstruction in favour of a tragic Homeric narrative of destruction. William Drummond uses the narrative implications of Henry's death to sketch an epic outline for his lost biography:

---

[46]G. B., *Cestria Lugens*, p. 243.

[47]Gorges, *Olympian Catastrophe*, ll. 1033–1044; pp. 175–176. This poem exists only in manuscript (Huntington MS Ellesmere 1130) and in modern editions. Upon hearing of Henry's death, his sister Elizabeth refused all food for days, and "not even the presence of her future husband could console her" (Williams, *Anne of Denmark*, p. 151).

[48]Campion, *Songs of Mourning*, C1r.

A booke had beene of thy illustrious deedes.
So to their nephewes aged Syres had told
The high exploits perform'd by thee of olde;
Townes raz'd, and rais'd, victorious, vanquish'd bands,
Fierce Tyrants flying, foyl'd, kild by thy hands.
And in deare Arras, Virgins faire had wrought
The Bayes and Trophees to thy countrie brought:
While some great *Homer* imping wings to fame,
Deafe *Nilus* dwellers had made heare thy name.[49]

At least some of the pathos of Henry's death derives from his elegists' disappointment at their loss of heroic material for these unwritten texts. While calling on virgins and poets, young and old alike, to recount Henry's brave deeds, Drummond evidently succeeded only in intimidating his countrymen. Henry's elegists knew that their genre was inadequate compared to the heroic narratives his life might have inspired. Few were prepared to undertake this epic, least of all Henry's first true biographer John Hawkins, who hesitated to write what he calls "so high a task, (which rather would become some *Homer, Virgil, Demosthenes, Cicero*, or rather some one in whom all their excellencies are combined, to performe aright)."[50] The poet John Taylor protested that Henry's worth surpasses poetry's capacity to express it ("Not any Poets all-reuiuing pen / Can write vnparalel'd Prince *Henries* praise"), though he invoked greater poets who might be up to the task ("that I could to *Virgills* veine aspire, / Or *Homers* Verse").[51] Much of this humility is the conventional posture of poets deliberately limiting their readers' expectations. Their references to epic poets nonetheless suggest that Henry's life was widely expected to have fit this specific generic mould. The difficulty these poets anticipated was not in writing this Henriad, but in forming an epic from such disappointing source-material.

John Webster was unimpressed by their results, dismissing many of the elegies for Henry as "scraps of commendation more base / Then are the ragges they are writ on, ô disgrace / To nobler Poesie." He went on to praise the prince as "a reuerend subiect to be pend / Onely by his sweet *Homer* and my frend."[52] Webster's "frend" is George Chapman, who like Drummond inspired rampant anxiety among the prince's elegists.[53] Unlike

---

[49]Drummond, *Teares on the death of Meliades*, A2v.

[50]Hawkins, *Life and Death,* p. 3. This book is based on BL Add. MS 30075; a copy (BL Add. MS 11532) is dated 1613.

[51]Taylor, *Great Britaine*, A3r.

[52]Webster, *Monvmental Colvmne*, C1r.

[53]Webster thus suggests that the *Iliad* is Henry's ideal biography. The identification

Drummond, however, Chapman actually provided Henry with an epic and a model for the prince's ideal narrative. His translations of Homer's Iliad, dedicated to Henry in 1609 and again in 1611, encouraged this "high borne prince of men" to govern himself by the classical models associated with this text.[54] Yet Chapman's epistle does not advise Henry to imitate Homer's characters themselves, owing perhaps to a New Trojan's ambivalence toward the Greek aggressors, or toward Hector's vulnerability. Instead, Chapman urges Henry to emulate such "Princely presidents" as Alexander the Great, Homer's ideal reader.[55] According to Chapman, Alexander's admiration for Achilles began with his reading of Homer, where he found

> *him* reuiu'd
> For whose life, *Alexander* would haue giuen
> One of his kingdomes: who (as sent from heauen,
> And thinking well, that so diuine a creature
> VVould neuer more enrich the race of Nature)
> Kept as his Crowne his workes; and thought them still
> His Angels; in all power, to rule his will.
> And would affirme that *Homers* poesie
> Did more aduance his Asian victorie
> Then all his Armies. O! tis wondrous much
> (Though nothing prisde) that the right vertuous touch
> Of a well written soule, to vertue moues.
> Nor haue we soules to purpose, if their loues
> Of fitting obiects be not so inflam'd.[56]

Chapman emphasizes the influence of Homer's text on its most famous reader in order to show Prince Henry how exemplarity works. His apostrophe to exemplarity as a "touch" of the reader's soul by "a well written soule" insinuates his poetry into a causal relationship with Henry's future heroism. If Henry follows Alexander and allows this text "to rule his will," Achilles' "diuine" example will surely inspire more worldly conquests in the future. Because Chapman aims to turn Henry into his own model reader, he says nothing of Alexander's "Asian victorie" beyond its indebt-

---

comes from David Gunby's commentary on Webster's *Monvmental Colvmne* in *The Works of John Webster*, forthcoming from Cambridge University Press, which he kindly allowed me to consult; for corroboration, see Webster, *Complete Works*, ed. Lucas, vol. III, p. 289.

[54]Chapman translated twelve books of Homer's *Iliad* as *Homer Prince of Poets* (1609) and the remainder as *Iliads of Homer Prince of Poets* (1611).

[55]Chapman, *Iliads of Homer*, *2r.

[56]Chapman, *Iliads of Homer*, *2r–*2v.

edness to a reading of Homer; he relies on readers to recall these victories in order to conceive the shape of Henry's future.

Chapman's translation, and its selective treatment of Alexander in its dedication to Prince Henry, are essential to understanding both the workings and the risks of exemplarity. First, its use of Alexander's biography concurs with Hampton's description of the exemplar's life constituting a "multitude of discrete metonymically related segments or moments."[57] Chapman parcels out a discrete segment of Alexander's life, his reading of Homer, because this is all he needs (he hopes) to convince Henry that Chapman's text can play a similar role. By imitating one of these "metonymically related segments," which attempts to encapsulate an exemplar fully, the reader will ultimately resemble his model. Exemplarity's willingly derivative object must be judged against this model to gauge the success or failure of this resemblance. This system's shortcomings should be evident to any translator, including Chapman, who knows that a source-text is greater than the sum of its linguistic parts and literary style, and that much is lost in the translation.

To give distant texts a local immediacy through *translatio*, in its various forms, is also the aim of humanist translation. Exemplarity is at bottom a humanist undertaking, insofar as it attempts to give remote narratives and experiences a local immediacy through practical imitation. It assumes the same risks and rewards of humanist translation, including its vulnerability to the criticism that its object may not live up to its subject, just as a translated text may fall short of its source. Thomas Greene has argued that humanist texts rely on "precarious lifelines, imitations of cultural sequence, defining each work . . . as a vulnerable extension out of the remote into a self-creating, self-vindicating present."[58] Panegyric specializes in self-vindication, in its assumptions that the future will always resemble the past. But after witnessing panegyric's spectacular failure, we must conclude that it cannot effect change in the world if this world will not cooperate. In spite of its prescriptions and its didactic aims, panegyric makes nothing happen.

Neither does elegy, whose dead subject is hardly amenable to being taught how to live. Elegy forces poets to approximate their occasional representations to the truth, to temper their hyperbole with the experience of failure. With failure as its premise, elegy deals not only with what might have been, but also with what truly happened. In John Browne's elegy, for

---

[57] Hampton, *Writing from History*, p. 26.
[58] Greene, "Erasmus' 'Festina lente,'" p. 17. In Greene's formulation, the humanist text is vulnerable because it risks denigrating its source, "falling into travesty or pollution" (p. 14).

example, Henry is made to begin by coveting the glittering trophies and grand monuments of his exemplars, only to vanish, leaving scarcely a trace behind:

> *Flos Iuuenum Henricus templo residebat Honoris*
>   *Magnorum aspiciens clara trophæa virum.*
> *Cæsaris hic laudes, illic sæva arma Britanni*
>   *Arthuri, Macedum visa et imago ducis.*
> *Hæc ait ostendunt fortes, Martisque nepotes,*
>   *Dignaque supremo sunt monumenta Ioue.*
> *Vos tamen O cæli Reges modo cedite vitam,*
>   *Ac laudes æquas reddere spero meas.*
> *Dixit, sed subito tenues vanescit in auras,*
>   *Vitaque crudeli reddita præda neci.*
> [Henry, the flower of youth, was sitting in the Temple of Honour
>   Viewing the bright trophies of great men.
> Here the glories of Caesar, there the savage arms of British
>   Arthur, and the image seen of the Macedons' general.
> "These," he said, "show the brave, and grandsons of Mars,
>   And are worthy monuments to highest Jove.
> Yet you, O Kings of heaven, now yield your life,
>   And I hope to render my glories equal."
> He spoke, but suddenly vanishes into thin wind,
>   And life was rendered prey to cruel slaughter.][59]

Browne telescopes the prince's life and unexpected death into a few lines, juxtaposing Henry's projected glory with his senseless death. His is the only elegy to depict Henry's moment of death, his sudden shift from one legacy to another. By presenting this immediate event rather than a reflection after the fact, Browne forces the reader to confront Henry's unavoidable legacy of failure. Like Dekker's House of Fame, Browne's Temple of Honour is a place for young men to find models of both martial heroism and worthy reputations. More crucial than any similarity, however, is this difference: Browne's "glories" are mere vainglory, as insubstantial as the wind.

With an immediacy found in only one other elegy that we have considered—Heywood's tragedy of "these mortall brals"—Browne highlights the crisis exemplarity faced after Henry's death. After a lifetime of expectations and exhortations had suddenly collapsed, these elegies reveal how swiftly representations of Henry shifted their gaze from forward to reverse, optimism to pessimism, and inspiration to caution. Henry's premature death earned him the rare misfortune of becoming an exemplar before his time, not of virtue but of vulnerability. It takes Browne's representation

---

[59]Lawson, "*Flos Iuuenum Henricus*," F2v–F3r. I thank Irina A. Dumitrescu for this translation.

of Henry's final moments to appreciate how deceptive the poets' exemplars of past glory can be. Their lives, distorted by eulogistic narratives which smooth over inconsistencies and occasional rough patches, leave present readers and audiences unconfronted by their own vulnerability.[60]

WORKS CITED

G. B. " *'Cestria Lugens': A Collection of epitaphs and elegies on Prince Henry by one 'G.B.'* " Dennis Kay. *Melodious Tears: The English Funeral Elegy from Spenser to Milton.* Oxford: Clarendon, 1990. Appendix A. 233–250.

Bergeron, David M. "The Emblematic Nature of English Civic Pageantry." *Renaissance Drama* n.s. 1 (1968): 167–198.

Bergeron, David M. *English Civic Pageantry, 1558–1642.* Columbia: University of South Carolina Press, 1971.

Bergeron, David M. "Prince Henry and English Civic Pageantry." *Tennessee Studies in Literature* 13 (1968): 109–116.

Bergeron, David M. "Symbolic Landscape in English Civic Pageantry." *Renaissance Quarterly* 22 (1969): 32–27.

Birch, Thomas. *The Life of Henry Prince of Wales, Eldest Son of King James I.* London, 1760. Wing C6330.

Bridges, Egerton. *Restituta; or, Titles, Extracts, and Characters of Old Books in English Literature, Revived.* 4 vols. London: Longman, 1814–1816.

Browne, John. "*Flos Iuuenum Henricus templo residebat Honoris . . . .*" *Epicedivm Cantabrigiense, In obitum immaturum, semperq; deflendum, Henrici, Illustrissimi Principis Walliae, &c.* Cambridge, 1612. STC 4481. F2v–F3r.

Calendar of State Papers–Venice. Ed. Rawdon Brown and G. C. Bentinck. 38 vols. London: H.M. Stationery Office, 1864–1947.

Campion, John. *Songs of Mourning: Bevvailing the vntimely death of Prince Henry. VVorded by Tho. Campion. And set forth to bee sung with one voyce to the Lute, or Violl: By John Coprario.* London, 1613. STC 4546.

Chapman, George. *Homer Prince of Poets: Translated according to the Greeke. in twelue Bookes of his Iliads.* London, 1609. STC 13633.

Chapman, George. *The Iliads of Homer Prince of Poets. Neuer before in any languag* [sic] *truely translated.* London, 1611. STC 13634.

Clode, Charles M. *The Early History of the Guild of Merchant Taylors of the Fraternity of St. John the Baptist, London.* 2 vols. London: Harrison, 1888.

Cornwallis, Charles. *A Discourse of the Most Illustrious Prince, Henry, late Prince of Wales. Written, Anno 1626.* London, 1641. Wing C6329.

Dekker, Thomas. *The Magnificent Entertainment. The Dramatic Works of Thomas Dekker.* Ed. Fredson Bowers. 4 vols. Cambridge: Cambridge University Press, 1953–1961. 2:229–309.

Dekker, Thomas. *Nevves from Graues-end: Sent to Nobody.* London, 1604. STC 12199.

---

[60]I am grateful to James Carscallen and the editors of this volume for commenting on previous versions of this article.

Dekker, Thomas. *Troia-Noua Triumphans. London Triumphing, Or, The Solemne, Magnificent, and Memorable Receiuing of that worthy Gentleman, Sir Iohn Svvinerton Knight, into the Citty of London . . . . The Dramatic Works of Thomas Dekker.* Ed. Fredson Bowers. 4 vols. Cambridge: Cambridge University Press, 1953–1961. 3:225–247.

Drayton, Michael. *A Paean Trivmphall. Composed for the Societie of the Goldsmiths of London.* London, 1604. STC 7215.

Drummond, William of Hawthornden. *Teares on the death of Meliades.* Edinburgh, 1613. STC 7257.

Edmond, John Philip. "Elegies and other tracts issued on the death of Henry, Prince of Wales, 1612." *Publications of the Edinburgh Bibliographical Society* 6 (1901–1904): 141–158.

Gelley, Alexander. Introduction. *Unruly Examples: On the Rhetoric of Exemplarity.* Ed. Gelley. Stanford: Stanford University Press, 1995. 1–24.

Gorges, Arthur. *The Olympian Catastrophe. The Poems of Sir Arthur Gorges.* Ed. Helen Estabrook Sandison. Oxford: Clarendon, 1953. 137–182.

Great Brittans Mourning Garment. Given To all faithfull sorrowfull Subiects at the Funerall Of Prince Henry. London, 1612. STC 13158.

Greene, Thomas M. "Erasmus' 'Festina lente': Vulnerabilities of the Humanist Text." *Mimesis: From Mirror to Method, Augustine to Descartes.* Eds. John D. Lyons and Stephen G. Nichols, Jr. Hanover: University Press of New England, 1982. 132–148. Rpt. in Greene, *The Vulnerable Text: Essays on Renaissance Literature.* New York: Columbia University Press, 1986. 1–17.

Hampton, Timothy. *Writing from History: The Rhetoric of Exemplarity in Renaissance Literature.* Ithaca: Cornell University Press, 1990.

Hawkins, John. *The Life and Death of ovr Late most Incomparable and Heroique Prince, Henry Prince of Wales.* London, 1641. Wing C6330.

Haydon(e), William. *The Trve Picture and Relation of Prince Henry His Noble and Vertuous disposition.* Leiden, 1634. STC 12581.

Heaton, Gabriel and James Knowles. "'Entertainment Perfect': Ben Jonson and Corporate Hospitality." *The Review of English Studies* n.s. 54 (2003): 587–600.

Herbert, William. *A Prophesie of Cadwallader, last King of the Britaines.* London, 1604. STC 12752.

Heywood, Thomas. *A Fvnerall Elegie, Vpon the death of the late most hopefull and illustrious Prince, Henry, Prince of Wales.* London, 1613. STC 13323.

Heywood, Thomas. *Troia Britanica: Or, Great Britaines Troy.* London, 1609. STC 13366.

Hoy, Cyrus. *Introductions, Notes, and Commentaries to Texts in* The Dramatic Works of Thomas Dekker. 4 vols. Cambridge: Cambridge University Press, 1980.

James VI and I. *Basilicon Doron. Political Writings.* Ed. Johann P. Sommerville. Cambridge Texts in the History of Political Thought. Cambridge: Cambridge University Press, 1994. 1–61.

James VI and I. *The Kings Maiesties Speech, as it was deliuered by him in the vpper house of the Parliament, to the Lords Spirituall and Temporall, and to the Knights, Citizens, and Burgesses there assembled, On Munday the 19. day of March 1603.* London, 1604. STC 14390.

Kay, Dennis. *Melodious Tears: The English Funeral Elegy from Spenser to Milton*. Oxford: Clarendon, 1990.

Lawson, Charles. "*Fvneris infandi coram tristissimus adsum . . . .*" *Epicedivm Cantabrigiense, In obitum immaturum, semperq; deflendum, Henrici, Illustrissimi Principis Walliae, &c*. Cambridge, 1612. STC 4481. I1v–I3r.

Manley, Lawrence. *Literature and Culture in Early Modern London*. Cambridge: Cambridge University Press, 1995.

Mayerne, Theodore Turquet de. *The Relation of the Sicknes and Death of the most Illustrious Henry, Prince of Walles, &c. Together With the opening of his Body*. William Haydon. *The Trve Picture and Relation of Prince Henry*. Leyden, 1634. STC 12581. E1r–F3v.

Middleton, Thomas. *Micro-cynicon. Sixe Snarling Satyres. Insatiat Cron. Prodigall Zodon. Insolent Superbia. Cheating Droone. Ingling Pyander. Wise Innocent*. London, 1599. STC 17154.

Moore, Norman. *The History of the Study of Medicine in the British Isles*. Oxford: Clarendon, 1908.

Nance, Brian. *Turquet de Mayerne as Baroque Physician: The Art of Medical Portraiture*. *Clio Medica* 65. Amsterdam: Rodopi, 2001.

Nashe, Thomas. *Pierce Penilesse his Supplication to the Diuell. The Works of Thomas Nashe*. Ed. Ronald B. McKerrow. 5 vols. 1903–1910. Rpt. and ed. F. P. Wilson. Oxford: Basil Blackwell, 1966. 1:137–245.

Niccols, Richard. *The Three Sisters Teares. Shed at the Late Solemne Funerals of the Royall deceased Henry, Prince of Wales, &c*. London, 1613. STC 18525.

Nichols, John. *The Progresses, Processions, and Magnificent Festivities of King James the First, his Royal Consort, Family, and Court*. 4 vols. 1828. Rpt. New York: Kraus, 1966.

Peele, George. *Decensus Astrææ* [sic]. *The Device of a Pageant*. London, 1591. STC 19532.

Petowe, Henry. *Englands Cæsar. His Maiesties most Royall Coronation*. London, 1603. STC 19806.

Pigman, G. W., III. *Grief and English Renaissance Elegy*. Cambridge: Cambridge University Press, 1985.

Price, Daniel. *Spiritvall Odovrs to the Memory of Prince Henry in fovre of the last sermons preached at St James after his Highnesse death*. Oxford, 1613. STC 20304.

Price, Daniel. *Teares shed over Abner. The Sermon Preached on the Sunday before the Prince his funerall in St. James Chappell before the body*. [In] *Spiritvall Odovrs*. Oxford, 1613. STC 20304. L4r–P2v.

Shakespeare, William. *Troilus and Cressida*. The Arden Shakespeare. Ed. David Bevington. Walton-on-Thames: Thomas Nelson, 1998.

Strong, Roy. *Henry, Prince of Wales and England's Lost Renaissance*. 1986. Rpt. London: Pimlico, 2000.

Taylor, John. *Great Britaine, All in Blacke*. London, 1612. STC 23760.

Webster, John. *The Complete Works of John Webster*. Ed. F. L. Lucas. 4 vols. London: Chatto and Windus, 1927.

Webster, John. *A Monvmental Colvmne, Erected to the liuing Memory of the euer-glorious Henry, late Prince of Wales*. London, 1613. STC 25174.

Webster, John. *Monuments of Honor*. London, 1624. STC 25175.

Werner, Hans. "A German Eye-witness to *Troia-Nova Triumphans*: Is Dekker's Text a Reliable Description of the Event?" *Notes and Queries* 244; n.s. 46 (2002): 251–254.

Williams, Ethel Carleton. *Anne of Denmark, Wife of James VI of Scotland: James I of England*. London: Longman, 1970.

Wither, George. *Prince Henries Obseqvies or Movrnefvll Elegies vpon his Death: VVith A supposed Inter-locution betweene the Ghost of Prince Henrie and Great Brittaine*. London, 1612. STC 25915.

Index

"A Rí ríchid réidig dam" 85–86

Abelard, Jacques 70

Abray, Lorna Jane 7, 8, 133–148

Achates 183

Achilles 7, 22, 24, 43, 45, 117, 121, 125, 129, 140, 141, 151, 152, 154, 167, 168, 172, 196, 198, 204, 226, 270, 276, 284

adaptation 1, 4–5, 8, 17, 82–83, 85, 90, 117

— into Irish vernacular 90, 93. See also Trojan legends.

Aeneas 1, 9, 15, 17, 18, 22, 23, 31, 85, 86, 100, 117, 121, 137, 128, 141, 153, 182–184, 187, 190, 198, 199, 215, 216, 221, 222, 224, 225, 226, 230, 233, 239, 256, 282

— as traitor 3, 126–129, 173; Senecan *nuntius*, shapes Hamlet 172–173; linked to English throne 275

Aeschylus 39

Africa 183

Agamemnon 22, 150, 158

"Ages of man," Renaissance theories of maturation 137–138, 143

Agincourt, Battle of 144

Alamanni, Niccolò 180

Alan of Lille 26, 35

Alexander the Great 48, 83, 136, 157, 271, 276, 284–285

allegory, in Goethe 43–44

Alma 244, 245, 246

Amazons 141, 146, 198

America, in Spenser 246

Amoret 33, 34

anatomy theatre, early modern 3

Anchises 173, 182, 230, 243

Ancien Régime 151

Andromache (Andromaque) 51, 140, 141, 151, 154, 155, 156, 168

Anglo, Sydney 259

Anne of Brittany (w. of Louis XII of France) 70

Antenor 15, 99, 101, 102, 105, 117, 121, 126, 127, 128

Antioch 73

antiquity 67, 69, 71, 72, 76

— changing attitudes toward in Venice 105; projections of current troubles onto 159

Aphrodite 22, 45

Arachne 209

archaeological ruins, Troy and ancient provenance 1, 97

architecture, Venetian and identity 111

Ariosto, Ludovico 28, 29, 30, 71, 72, 199, 216, 225–226, 227, 229

Aristotle 26, 40, 138

— aesthetic terms of 197, 202, 203, 205, 206

Armstrong, Elizabeth 64

Arnaldi, Girolamo 104

Artegal 5, 29, 30, 31, 32, 225

Arthur 18, 36, 225, 244, 245, 259, 286

Arthurian romance 89

Ascanius 17

Asia 72

assimilation, and Ireland 81

Astolfo 225, 226

Astyanax 51, 154, 155, 168, 169

Athena 58, 123, 209

Athens, fall of 157

Atkinson, James 67

Attila the Hun 103

Atwood, E. B. 119, 129

Aubigné, Aggripa d' 155

audience 2, 3, 4, 53, 83–84, 117, 120–121, 123, 141, 163, 222–223, 278

Auerbach, Erna 260

Augustine (St) 163

— City of God 35; *Confessions* 163, 174; *De Trinitate* 163

Augustus Caesar 240

authority, invocation of classical past 97; religious and Venice 102, 104

Ayscu, Edward 260

Babel, Tower of 75, 76
Bacon, Francis 193–194, 206
Baines, Richard 50
Bakhtin, Mikhail 120
Baldwin, T. W. 196, 197
Bale, John 263
barbarians, invaders of Rome 157
barbarous language 70
Barnicle, Mary Elizabeth 117, 119
Baron, Frank 56
Barraclough, Geoffrey 28
Battle of Agincourt 144
Battle of Bosworth 18
Battle of Kinsale 82
battles, representation and burlesque 121
Bavo 19
Bawcutt, Priscilla 180
Bayot, Alphonse 20
Beaune, Colette 137
Beaune, Regnaud de 149
Bélanger, Stéphanie 8, 149–160
belatedness, and historical mediation 40, 44
Belgian origin of Gaul 70
Bellamy, Elizabeth Jane 10, 215–235
Benoît de Sainte-Maure 23, 82–83, 99, 118, 229, 230
Benson, C. David 4, 120
Berger, Harry 218, 220, 221, 222
Bergeron, David 254, 255, 264, 273
Bernardus Silvestris 199
Best, R. I. 84, 86
Bevington, David 46
Bible 3, 34
biblical history, and Ireland's past 85
Birch, Thomas 274
blank verse 9, 177, 180, 181
Blasset 65, 69
Blumenfeld-Kosinski, Renate 70
Boccaccio, Giovanni 19, 21, 134
Boethius 124
Boiardo, Matteo (count) 27
Bono, Barbara 159
Book of Common Prayer 258
Bosworth, Battle of 18
Bourges, Archbishop of 149

Bouwsma, William 71
Bowers, Fredson 157
Bradamante 27, 28
Bradbury, Nancy 121, 129
Bradshaw, Brendan 82, 93
Brandt, Bruce 46
Branyan, Richard 253
Bridges, Egerton 279
Briseida 23
Britain, attempted union of 258, 260, 264, 266; genealogical link with Troy 7, 31, 224
Britomart 5, 10, 29–34, 216–227, 229, 233, 234, 242, 243, 244
Brown, Patricia 105, 111, 112
Brown-Grant, Rosalind 134, 138
Browne, John 272, 285–286
Bruscagli, Riccardo 27
Brutus (Brute) 1, 9, 11, 15, 17, 29, 215, 216, 224, 225, 233, 245, 251, 253, 254, 255, 256, 257, 259, 260, 261, 262, 263, 264, 266, 271, 275, 282
Budé, Guillaume 65
Burel, Jean 152, 155
Burgundy, Dukes of. See Philip the Bold and Philip the Good.
Burke, Peter 65
burlesque 7, 117–130
Burrow, Colin 167
Burton, Richard 45
Busyrane 33–35
Byrne, Francis John 85
Byrnes, Edward 124
Byron, George Gordon, Lord 44
Byzantine Empire 97, 110, 111

Cadwalader 259
Cairns, Huntington 50
Calasso, Roberto 43, 50, 51, 53–54
Calvin, Jean 5, 44, 48–50, 53, 59
Cambridge 44, 50
Camden, William 11, 260, 261
Campion, Thomas 178, 181, 282
Carile, Antonio 97, 99, 102, 103, 104
Carney, James 87
carnivalesque 76, 120
Carscallen, James 4–5, 10, 15–38
Carthage 17, 20, 173, 182, 183, 186, 190

Cassandra 150, 153
Cassius 173
Castelneau, Michel de 75
Castiglione, Baldassare 93
Caxton, William 5, 23, 24, 90, 91, 166, 230
Celtic (language) as origin of French 77
Celts, as ancestors of Gauls 70
Chambers, David 104, 108, 110
chansons de geste 26, 27, 28, 30
Chapman, George 194, 196, 205, 272, 283–284
Chariclea 27
Charlemagne (emp.) 19, 27, 28, 36, 70, 137, 144
Charles V of France, subject of Christine de Pizan 135, 144–145, 146
Charles VI of France 8, 143
Charles IX of France 76
chastity 30–33
Chaucer, Geoffrey 4, 178, 181
— *Book of the Duchess* 124; *Canterbury Tales* 227–228; *House of Fame* 10, 124, 217, 227–228, 229, 232–234, 265; *Troilus and Creseyde* 3–4, 24, 33, 34, 189, 230
Chaurand, Jacques 64
chivalry 5, 25, 28, 45, 133, 270
— in France 133, 136, 140, 143, 144
Chrétien de Troyes 4, 18, 138
Christianity, and transformation 19
Christine de Pizan 7–8, 89, 133–148
— *Book of the Body Politic* 135; *Book of the City of Ladies* 134, 136, 137, 142, 145; *Book of the Deeds of Arms and Chivalry* 135; *Charles V* 13, 135, 137, 144; *Christine's Vision* 135, 145–146; "Les enseignemens moraux" 138; *Epistre Othea* 136, 138–140; *Long Road of Learning* 135; *Mutacion de Fortune* 134, 135, 136 137, 140–141, 145
chronicles, and Faeryland 246; and medieval and Trojan origins 97, 102, 104, 233–234, 256, 263; and Venetian liberty and settlement 97,

98 101; in Ireland 89; medieval and early modern 256
Cicero 162, 283
civilization, eclipse of and Rome 94
Clann Ollaman Uaisle Emna 85–86
Claudius (character) 8, 165, 169, 172
Clement (pseudo-Clementine) 56, 58
Clément, Louis 64
Clerico, Geneviève 68
Clode, Charles 265, 266, 274
Cohen, Paul 4, 5–6, 63–80
Columcille (St) 92
conquest, and Hölderlin 40–41; and Roman Empire 43; by Franks 43
consolation 149, 182–183
— epic inadequate for 283–284
Constantine (emp.) 19, 111
Constantinople 20, 110
Contarini, Gasparo 6–7, 105, 106–109, 112
Cooper, John 178
Corbinelli, Jacques 74
Corineus 259
Corkery, Daniel 81–82, 93
Cornwallis, Charles 279
Cosimo I de' Medici (grand duke) 72
Cotton, Robert 11, 259, 260
Cracow 57
Craik, T. W. 46
Crane, Hart 47
Crick, Julia 256, 261
Crouzet, Denis 149, 152
crowds 258
Crusade, Fourth 110, 111
cultural identity 255, 263
cultural legitimacy, and Trojan legends 5, 39, 69
Cupid 23, 33
Cyprus 73

da Canal, Martin 97, 99, 103
Daedalus 199
Dandolo, Andrea 104, 111
Daniel, Samuel 11, 257, 258
Dante 74
Dares Phrygius 6, 16, 23, 82, 91, 118, 123, 125, 228–229
Das, Sheila 4, 6–7, 97–114

Day, John 177, 178
de Brún, Pádraig 88, 93, 94
death, glory of 153
Dekker, Thomas 254, 269, 272, 286
— *Troia-Noua Triumphans* 273–275, 277, 280
Delaruelle, Louis 65
Demazière, Colette 67
democracy 67
demonology 44–50
Demosthenes 283
Desan, Philippe 68
Descartes, René 193
Deschamps, Eustace 137
Desmond, Thomas FitzGerald, Earl of 87
destiny 7, 17–19, 22, 24, 27–32, 34, 149, 166–167
Diacono 97
dialects 63, 77
Diana 17, 257
Dictys of Crete 16, 118, 125, 127, 128, 228–229
Dido 9, 22, 23, 35, 168, 173, 182, 186, 187, 197, 217, 221, 222, 230, 233
Diels, Hermann 55
Dillon, Myles 88
"discursive hybridity" 4, 48
divine retribution 149, 157, 159
divine, the 39–60
Douglas, Gavin 8–9, 166, 179–180, 181, 183, 184–188
Doutrepont, Georges 20
Drayton, Michael 11, 257, 258, 263, 272, 275
dreaming, and Troy materials 124–125
Druids 73
Drummond, William 271, 272, 277, 282, 283
Dryden, John 177
Du Bellay, Joachim 71
Dubois, Claude-Gilbert 68
Dunn, Charles 124
Dutton, Richard 258, 259, 263

Échecs amoureux (trans. Lydgate?) 26
Edinburgh 279
Edmond, John 279

education, function of and Troy 8
Edward IV of England 259
Edwards, Mark 56
Egypt 49, 51, 260
ekphrasis 9, 183, 190–191, 194–212
elegy 11, 271, 272–273, 276, 279, 285–286
Eliot, T. S. 21
Elizabeth I of England 9, 10, 36–37, 215, 218, 238, 244, 245, 259
— claims of Trojan ancestry 219; linked to Jove and Troy 11; myths of as ruler 248–249, 250
Elizabeth (d. of James VI and I) 274
eloquence 100, 201
empire, and England 240; and transference of cultural legitimacy 5; and Trojan legends as narrative frame 2, 3, 4, 11, 39, 199
England 9, 81, 189, 237, 242, 257, 258
— and empire 237–238; and national security and Troy and theatres 10; and Troynovant and Spenser 31, 238
epic 71, 84–94, 199, 215, 218, 225, 228, 283
Epimeleia 265
Erasmus, Desiderus 163–164, 285
Erbse, Harmut 228
Erminia 30
eschatology 150, 182
Este (ruling house of Ferrara), descended from Roland 72
Estienne, Henri 63–66, 71, 74, 75, 76
Estienne, Robert 63, 64, 65
etymology 63, 65, 68
eucharist, the 48, 50
Euripides 5, 17, 22, 44, 60
— *Helen* 51, 54; *The Trojan Women* 51–52
Europa 241
Europe 65, 67, 74
Eudoxus 250, 251
exemplarity 7, 9–11, 200, 222–225, 263, 271, 277–287

fabliau 221
Fairholt, F. W. 256
Fairley, Barker 42, 43
Fall of Troy. See Troy.

Falstaff 35

fame 226, 228–230, 231–232, 233, 264, 265

Fauchet, Claude 68, 73, 74

Faustbook 58

Faustus, legend of 42, 44–60; magician, narratives of 56–59

Favyn, André 72, 73

Federico, Sylvia 1, 2, 4

Ferdinand of Aragon 108

Ferrara 72

Filoramo, Giovanni 51, 58

Fineman, Joel 195, 200, 206

Flood, the 19

Florence 72

Foley, Stephen 178, 181

Forhan, Kate 133, 144

Forsyth, Neil 44

fortune 24, 33–34

— wheel of 144

Foucault, Michel 216

Foxe, John 164

France 1, 4, 8, 63, 66, 81, 155, 156, 158, 239, 242

— as origin of civilization 73; history of 74; linguistic history of 5; Trojan foundations of 8

Francion (Francus) 1, 5, 8, 15, 19, 65, 69, 71, 76, 137, 143, 215

Franklin, Julian 68

Frazer, R. M. 82

Frederick V, elector palatine 273–274

French, ancestry of 72

French (language) 5, 63–69, 71, 73, 77

French monarchy, founding of 159

French poetry, history of 73

French, A. L. 46

Freud, Sigmund 2

friendship, in Spenser 30–33

Fumaroli, Marc 67, 74

future, the 8, 9, 10, 18, 31, 32, 35, 100, 269–287

Gadoffre, Gilbert 67

Gaeta, Franco 109

Galileo 199

Gardner, Helen 46

Garnier, Robert 8, 149–160

Garrisson, Janine 152

Gascoigne, George 221

Gaul, as origin of Greek culture 72

Gauls, Celtic origins of 68

Gawain 138

Gelley, Alexander 272

Gelli, Giovanni Battista 72

gender 41–43, 59, 133, 194, 201–202, 204–205, 220–227

— identity, topsy-turvy in magical kingdoms 124

genealogy 1, 3, 19, 20, 27, 69–70, 129–130, 216, 218–221, 234, 243, 259

generosity 154

genre, and exemplarity 272–273

Geoffrey of Monmouth 17, 29, 129–130, 225, 233, 256, 261, 263, 271

Gerald of Wales 89, 261

German (language) 71, 77

Germany 4, 39–44, 56, 72, 81

Gertrude 8, 165, 169

Giambullari, Pier Francesco 72

Gilbert, Felix 108

Gill, Roma 46

Girard, René 204

Giustiniani, Bernardo 6, 105, 112

Gloriana 29, 33, 36

gnosticism, and Trojan materials 39, 44–48, 51, 55–60

Godfrey of Bouillon 19–20, 137

gods, the 150, 154, 157, 158

Goethe, Johann Wolfgang von 5, 39–44, 55, 59

Gog and Magog 256, 259

Goldberg, Jonathan 189

Golden Age 26, 237, 240, 245, 246, 247, 248, 252

Gombrich, Ernst 211

Gorboduc 178

Gordon, D. J. 254, 263

Gorges, Arthur 271, 272, 282

Gorgias 5, 52–53, 54–55, 59

Goudelin [Goudouli], Pierre 75, 76

Gower, John 230

Grafton, Richard 262

grammar 67, 68, 73

Gransden, Antonia 261
Grant, Edward 262
Great Brittans Mourning Garment 276
Greece 5, 74, 83, 85, 84, 123
— classical as linked to Germany 39–44, 59
Greek (language) 63, 64, 65, 66, 67, 68, 76, 72, 77
Greek culture, as derivation from Gallic 72
Greek origin of France, myth of 71
Greeks 102
— cruelty of 154
Greenblatt, Stephen 55
Greene, Thomas 60, 165, 285
Greg, W. W. 46, 48
Grendler, Paul 107
grief, destruction of Troy and Spenser 31; Hecuba's and Lucrece's 205; Helen of Troy and Marlowe 49–50; Lucrece's 195–196; Menelaus' 49; Priam's 198; rhetorical 202; Troy and memory of 190–191
Guichard, Robert 73
Guido delle Colonne 15, 24, 33, 120–121, 125, 128, 230
Guillaume, Jean 204
Gunby, David 284
Gunpowder Plot 266
Gurevic, Aron 120
Guy-Bray, Stephen 8–9, 177–192
Guyon 244, 245, 246

Hadas, Moses 15
Hadrian's Wall 258
Hager, Alan 180
Hamilton, A. C. 215–216, 238
Hamilton, Edith 50
Hamlet 208, 209, 210, 211
Hampton, Timothy 223, 271–272, 285
happiness, transience of and Troy 190
Hardison, O. B. 180, 181
Harmening, Dieter 56
Harry, George 260
Harvey, Gabriel 163, 166, 195
Hawkins, John 279, 283
Hay, Denys 97
Haydon, William 278, 279

Hazlitt, William 170
Headley, John 56
Hebrew (language) 71, 72, 75, 77
Hector 7, 8, 10, 11, 24, 25, 27, 65, 71, 84, 85, 117, 121, 122, 125, 126, 129, 133–147, 150–152, 154, 156, 218, 222, 226, 270, 271, 276, 281, 282, 284
— as a model of knighthood 136; as exemplar 276; as masculine idol for Christine de Pizan 141; as model for Christine de Pizan's son 137–140; attacked by Achilles in *Seege or Batayle of Troy* 117; Christine de Pizan's treatment of as cautionary tale 134–147; death of 11, 153, 269, 281; in battle 131; parodic humiliation of in *Seege or Batayle of Troy* 126, 129; physiological situation in Christine de Pizan 138; representation of in Christine de Pizan 7, 133
Hecuba 118, 126, 142, 150, 151, 155–158, 161, 167, 169, 172, 173, 205, 206
Heffernan, James 194, 206
Heidegger, Martin 39, 40
Heidelberg 57
Helen of Troy 5, 20, 22, 24–25, 32, 39–60, 117, 123, 126, 128, 202, 206, 217, 218, 221, 230, 242
— abduction of 52–53; abduction reenacted in Spenser 217–218; and gnosticism 55–60; and hermeneutics of eroticism 59; as phantom image 50; dematerialization of 49; in Goethe 43
Helfer, Rebeca 10–11, 237–252
Heliodorus 4, 26
Hellenists 63, 65, 72
Hellenore 32, 217, 218, 220, 221, 222, 242
Hennecke, E. 56
Henry I of England 17
Henry V of England 18
Henry VII of England 257, 259, 261, 265, 266, 271, 274, 275
Henry VIII of England 82, 261
Henry III of France 74

Henry, Françoise 87, 90
Henry, Prince of Wales (s. of James VI
    and I) 10, 269–290
— illness and death of 273, 278–279
Herbert, William 269, 271, 272, 276
Hercules 70, 72, 85, 90, 91, 276
hermeneutics, and Trojan materials
    54–55; ekphrasis as vehicle of 199,
    200, 208–209; of reading in Spenser
    224
Herodotus 51, 53
Hesione 16
Heywood, Thomas 168–170, 254, 264,
    272, 276, 280–281, 286
Higden, Ralph 89
high and low culture, and "serious"
    histories 120
Hilliard, Nicholas 259
Hindman, Sandra 133, 134, 138, 139
Hippolytus of Rome 56, 57
Hiscock, Andrew 8, 161–175, 181, 187
Histoire ancienne jusqu'à César 135
historiography and Trojan legends 4,
    76, 249, 254
— and Christian originary myth 104;
    and Venice 6, 103–113; Spenser
    parodies 244–245
history 64, 74–77, 266
— accuracy of 76; as oral performance
    121; British 10, 237, 261, 262, 263;
    Christine de Pizan's view of cyclic
    144; claims of universal 19;
    competing versions of 243;
    considered as fiction 237, 247;
    depiction of on Achilles' shield 199;
    linguistic 64–68, 74–76; mediation
    of 39–60; medieval 65, 74;
    narrating, and England 237; reality
    of 149, 259, 261; standards of
    evidence in 67; Trojan as extension
    of Roman 203; Venice and
    municipal 105
Hölderin, Friedrich 5, 39, 40–41,
    43–44, 59
Holinshed, Raphael 263
Holliday, Leonard 253, 254
Holy Grail, legend of 86
Holy Land 73

Holyoake, John 155, 159
Homer 1, 17, 22, 47–48, 50, 82, 204,
    276, 283, 284–285
— Iliad 21, 71, 76, 125, 151, 152,
    196–198, 221, 228–229, 270;
    Odyssey 21, 50, 53–54, 60, 83
Homeric poems 16
homosexuality 35
Honigmann, Ernst 46
Horace 161
Horatio 170, 174, 211
Horne, David 167
House of Commons 258
Howard, Deborah 111
Howe, P. P. 170
Hoy, Cyrus 274
Hughes, Paul 258, 266
Hugh Capet of France 68
Huit, C. 65
humanism 10–11, 67, 89, 93, 98, 105,
    112, 163, 285
— and exemplarity 223–225, 285; and
    historiography 98; and Italy 6; and
    memory 163–164
Humphries, Rolfe 231
Hungarian (language) 71
Hutson, Lorna 221
hybridity, discursive and Trojan legends
    4, 48
Hyginius 118

imagination 205, 266
— visual 193–194
imitation, of classical tales in Irish saga
    84; status of in Renaissance 193
imperial expansion, and Italian
    city-states 6
imperialism, and England 10, 250–252;
    and Ireland 250–242; and Venice
    98, 100, 111
India 244, 246
interiority 163, 167, 196, 206–207
Ireland 4, 6, 250–252
— and Spenser 237; and Tudor policy
    81; Anglo-Norman invasion of 82;
    Gaelic (period in history) 82, 86,
    89; Renaissance in 94; Republic of
    93

Irenaeus 56, 57, 58, 250, 251
Irish Renaissance 81–96
Iser, Wolfgang 206
Islam 20
Italian (language) 66, 74
Italians 70, 71
Italy 17, 72, 103, 106, 112, 183, 239,
    240

Jacoby, Susan 158
James (earl of Ormond) 78
James VI and I of Scotland and England
    10, 254, 257, 258, 259, 260, 264,
    265, 266
— *Basilicon Doron* 278; *Kings Maiesties
    Speech* 275
— ancestry and Troy 271, 274,
    281–282; royal entry 269, 275
James, Heather 4, 9, 200
Jason 16, 20, 33
Jean de Longuyon 136
Jean de Meun 26, 135, 221
Jerusalem 16, 20, 35–36, 73
Joan of Arc (St) 134, 144, 146
John the Baptist (St) 266
Johnson, Christopher 9, 193–212
Jones, Emrys 166
Jonson, Ben 55, 165, 171, 263, 264, 274
Jove 10, 11, 237, 238, 239, 241, 247,
    248, 249
Judgment of Paris 26, 35, 117,
    118–119, 121–130, 215
Julius Caesar 17, 18, 136, 240, 276
Julius II (pope) 108
Juno 23, 123, 215
Jupiter 18, 117, 122, 123
justice 15, 16, 34, 150, 153, 157, 159,
    248
— divine 5, 8, 51–52, 54
Justin Martyr (St) 56
Juvenal 89

Kahn, Coppélia 195
Kay, Dennis 280
Keating, Geoffrey 86
Keefer, Michael 4, 39–62
Keen, Maurice 137
Kelley, Donald 68

Kellogg, Judith 135, 137, 138, 144
Kempe, William 161
Kerrigan, John 167
Kibbee, Douglas A. 67, 68
Kiessling, Nicolas 46
Kildare, Earl of 89
King Arthur. See Arthur.
King, Margaret 134
kings of Britain, legendary 255
Kinney, Arthur 259, 263
Kinsale, Battle of 82
Kintgern, Eugene 163
Konrad von Wurzburg 118
Krakow. See Cracow.
Krier, Theresa 227
Krueger, Robert 138, 139
Krynen, Jacques 133, 137

L'Estoile, Pierre de 152
Lacan, Jacques 2
Lady Philosophy 124
Lady Reason 145, 146
Laertes 169, 170, 172
Lancashire, Anne 253
Lancelot (romance) 71
Lane, Frederic 110
language, and poststructuralism 194, 195
Lanham, Richard 195, 202
Lanquet, Hubert 262
Lanquet, Thomas 262
Laomoden 16, 33
Larkin, James 258, 266
Latin 63–69, 72, 76, 177
— as derivation from Greek 72; as origin
    of French 77; chronicle 119; classical
    adaptations from, into Irish 83;
    prosody 9; syntax 185–188
Latinists 72
Lattimore, Richard 49
Launay, Marie-Luce 71
Lavinia 201
Lawson, Charles 276–277, 286
Leabhar an Rátha 87
Leabhar Meig Shamhradháin 88
Leabhar na Carraigi, and ransom 90
Leabhar na hUidhre 87
League of Cambrai 108, 110
Lear 208

Leech, Clifford 46
Lefèvre, Raoul 20, 21, 23–24
"Legend of the Holy Grail" (French) 86
legend of Troy. See Troy.
Leland, John 262, 260
Lemaire de Belges, Jean 19, 21, 70, 75
Lercheimer, Augustin 56, 57
Léry, Jean de 155
Lévinas, Emmanuel 207
lexicon 65, 66, 67, 68, 74
liberty 102–103, 104, 112
— and Venice 6, 100, 108
libraries, and Ireland 88–89
Liburnio, Niccolò 180
Lim, Walter 251
Lindemann, Mary 138
lineage, expressed in literature and
    Faerie Queene 30; Trojan 97; Trojan
    and Venice 109
linguistic prestige 67, 69
linguistic treatises 3, 63–78
literacy practices 2, 4, 5
medieval storytelling 84
literary history 74, 178–179
— and historians 181; and Ireland 94;
    Shakespeare and 201
literary patronage, in late mediaeval
    Ireland 87
literary prestige 67
literary productivity, Irish investment in
    86
literary tradition, English, origin of 178
Livy 105, 197
Llwyd, Humphrey 262, 263
Lobanov-Rostovsky, Sergei 253
Logan, Oliver 108
logic, representational 210
logic treatises 161
London 9, 266, 269
— as Troynovant 9, 10, 18, 257, 264;
    theatres closed for plague 194
Loraux, Nicole 156
Lord Mayors' Shows 10, 253–260, 263,
    266
— (in 1604) 263; (in 1605) 253, 255,
    256, 264; (in 1612) 273–275,
    277–279, 280; (in 1633) 264

— and Henry of England 273–274;
    modern 256
Louis (St) 73
Louis (duke of Orléans) 8, 139, 143
Louis XII of France 108
love, and destiny 30; heroic 28; pageant
    of, and Troy materials 33
Lucan 83, 199
Lucas, F. L. 284
Lucian 72
Lucrece 9, 167, 193–211
Lusus 215
Luther, Martin 56, 57
Lycus 90
Lydgate, John 4, 24, 33, 34, 230
Lyte, Henry 259

Mac an Lega Ruadh, Illann 90
Mac an Lega, Uilliam 90–91
Mac Craith, Mícheál 82, 93
Mac Eoin, Gearóid 83
Mac Gearailt, Uáitéar 84
Mac Niocaill, Gearóid 89
Macedonia 72
Mackie, Hilary 228
MacLure, Millar 50
Malbecco 216, 217, 219, 221, 225, 226,
    231, 233
Maley, Willy 251
Malory, Thomas 5, 18
Mandeville, John 89
manhood, instruction in 139–140
Manley, Lawrence 46, 254, 273, 274,
    275
manuscript decoration 87
manuscripts 6, 86–93, 98, 99–101, 111,
    117–124, 126, 259, 278
Marchello-Nizia, Christiane 137–138
Marco (auth. of Codex Marco) 97, 99,
    100, 101, 102, 103, 107, 109, 111
Marcus, Leah 179, 190
Mark the Evangelist (St) 98, 99, 103,
    104, 109
— legend of in Giustiniani 106
Marlowe, Christopher 4, 166, 179, 194
— Dido, Queene of Carthage 45,
    167–168, 186; Doctor Faustus 5, 40,
    44–60

marriage, dynastic 20–21; in Spenser 35–36
Marseille 68, 77
Marsh-Micheli, Geneviève 87, 90
Martin, Carol 229
Marvell, Andrew 194
Mary I of England 259
masculinity 7–8, 133–146
— and violence 133
Mass, abomination of and Calvin 48; Latin 3
Massacre of Saint Bartholomew's Day 149
Mathey-Maille, Laurence 70
Matthieu, Abel 75
Maus, Katharine Eisaman 195
Maximilian I (emp.) 108
Maxwell, James 272
Mayerne, Theodore 270, 278–279
McCabe, Richard 243
McGillivray, Murray 131
Medici, Cosimo I (grand duke) 72
Megara 90
Meister, Ferdinand 82
Melanchthon, Philip 56–57
Melville, A. D. 241
memory, and knowledge 205; and pleasure 189; and translation 188, 189; ekphrasis and narrative of 174; exercises for and the public sphere 162; historical 39; in Faerie Queene 244; literary texts and despair 187; nature of and Troy 8; of the Trojan War 184; political and psychological dangers and Hamlet 165–168, 170–174; Troy and danger of 190
Mendelsohn, Daniel 1
Menelaus 39, 43, 45, 49, 50, 52, 54, 59, 276
Mephistopheles 42, 49
Merchant Taylors, guild of 253, 264, 265, 266
Mercury 117, 122, 123
Merlin 29, 35, 219, 225
Meyer, Paul 135
Middle Ages, as golden age for French letters 73, 74

Middleton, Thomas 254, 269
Miles, Brent 4, 81–96, 118
military conduct books, and Christine de Pizan 136
Millican, Charles 18
Milowicki, Edward 4
Milton, John 194
— Paradise Lost 178, 181, 199, 228
mimesis, as trap in Shakespeare 202; fantasy of possession and 204
Minerva 215
minstrels, and rumour 231; and Troy as burlesque entertainment 130; as corrupt figures in Seege or Batayle of Troye 120, 121, 123
misogyny, clerical tradition of and Christine de Pizan 134
modernity 185, 187
Moncrieff, Charles Scott 189
Montchrestien, Antoine de, Hector 8, 151, 152, 153; Lacènes 154
Montrose, Louis 215
Moore, Norman 279
Moors 72
More, Robert 56, 57
Muir, Edward 99, 111
Mulchrone, Kathleen 86
Munday, Anthony 11, 254, 256
— The Triumphes of Re-United Britannia 253–266
Munro, John 166
Mutability (character in Spenser) 237–239, 247–250
Myrick, Leslie 83, 86
myth 75, 76, 264
— and origins of people destined for greatness 4; anti-Roman 102; Christian and subsidence of Troy 103; construction of 106; foundational 3; functions of in Venetian historiography 103–113; of Trojan origin 1 (understood to be fictional 6); of Venice 6–7, 103–114; originary and Venice 107–113; Trojan foundational 103, 105; Troy and historiography of Venice 97; Tudor 15

Nakam, Géralde 155
Nance, Brian 279
narration, fall of Troy and literary
    strategies 222; of Trojan materials
    233
narrative, gendered in the rape of
    Lucrece 194–195; genealogical 225;
    structures of and Troy 15–16
Nashe, Thomas 177, 269, 271
nature, falsified in Spenser 34
Neptune 254
Newman, Jane 201
Niccols, Richard 273, 275, 277–278
Nichols, John 279
Nietzsche, Friedrich 40
Nimrod 75
Nine Worthies 222
— cult of 143
Noah 75, 256
— as founder of Tuscany 72
Nohrnberg, James 218
Nooteboom, Cees 177
Nuttall, A. D. 44, 50

Ó Buachalla, Breandán 93, 94
Ó Cianáin Miscellany 87–88, 91, 92
Ó Cianáin, Maoílechlainn 87–88, 92
Ó Cianáin, Tadhg 88
Ó Clabaigh, Colmán 89
Ó Domhnaill, Aodh Ruadh 87
Ó Domhnaill, Manus 92–93, 94
Ó Duibhghennán, Daelgus 88, 92
O'Brien, M. A. 84, 86
O'Connell, Michael 219, 221, 217, 246
O'Grady, Standish Hayes 89
Occitan (language) 75, 76
— origin of 77
Odysseus 154
Oenone 48, 223
Old Hamlet 165, 173
Ophelia 172
oral performance of Trojan materials,
    and Seege or Batayle of Troye 121, 123
oral tradition 2, 263
— and Irish epics 83–84
origins of languages topos 75
Orlando 28, 225
Orléans, Duke of. See Louis.

Ormond, Earl of. See James.
Ornstein, Robert 46
Orpheus 100
Othea 138, 139, 140
Ovid 197, 227
— Amores 221; Fasti 167; Heroides 15,
    217, 230 (and Seege or Batayle of
    Troye 118); Metamorphoses 23, 33,
    161, 168, 201–202, 209, 231–232,
    234, 240–241, 247
— and Spenser 217

Padua 101–102
pageantry, and Venice 111–112; civic
    254, 255, 265, 274
pageants, civic 269
— and royal panegyric 275; medieval
    259; Tudor 259
Painter, William 197
Palmer, Philip 56, 57
Pandarus 25
Paridell 10, 32, 215–229, 231, 233,
    234, 242, 243, 244
— Trojan origins of 218
Paris (character) 10, 16, 20, 22, 24, 26,
    45, 59, 117–126, 129, 206, 215,
    217, 218, 220–224, 230
Paris 63, 74
— founding of 71; Parliament of 72
Parker, Patricia 243
"Parricides of the Children of Tantalus"
    86
Parry, Graham 261
Parry, Milman 50
Pasquier, Estienne 77, 152
past, the 66
— and influence on the future 275; and
    relation to present 271;
    dissatisfaction in relation to,
    England 169; literary dialogue with
    181–182; medieval 67; memory of,
    Saint Augustine 174; power over
    the present 187; recollections of and
    translation 8
patriarchy, Trojan and Hamlet 172
Patroclus 141, 196
peace 28–29, 35, 100, 102–103, 108,
    112, 159

— Chapman admires Homer's 196; Christine's vision of 146
peace treaty, Antenor and Aeneas in favour of 128
Pearsall, Derek 119
Peele, George 167–168, 269
Peloponnesian Wars 157
Penthesilea 125, 137, 141, 198
Percival 138
Périon, Jacques 65
Peter (St) 56
Petersen, Wolfgang 1
Petowe, Henry 269
Petrarch 165, 188–189, 203
Phaer, Thomas 166
Philip II of Spain 259
Philip the Bold (duke of Burgundy) 8, 143
Philip the Good (duke of Burgundy) 20
philology 64, 66, 68, 76, 77
Philomela 201
Pigman, G. W. 279
pilgrimage 81
Plaisance, Michel 72
Plato 50, 193
pleasure, and demonology 47–48; and Helen of Troy 49; and ravishment of Helen 45; narrative in *The Rape of Lucrece* 195; related to narrative 53
pluralism, Venice and 107
poetics 266
poetry, and ordered speech 53, 54; role of, in state 10; truth content of 53–54, 217, 227–230, 231–234 (and ideology of Troy 10)
politics 67, 256, 266
— French 66
Polymestor 157, 158
Polyxena 125, 156, 168
Polonius 171, 173
Polyboetes 140
Polymester 168
Polytes 168
Poppe, Erich 88
Postel, Guillaume 65
postmodernism 179
Powell, Stephen 1–12

Priam 16, 17, 19, 20, 24, 84, 85, 91, 117, 123–128, 142, 151, 167, 168, 170, 171, 173, 190, 205, 207, 210, 218, 242, 281, 282
Price, Daniel 279, 280
prosody 178, 180, 181
— and Gavin Douglas, 184–188; and Goethe 39; and Irish texts 84–85; and translation, and *Aeneid* 8–9; in Virgil 199
psychoanalytic theory 2
Punic Wars 182, 187
Putnam, Michael 198, 199
Puttenham, George 162, 164, 205
Pygmalion 194
Pyrrhus 142, 151, 166–173

Quilligan, Maureen 133
Quint, David 226
Quintilian 162, 163

Raleigh, Walter, Spenser's letter to 32
Ramus, Peter 5, 72, 73, 75
rape 52–54, 58, 195, 200–202, 208–209, 217, 222, 241–242
Read, David 240, 250
readers 208, 210, 284–285
reading, as acting 206
Rechtien, John 164
reconstruction, Virgilian narrative of 282
relics, of St Mark the Evangelist 106
Renaissance, as term 190; vs. early modern, historiography of 180
representation, and ekphrasis 208, 209–211; and Troy 2; interrogation of in Shakespeare 195
retribution 8
revenge, Shakespeare and Troy 170; Troy and motives for 16
rhetoric 7, 54–55, 67
— and Paridell 220; treatises 3, 161–162; verbal 193
Rhetorica ad Herennium 162
Rich, Barnabe 3
Richardson, David 182
Richardson, Mark 166
Ricoeur, Paul 208–209
Ridley, Florence 180

Robert de Boron 4, 18
Roberts, Sasha 204
Robertson, Jean 254, 263
Robin Hood 254
Robinson, F. N. 230, 231, 232
Roche, Thomas 217, 219, 221
Roland 27, 72
Roman conquest of Gaul 68, 69
Roman d'Énéas 23
Roman Empire 104, 105, 106, 182
Roman literature, subject matter for
    students 161
Roman Senate 67
romance (genre) 23, 26–27, 254
— and Trojan War 23; Greek 26;
    history of, and *Seege or Batayle of
    Troye* 119; medieval cycles 18; *Seege
    or Batayle of Troye* and generic
    decorum 117
Romance languages 66
romans anciens 23
Romans 73
romantic medievalism 4, 5, 43
Rome 5, 41, 81, 83, 100, 101, 102,
    104, 108, 182, 186, 187, 189, 243
— another Troy 18; classical 69, 74; fall
    of 157; founding of 72, 159; in
    comparison to Venice and war 109
Romulus 239
Ronsard, Pierre de 71, 75, 76
Ross, Bianca 90
royal entries 263–264, 269
royal entry of James I of England
    263–264
Ruggiero 27, 28

Sabellico, Marcantonio 105
Sachs, Arieh 46
Sackville, Thomas and Thomas Norton
    178
saga in Irish 80
Saint Bartholomew's Day Massacre 149
saints' lives, in Irish literature 89
Sands, Donald 121
Saturn 117, 122, 123, 238
Satyrane 217, 221
Saxon invaders 29
Saxon kings of Britain 259

Saxon origins of England 260
Saxons 17
Scéla Alaxandair 83
Schiller, Friedrich von 208
Schliemann, Heinrich 1
Schofield, Scott 10, 253–268, 274
Schwyzer, Philip 262
Scotland 257
Scots 258
Scots (language) 8–9, 180
— translation into 166, 185
scribal authorship 118–120, 123
scribes, medieval in Ireland 81
Scripture, Jewish 16
Scudamore 32, 33, 34
seduction, and literary history 221;
    Ovidian in Spenser 220
Seege or Batayle of Troye 2, 7, 117–130
Selden, John 263
self-fashioning 265
— and translators 170–171; and
    Venetian myth 111; in *Hamlet*, and
    Troy 170–171
Seneca 150
Servius 198
Sessions, W. A. 180, 182, 191
settlement, Trojan and Venice 99, 101
settlers, in Venice 103, 106, 109
Shakespeare, William 4, 178, 179
— *Hamlet* 8, 209 (and memory
    164–174; sack of Troy as *locus
    amœnus* 166–174; various versions
    of 164–165); *Julius Caesar* 172–173;
    King Lear 208, 258; *The Rape of
    Lucrece* 9, 166, 194–212; *2 Henry VI*
    173; sonnets 189; *Troilus and
    Cressida* 3–4, 24, 25, 34, 269, 270,
    281
— and fall of Troy, site for political
    trauma 166, 170
Sharpe, Kevin 259
Shepard, Alan 1–12
Sicanus 15
Sicily 15, 73
Sidney, Philip 179, 193, 262
Simon Magus 56–57
Simpson, James 190
sin, original 47, 147

Sinistrari, Ludovico 46–47
Sir Orfeo 124
Smuts, R. Malcolm 255
social imaginary 2–4, 7
— and London and Spanish Armada 9–10
sodomy, and demonology 47; linked to necromancy 56
Solente, Suzanne 135
sorcery, and poetic incantation 53
soul, Christian, in Christine de Pizan 139
Southampton, Henry Wriothesley, Earl of 195
sovereignty, and Venice 101
Spanish (language) 66
Sparta, fall of 157
Speed, John 261
Speght, Thomas 229
Spenser, Edmund 4, 10–11, 179, 194
— *The Faerie Queene* 2, 4–5, 10, 200, 215 (and England's history 238–252); *A View of the Present State of Ireland* 250–252
— and ekphrasis 204; and story of Troy 15; classical genealogy as writer 217; influenced by Ariosto 28–29
spirituality, classicizing 40–42
Sprague, Rosamond 53, 55
Stachniewski, John 50
Stanford, W. B. 83
Statius, *Achilleid* 83; *Thebaid* 83 (and *Seege or Batayle of Troye* 118)
Stesichorus 50, 51, 52, 58
Stevens, Linton 66
Stokes, Whitley 84
storytelling, and social imaginary 4
Stow, John 253, 262, 263
Strong, Roy 278
Stuart, dynasty of 258, 259
suffering 149
suicide 195, 210
Surrey, Henry Howard, Earl of 166, 177, 259
— and *Aeneid* 8–9, 177–191
Suzuki, Mihoko 217, 219, 221, 222, 227
Swift, Jonathan 46
Swinnerton, John 11, 273–274, 279

Synon 169, 207, 208
Szönyi, György 46

Taddei, Ilaria 137
Táin Bó Cúailnge 83–84
"Tale of the Minotaur" 86
Tarquin 167, 200, 206, 207, 208
Tasso 19, 20, 30, 32
Tavoni, Mirko 72
Taylor, Andrew 121
Taylor, Charles 2–3
Taylor, Elizabeth 45
Taylor, John 283
temporality 266
Tennyson, Alfred Lord 26
Terence 89
Tereus 201
Teskey, Gordon 228
theatricality, and grief for Troy 205; energized by Troy legends 169–170
Thebes 157
Thetis 118, 129
Thomas, Vivien 166, 168
Thrace 72
time, narrative 194
Titan 238
Titus 201
Togail Troí 6, 81–94, 118
— manuscript history of 83–91
Tolus (founder of Toulouse) 75
Tottel, Richard 177, 178
Toulouse 75, 76
Tournament of Tottenham 121
translatio imperii 11, 68, 70, 243
translatio studii 68, 73
translation 8, 9, 11, 68, 82, 88, 90, 92–94, 170, 177–191, 242, 285
— act of 177; and Surrey 177–191, esp. 182; as school exercises 161; choices in, and Irish literature 91; classical texts into Irish 94; from classical sources 82; from Greek 88; into English 177; latitude in and *Seege or Batayle of Troye* 118; of *Aeneid* 182; of Dares 20; practice of 182; techniques of, Douglas and Surrey 185–188
transubstantiation, and Calvin 48
Trippault, Léon 64

Trissino, Giangiorgio 180
Tristan (romance) 71
Tristram, Hildegard 83, 84
Troilus 23, 24, 25
Trojan ancestry. See Trojan origin.
Trojan genealogy. See Trojan origin.
Trojan horse 128, 191, 207
Trojan legends, affiliation and
    appropriation 3, 4, 100; and
    Giustiniani 105–106; and national
    identity 3; and Venetian patriotism
    98, 112; anti-Trojan stance of
    Christine de Pizan 135; as love
    story 21–39; boredom with
    203–231, 234; ekphrasis of and
    Shakespeare 195; exhaustion of 10;
    ideological burdens 216; in English
    history 247; obsolescence of, for
    England 10; reception of, in Ireland
    6; related to Wars of Religion 157;
    signs of exhaustion 6; sources for
    Christine de Pizan 133–147;
    Spenser's doubt 240–241; structure
    21–37; survey of 15–37
Trojan origin, and crusade 20; and
    French nobility 143–144; and royal
    houses 215; Britomart and Paridell
    218; claims of 15; of Britain
    254-255, 259, 260, 261; of Brittany
    70; of England 239; of France 65,
    66, 69, 70, 72, 75, 151; of French
    (language) 75; of Venice 105;
    reproduced in English history 244
Trojan War 150, 151
— alleged eyewitness reports of 16; and
    love 15; a cause of 20; eyewitnesses
    of 232; related to Jewish Wisdom
    literature 58–60; represented in
    literature 90–91; Virgil's ekphrasis
    and Shakespeare 197
Trojanksa Prica 118
Trojans 151, 154
— as chosen people 16–17; defeated 8
Trójumanna Saga 118
Troy, as para-scripture 35; competing
    literary traditions 1; defeat of 149;
    destruction of 117, 182 (and blame
    for: House of Laemadon 130);

exiles from 256, 257, 260; fall of
    82, 195–196, 218, 239, 242, 270
    (analogy with Fall of Man 35, 167;
    paintings of 183); history of
    216–217; medieval tradition of
    82–83; refounding of 17, 70; ruins
    of 1, 159; sack of 71 (in Marlowe
    45); siege of 51, 75, 167 (and
    Calvin 49; in *Rape of Lucrece*
    202–203). See also Trojan legends,
    Trojan origin, Trojan War, Trojans.
Troyer, Pamela 7, 117–131
Troynovant (London) 17, 215, 216,
    220, 243, 276, 257, 264
— and Virgilian ekphrasis 196; in
    Spenser 218, 246; Shakespeare and
    the myth of 200, 204
Trudeau, Danielle 67
Tudor myth 15
Tuscany, founding of 72
Twyne [Twynne], Thomas 166, 262
Tydeman, William 166, 168
typology, and Troy 18–19

Ullyot, Michael 10, 225, 269–290
Untersteiner, Mario 53, 55

Vegetius 144
— on war, and Christine 136
Venice, Republic of 4, 6, 15, 97–114
— and construction of new Troy 100;
    and empire 109; as maritime power
    109–110; colonized 101;
    historiography of 98–114; myth of
    6–7, 103–114; origin of 105;
    prosperity of and Trojan myth 110
Venus 18, 33, 117, 122, 123, 139, 196,
    197, 215, 231, 234, 241
Vergil, Polydore 11, 261, 262
verisimilitude 158
vernacular 63, 66, 67, 74, 83
Verstegan, Richard 260
Vickers, Nancy 204
Viking raiders, and Ireland 94
Virgil 1, 10, 17, 19, 24, 36, 89, 102,
    217, 225, 227, 276
— *Aeneid* 15–16, 17, 26, 71, 76, 83, 84,
    99, 118, 161, 177, 180, 182, 187,

189, 196–199, 221, 230–232, 239,
242, 245, 247, 249, 264, 282;
Eclogues 249
Virginia (American colony) 244
Vogler, Candace 2–3

Wales 257
Walters, Lori 145
Waquet, Françoise 65, 67
war 3, 47, 8, 120, 186–187
— and Rome 108; as game 25; perils of
and Christine de Pizan 133. See
also Trojan War and Wars of
Religion.
Warner, Marina 137, 146
Wars of Religion (French) 8, 149, 150,
153, 159
Watkins, John 204, 217
Webster, John 254, 272, 274, 283
Weimann, Robert 210

Weiss, Roberto 66
Werner, Hans 274
Willard, Charity 134, 135, 136, 141
William of Newburgh 261
William I of England (the Conqueror) 73
Williams, Ethel 282
Wills, Garry 98, 99, 111
Wilson, Robert Rawdon 4
Winckelmann, Johann 39
Wither, George 270, 272, 277, 280
Withington, Robert 254
Wittenberg 57
Wolfthal, Diane 138
Worcester, Edward Somerset, Earl of 276
Wyatt, Thomas 178, 188–189

Yates, Frances 98, 240, 249

Zeus 50, 51, 52

Publications of the
Centre for Reformation and Renaissance Studies

Renaissance and Reformation Texts in Translation

Du Bellay, Ronsard, Sébillet. *Poetry and Language in 16th-Century France*. Trans. and Intro. by Laura Willett (2004), pp.116. ISBN 0-7727-2021-5

Girolamo Savonarola. *A Guide to Righteous Living and Other Works*. Trans. and Intro. by Konrad Eisenbichler (2003), pp. 243. ISBN 0-7727-2020-7

Godly Magistrates and Church Order: Johannes Brenz and the Establishment of the Lutheran Territorial Church in Germany, 1524-1559. Trans. & Ed. J.M. Estes (2001), pp. 219. ISBN 0-7727-2017-7

Giovanni Della Casa. *Galateo: A Renaissance Treatise on Manners*. Trans. & Ed. K. Eisenbichler and K.R. Bartlett. 3rd ed. (2001), pp. 98. ISBN 0-9697512-2-2

Romeo and Juliet Before Shakespeare: Four Stories of Star-Crossed Love. Trans. & Ed. N. Prunster (2000), pp. 127. ISBN 0-7727-2015-0

Jean Bodin. *On the Demon-Mania of Witches*. Abridged, trans. & ed. R.A. Scott and J.L. Pearl (1995), pp. 219. ISBN 0-9697512-5-7

Whether Secular Government Has the Right to Wield the Sword in Matters of Faith: A Controversy in Nürnberg in 1530. Five Documents trans. & Ed J.M. Estes (1994), pp. 118. ISBN 0-9697512-4-9

Lorenzo Valla. *'The Profession of the Religious' and Selections from 'The Falsely-Believed and Forged Donation of Constantine'*. Trans. & ed. O.Z. Pugliese. 2nd ed. (1994), pp. 114. ISBN 0-9697512-3-0

A. Karlstadt, H. Emser, J. Eck. *A Reformation Debate: Karlstadt, Emser and Eck on Sacred Images*. Trans. & Ed. B. Mangrum and G. Scavizzi. 2nd edition (1991), pp. 112. ISBN 0-9697512-7-3

Nicholas of Cusa. *The Layman on Wisdom and the Mind*. Trans. M.L. Führer (1989) pp. 112. ISBN 0-919473-56-3

Bernardino Ochino. *Seven Dialogues*. Trans. & Ed. R. Belladonna (1988), pp. xlviii, 96. ISBN 0-919473-63-6

Tudor and Stuart Texts

The Queen's Majesty's Passage & Related Documents. Ed. & Intro by Germaine Warkentin. (2004), pp. 158. ISBN 0-7727-2024-X

Early Stuart Pastoral: 'The Shepherd's Pipe' by William Browne and others, and 'The Shepherd's Hunting' by George Wither. Ed. & Intro by J. Doelman (1999), pp. 196. ISBN 0-9697512-9-X

The Trial of Nicholas Throckmorton. A modernized edition. Ed. & Intro by A. Patterson. (1998), pp. 108. ISBN 0-9697512-8-1

James I. *The True Law of Free Monarchies* and *Basilikon Doron.* Ed. & Intro by D. Fischlin and M. Fortier (1996), pp. 181. ISBN 0-9697512-6-5

Essays and Studies

A Renaissance of Conflicts: Visions and Revisions of Law and Society in Italy and Spain. Ed. John Marino and Thomas Kuehn. (2004), pp. 456. ISBN 0-7727-2022-3.

The Renaissance in the Nineteenth Century / Le XIXe siècle renaissant. Ed. Y. Portebois and N. Terpstra (2003), pp.302. ISBN 0-7727-2019-3

The Premodern Teenager: Youth in Society 1150-1650. Ed. K. Eisenbichler (2002), pp. 349. ISBN 0-7727-2018-5

Occasional Publications

Annotated Catalogue of Editions of Erasmus at the Centre for Reformation and Renaissance Studies, Toronto. Comp. J. Glomski and E. Rummel (1994), pp. 153. ISBN 0-9697512-1-4

Register of Sermons Preached at St. Paul's Cross (1534-1642). Comp. M. MacLure. Revised by P. Pauls and J.C. Boswell (1989), pp. 152. ISBN 0-919473-48-2

Language and Literature. Early Printed Books at the CRRS. Comp. W.R. Bowen and K. Eisenbichler (1986), pp. ix, 112. ISBN 0-7727-2009-6

Published Books (1499-1700) on Science, Medicine and Natural History at the CRRS Comp. W.R. Bowen and K. Eisenbichler (1986), pp. ix, 35. ISBN 0-7727-2005-3

Bibles, Theological Treatises and Other Religious Literature, 1492-1700, at the CRRS. Comp. K. Eisenbichler et al. (1981), pp. 94. ISBN 0-7727-2002-9

Humanist Editions of Statutes and Histories at the CRRS. Comp. K. Eisenbichler et al. (1980), pp. xxi, 63. ISBN 0-7727-2001-0

Humanist Editions of the Classics at the CRRS. Comp. N.L. Anderson et al. (1979), pp. ix, 71. ISBN 0-7727-2000-2

To order books, and for additional information, contact:

CRRS Publications, Victoria University
71 Queen's Park, Toronto ON, M5S 1K7, CANADA
tel: (416) 585-4465 / fax: (416) 585-4430
e-mail: <crrs.publications@utoronto.ca> / web: www.crrs.ca